Victorian Science Fiction in the UK:
the Discourses of Knowledge and of Power

A
Reference
Publication
in Science Fiction

L. W. Currey
Advisory Editor

Victorian Science Fiction in the UK:
the Discourses of Knowledge and of Power

Darko Suvin

G.K. Hall & Co.   Boston
1983

The Limits of the Genre is reprinted in a somewhat altered form from *Science-Fiction Studies* 5 (1978) :45-57, by permission of the editors.

Library of Congress Cataloging in Publication Data

Suvin, Darko, 1930–
 Victorian science fiction in the UK

 Includes index.
 1. English fiction—19th century—History and
criticism. 2. Science fiction, English—History and
criticism. 3. English fiction—19th century—Bio-
bibliography. 4. Science fiction, English—Bio-
bibliography. 5. Authors, English—19th century—
Biography. I. Title.
PR878.S35S8 1983   823'.0876'09   83-10768
ISBN 0-8161-8435-6

Writers are really people who write books
not because they are poor, but because
they are dissatisfied with the books which
they could buy but do not like.

W. Benjamin

Is it crazy enough?

N. Bohr

I hope the dissatisfied craziness of this work makes it fit for
dedication:

— to MARC ANGENOT, master of European intertextuality;
— to DALE MULLEN, master of American civic imagination;
— and to NENA, for all the spaces in between.

Contents

The Author

Darko Suvin, a native of Zagreb, Yugoslavia, studied English and French and natural sciences at the universities of Zagreb, Bristol (U.K.), the Sorbonne (France), and Yale before getting his Ph.D. in Comparative Literature. He has taught drama and literature at the universities of Zagreb, Massachusetts, Indiana, and since 1968 at McGill University, Montreal, where he is a full professor of English and comparative literature. He has written or edited a dozen books, and published approximately 300 articles in books and periodicals on dramaturgy, Brecht, and Science Fiction as well as on the theory of social discourse. He coedited the journal <u>Science-Fiction Studies</u> 1973–81 (largely collected in two G. K. Hall reprints with the same title in 1976 and 1978), edited <u>H. G. Wells and Modern Science Fiction</u>, and wrote <u>Metamorphoses of Science Fiction</u> (Yale UP, 1979, also published in French, German, and Spanish, forthcoming in Italian and Portuguese), as well as working on Russian and other Slavic SF. He has been vice-president of the Science Fiction Research Association, and is a recipient of its Pilgrim Award in 1979 for his contribution to S-F scholarship.

Preface

> To articulate historical-
> ly past matters does not
> mean to understand 'how
> it really happened.' It
> means to take hold of a
> memory as it flares up at
> a moment of danger.
>
> W. Benjamin, "On the Con-
> cept of History"

This book has arisen as a continuation of my interest in
the history and theory of Science Fiction (SF) evident in
my book Metamorphoses of Science Fiction--and indeed in
response to some dilemmas experienced while writing its
chapters on and leading up to H.G. Wells. At that point I
became increasingly and uncomfortably aware that I was dealing only with the tip of an S-F iceberg in the 19th
century. Even before finishing that first book, I therefore set to work collecting indications on just how large
that iceberg was. It proved to be tremendous, practically
an occulted continent. Initially, I naively thought that
a second bibliography could easily be compiled for the
books published in the USA, and that both would be carried
to about 1915. I found out that the material was just too
large to be dealt with by a single person and project (and
on top of dealing with other projects in other fields).
Even so, the research took a respectable chunk out of six
summers in major British libraries, and much occasional
time in between. The present Part I, Section A of this
book--the primary bibliography of S-F books published in
the UK between 1848 and 1900, as well as the four subsidiary lists and reflections on the limits of the genre at the
time--was the result. Before that part was finished, I was
hooked, and I went on to work in 1979 and the first half of
1980 on Part I, subsection B.1 of this book, the biographi-

cal sketches of Victorian S-F writers. On sabbatical in
London for the best part of 14 months in 1980/81, I found
that I had to largely recast and fill in these sketches
with help of further indications from a systematic perusal
of all the Victorian yearly registers of professions as
well as from friendly and knowledgeable British counselors.
The sketches then logically issued in their valorization,
the social classification of S-F writers (Part I, subsection B.2).

By then, it was winter 1980, and it had become painfully
clear that, having amassed all this data, I was committed
to bite the bullet and provide an at least partial explanation that made sense of it. Frederic Harrison's stern epigraph to Part II, section A, warned me (these great bourgeois Victorians are hard task-masters!) that otherwise I
would have merely encumbered the future with useless
rubbish. In fact, this Part II then became an experiment
in dealing with a large body of paraliterature. If I had
earlier been just barely able to deal with Wells--or
Morris, or even Verne and Bellamy--by a methodology which
only somewhat bent the tried approaches to "high lit," this
was evidently impossible here. The present Part II--whose
spiraling from history to theory, from addressee to address-
or, from text to context, should speak for itself--is the
result of that experiment in both how can one study and
what is the use of studying paraliterature.

For better or worse, then, I think I may claim that--like
much fiction of our times--I have broken some genre compart-
mentalizations. I confess I had no advance master-plan.
Simply, the logic of my research and subject-matter dic-
tated that sacrosanct distinctions between "preliminary"
bibliographies or biographies and imperial, lofty, but
often unverifiable theories be put into question or into
crisis. Both of these scholarly genres meet here in the
historical interpretation. Both (ideally) cross-fertilize
each other: the annotations of the main bibliography, the
insert about the limits of SF, the study of social classification of the writers--all these are as essayistic (or
studious) as Part II. Conversely, the interpretation in
that Part is constantly referring back to the bibliographies and biographies. My long-suffering editors gently
pointed out that fact, hinting that I could have unified
the bibliographic and note styles from various sections.
But once my mélange of genres proved unavoidable, it was
woven with some care. My various sections communicate
through overt or covert networks of juxtaposition, rein-
forcement, calling into doubt, and reaffirmation--the picky
pinpointing and the theoretical speculation lending dignity

to each other, I trust. Thus, the differences, for example, in reference styles (all explained in their several
places), flow out of the different functions of the sections. I can only hope it all comes together eventually,
so that the reader's forbearance in shuttling back and
forth is at the end rewarded. I wish I could have done
this as a hologram; in the meantime, I warn that the book's
structure is often spiral rather than linear, multicausal
rather than unicausal.

A special mention is due of the sketch of 19th-century SF
and the book trade by John Sutherland. Dr. Sutherland, of
the Department of English, University College, London
University, is perhaps the foremost authority today on this
subject, about which my book is otherwise (out of sheer
ignorance) silent. His survey is a precious indication of
directions to follow, on which I have relied in my conclusions, and it is in my opinion a significant addition to
this book's polyphony.

Thus, my perspective is one of a "social formalism,"
which holds that it is the literary form which can be
questioned as to the societal significance. In this work,
it is applied to a somewhat unorthodox goal--to identify an
almost unknown, and yet historically significant, genre
delimited in space, time, intertextual affinities, and
structures of feeling or ideological horizons. Historically significant means, in keeping with Benjamin's epigraph,
that 19th-century SF is interesting for us today as the
spacetime (or, in Bakhtin's term, the chronotope) where one
can most palpably observe some central tendencies still at
work in SF; indeed, in some important ways at work in all
mass or "popular" literature of the last 100 years. What
is observable here is how and why some fundamental ideological vectors of hegemony, alternative, and cooptation shape
a social discourse between the poles of power and
knowledge. Yet at the same time, this urgent discursive
polarization between domination and liberation may be seen
in the estranging--distanced and therefore cognitively fer-
tile--situation of our ancestral century.

This is to say that I did not conceive of my task--even
in the interpretive study of Part II--so much as one of
writing a positivistic or "objective" history of British SF
in a given period; rather, I wanted to sublate--both
include and supersede--such a history. I wanted to "take
hold of a (buried) memory" in order to have it "flare up at
a moment of danger"--these 1980s. That is why I deal with
SF as part of social discourse, and include all texts
actually published in the UK rather than only those by UK
writers. Further, having delimited my textual set, I

wanted to tease out its <u>key problems</u> and to indicate their shape and import. Their critical understanding necessarily focusses on the interaction between what the texts pose and what they presuppose (see Part II, section C.1). No doubt, in a situation where initial delimitations of Victorian SF were largely lacking, I had to shoulder a first registration with attendant commentary, as well as a critique that went beyond the registration and valorized the commentary. If one wishes this commentary to draw equally upon text and context, formal (generic) and thematic considerations within a narrative logic, cognition and ideology--this may grow time and space-consuming (it takes a good slice of one's life). But such a lengthy, and for one individual perhaps cumbersome, approach is not necessarily bad; it has, in fact, confirmed my long-standing suspicion that commentary can be disjoined from critique only for very brief stretches: "Finally, the full insight into the actual situation of things at hand (<u>Sachgehalt</u>) will coincide with the full insight into their truthfulness (<u>Wahrheitsgehalt</u>)" (Benjamin). The posed and the presupposed are--in literature, at least--in a feedback loop, in an interaction that unfolds within the crucial interpretive horizon of the great collective and class discourses, in which a text is little more than an individual utterance whose narrative patterns are to be understood as a significant enactment of the societal within the formal.

From this it follows that any significant fictional text or group of texts can be centrally interpreted only in interaction with the interpreter's philosophy of history-- that is, her/his view of the formal patterns enacting the ideological systems in the discourse at hand. Whoever pretends to an "objective" neutrality, from whose point of view he can condemn others as "biased," is fooling either himself or others--usually both. All of which is to be proved.

Acknowledgments

The gestation of this book was longer and more complex than usual. Therefore, I have incurred more numerous and deeper debts than usual. Some are buried amid private correspondence of seven or nine years ago; my sincere apologies to anybody I disgracefully forgot.

The whole work was made possible, to begin with, by my teaching institutions, the Department of English and the Comparative Literature Program of McGill University, which have systematically encouraged me to teach various aspects of science fiction and narrative theory at both the undergraduate and graduate level, in possibly indirect but certainly fruitful feedback with this research. My thanks go to the chairmen of these units in these years, George Szanto, Don Theall, Peter Ohlin, and David Williams. The McGill Faculty of Graduate Studies and Research also gave me, for successive stages of work on this project, parts of three Humanities Research grants for some research expenses. Major financial support was provided by the Social Sciences and Humanities Research Council of Canada in several grants. A two-year grant, 1974-1976, to Professor M. Angenot and myself resulted in the identification of almost all the works in my primary bibliography, the annotation of about half of them, and the help of a research assistant, M.E. Papke. Work on other projects funded by the same body incidentally allowed further visits to major libraries and gathering of data, but the whole of the present book was finished on its Leave Fellowship, 1980-1981, spent mostly in London, and in the months following. The Montreal Inter-University Centre for European Studies gave me between those two dates a travel grant in partial defrayment of expenses for two weeks of research in Europe. Without such financial support, in particular from the S.S.H.R.C., this project would not have been feasible.

My thanks go to the staff of the following libraries: primarily, the British Library and various London University libraries; further, the L.S.E., the Bodleian, Oxford,

and University of Cambridge libraries, UK; the Library of
Congress, New York Public Library, and Yale University
libraries, USA; the Bibliothèque nationale, Paris; and for
theoretical literature connected with the interpretive
part, the national or university libraries at Marbach and
München, West Germany, Milan and Florence, Italy, and for
Slavic materials Zagreb, Yugoslavia. The University of
Sydney Library kindly loaned me the rare Larnach checklist.
Beside the London sources, my greatest debt is to the
McLennan Library of McGill University, and in particular
to its Inter-Library Loans Division as well as to Hélène
Bertrand and others in its Acquisition Department. Further, my thanks go to my G.K. Hall editors. The external
editor, Lloyd W. Currey, counselled and supported the impre-
visible evolution of the whole work, as well as sharing
with me the benefit of his unrivalled bibliographic
knowledge of SF, which has opened to me several avenues of
investigation and spared me several bad blunders in the
bibliography and the biographies; Mr. Currey has, together
with David Hartwell, further stimulated all researchers on
19th-century SF by editing the Gregg Press reprints. Tom
Beeler, Meghan Robinson Wander, and Janice Meagher of G.K.
Hall kindly helped with books and counsel during my final
shaping of this work. The actual manuscript editors,
Borgna Brunner, Michael Sims, and Linda Smith, were helpful
and very patient. Finally, Patrick Parrinder as well as
three persons named in my dedication read all phases and
stages of this work; I learned from their raised eyebrows.
     For the bibliographical section, my thanks go, beside
L.W. Currey and R.D. Mullen, to Elizabeth Silvester and
Irena Žantovskà Murray (the latter my pleasant collaborator on earlier ventures also), for help in organizing the
primary bibliography and formulating its introduction, and
for other bibliographic guidance; to Professors Kenneth
Roemer, Lyman Tower Sargent, and Arthur O. Lewis, Jr., and
to John Eggeling, for information on and help with obtain-
ing the primary texts; and to George Locke for information
on these texts, given during several interviews.
     For the biographical sketches, my thanks go to my
research assistants M.E. Papke and Barbara L. Campbell.
After I had with their help established the biographical
sources, their first perusal and the first formulation of a
great number of entries were done by my last research
assistant in Montreal, 1979-1980, Julie Adam. Though
almost all were subsequently rewritten and many were
radically changed by new data gathered in London, I wish to
acknowledge a particular debt to her work. Professor
Sargent again helped with some information from his wide

knowledge of the field, and Professor Roemer on top of that
kindly sent me a chapter of his dissertation interpreting
the social classification of US utopian writers. In London,
W.O.G. Lofts is to be thanked for some additional
information on F.H. Atkins, John Clute for sharing with me
data he is preparing for publication, and, most importantly, John Eggeling for generously supplying additional
information and leads on more than a dozen writers, which
enabled me to completely reconstruct their biographies in
some cases (e.g., for Chilton, Cromie, Greer, Murphy) and
to add new entries in other cases.

For Part II, the interpretive essay was also read by John
Clute, Charles Elkins, Fredric Jameson, David Ketterer,
Robert M. Philmus, John Sutherland, and George Szanto,
whose comments helped; Charles Elkins chaired the MLA section on science fiction in 1979 where I first presented
some of my findings, while George Szanto's counsel was crucial in resolving some dilemmas in my conclusion. Dr. John
Sutherland not only was persuaded to grace the pages of
this book by a contribution of his own (discussed in the
Preface), he also--with the concurrence of Professor
Randolph Quirk--was instrumental in making me an honorary
fellow of University College, London, during my sabbatical
year; a signal honor in itself, it much facilitated my
access to London University libraries, and I owe him
special thanks for all he did. The section on the social
addressees of Victorian fiction was much helped also by the
counsel of Michael Green, E.J. Hobsbawm, Louis James,
Victor Neufeld, Raphael Samuel, Tom Wengraf, and Peter
Widdowson. Dr. Elizabeth James of the British Library and
Elizabeth Silvester were involved in a valiant if unsuccessful effort at clearing up dilemmas of Victorian book-
publishing statistics. Professor Merritt Abrash kindly
shared with me his unpublished paper on Walter Besant, and
Professor David Stafford on Edwardian spy scares with roots
in Le Queux, while Rafail Nudelman of Ramat-Gan, Israel,
discussed with me some points of S-F theory involved. My
thanks go to Hectorine Léger for typing beyond the call of
duty.

It is unclear to me how I should be able to do anything
else in my life if I were called upon to repay all these
debts. I can only thank them most sincerely, one and all.
It might be more than usually necessary to add that none of
the above people or institutions bears any responsibility
for the mistakes that almost certainly remain in this book.
Va, canzonetta mia: if thou art not well licked into
shape by now, it is not for want of generous help, but obviously a genetic burden bequeathed by your begetter.

Part I: Identification of the Science-Fiction Books and Writers

O bibliographers, I pity you
You will go under.

H. M. Enzensberger, *The Wreck of the "Titanic"*

A. Bibliographical Study
1. Introduction

This bibliography attempts to record all the first editions
of English-language science fiction (SF) in book form published in and/or registered as imported into the United
Kingdom in the years 1848 to 1900 inclusive. Much about
the Bibliography should be self-explanatory. I will here
note only the salient aspects of how the field covered was
constituted (scope), and then proceed to some aspects of
the style (format).

Scope

I have taken "book" to mean any independently bound,
printed, nonperiodical publication whose text is larger
than 16 printed pages; smaller works have been designated
"pamphlets," and an unannotated list of them is appended.
"Novel" means a fictitious prose-work with characters
(or, more precisely, narrative agents) in one single plot
of a certain length; as everybody who has tried to separate
the so-called "long stories" from brief novels knows, the
above definition is not only imprecise but also in some
ways incorrect--for length is not the only and perhaps not
the best way of delimiting them (some internal formal
features are probably more relevant). In this Bibliography
I decided to treat as novels all fictitious prose-works
with a single plot taking up (at least) one whole book as
defined above. The Bibliography is nonetheless not called
a bibliography of novels but of books because stories published in books are also included in it on a selective
basis. I have included stories from collections in the
following three cases: 1) if the stories were long; 2) if
they were of significance in the development of SF; 3) if
there were two or more stories in a single book. However,
the reader is hereby duly warned that this Bibliography has
not sought for, nor does it pretend to give, any full overview of S-F stories in the period covered--a task that

would require the inclusion of stories published in periodicals, besides those collected in books.

"Science Fiction" is taken to mean, in brief, all such fictional works in which an imaginary, nonexisting but not impossible, novelty or novum is narratively dominant or hegemonic, whether it be of a sociopolitical nature (as in utopian fiction), or of a natural-science-cum-technological nature, or indeed a fairly abstract--for example, mathematical or philosophical--parable on the possibilities of novel relationships of psychozoa (intelligent beings) to each other and the universe. Any such delimitation raises a host of hotly debated points. I have explained my position at length in Metamorphoses of Science Fiction (see in the "Sources" following), as well as in the essays "The Riverside Trees, or SF and Utopia," Minnesota Review, n.s. 2-3 (1974), 108-15; "On What Is and What Is Not a SF Narration," SFS, no. 14 (1978), 45-57; and "The State of the Art in Science-Fiction Theory," SFS, no. 17 (1979), 32-45; subsection 3 to this bibliography--dealing with books which some bibliographies do not differentiate from SF but which have not been retained in this bibliography--reprints as its first part the second of the above essays. This position entails excluding so-called "science-fantasy" (e.g., Dr. Jekyll and Mr. Hyde); it further excludes the "lost race" tales--unless they also contain some other S-F novum such as a singularly different technology or social organization. A fair number of such cases are marginal, and decision has to be made by following one's critical "nose"; in such cases I have preferred undue inclusion with an appropriate final note to exclusion, but I readily acknowledge that here or there the choice could have been different. I cannot forbear adding here that any historically oriented enterprise, such as this one (using the term historical in opposition to a-historical or bereft of historical consciousness), convincingly demonstrates the unavoidable necessity of theoretically clear delimitation--and also definition--of SF.

Two classes of works which are, according to the above, SF have not been retained in the annotated bibliography for pragmatic reasons. The first is constituted by juvenile penny paperback series, of which at least the Aldine Boys' First-Rate Pocket Library and the Aldine Romance of Invention, Travel, and Adventure Library contain one or more S-F titles (e.g., The Steam Man of the Prairies). Systematic investigation into this domain in the UK is seriously hampered by the difficulties of identifying and finding complete sets of such series, and needs a separate effort. The second of these classes is constituted by those "future

war" tales which, except for the purely political aspect of
who wars with whom with what final redrawing of boundaries,
do not contain any further S-F novum, such as a significantly different technology employed during or social organization arising out of the future war. I felt that such
future works have been adequately covered by Professor I.F.
Clarke's annotated bibliography (see the list following)
and his other publications also referred to in this work.
I have therefore only listed the omissions in an appendix.
Having made this decision, its logic led me to include into
that appendix two titles from the curious and interesting
subgenre, so far much too little if at all noticed, the
"future civil war in Ireland," which flourished during the
Home Rule debates.

"Published and/or registered as imports in the UK" is a
category reflecting the basic horizon explained in this
work's interpretive essay. In some cases the publication
consisted simply in the wholesale importation of a work
from the USA (which is in the following list indicated by
the initials US before the date of publication), as evidenced either by an entry in the English Catalogue or by
the work's having a US/UK imprint. My reason for counting
such works as UK books is simple: I am not interested primarily in any "national genius," but in actual historical
availability to the UK readers of new fiction. This is
another category which not only permits some significant
insights but raises further questions too. For one thing,
how accessible were, in the everyday reality of a UK
reader, the titles of a publisher marked as publishing
simultaneously in the USA and the UK? For another, how
many of the works not registered as imports in the English
Catalogue were nonetheless also accessible (this category,
too, practically concerns US books)? All such queries
remain a subject for further sociological investigations
which I dearly hope will soon be undertaken; again, I have
preferred to sin by commission rather than by omission.

Format

The entries are chronological, and within each year alpha-
betical by the author's last name; due to the paucity of
entries for 1848-1870, these are not further subdivided by
year numbers. Pseudonyms in the form of a proper name are
for purposes of alphabetization treated as other proper
names; pseudonyms in the form of other nominal syntagms are
inserted by the first letter of the first word except for
"A" and "The"; pseudonyms in the form of initials are in-

serted by the first initial (e.g., X.Y.Z. is inserted as X and not as Z).

In the entry, the name--outside of any possibly existing square brackets--is such as on the title-page of the actual book, except that no titles, for example "Captain" or "Lady," have been retained unless they indicated the author's sex which was otherwise unclear. The full and exact form of the author's name has been filled in with help of square brackets whenever known. Incorrect or dubious attribution is indicated by a parenthesis following the name and preceding the title (and as a rule discussed in the biographical Part II of this work), with the incorrect function of "ed." put into quotation marks as in this sentence. The parenthesized entry indicating that the name is a pseudonym is in cases of my greater uncertainty supplied with a question mark (see for each also the discussions in the biographies).

The title is entered verbatim, with all the subtitles as found in the book. Only the punctuation has been standardized, inasmuch as at the beginning of any subtitle a colon has been added in lieu of other punctuation marks, and a comma after any "or." If the subtitle ends in "by" followed with a putative author's name (true or pseudonymous), this has been replaced with three dots and the name transferred to the name part of the entry. The initial capital letters have also been unified.

The place and time, publisher, and pagination are, in keeping with the scope of this bibliography, those of the first UK edition to be found. When the year is not indicated on the front or back pages of the book itself, it is identified from information in the bibliographical sources listed (usually the British Museum or National Union catalogs) or--much more rarely--from internal evidence, and enclosed in square brackets. Most of these year-identifications are reasonably secure, but a few might err by one year; in the case of hesitation, I have chosen the most likely date and accompanied it by a question mark. It should be mentioned that a few titles purporting to report from the future have deliberately false dates: this has been noted by following any such date with the correct date preceded by "i.e.," all in square brackets; square brackets with a different date but without "i.e." indicate simply miscalculation by the publisher, usually testified to by the library arrival date stamped in the book. In the case of titles originally published outside the UK, they have been entered in this bibliography by the year of UK publication (or, for US titles only, by the year of importation into the UK as evidenced by the English Catalogue--which

ever came first); a publisher who regularly published both
in the USA and UK (e.g., Neely) was treated as having his
titles published in the UK in the same year unless there
was evidence to the contrary.   Information about the original publication has been given in a parenthesis toward the
end of the entry, except in cases of English-language publication elsewhere (as a rule in USA) the same year under the
same title, in which case further bibliographical research
is necessary to establish the primacy--research which was
not within the scope of this project.   The name of the
publishing company has been reduced to the last names or
other indications for the first two partners (e.g., Low,
Marston) and linked by a comma or an "&"; an "and" in the
entry for publishers indicates the collaboration of several
publishing companies in that title.

The pagination includes significant prefatory matter in
roman numerals.   In the case of stories, their pagination
within the book has as a rule been indicated.   In the case
of several S-F stories within the same title, the entry
includes at its end a partial list of contents with the
titles of the pertinent stories.

Also included are unannotated lists of "future war" tales
without any other technological or sociopolitical novelty,
of titles not found, and of S-F pamphlets, an annotated
list of titles sometimes not differentiated from SF but not
retained in this bibliography, and last, but not least, Dr.
John Sutherland's comment on 19th-century SF and the book-
trade, which provides the basis for a very necessary
further discussion on matters I was too ignorant to tackle.

Sources for Finding S-F Titles Published in the UK, 1848–1900

Bailey, James Osler.   "Scientific Fiction in English:
    1817-1914: A Study of Trends and Forms."   Ph.D. disserta-
    tion, University of North Carolina, 1934.

Bailey, J[ames] O[sler].   Pilgrims Through Space and
    Time.   New York: Argus Books, 1947.   Reprint. Westport,
    CT: Greenwood Press, 1972.

Bleiler, E[verett] F.   The Checklist of Science-Fiction
    and Supernatural Fiction.   Glen Rock, NJ: Firebell,
    1978.

Botros Samaan, Angele.   "The Novel of Utopianism and Prophe-
    cy from Lytton (1871) to Orwell (1949):   With Special

Reference to Its Reception." Ph.D. dissertation, University of London, 1962.

British Museum: General Catalogue of Printed Books to 1955, 263 vols. London: The Trustees of the British Museum, 1959-1966.

Christensen, John Michael. "Utopia and the Late Victorians: A Study of Popular Literature, 1870-1900." Ph.D. dissertation, Northwestern University, 1974.

Clareson, Thomas D. "An Annotated Checklist of American Science Fiction: 1880-1915." Extrapolation 1, no. 1 (1959), 5-20.

Clarke, I[gnatius] F. Tale of the Future: From the Beginning to the Present Day. . . . 3d ed. London: The Library Association, 1978.

Day, Bradford M. Supplemental Checklist of Fantastic Literature. Hackensack, NJ: Wehman Bros., 1963.

Dupont, V. L'Utopie et le Roman Utopique dans la Littérature Anglaise. Toulouse and Paris: Didier, 1941.

The English Catalogue of Books. . . . [various subtitles], vols. 1-6. Millwood, NY: Kraus Reprint, 1976.

Greaves, Roger. "Bibliography," in Jean Jules-Verne, Jules Verne. New York: Taplinger, 1976, pp. 228-36.

Henkin, Leo J. "Problems and Digressions in the Victorian Novel (1860-1900)--Part XIII, Part XIV." Bulletin of Bibliography 19, no. 6 (1945), 156-59; no. 8 (1945), 202-03.

Larnach, S.L. Materials Toward a Checklist of Australian Fantasy (to 1937). Sydney: Futurian Press, [1950].

Locke, George. Ferret Fantasy's Christmas Annual for 1972. London: Ferret Fantasy, 1972.

_____. Ferret Fantasy's Christmas Annual for 1973. London: Ferret Fantasy, 1973.

_____. A Spectrum of Fantasy. London: Ferret Fantasy, 1980.

_____. Voyages in Space: A Bibliography of Interplane-
tary Fiction 1801-1914. London: Ferret Fantasy, 1975.

Messac, Régis. Esquisse d'une chrono-bibliographie des
utopies. Lausanne: Club Futopia, 2962 [i.e., 1962].

Moskowitz, Sam. Explorers of the Infinite. Cleveland
and New York: World, [1963].

_____. Science Fiction by Gaslight: A History and
Anthology of Science Fiction in the Popular Magazines,
1891-1911. Cleveland and New York: World, 1969.

Newman, John. "America at War: Horror Stories for a Society." Extrapolation 16, no. 1 (1974), 33-41; 16, no. 2
(1975), 164-72.

Reginald, Robert. Science Fiction and Fantasy Literature
1700-1979, vol. 1. Detroit: Gale Research, 1979.

Roemer, Kenneth M. The Obsolete Necessity: America in
Utopian Writings, 1888-1900. [Kent, OH]: Kent State
University Press, 1976.

Rooney, Charles J., Jr. "Utopian Literature as a Reflection of Social Forces in America, 1865-1917." Ph.D.
dissertation, George Washington University, 1968.

Sargent, Lyman Tower. British and American Utopian Literature 1516-1975: An Annotated Bibliography. Boston:
G.K. Hall, 1979.

Shurter, Robert L. "The Utopian Novel in America, 1865-
1900." Ph.D. dissertation, Western Reserve University,
1936.

Teitler, Stuart. Eureka! Berkeley, CA: Kaleidoscope
Books, 1975 (catalog no. 29).

_____. Great Grandad's Secret Cabinet 1835-1918.
Watertown, MA: Kaleidoscope Books, 1974 (catalog no.
27).

_____. The Invasion . . . and Other Speculations.
Berkeley, CA: Kaleidoscope Books, [1977] (catalog no.
32).

With all entries in the bibliography, the biography of the

author (when known) might also be consulted. It was found convenient in some entries on major authors to refer, for further discussion and copious secondary literature, to two books of mine, abbreviated as:

MOSF = Suvin, Darko. <u>Metamorphoses of Science Fiction: On the Poetics and History of Literary Genre.</u> New Haven and London: Yale University Press, 1979.

WMSF = Suvin, Darko, with Robert M. Philmus. <u>H.G. Wells and Modern Science Fiction.</u> Lewisburg: Bucknell University Press; and London: Associated University Presses, 1977.

2. Bibliography of S-F Books Published in the UK, 1848–1900

1848–1870

Forrest, Henry J. <u>A Dream of Reform</u>. London: Chapman, 1848. 162 pp.
Utopian dream of arriving at planet with limitations on wealth, small workshops, political and ethical reforms. Mostly lectures by "Kindly."

Lamartine [de Prat], [Marie Louis] Alphonse de (attributed to). <u>France and England: A Vision of the Future</u>. London: Clarke, 1848. 155 pp.
Found manuscript describes hashish visions of 1943 politics, dominated by "Ibergallitalian" confederation, Germany, and USA as against England and Russia, and by middle classes instead of capitalists. (French original, claimed in the "translator's preface" to be Lamartine's from 1843, could not be found in his works.)

Rowcroft, Charles. <u>The Triumph of Woman: A Christmas Story</u>. London: Parry, 1848. 271 pp.
Comic German visited by Neptunian who transmutes copper into gold, travels by magnetism plus power of will, discusses science. Coming from planet without women, visitor succumbs to charms of German's daughter. Incidental satire of erotical and other manners.

<u>The Last Peer: A Novel</u>. London: Newby, 1851. 3 vols. 368+384+368 pp.
In 20th century aristocracy is dispossessed, merchants, unemployment, and crime thrive. Sentimental melodrama à la Sue, some technological improvements mentioned. Moral: upper class is perfect, bourgeoisie and lower class good if they keep their place.

Poe, Edgar Allan. <u>Tales of Mystery, Imagination and Humour</u>, in <u>Readable Book</u>, vols. 1 and 9. London: Vize-

telly, 1852 (US originals 1835 ff.). Contains among
other: "MS Found in a Bottle," "The Unparallelled Adven-
ture of One Hans Pfaall," "Mellonta Tauta," "Mesmeric
Revelation," "Strange Case of M. Valdemar," "Von
Kempelen's Discovery," and "The Conversation of Eiros and
Charmion."
Poe's well-known tales. For argument about which are SF,
see MOSF.

Pemberton, Robert. The Happy Colony. London: Saunders
   & Otley, 1854. 217 pp.
Detailed pro-labor plans of perfect utopian colony. Pseu-
dodialogs, only marginally fiction.

[Whiting, Sydney.] Heliondé: or, Adventures in the
   Sun. London: Chapman & Hall, 1855. 424 pp.
Narrator drawn to Sun after water-cure, dissolved into
"vapours." Description of Sun as ball of electric light,
of people with musical language inflections and living on
odors (echoes from Cyrano are unmistakable), of Heliopo-
lis, fauna, flora, and the Court. Love romance with princess, full of flowers and sighs. All was a dream.

Imaginary History of the Next Thirty Years. London:
   Low, and Edinburgh: Menzies, [1857]. 72 pp.
Semiliberal forecasts of reforms, nations becoming politi-
cally independent, and some technological improvements.
Much Anglo-Saxon chauvinism.

Lang, Herrmann (pseud.). The Air Battle: A Vision of the
   Future. London: Penny, 1859. [ii+]112 pp.
5,000 years in the future geological and political
changes have left the dark-skinned empires of Brazilia,
Madeira, and Sahara contending for supremacy in naval and
air battles. Melodramatic love-and-hate plot with nasty
Jew and Irishman, comic black servant, yet also happy
ending with racial intermarriage. Nonetheless a remarkable work, not only historically pioneering but also one of
the first narratively successful S-F romances set in the
future.

Trueman, Chrysostom, "ed." (pseud.). The History of a
   Voyage to the Moon: With an Account of the Adventurers'
   Subsequent Discoveries. London: Lockwood, 1864. 204
   pp.
Part 1, "The Voyage": narrator finds manuscript about
levitation, together with friend finds, after many discussions and adventures, two minerals in California which,

when mixed together, produce "repulsion." They build an "island earth" with all scientific frills, including plants for oxygen, fly from Earth to Moon with much metaphysical speculation on the way. Part 2, "The Ideal Life": utopia on further hemisphere with small people who have a much higher capacity for pleasure, no diseases or predators known, one language, one sea. Politically a self-governing federation of workmen without economic distinctions or sexual roles, short working time. Lunarians die painlessly at about 70 years; since they are amnesiac reincarnations of select Earthmen, perhaps they reincarnate again elsewhere. Narrative put into metal balls and Moon volcano at eruption, arrives to "Trueman" on Earth. Certainly the most significant S-F novel between Shelley and the 1870s, it influenced both Verne and Wells.

Hayward, William S[tephens]. The Cloud King: or, Up in the Air and Down in the Sea: Being a History of the Wonderful Adventures of Victor Volans. London: Clarke, and Darton & Stodge, 1865. 356 pp.
Hidden valley in Africa with spots of lower gravitation and beautiful ageless people. Balloons, undersea voyage, unknown marine animal. (Apparently two identical editions in the same year, but this could not be verified.)

Chatelain, Madame [Clara] de. The Sedan-Chair, and Sir Wilfred's Seven Flights. London: Routledge, 1866. 300 pp.
Two long stories: the first a magic sedan-chair in Renaissance England; the second, seven flights by means of it, including to underwater city (lost race plus ancient gods), to Golden City, to Mercury with fire-people, to Moon where thoughts are visible and to Saturn with less dense matter and rejuvenation, to pyramid with arrested time. Juveniles, very marginal.

Heliomanes (pseud.). A Journey to the Sun. London: Cornish, 1866. 29 pp.
Flight using compressed air and endangered by comets and meteors. Above Sun surface is a molten metal shell. Generally topsy-turvy life, with some political satire.

Lord Macaulay's New Zealander (pseud. of Frederick Gale). The History of the English Revolution of 1867. Edited by Wykehamicus Friedrich (pseud. of same). Westminster: King, 3867 [i.e., 1867]. 31 pp.
Satire on Reform Bill of 1867: Church and State abolished by new government, but armed forces and banks stand

firm so that finally the old order is reestablished.

Mohoao (pseud. of Edwin Fairburn). The Ships of Tarshish: A Sequel to Sue's "Wandering Jew." London: Hall, 1867. 104 pp.
English descendant of Wandering Jew builds fire-spewing ironclads and saves England. (Reprint in 1884 adds a 32 page Prologue on how the 1867 printing was not put on sale before, and on mystical connection between England and Israel.)

[Helps, Arthur.] Realmah. London: Macmillan, 1868. 2 vols., 299+320 pp.
Tale of prehistoric tribe, its politics, wars, and religion, in upper-class bantering dialogue. Protagonist invents use of iron and becomes king.

O'Neil, Henry [Nelson]. 2000 Years Hence. London: Chapman & Hall, [1868]. 351 pp.
In 3867, when Britain is depopulated and colder, its New Zealander governor writes a history of its 19th century. Description by sectors, against reforms of 1832 and 1867. Little coherence.

1871-1879

[Bulwer-Lytton, Edward George Earle Lytton.] The Coming Race. Edinburgh and London: Blackwood, 1871. 292 pp.
Subterranean race in biological control of mysterious energy "vril" which makes work and a "separate working class" unnecessary and deviance impossible. Collective social organization, some gender-role reversal (e.g., in courtship); domestic robots, flying machines, and sleep-teaching; incidental satire on Darwinism and democracy. The "endangered narrator" ploy and the demagogic mixture of utopianism, sensationalism, and elitist political reactionariness or indeed semioccultism made for this novel's instant popularity. Together with Butler 1872, Chesney 1871, and Verne 1872 (q.v., all), it sparked the publishing revival of an SF suggesting, but also warning against, significantly different relations, and fusing new gadgetry with sentimental and/or horrific melodrama.

[Chesney, George Tomkyns.] The Battle of Dorking: Reminiscences of a Volunteer. Edinburgh and London: Blackwood, 1871. 64 pp.
Reminiscences 50 years later on terrible defeat of valiant but unprepared British by German invasion; lack of

preparation blamed on the rise of irresponsible "lower classes." England stripped of all colonies, trade, and wealth. Provoked immediately a torrent of variations and rebuttals, and became fountainhead of subgenre of future war" (see Introduction, biography, and MOSF).

[Harting, Pieter.] Anno Domini 2071. London: n.p., 1871. 128 pp. (Dutch original as Dr. Dioscorides, Anno 2065, 1865.)
Dream of visit to 21st century and balloon-voyage with Roger Bacon. New technologies, new source of energy, and world peace, but all on unchanging basis of liberalism, competitive capitalism, and industry.

Hemyng, [Samuel] Bracebridge. The Commune in London: or, Thirty Years Hence: A Chapter of Anticipated History. London: Clarke, [1871?]. 45 pp.
Sensationalist and muddled anticommunist description, mostly of gory fighting and horrors.

His Royal Highness Mammoth Martinet, alias Moho-Yoho-Me-Oo-Oo (pseud.). The Gorilla Origin of Man: or, The Darwin Theory of Development, Confirmed From Recent Travels in the New World Called Myu-me-ae-nia, or Gossipland. London: Farrah, 1871. 168 pp.
Semi-allegorical satire, set in concave world beyond the polar sea, of British customs and politics. Both science, materialism, communism, the slum mobs and Thiers's "butchery," armies, churches, courts satirized.

The Island of Atlantis: A Personal Narrative of the Travels and Wonderful Adventures of Lord Arthur A.....y, of Phantom Castle, Ben Nevis. [London?: n.p.], 1871. 59 pp.
In 1840s Rosicrucians live on huge Atlantic floating island, have airships, submarines, camouflage, elixir of life, Philosopher's Stone, most of it explained scientifically. They defeat rebel sorcerer faction, are translated to Sun/Heaven. Marginal.

J.W.M. The Coming Cromwell. London: British & Colonial Pub., 1871. 48 pp.
Unclear narration of a new "Cromwell" winning a new civil war of communists and middle classes against monarchist North, proclaiming republic and Irish Home Rule. War against Germany which supports monarchists results in German Republic.

Maguire, John Francis. The Next Generation. London:
    Hurst & Blackett, 1871. 3 vols., 330+337+330 pp.
Sentimental and parliamentary manoeuvers in 1892, when
women lead House of Commons, Ireland has Home Rule, steam
balloons and the Channel Tunnel facilitate communication,
British Empire rules China, and things are hunky-dory.

McCauley, Motly Ranke (pseud.). Chapters From Future His-
    tory: The Battle of Berlin (Die Schlacht von Königs-
    berg). London: Tinsley Bros., 1890 [i.e., 1871]. 54
    pp.
Germany and Russia war on Britain. Civil war in Germany
culminates in battle of republicans and British against
king and Russians. All Europe turns republican.

[Butler, Samuel.] Erewhon: or, Over the Range. London:
    Trübner, 1872. viii+246 pp.
Country on the antipodes with reversal in the social role
of illness versus crime, reason versus unreason, religion
versus banking; the changes are not only mutually incompatible but also hesitate between satire, cynicism, and
amusing paradox. Most famous part applies Darwinist evolution to machines, banned to avoid enslavement of man. Popularity of the novel prompted many variations on similar
themes.

Verne, Jules. Journey to the Centre of the Earth. Lon-
    don: Griffith & Farran, 1872. 384 pp. (French original
    Voyage au centre de la Terre, 1864).
Verne's first S-F novel and translation in the UK, one of
his most splendid epics of voyage inscribed into the space
of quantifying, measuring, and classificatory pre-Darwinian
sciences--here geology. The voyage is the spatial parallel
of solving the initial scientific dilemma or riddle, and it
draws its excitement from the prestige of mid-19th-century
science. This formula had a strong impact, and Vernean
combinations of liberal utopianism, quantifying gadgetry,
and adventurous voyage found very many inferior imitators.
(See for more on Verne MOSF and the bibliography in it.)

[Dudgeon, Robert Ellis.] Colymbia. London: Trübner,
    1873. 255 pp.
An underwater race, its institutions and some technologi-
cal adaptations. Much water/air parallelism, some sub-
Butlerian satire on religion, etc.

Hermes (pseud. of Benjamin Lumley). Another World: or,
    Fragments From the Star City of Montalluyah. London:

Tinsley, [1873].   306 pp.
Autobiographical fragment by supreme ruler of planet
(probably Mars). Emphasis on electricity for locomotion, lessening weight, optics, medicine, music; also on
teaching, marriage, Baconian knowledge, and new instruments.

Jenkins, [John] Edward. Little Hodge. London: King,
    1873. 108 pp.
Scenes from country life in future year 18--, in effec-
tive local dialect. Agricultural strike viewed with
Dickensian sympathy as against bureaucratic centralization.
Solutions are class reconciliation, reform, and emigration
to USA. Ten years later everything is rosy.

Maitland, Edward. By and By: An Historical Romance of
    the Future. London: Bentley, 1873. 3 vols., iv+1,034
    pp.
Long, ambitious, in places ingenious ideological melodrama focused on political and moral adventures of young,
rich, multiracial, and royal superhero in a world of
African empires, united Europe, capitalist Jews in Palestine, and a generally enlightened international order.
Electromagnetic flying machines and communication coexist
with talismans, a superrace of "angels" favoring hero, his
final ascension into death, and other mystic hints. Social
classes are reconciled in a corporative neocapitalism, with
partnership of capital and labor and enterprises such as a
Sahara Sea, based on a religious renovation and clerisy
reconciling love and "higher" science as against animal
instincts and cold reason (incarnated in the hero's two
wives). The lengthy alternatives to and criticisms of
Victorian starchiness in political and family life are
occasionally bold, approaching some ideas of the "utopian
socialists," but frequently mawkish, preachy, and imperialist. Important and representative precursor of similar
ideological blind alleys in SF.

Verne, Jules. From the Earth to the Moon Direct in 97
    Hours 20 Minutes; and A Trip Around It. London: Low,
    Marston, 1873. 323 pp. (French original De la Terre à
    la Lune, 1865, and Autour de la Lune, 1870.)
Exciting adventures combining Yankee technological triumphs with Gallic exuberance, and dipping a cautious toe
into interplanetary space without violating the safely
circular nature of the voyage. Grafted--as all Verne--on
previous S-F tradition (including Poe and "Trueman"), in
turn gave it strong further impetus and inflection.

_____. Twenty Thousand Leagues Under the Seas. London: Low, Marston, 1873. 303 pp. (French original Vingt mille lieues sous les mers, 1870.)
Probably Verne's best novel, combining marine sciences with revolutionary liberalism, the electric submarine with a Byronic freedom-fighter corsair, the Ulysses tradition of circumnavigation with that of attaining the still point of the Pole.

Back Again: or, Five Years of Liberal Rule: 1880-5: A Forecast. London: Low, Marston, 1880 [1874]. 32 pp.
Liberals disarm, lose many colonies which join USA, other powers divide Europe and Asia.

[Blair, Andrew.] Annals of the Twenty-Ninth Century: or, The Autobiography of the Tenth President of the World-Republic. London: Tinsley, 1874. 3 vols., 260+248+250 pp.
Utopian projections in turgid pseudoclassical style. After political and geological cataclysms, a united world realizes scientific wonders of training working animals, leveling mountains, clearing satellites near Earth, trying out a Vernean Moon-gun, and boring through Earth. Planets reached: Moon with animals, plants, and corridors, Venusians unfallen and angel-like, Mercurians even superior, travel to Jupiter. Difficult to stomach, but a link between Verne and Wells.

Collins, [Edward James] Mortimer. Transmigration. London: Hurst & Blackett, 1874. 3 vols., 320+264+292 pp.
In volume 2, narrator after death reincarnates on Mars where life is Epicurean, money abolished, and Troy, Rome, Childland, troubadour château, etc., are to be found. In volume 3, reborn on Earth, he marries granddaughter of volume 1 sweetheart. Marginal.

L[ach-] S[zyrma], W[ladislas] S[omerville]. A Voice From Another World. Oxford and London: Parker, 1874. 68 pp.
Could not be checked, but apparently the nucleus (chapter 7) of the author's later Aleriel (q.v., 1883), reporting the protagonist's visit on Earth.

[Davis, Ellis James.] Pyrna: A Commune: or, Under the Ice. London: Bickers, 1875. 142 pp.
Deist and rationalist utopia under alpine glacier. Community of goods, obligation to work, planned welfare state, collective education, Christian brotherliness, geometrical

city. Pyrnians have adapted by lowering their animal warmth. Guide explains all to only gradually persuaded visitor.

Etymonia. London: Tinsley, 1875. 258 pp.
Narrator castaway on island updating More, only even more geometrical. Federation of self-governing communes, equality, uniformity, rule of elders, agricultural economy, but also sexual freedom and population control. Fight against invaders who take narrator out.

In the Future: A Sketch in Ten Chapters. London: [The Hampstead and Highgate] "Express," [1875?]. 66 pp.
As backlash to radical revolution, federal monarchy is constituted in area of ancient Hellenistic and Roman empires and on their "pagan" rationalist principles. Omnipotent State owns all land and capital, divides men and women into professional castes (including yellow race immigrants as manual laborers). Opposed by Russia and assorted Christian liberals, Moslem constitutionalists, and libertarian anarchists (Jews are treated more leniently).

Penrice, Arthur (pseud.). Skyward and Earthward. London: Tinsley, 1875. 279 pp.
Narrator with friends flies in improved balloon to Moon--where they find telepathic inhabitants in caves--Mars, Jupiter moon, and back.

Verne, Jules. The Mysterious Island. London: Low, Marston, 1875. 304 pp. (French original L'Ile mystérieuse, 1875.)
Shipwrecked group recreates in its mastering of nature by means of scientific know-how and technological organization the rise of bourgeois civilization in the key of liberal utopianism, without social conflicts or any class, sexual, or national enslavement. The island location both permits this long parable and makes evident its final sterility, which can only be overcome by melodramatic plot tricks of hidden benefactor and natural catastrophe.

Collens, T[homas] Wharton. Eden of Labor: or, the Christian Utopia. Philadelphia: Baird, 1876. 228 pp. EC 1876.
After expulsion from Eden of Rest, antediluvian Eden of Labor--where labor is the measure of all exchangeable value--is supplanted by Cain-descended caste society with "our present institutions" based on private property of land, which provokes the Flood. Imaginary economics plus a

bit of imaginary history with wars and revolts, all framed
by theoretical chapters of Christian socialism. Imaginary
history on the verge of becoming fiction.

Soleman, William. Caxtonia's Cabinet. London:. Provost,
    1876. 40 pp.
Comic story of woman elected as Tory prime minister,
names cabinet by looks; various nonsensical bills passed.
All was a dream.

Merlin Nostradamus (pseud. of Frances Power Cobbe). The
    Age of Science: A Newspaper of the Twentieth Century.
    London: Ward, Lock, [1877]. 50 pp.
New Year 1977 issue of newspaper details an age dominated
by medicine and science. Some changes in international
politics. Dull pseudosatire.

Verne, Jules. The Child of the Cavern: or, Strange Do-
    ings Underground. London: Low, Marston, 1877. 246 pp.
    (French original Les Indes Noires, 1877.)
Underground mining city and microcosm of darkness and
closure with emblematic old man and maiden. The otherness
of the locale approaches SF, if only obliquely.

About, Edmond [François Valentin]. Colonel Fougas' Mis-
    take: A Novel. London: Remington, 1878. 2 vols.,
    244+255 pp. (French original L'Homme à l'oreille cas-
    sée, 1862; US edition as The Man With the Broken Ear,
    1867.)
Napoleon's colonel, "dessicated" in 1813, is resuscitated
in 1859, brimful of patriotism and enthusiasm for the homonymous granddaughter of his earlier beloved.

Verne, Jules. Hector Servadac: or, The Career of a
    Comet. London: Low, Marston, 1878. 370 pp. (French
    original with same title, 1877; US edition, 1877.)
Comet circling within solar system tears off chunk of
Earth. First clear sign of Verne's decline, with chauvinism replacing the euphoria of earlier space voyages, it is
still very interesting as parable of obstacles to circulation centered on hoarding gold, with a memorable congealed
sea.

[Chesney, George Tomkyns.] The New Ordeal. Edinburgh
    and London: Blackwood, 1879. 140 pp.
New explosives make war impossible. It is replaced by
combat of 105 national champions, with spectators; Britain
wins.

Payn, James. High Spirits: Being Certain Stories Written
   in Them, vol. 3. London: Chatto & Windus, 1879. 293
   pp. Contains among others: "The Fatal Curiosity, or a
   Hundred Years Hence" (pp. 113-219) and "The Cruise of the
   Anti-Torpedo" (pp. 221-93).
   Comic stories. In first: 1979 sees coal worth its
weight in diamonds, sermons and mountain air piped into
homes, a kind of TV, food pills, air travel, status based
on ideas, cooperation of capital and labor. In second (published separately 1871, see Appendix): new submarine with
gun sinks German navy after Battle of Dorking, with some US
help, and liberates Britain.

Verne, Jules. The Begum's Fortune. London: Low,
   Marston, 1880 [1879]. 272 pp. (French original Les
   Cinq cents millions de la Bégum, 1879; US edition as
   The 500 Millions of the Begum, 1879.)
   Teutonic autocratic Steel-City, built around a factory
for supercannons by evil scientist boss, is foiled by our
hero and vaguely balanced by the rosewater suburbanite
colony of France-Ville. For all the melodrama, the foretaste of a captive labor-force that builds ballistic MIRVs
using asphyxiating cold has impressive sequences.

[Watson, Henry Crocker Marriott.] Erchomenon: or, The
   Republic of Materialism. London: Low, Marston, 1879.
   viii+226 pp.
   In 600 years, year 550 of the Commune, Germany and Russia
rule Europe, USA the New World, sick people and unfit
babies are killed off, religion and nuclear family have
been destroyed, positivism and Darwinism dominate, and
women smoke. Gas-filled aerial machines, phonographs, tele-
microphones. Small Christian community holds out amid
gambling, drinking, fornication, and suicides at large.
Finally the Last Judgment arrives, but it was all a dream.

                              1880

Greg, Percy, "ed." (written by). Across the Zodiac: The
   Story of a Wrecked Record. London: Trübner, 1880. 2
   vols., 296+288 pp.
   Manuscript, found after mysterious catastrophe in Pacific, describes how repulsion-force takes vessel to
science-dominated Mars with electricity, vessels for all
elements, trained working animals, telephones, etc. Martian history has developed from class society through horrible democratic communism to listless materialist and
rationalist autocracy. A religious secret society stages

uprising with help of hero, who finally flies to Earth.
Much violent sermonizing against unspiritual science, communism, and sex equality, and a mawkish yet sadistic love
subplot with polygamy and a child-bride. Nonetheless historically important if not successful attempt at combining
Vernean strange invention, social anatomy, and historico-
sentimental adventure, which clearly influenced Wells.

Hay, William Delisle. The Doom of the Great City: Being
the Narrative of a Survivor Written A.D. 1942. London:
Newman, [1880]. 52 pp.
Immorality of London society punished by killer fog in
1882, strewing its streets with corpses. Preachy, clerical
antimaterialism.

Ryan, G.H. Fifteen Months in the Moon: Giving a Full
Description of its Inhabitants: Their Appearance: Customs: Laws: Modes of Locomotion: Animals: Plants,
etc. London: Ryan, [1880]. 96 pp.
Narrator levitates to the Moon, whose inhabitants have
sixth sense, electricity, monorails, airflight, diamond
manufacture. Poor story.

1881

Hay, William Delisle. Three Hundred Years Hence: or, A
Voice From Posterity. London: Newman, 1881. xv+356
pp.
Atlantean 22nd-century lectures on history determined by
overpopulation, which leads to national and civil wars with
new weapons. United white "socialism" discovers a new
force and transfers much population to undersea cities,
wipes out yellow and black races. Fine example of proto-
fascist racism, exemplary and influential in spite (or
because?) of its awkward style.

Lang-Tung (pseud.). The Decline and Fall of the British
Empire: Being a History of England Between the Years
1840-1981: Written for the Use of Junior Classes in
Schools. London: White, 1881. 32 pp.
Chinese historiographer in 2881 details fall of Britain
into barbarism because of liberals, suffragettes, and
"Social Communists" who introduce free love and atheism
after civil war; even climate changes to colder. Christian-
ized Chinese send missionaries to the barbarians.

M. Pee (pseud.). Hibernia's House: The Irish Commons
Assembled at Dublin: Extraordinary Debate: Amusing

Scenes in the House. London: Allen, [1881]. 30 pp.
Newspaper report from 1990 of silly debate by boorish
Micks in Irish brogue.

Robinson, Phil[ip Stewart]. Under the Punkah. London:
Low, Marston, 1881. vii+255 pp. Contains among others:
"The Man-eating Tree" (pp. 1–13) and "The Hunting of the
Soko" (pp. 35–63).
First story on carnivorous plant, second on apeman.

1882

[Besant, Walter.] The Revolt of Man. Edinburgh and
London: Blackwood, 1882. 358 pp.
In future England women rule, badly of course, having all
the prerogatives that are now male--leading positions in
politics, armed forces, religion, etc. After feeble plot-
intrigues men revolt and restore the "natural order" where
women are again housewives, which most of them wanted anyway. Such a natural love triumphs for our heroes too.
Rather brainless attempt at satire.

The Dawn of the 20th Century: A Novel, Social and Political. London: Remington, 1882. 3 vols., 277+236+268
pp.
Politics from right-wing, Irish landlord point of view,
using clumsy love-plot and clumsy dialogue. In 1900 all
religions join Church of England, England leads European
federation, colonies abound, "photophones" are used. (Not
identical to same title in 1888, q. v.)

Green, Nunsowe (pseud.). A Thousand Years Hence: Being
Personal Experiences as Narrated by. . . . London:
Low, Marston, 1882. xii+397 pp.
Framework discussion on the future with a group of
friends of different interests, jumps to 2882. Horrendous
overpopulation, welfare state, new energy, universal education and peace, artificial food, oceans filled in,
flights to planets--all happened in 20th-21st century.
In each succeeding century one new aspect presented. Much
detail of life on other planets, culminating in another
jump to 3882: "higher life," on planets nearer to
respective suns, is in the universe always in charge of
outer-planet life. Man in the Moon died out, Venus men
more advanced, Mars repeats English history, "Solars" have
an extra sense which can calculate the future. All was a
dream. A wealth of ideas prefiguring much modern SF, if
somewhat disjointedly.

Grip (pseud. of Edgar Luderne Welch). The Monster Munici-
    pality: or, Gog and Magog Reformed: A Dream. London:
    Low, Marston, 1882. 128 pp.
Dream of London municipality under Radicals after self-
government reform of 1885. Confiscations, corruption, high
taxes, finally it is dissolved.

Trollope, Anthony. The Fixed Period: A Novel. Edin-
    burgh and London: Blackwood, 1882. 2 vols., 200+203 pp.
Antipodean British settlement adopts in the 1980s age of
67.5 years as "fixed period" for economic euthanasia.
Narration by leading exponent of the measure, which is
scuttled by UK forces reannexing the settlement, is the
only device of interest beyond initial idea.

1883

The Battle of the Moy: or, How Ireland Gained Her Indepen-
    dence 1892-1894. London: Sonnenschein, 1883. 123 pp.
Home-Rule Ireland repeals union with England during UK-
German war. Irish army with German support wins battle,
described at length. New republic confiscates alien possessions, prosperity ensues.

Lach-Szyrma, W[ladislaw] S[omerville]. Aleriel: or, A
    Voyage to Other Worlds: A Tale. London: Wyman & Sons,
    1883. 220 pp.
Winged and godly Venusian with psychic powers comes to
Earth. Rest of book is manuscript of his travels in the
solar system where life is universal. Tropical Venus is
without sin and death; Mars in the next stage awaiting
Earth, with one state, language, and religion, electric
locomotion; Jupiter with rational ocean-dwellers and undersea city; Saturn and its moon. Clearly influenced Wells.
(Expanded from the author's A Voice from Another World,
1874, which was apparently only the Earth visit.)

Ulidia (pseud.). The Battle of Newry: or, The Result of
    Thirty Years' Liberal Legislation. Dublin: Hodges,
    Figgis, 1883. 42 pp.
In 1910 Liberals abolish House of Lords and confiscate
their estates, aristocracy emigrates to USA. New Parliament dispossesses Irish landlords, Ulster revolts, is
joined by Scotland, the king, and armed forces, and wins.
Upper class reinstituted, prosperity reappears, and "the
great class struggle . . . between the rich and poor" dies
out. But for this ending, a remarkably realistic right-
wing scenario. (First edition could not be found, probably

also in 1883, possibly in London?)

[Welch, Edgar Luderne?] Politics and Life in Mars: A Story of a Neighbouring Planet. London: Low, Marston, 1883. 201 pp.
Technologically and politically advanced Mars (in medicine, travel, religion, political and economic democracy, women's rights, universal peace with international police) is used to satirize Earth institutions, in particular English politics and the subjection of Ireland. Some remarkable utopian-socialist traits, which lead me to query the identification of the author (see "Grip," 1882, "Gay," 1887, and the biographical entry).

1884

Allen, [Charles] Grant [Blairfindie]. Strange Stories. London: Chatto & Windus, 1884. vi+356 pp. Contains among others: "Pausodyne" (pp. 234-54) and "The Child of the Phalanstery" (pp. 301-20).
First story on suspended animation, second on euthanasia of deformed child in future collectivist world.

Bellamy, Edward. Dr. Heidenhoff's Process. Edinburgh: Douglas, 1884. 234 pp. (US original, 1880).
Invention permits erasure of painful memories. All was a dream.

[Brookfield, Arthur Montagu.] Simiocracy: A Fragment From Future History. Edinburgh and London: Blackwood, 1884. 186 pp.
Satire against radical liberals who admit orang-outangs to equality with men and import millions to vote for them. England subjugated.

An Eye-Witness (pseud. of ? Fairfield?). The Socialist Revolution of 1888, by. . . . London: Harrison, 1884. 35 pp.
Socialists come to power in England, but in spite of their good will become detested due to loss of affluence and State supervision. Finally they are turned out of office peacefully, Irish Home Rule is retained. Not unshrewd critique.

Hoffmann, E[rnst] T[heodor] A[madeus]. "The Sandman," in his Weird Tales. London: Nimmo, 1885 [1884]. Vol. 1, pp. 173-222. (German original "Der Sandmann," 1817; US in Hoffmann's Strange Stories, 1855.)

Romantic story of lovely woman who turns out to be a horrible mechanical construct by malignant scientist. Oscillating between fiends and physics, but great influence down
to Čapek. Marginal.

Robinson, E[dward] A., and G[eorge] A. Wall. The Disk: A
   Prophetic Reflection. London: Griffith, Farran, 1884.
   xi+182 pp.
   Inventor and businessman friend develop "photoelectro-
phone" TV. Concurrently Panama sinks, Europe grows colder.
Second invention prolongs life by preserving organic matter. Sentimental melodrama around inventor's wife, he is
killed in explosion.

A Square (pseud. of Edwin Abbott Abbott). Flatland: A
   Romance of Many Dimensions. London: Seeley, 1884.
   viii+100 pp.
   Narrator in worlds of dimensions: Pointland, Lineland,
Flatland, Spaceland, peopled by geometrical figures. Used
for acute analogies to human class perception, conceiving,
and behavior, and radical social satire. A pioneer of SF
as cognitive parable, and the culmination of UK SF up to
that time.

[Wise, Clement.] Darkness and Dawn: The Peaceful Birth
   of a New Age. London: Paul, Trench, 1884. 141 pp.
   Christian communist tract against capitalist pillage,
abolished by rich aristocrat giving example of renunciation. Universal state ownership, equality, and work, inheritance abolished. Turgid writing, most of it not fiction.
Marginal.

                            1885

The Battle of To-Morrow. London: Chappel, 1885. 54 pp.
   UK in 1890 wars with Russia over India and with France
over the Netherlands, and loses with great slaughter.

Coverdale, Henry Standish (pseud.). The Fall of the Great
   Republic (1886-88) by Sir Henry Standish Coverdale Inten-
   dant for the Board of European Administration in the
   Province of New York: By Permission of the Bureau of
   Press Censorship: New York 1895. London: Low,
   Marston, 1885. 226 pp.
   After hard times in USA 1882-1887, combination of radical
immigrants, socialist poison, and corrupt morals leads to
left-wing revolts and then to war with UK and Europe. They
occupy USA to protect business and order.

An Ex-M.P. (pseud.). A Radical Nightmare: or, England
  Forty Years Hence. London: Field & Tuer, and Simpkin,
  Marshall, [1885]. 62 pp.
In 1925 Germany has conquered France, shattered by civil
war. Britain is radical republic with female equality and
atheism because radicals won 1885 election, so "take care
for whom you vote."

Gillmore, Parker. The Amphibion's Voyage. London:
  Allen, 1885. 366 pp.
Travel in amphibious vessel.

Greer, T[h]om[as]. A Modern Daedalus. London: Griffith, Farran, 1885. xvi+261 pp.
Hero invents winged flight, English government tries to
appropriate it but he escapes to Ireland and trains squad
who bomb English armed forces with dynamite. Ireland gains
independence, flying will be used for the original peaceful
purposes. In story, and in introduction set in 1887, narrator proclaims preference for equal Anglo-Irish union by
peaceful means.

Jefferies, [John] Richard. After London: or, Wild
  England. London: Cassell, 1885. vii+442 pp.
Fall of modern civilization results in new barbarism.
The reassertion of intensely rendered wild life, roving
tribes and individuals, legends about the "ancients" and
the poisonous site of their old metropolis, new geopolitics
superimposed on old maps--all of these prefigure much subsequent SF. Plot is the affirmation of our hero on his
adventurous journey. Unequal, but still a minor masterpiece.

John Haile: A Story of Successful Failure. London:
  Low, Marston, 1885. 3 vols., 248+243+256 pp.
Melodrama of love and politics around two foundling boys,
whose blood will out. Rise of nouveau riches and workers,
downfall of nobility and religion, victorious war of 1889
squandered by Liberals. Three parties from the three
social classes in 1901. One protagonist becomes Radical
leader, the other a poet; Radicals and Conservatives should
ally against spineless merchants. Confused Social-
Darwinism.

The New Democracy: A Fragment of Caucusian History. London: Low, Marston, 1885. 155 pp.
Narrator shipwrecked on island of Caucusia, finds female
equality and electric locomotion. Mostly political satire:

queen a machine puppet, hero campaigns against too much democracy which breeds despotic plot by radical leader, his love rival. Finally hero kidnapped and put to sea.

S.L.S. (pseud. of John St. Loe Strachey). The Great Bread Riots: or, What Came of Fair Trade. London: Simpkin, Marshall, 1885. 60 pp.
Retrospective from 1934: abolition of free trade resulted in disastrous inflation and socialist-anarchist riots, quelled by upper-class plot.

1886

Adeler, Max (pseud. of Charles Heber Clark), and Other Popular Authors. A Desperate Adventure and Other Stories. London and New York: Ward, Lock, [1886]. 2 vols., viii+ 122+255 pp. Contains among others: Adeler's "A Desperate Adventure" (1:110-22, earlier UK publication in his Transformations, London: Ward, Lock, [1883]; [Henry Frith's?] "What It Must Come To: or, Four Hundred Years Hence" (2:165-73)--both here anonymous.
First story: five would-be suicides fly to North Pole in a balloon, all change their minds. Second story: future with mechanical servants and writing machines, people flying, solar energy, recorded singing and marriage proposal.

Brydges, Harold (pseud. of James Howard Bridge). A Fortnight in Heaven: An Unconventional Romance. London: Low, Marston, 1886. vii+177 pp.
"Spiritual double" of old sea-dog visits Jupiter, which is Heaven and also a giant replica of USA, but ruled by wicked State communism. In England, upper classes abolished in 20th century, Spencerian progress with some technological novelties. Rather incoherent.

Burnaby, Fred[erick Gustavus]. Our Radicals: A Tale of Love and Politics. Edited by J. Percival Hughes. London: Bentley, 1886. 2 vols., 255+261 pp.
Posthumously edited, alternative political present of Radical rule which gave self-government to Ireland and led to upper-class and army insurrection. Story told from their point of view, with Fenian plots, disguises, and dastardries, mob socialist revolt; gallant general puts Radicals and Irish down and becomes dictator under the queen.

Carne-Ross, Joseph, "ed." (written by). Quintura: Its

Singular People and Remarkable Customs. London: Maxwell, [1886]. 191 pp.
Found manuscript describing Butlerian tongue-in-cheek island through dialogues with a guide. Stress on medicine and family, some satire of English politics.

Genone, Hudor (pseud. of William James Roe). Inquirendo Island. New York and London: Putnam's, 1886. 347 pp.
Shipwreck in Atlantic on Butlerian island where a peculiar mathematics serves as religion.

The Great Irish Rebellion of 1886: Retold by a Landlord. London: Harrison & Sons, 1886. 48 pp.
Orangeman's diary-letter on antilandlord revolt after Home Rule; after initial success, the English reconquer Ireland. Uchronia, with strong class hatred from above.

Hinton, C[harles] H[oward]. Scientific Romances: First Series. London: Sonnenschein, 1886. 229 pp.
Reorientation of perception by means of analogy, mainly from physics. Straight exposition except for "The Persian King" (pp. 33-128): if pain and pleasure could be subjected to thermodynamic calculus, would natives of a closed valley suspect the presence of an invisible king with powers to siphon off pain by reasoning backwards from his effect? Probably influenced Wells.

In the Year One (A.D. 1888) of Home Rule "de jure": A Drive in the West of Ireland: Is It Possible? Is It Probable? London: Allen, and Dublin: McGee, [1886]. 31 pp.
Scary picture of mob rule, violence, and rampant atheism in self-governing Ireland.

Innominatus (pseud. of Edward Heneage Dering). In the Light of the Twentieth Century. London: Hodges, 1886. 155 pp.
Dream-vision of 1960 when state control, free love, and paganism reign, better people long for religion of a Catholic kind. Mob uprising, narrator awakes as he is being killed. Some aspects prefigure Morris closely.

Lang, Andrew. "The Romance of the First Radical," in his In the Wrong Paradise and Other Stories. London: Kegan Paul, Trench, 1886, pp. 177-209.
Possibly the first short story of prehistoric men and one of the most forceful, openly displaying the analogy to the present. "Radical" young hero Why-Why and bride keep trans-

gressing the stultifying customs, and are finally killed by the tribe and its high priests; their martyrdom is today bearing fruit. Bitter-sweet satire.

Lee, Thomas, "ed." (written by). Falsivir's Travels: The Remarkable Adventures of John Falsivir, Seaman, at the North Pole and in the Interior of the Earth: With a Description of the Wonderful People and the Things He Discovered There. London: Published for the Proprietor, 1886. iv+122 pp.
Polar continent leads to Swiftian country in Symmesian hole under an inner sun, whose people are in alternate generations normal and giant-sized. Satire on religion enslaving giants: narrator expelled by priests. One of the most noteworthy tales of its kind.

Lester, Edward. The Siege of Bodike: A Prophecy of Ireland's Future. Manchester and London: Heywood, 1886. 140 pp.
Love and political plots in Home-Rule Ireland. Hero-narrator helps--on horse and in balloon--to suppress rebellion and gains fair lady. Union with UK restored along with landlords and improvements in economy and education.

Miller, Joaquin (pseud. of Cincinnatus Hiner Miller). The Destruction of Gotham. New York and London: Funk & Wagnalls, 1886. 214 pp.
Dickensian tale with seduced girl and noble reporter who befriends her, issues into alternate history; in the last chapter mob burns down New York City. Well written though sentimental. Marginal.

Minto, William. The Crack of Doom: A Novel. Edinburgh and London: Blackwood, 1886. 3 vols., 304+298+284 pp.
Mainly mundane romance with love intrigues. Discovery of comet leads to public agitation--insofar marginal SF.

[Moore, G.H.] Opening and Proceedings of the Irish Parliament: Two Visions. London: Reeves & Turner, 1886. 23 pp.
Two views: "the dark seer" in 1887--riots by Irish-Americans, fights in parliament, English troops restore order; "the bright seer" in 1894--amity of England and Ireland, upper and lower classes.

Newry Bridge: or, Ireland in 1887. Edinburgh and London: Blackwood & Sons, 1886. 72 pp.
Reminiscences of awful results of Home Rule: Ulster re-

bels, wins civil war in crucial battle, Ireland returns to British Empire.

Verne, Jules. Mathias Sandorf. London: Low, Marston, 1886. 2 vols., 192+199 pp. (French original with same title, 1885; US edition, 1885.)
Political and sentimental dastardry foiled by our hero who founds an island-colony in the Mediterranean defended by electric super-submarines. Marginal.

Watlock, W.A. The Next 'Ninety Three: or, Crown, Commune, and Colony: Told in a Citizen's Diary. London: Field & Tuer, [1886]. 36 pp.
Diary of supporter of 1893 law enforcing egalitarianism. Total State control, much oppression, 4 hours work per day. Legion of colonials restores old regime. Intelligent anti-revolutionary tale.

1887

A Captain of the Royal Navy (pseud.). The Battle off Worthing: Why the Invaders Never Got to Dorking: A Prophecy. London: London Literary Society, 1887. 96 pp.
Retrospect from 1900 on how Royal Navy prevented invasion.

Collingwood, Harry (pseud. of William Joseph Cosens Lancaster). The Log of the "Flying Fish": A Story of Aerial and Submarine Peril and Adventure. London: Blackie, 1887. 384 pp.
German professor invents new light metal and crystal source of gas and electricity for Vernean amphibious vessel. Adventures on North Pole island in warm sea with mammoths and diamonds, in Africa where unicorns and ruins of Ophir are found, on Mt. Everest.

Courteney, Luke Theophilus (pseud. of Alfred Taylor Schofield). Travels in the Interior: or, The Wonderful Adventures of Luke and Belinda: Edited by a London Physician. London: Ward & Downey, 1887. 316 pp.
Manuscript found at a physician's about our protagonists dwindling to 1/50 inch and traveling through the human body. All was a dream.

Curwen, Henry. Zit and Xoe: Their Early Experience. Edinburgh: Blackwood & Sons, 1887. 131 pp.
Mawkishly comic tale of first man and woman descended

from apes yet with all the Victorian petty-bourgeois habits
and opinions. They evolve whole prehistoric society up to
the rise of theft.

Dodd, Anna Bowman. The Republic of the Future: or, Socialism a Reality. New York: Cassell, 1887. 86 pp. EC
1887.
Letters of Swedish nobleman from 2050 USA. State runs
economy and educates children, life is equalized, dull,
mechanized, electrified, people are apathetic. Women don't
cook but work, learning, and travel are forbidden. Perfunctory panorama with little plot.

E.W. (pseud. of Elizabeth Waterhouse). The Island of Anarchy: A Fragment of History in the Twentieth Century.
Reading: Miss Langley, Lovejoy's Library, 1887. 105 pp.
Government of young people returns women to homes and
exiles all subversives to Pacific island. There, peaceful
English Christian communists led by venerable sage are
killed off by violent continental socialists and nihilists,
who are in turn menaced by Dacoits. Finally earthquake
swallows the island except for dying Russian prince-
anarchist who tells their story. Very right-wing but interesting.

[Fox, Samuel Middleton.] Our Own Pompeii: A Romance of
Tomorrow. Edinburgh and London: Blackwood, 1887. 2
vols., 248+250 pp.
Satire within political and love intrigues. Hellenic-
type pleasure city of art built on the Riviera by high
society, abandoned as too expensive.

Gay, J. Drew (pseud. of Edgar Luderne Welch). The Mystery
of the Shroud: A Tale of Socialism. Bristol: Arrowsmith, and London: Simpkin, Marshall, [1887]. 134 pp.
Dastardly secret society, under cover of fog from cheap
coal discovered in England, plans to overthrow government,
but is foiled. Quite badly composed.

Genone, Hudor (pseud. of William James Roe). Bellona's
Husband: A Romance. London and New York: Putnam,
1887. 332 pp.
Professor invents metal "buoyant" to gravity. Flippant
narration by capitalist protagonist plus comments of manuscript finder expressing various doubts. Humans on Mars
have thought-reading device, live backward from old age to
youth. Some satire of law, medicine, and church, all rather disjointed.

[Hudson, William Henry.] A Crystal Age. London: Unwin, 1887. 287 pp.
Narrator awakes in pastoral future based on beehive-type matriarchal family where only one woman (or man) is sexed. Well rendered if ultimately ambiguous and self-defeating equation of modern civilization with sexual passion, simultaneously sick and indispensably sweet for hero. Only solution is death. Significant S-F milestone.

[Jackson, Edward Payson.] A Demigod: A Novel. New York: Harper & Bros., 1887. 337 pp. EC 1887.
Artificial selection (unexplained) produces perfect if socially naive man in remote part of Greece, who makes artificial diamonds.

Man Abroad: A Yarn of Some Other Century. London: Low, Marston, 1887. 114 pp. (US original, 1886.)
Mostly parallel to US politics in future US of Earth, both internally and in relation to other planets and wars with them. Asteroid of Henrygeorgia with small landholders helps in reforming political corruption. Politically but not narratively interesting--mainly long speeches.

North, Delaval. The Last Man in London. London: Hodder & Stoughton, 1887. 118 pp.
Found manuscript with vision of 7 days in empty London.

O'Brien, Fitz-James. The Diamond Lens, With Other Stories. Edited by W. Winter. London: Ward & Downey, 1887. xx+337 pp. Contains among others: "The Diamond Lens" (US original in Atlantic Tales, 1866) and "What Was It?" (US original in The Poems and Stories of Fitz-James O'Brien, 1881).
First story: microscopist falls in love with sylphlike woman seen in drop of water under supermicroscope constructed at the price of murder. Woman dies when water evaporates, narrator crazed. Though still using some spiritualism, this somber tale of elective affinity with creature from different microcosm is a minor masterpiece of early SF. Second story: invisible ghoul from another dimension captured and starved to death.

Verne, Jules. The Clipper of the Clouds. London: Low, Marston, 1887. viii+234 pp. (French original Robur le Conquérant, 1886.)
Flying machine heavier than air takes kidnapped Americans around the world. Protagonist with allegorical name realizes that "science should not overtake ethics" in a

civilization of selfishly opposed interests.

Watten, Bower (pseud. of John King Grant). <u>Stratharran:
or, The Crofters' Revolt</u>. Edinburgh: Oliphant, Anderson, 1887. 190 pp.
Politics and love in Scotland. Year of events unclear,
possibly marginal SF.

Westall, William [Bury]. <u>A Queer Race: The Story of a
Strange People</u>. London and New York: Cassell, 1887.
303 pp.
Descendants of shipwrecked Englishmen on tropical island
have as servants piebald race with better hearing and
sight. Love and adventures of our hero, happy ending.

                              1888

Besant, Walter. <u>The Inner House</u>. Arrowsmith's Christmas
Annual 1888. Bristol and London: Arrowsmith, 1888. 198
pp.
Discovery of immortality ushers in socialism with little
work, no emotions of religion, laughter, and love, euthanasia of old people, uniformity, and rule of physicians.
Dissenters perusing old books rediscover love, honor of
battle, and dignity of death, revive discontent of former
upper class, who revolt to regain land, wealth, arts, amuse-
ment, and love. First-person narration by archvillain
ex-servant. Rebels succeed and secede. A clumsy prefiguration of Orwell, and a clear influence on some elements in
Morris.

<u>The Dawn of the Twentieth Century: 1st January 1901</u>.
London: Field & Tuer, and Simpkin, Marshall, and Hamilton, Adams, 1888. 156 pp.
Series of UK ministerial reports on state of world and
country. Map of Europe slightly different, in the Empire
everything is perfect.

△ (pseud. of Arthur Conan Doyle). "The Great Keinplatz
Experiment," in <u>Dreamland and Ghostland</u> (anonymous
anthology by various hands), vol. 3. London: Redway,
[1888], pp. 64–91.
German professor exchanges souls with his student by
mesmerism.

[De Mille, James.] <u>A Strange Manuscript Found in a Copper
Cylinder</u>. London: Chatto & Windus, 1888. viii+291 pp.
Manuscript, interrupted by discussions of finders who

don't finish reading it, tells of a South Pole people, with Semitic language, found by shipwrecked narrator and his adventures among them. Theocracy celebrating darkness, death, and poverty, with human sacrifices and ichthyosaurus hunt, is horrible but fascinating. For all echoes from More to Poe, the consistency of this inverted world makes for one of the most interesting works of the kind.

"Down With England!" London: Chapman & Hall, 1888. 152 pp. (French original Plus d'Angleterre, 1887.)
Vindictive tale of total British defeat by France and loss of whole Empire.

Grove, W. A Mexican Mystery. London: Digby & Long, [1888]. 144 pp.
Automatic self-feeding locomotive becomes alive and fights off attackers.

Henry, Edgar (pseud. of Albion Winegar Tourgée). '89: Edited From the Original Manuscript. London: Cassell, 1891 [i.e., 1888]. 498 pp.
Narrator founds Order to revive the US South by playing on class divisions in the North and allying with capital against blacks and labor. Communication unions bought off, lock-out and "mercenaries" crush labor, introducing "a new Feudalism." Remarkable foretaste of London's Iron Heel.

Lyon, E[dmund] D[avid]. Ireland's Dream: A Romance of the Future. London: Sonnenschein, Lowrey, 1888. 2 vols., 520 pp.
Melodramatic loves and fights amid horrible lawlessness of newly independent Ireland. Orangemen successfully re- sist Dublin, Irish-American gangsters loot and rape, final- ly Britain restores order. As agitation resumes, our heroes are off to Australia.

MacKay, Donald. The Dynamite Ship. London: Page, Pratt, 1888. 209 pp.
Irish revolutionaries with new dynamite gun on ship in Thames bombard stubborn London and extort independence after much devastation.

Morris, William. "A Dream of John Ball," in his A Dream of John Ball and A King's Lesson. London: Reeves & Turner, 1888, pp. 1-111.
Narrator finds himself amid Peasant Revolt in 14th cen- tury, as visitor from the future discusses historical evolu- tion with its ideologist John Ball, finally awakens. One

of the most beautiful S-F tales of the period, if only marginal.

[Nicholson, Joseph Shield.] <u>Thoth: A Romance</u>. Edinburgh and London: Blackwood, 1888. 209 pp.
At time of Pericles, Athenian beauty kidnapped to city in desert, with submarines, airships, electric light, and other modern devices, all provided long ago by Egyptian Thoth the First; he and his descendants are in suspended animation. Static perfection with misogyny leads to degeneration, "Thoth-at-present," in love with Athenian, determines to reverse the policy, fights with awakened ancestors, city destroyed.

One Who Was There (pseud.). <u>The Great Irish "Wake."</u> [London and New York]: Clement-Smith, 1888. 23 pp.
Reminiscences from 1950 on Irish secession in 1890. Gladstone becomes minister in Ireland, Ulster revolts, after battles Ireland reenters UK.

Payn, James. <u>The Eavesdropper: An Unparalleled Experience</u>. London: Smith, Elder, 1888. 122 pp.
Feeble comedy built on invisibility caused by fernseed paste. Marginal.

Richardson, Benjamin Ward. <u>The Son of a Star: A Romance of the Second Century</u>. London: Longmans, Green, 1888. 3 vols., 286+293+307 pp.
Long historical romance of the Bar Kochba rebellion. One episode is voyage by submarine to island of peace and beauty, without commerce and property. Marginal.

Stewart, Stanley, and Ritson Stewart. <u>The Professor's Last Experiment</u>. London: Sonnenschein, 1888. 129 pp.
Winged, thought-reading "Marsman," trying to contact humans, has wings cut off by fanatical vivisecting professor, who gets killed; Martian escapes.

Vetch, Thomas (pseud.?). <u>The Amber City: Being Some Account of the Adventures of a Steam Crocodile in Central Africa</u>. London: Biggs & Dibenham, [1888]. 291 pp.
Ship fuelled with reusable hydrocarbons, with balloon floats for short flights, finds village with amber buildings. Inferior combination of Verne and Haggard.

Watson, H[enry] B[rereton] Marriott. <u>Marahuna: A Romance</u>. London: Longmans, Green, 1888. 298 pp.
Darwinian finds fire island in Antarctic and fire-maiden,

without sentiments or fear of death, who becomes candid glance at England. In spite of metaphors of heat and passion the possibilities of Homo igneus are evaded: she kills narrator's pure English girl friend and is consumed by volcano.

1889

Bellamy, Edward. Looking Backward, 2000-1887. London: Reeves, [1889]. x+249 pp. (US original, 1888.)
The famous US utopian anticipation which initiated a flood of nearly 200 others. Economic blueprint of State planning and universal civic service making for full security is integrated into sentimental story of Julian West who awakes from mesmeric sleep. He undergoes change of loyalties to this Christian socialism—which came about by peaceful and instantaneous recognition of capitalism's folly—through his host's lectures and daughter's healing love. Bellamy's strength is in fusing the US traditions of unknown worlds or possibilities and of organizing a new world. Transforming stimuli from Hawthorne and Irving, About and "Thiusen" (q.v. both, 1878 and 1890), he will bequeath the materialist view of history as coherent succession of social relations and institutions to Morris and Wells (q.v. both, 1891 and 1895), and thence to all subsequent SF. (For more on Bellamy see MOSF and bibliography therein.)

Bleunard, Albert. Babylon Electrified: The History of an Expedition Undertaken to Restore Ancient Babylon by the Power of Electricity, and How It Resulted. London: Chapman & Hall, 1890 [1889]. 304 pp. (French original La Babylone électrique, 1888.)
Hydro-power, gasoline, and new battery transforming light into electricity lead to technological transformation of Mesopotamia, hindered by unsatisfied workers and natives. Moral: the country will first have to be conquered as colony.

Corbett, Mrs. George (i.e., Elizabeth Burgoyne Corbett). New Amazonia: A Foretaste of the Future. London: Tower, and Newcastle-on-Tyne: Lambert, [1889]. 146 pp.
Dream of woman narrator awakening 600 years in the future among 7-foot women in what had been Ireland. A silly male dandy arrives into the future simultaneously. History of future and conversation with guide: "nerve rejuvenation" for growth; State is Mother; war, monarchy, and poverty abolished; pantheism; vegetarianism; punishment for illegit-

imate children; narrator awakens.

Cromie, Robert. For England's Sake. London: Warne, 1889. 154 pp.
Russian invasion of India 189- foiled by loyal native elite.

Dalton, Henry Robert S[amuel]. Lesbia Newman: A Novel. London: Redway, 1889. 327 pp.
After war of 1890s, when England lost Ireland to USA and important possessions to France and Russia, changes in mores ensued. Girl educated in unorthodox ways brings about women-worship at Ecumenical Council of 1900.

Grove, W. The Wreck of a World. Long's Albion Library, vol. 2. London: Digby & Long, 1889. 151 pp.
Continuation of author's earlier book (q.v., 1888). Anglo-American confederation and Germany dominate world of 1948, with engineering advances including some automation. Machines acquire life and progeny, attack men, after battles US evacuated, our protagonists settle happily in Hawaii after the fashion of More's Utopia, with man-machine struggle unresolved.

Hyne, Charles J[ohn Cutcliffe Wright]. Beneath Your Very Boots: Being a Few Striking Episodes From the Life of Anthony Merlwood Haltoun, Esq.. London: Digby & Long, [1889]. 388 pp.
Race below England uses Earth heat as energy, manufactures diamonds. Theocratic dictatorship, narrator invents boring-machine and is rewarded by pleasure drug. Rebellion against theocracy quelled, he escapes with underground woman.

Laurie, André (pseud. of Paschal Grousset). The Conquest of the Moon: A Story of the Bayouda. London: Low, Marston, 1889. 354 pp. (French original Les Exilés de la Terre, 1888.)
Wildly melodramatic story, beginning in Sudan amid Mahdi uprising, of how the Moon was pulled down by means of a great magnet, with vile dwarf-magicians and a set of pure heroes who get marooned on the Moon, find geysers, remnants of giant Selenites. All main devices from Verne and Flammarion, with inverisimilitudes added.

MacColl, Hugh. Mr. Stranger's Sealed Packet. London: Chatto & Windus, 1889. 338 pp.
Manuscript found by narrator telling of Stranger's con-

structing an antigravity machine and flying to Mars. Finds
blue humans in welfare-state city with synthetic food, electricity, etc., flying monsters, also wandering warrior
tribes. Betrothal to beautiful Martian girl, adventures,
much aerial cavorting. Visits Earth with wife, she dies of
disease, he returns to Mars, machine accidentally lost.
Clearly influenced Wells, but also a precursor of E.R.
Burroughs.

Mitchell, John Ames, "ed." (written by). The Last Ameri-
    can: A Fragment From the Journal of Khan-li, Prince of
    Dimph-Yoo-Chur, and Admiral in the Persian Navy. New
    York: Stokes, 1889. 78 pp. EC 1889.
Persian navy in 30th century finds ruined USA and kills
the last American. US decay due to greed, climate, and bad
European (in particular Irish) influences. Not inelegant
satire.

Murray, G[eorge] G[ilbert] A[imé]. Gobi or Shamo: A
    Story of Three Songs. London: Longmans, Green, 1889.
    376 pp.
Descendants of Hellenes found in Gobi, combining ancient
ethics with great scientific advances, notably explosive
based on "light force." Satire on Europe and against industry. Uprising of neighboring barbarians, fights, and
pursuits.

Stockton, Frank R[ichard]. The Great War Syndicate. Lon-
    don: Longmans, Green, 1889. 160 pp.
Capitalist syndicate hires itself out to the US government and wins war against Britain by means of superweapons,
including a "motor bomb"; the vanquished join in partnership to rule the world. Domesticated in USA the "future
war" subgenre, with its shallow conception of imperial
politics and decisive gadgetry.

The Swoop of the Eagles: An Episode From the Secret
    History of Europe. London: Ward & Downey, 1889. 88
    pp.
Satire on UK bureaucracy and politics when attacked by
Europe. Though unprepared, the English are saved by firm
of international bankers.

Twain, Mark (pseud. of Samuel Langhorne Clemens). A
    Yankee at the Court of King Arthur. London: Chatto &
    Windus, 1889. xvi+525 pp. (US original as A Connecti-
    cut Yankee in King Arthur's Court, same year.)
The classic "dark" epoch-collision projected backward in

history. An ambiguous bourgeois activist intervenes
against feudalism by introducing a patent office, special
schools, sensational newspapers, ads, and stock-market speculation. Yet the Swiftian burlesque and democratic indigna-
tion finally give place to pessimism about humanity, and
the small elite of budding technocrats perishes in carnage.
The narrator escapes first from history into private life,
then into dreams and drifting between historical epochs.
The horizon of havoc, the hero battling against the age,
the problems of outside intervention, even the major blind
spot of relations between hero and the people, make this
the first (and still among the best) of all the "new maps
of hell." (See for more on Twain MOSF and bibliography
therein.)

Vogel, Julius. Anno Domini 2000: or, Woman's Destiny.
  London: Hutchinson, 1889. 331 pp.
  Equally indigestible love and politics in 20th century:
great bankers are beneficent, while lady ministers and
presidents fall in love with handsome heroes.

Widnall, Samuel Page. A Mystery of Sixty Centuries: or,
  A Modern St. George and the Dragon: A Romance. Grant-
  chester: The Author, 1889. 195 pp.
  African adventures in valley of giants or missing links
and pterodactyls. Valley destroyed, hero escapes through
cavern.

Yelverton, Christopher. Oneiros: or, Some Questions of
  the Day. London: Kegan Paul, Trench, 1889. xi+264 pp.
  Utopian blueprints of and speeches from cicerone about
reformer Oneiros who abolishes poverty by decrees. Thinly
veiled by narrator's soul-flight during sickness to planet
1,000 years in advance, and a rudimentary love-interest.
Very marginal.

                          1890

Cobban, J[ames] MacLaren. Master of His Fate. Edinburgh
  and London: Blackwood & Sons, 1890, 247 pp.
  Nervous force magnetically transfused from young people
to wicked doctor who repents and dies suddenly aged. Clear
echo of Dr. Jekyll and Mr. Hyde, but SF.

Cole, Cyrus. The Auroraphone: A Romance. Chicago:
  Kerr, 1890. 249 pp. EC 1890.
  Telegraphic messages through Aurora Borealis from Saturn,
where enterprises are managed as stated in Bellamy, issuing

in revolt of electric robots. Muddled, especially in frequent discussions of religion.

Cromie, Robert. A Plunge Into Space. London and New
   York: Warne, 1890. 240 pp.
Scientist discovers origin of force, casts globe insulated from Earth's attraction, travels with 6 friends to desert Mars. On its poles, perfect people live without politics or money, with TV and airships, but in dawn of decay. Romance between Earthman and Martian girl who stows away on return trip and finally sacrifices herself; globe destroyed. Much sentimentality, but historically interesting halfway position between Verne (who wrote preface to 1891 edition) and Wells.

Dixie, Florence [Caroline]. Gloriana: or, The Revolution
   of 1900. London: Henry, 1890. x+350 pp.
Preface on equal rights for women and amity to men. Rich young heroine organizes women's movement, disguised as man becomes Prime Minister, brings about woman suffrage. When proposing law of full equality, dastardly intriguers learn her secret but her popularity and romance with a duke aid her to escape from jail and win. Epilog in 1999, overview of prosperous England and Federated Empire. Lots of melodrama à la Sue, but not without interest.

Laurie, André (pseud. of Paschal Grousset). New York to
   Brest in Seven Hours. London: Low, Marston, 1890. 302
   pp. (French original De New York à Brest en sept
   heures, [1889].)
Undersea pipeline across the Atlantic with Niagara Falls as propelling force. Love story of French inventor and daughter of Yankee financier. Two blackest villains foiled by our hero whizzing through pipeline.

[Nicholson, Joseph Shield.] Toxar: A Romance. London:
   Longmans, Green, 1890. 289 pp.
In Hellenic-Barbaric times, last survivor of different human race--with jewel growing from his forehead which permits him to read feelings--is involved in adventure, power, and love intrigues at a court. Marginal.

Smith, Artegall (pseud. of Philip Norton). Sub Sole: or,
   Under the Sun: Missionary Adventures in the Great
   Sahara. London: Nisbet, [1890]. 256 pp.
Superscientific civilization in a city within illuminated cavern under Sahara. Very pious, anti-Catholic, jingoistic, pro-Jewish. Wandering Jew shows Smith way through

Africa to oligarchic city of lost tribes of Israel, narrator plants the flag and weds Jew's daughter.

Thiusen, Ismar (pseud. of John Macnie). Looking Forward: or, The Diothas: or, A Far Look Ahead. London: Putnam, 1890. iv+358 pp. (US original as The Diothas . . ., 1883.)
Hero mesmerized into society of 96th century, when New York is built on five fathoms of destroyed cities and Manhattan one huge warehouse. Cultivated people with private property but limit on inheritance, new technology, 3-4 hours' work daily, electricity for locomotion and instead of factories, music by "telephone," chemical synthesis of foods, public service for young males, each person having later several occupations, stereo movies, TV. Against absolutism (whole world republican), plutocracy, catholicism, socialism; emphasis on family and sexual repression. Love story with reincarnation of 19th-century fiancée, who turns out to be hero's descendant; but he awakens and marries the prototype. Hero's position in new age unclear; many petty bourgeois eccentricities; nonetheless not uninteresting in itself and as a source for Bellamy (see for that MOSF).

Walsh, Rupert. The Fate of the Triple Alliance: A Jeu D'Esprit. London: Simpkin, Marshall, 1890. 64 pp.
Comic sketch of 1890 war of European powers, with good predictive score as to national alignments for World War 1. Use of electric bayonet and paper armor. Anti-War Union halts war by general strike.

[Watson, Henry Crocker Marriott.] The Decline and Fall of the British Empire: or, The Witch's Cavern. London: Trischler, 1890. 291 pp.
Australian professor gives overview of politics and life in 2990, when climate has changed, England is rural, London snowbound backwater with poor people. Muddled dream of old glory and love melodrama by narrator who defends God and capitalism against successful socialist uprising in 20th century, is saved by witch's ring.

1891

Bland, C[harles] A[shwold]. Independence: A Retrospect: From the "Reminiscences, Home and Colonial." London: Harrison & Sons, [1891]. 56 pp.
Australia secedes as republic in 1895, gets into financial and international trouble, is readmitted into Empire.

Boisgilbert, Edmund (pseud. of Ignatius Loyola Donnelly). Caesar's Column: A Story of the Twentieth Century. London: Low, Marston, 1891. 267 pp. (US original, 1890.)
Populist melodrama of broadest brush against both wicked (largely Jewish) US capitalists and bloodthirsty working-class revolution by Brotherhood of Destruction, resulting in downfall of civilization. Clumsy narrative in letters by hero from New York, plus his diary after retreating into a Swiss colony in Uganda, where a small proprietors' utopia is achieved. Both in narrative sweep and ideology midway between Bellamy and Jack London.

Clarke, Percy, "ed." (written by). The Valley Council: or, Leaves From the Journal of Thomas Bateman of Canbelego Station, N.S.W. London: Low, Marston, 1891. 356 pp.
Totally collectivist and egalitarian but despotic state in valley in Australian desert, with female equality, daily change of occupations and homes, based on electricity (including subterranean railway). Inhabitants vegetarian, cannot stand loud sounds and sight of blood, but cruel. Our heroes foment civil war against beautiful woman and escape. Valley is reformed.

Donnelly, Ignatius [Loyola]. Doctor Huguet. London: Low, Marston, [1891?]. 309 pp.
Metempsychosis of liberal Southerner into black man, organizes school against brutal repression, while being shot returns to original body. Happy ending of love-subplot, his bride and he pledge themselves to "the up-building of the negro race." Marginal.

Doyle, A[rthur] Conan. The Doings of Raffles Haw. London, Paris, and Melbourne: Cassell, [1891?]. 256 pp.
Billionaire uses electricity for everything including transmutation of metals to gold. His indiscriminate charity saps people's self-reliance, wealth alienates him. Destroys secret and dies.

Fiske, Amos K[idder]. Beyond the Bourn: Reports of a Traveller Returned From "the Undiscovered Country," Submitted to the World by. . . . New York: Fords, Howard, 1891. 222 pp. EC 1890-1897 [1891?].
Manuscript from a visitor to life after death, including life on many planets. One planet utopian, people are perfected in sentimental Christian vein. Marginal.

Flammarion, [Nicolas] Camille. <u>Urania: A Romance</u>. Lon-
    don: Chatto & Windus, 1891. 245 pp. (French original
    <u>Uranie</u>, 1889; US edition, 1890.)
In three parts: 1) Muse of astronomy takes narrator to
other solar systems, he sees aliens with different organs,
androgynous, with telepathy, in chrysalids, souls transmi-
grating. 2) Spiritualist narration. 3) Narrator finds himself on Mars without base matter, meets dead friends who
have changed sexes and become flowerlike intelligent
beings. Popular narrative recipe of mixing astronomy with
spiritualism made Flammarion world-wide success.

Folingsby, Kenneth. <u>Meda: A Tale of the Future</u>. Glas-
    gow: Aird & Cogshill, [1891]. 325 pp.
Narrator has trance vision of 56th century where small
people are nourished from atmosphere, have larger heads and
chests, reduced bellies, and almost no weight because of
"force of intelligence," which divides them into three
classes and allows them to control electromagnetism. New
artificial language, new religion, no money, elitism. In
4200 cosmic catastrophes changed lay of land, Earth axis,
and atmosphere. Much incoherence and moralizing, but a
link between Bulwer and Wells. (Seen in London 1892
edition.)

Gould, F[rederick] J[ames]. <u>The Agnostic Island</u>. Lon-
    don: Watts, [1891]. 124 pp.
Three Christian missionaries find sobriety and education
on Agnostic Island in Oceania. Long debates and sermons,
some love-interest and adventure with natives. Youngest
missionary converts to agnosticism. Barely fiction, very
marginal.

Herbert, William (pseud.). <u>The World Grown Young: Being
    a Brief Record of Reforms Carried Out From 1894-1914 by
    the Late Mr. Philip Adams: Millionaire and Philanthro-
    pist</u>. London: Allen, 1891. viii+304 pp.
Survey by Adams's secretary: richest Englishman brings
affluence, reforms in politics, education, and dress, parti-
tions Ireland, finally nationalizes main branches of
economy, defeats Russia and US, the latter is admitted into
British League. Neither plot nor intelligence alleviates
this volume.

Hertzka, Theodor. <u>Freeland: A Social Anticipation</u>.
    London: Chatto & Windus, 1891. vi+443 pp. (German
    original <u>Freiland</u>, 1890.)
Mixture of cooperative, corporative, and State capitalism

in East African "utopian" colony; imperialist, sexually repressive, and insipid. After defeat of Abyssinia whole world converts to its model.

Hume, Fergus W[illiam]. The Year of Miracle: A Tale of the Year One Thousand Nine Hundred. London: Routledge, 1891. 148 pp.
A fanatical, pseudosocialist Prophet of Doom spreads plague germs in London. Eventually, ideal state emerges, without slums or empires, not at all clearly delineated. Interwoven with love melodrama of good versus bad sister. Perfunctory and sensationalist.

The Ingathering: A Fiction of Social Economy. London: Waterlow & Sons, 1891. 56 pp.
Neomediaeval enlarged-family type community on land contrasted to towns with poor and lawless revolutionaries, whose dastardly attack is foiled. Much lecturing in clumsy story.

Jerome, J[erome] K[lapka]. "The New Utopia," in his Diary of a Pilgrimage. Bristol: Arrowsmith, and London: Simpkin, Marshall, 1891, pp. 259-79.
Narrator dreams of awakening in 29th century as exhibit in glass case. After revolution of 1899 people have numbers instead of names, unisex dress and appearance, lead anthill life with clock-regulated activities, scientific procreation, no marriage, beauty, or art, operations for the strong and clever. Cheap jibes, but a source both for Wells and Zamiatin.

Michaelis, Richard C. Looking Further Forward: An Answer to Looking backward by Edward Bellamy. The Bellamy Library, no. 10. London: Reeves, 1891. 110 pp. (US original, 1890.)
Continuation and reversal of Bellamy's plot (q.v., 1889): discharged professor reveals to West that his guide is spokesman of oligarchy and corruption reigns. Communist Radicals pressing for free love etc. revolt to kill West and bride, he awakes.

Middleton, W[illiam] H. "A Living Hidden City in South Africa," in his An Account of an Extraordinary Living Hidden City in Central Africa and Gatherings From South Africa. London: King, Sell, [1891], pp. 97-135.
Found manuscript about utopian city. Inhabitants believe in reincarnation, practice free love, gender apartheid, and

infant euthanasia. It is described by one of them traveling abroad.

Miller, George Noyes. The Strike of a Sex. London:
Reynolds, 1891. 63 pp. (US original, 1890.)
Dream of city where all women strike for legal equality
and right of determining childbirth. Consequences of their
secession are economic and sentimental, not sexual; demands
granted in referendum.

Morgan, Arthur, and Charles R. Brown. The Disintegrator:
A Romance of Modern Science. London: Digby & Long,
[1891?]. 220 pp.
Apparatus for disintegrating and then reintegrating people in melodramatic triangle stockbroker villain-girl-hero.
Each person's "spirit" has to be present at reintegration
if intelligence is to be restored to body; apparatus in
communication with spirit world. Semioccult, marginal.

Morris, William. News From Nowhere: An Epoch of Rest:
Being Some Chapters From a Utopian Romance. London:
Reeves & Turner, 1891. 238 pp.
Narrator awakens in dream-vision of 2003 England without
ugliness in nature or human relations, in deurbanized,
fully self-governing classless society, hears history of
the first realistic revolution in utopian fiction, and
travels up the newly fertile Thames with newfound friends
in garden England. Its people have regained the freshness
of a "second childhood," but narrator is unfit to live
there and returns to bear witness. Technology and industry
practically absent, economics not discussed; nonetheless
the finest "Earthly Paradise" utopia so far, a masterpiece
of lucid and warm writing, a rebuttal-complement to
Bellamy, and a source of such key S-F elements as the believable and justified revolution and the suffering narrator as bearer of collective values (both transmuted by
Wells). (See on Morris also MOSF and bibliography
therein.)

Oakhurst, William. The Universal Strike of 1899. London: Reeves, 1891. 89 pp.
Workers' International masterminded by its secretary
calls strike which in places turns to drunken riot. Secretary dies of exhaustion, strike ends in time to prevent
Russian invasion. Christian socialist tone, no sympathy
for strike but much for strikers.

[Rickett, Joseph Compton.] The Christ That Is To Be: A

Latter-day Romance. London: Chapman, 1891. 350 pp.
Christ returns in 2100 London, a decadent guild-cum-welfare State Britain overshadowed by China. Miracles, persecution, final disappearance. Disciples, including narrator, left expecting return, all with parallels to first coming. Interesting.

Rustoff, Michael (pseud.?). What Will Mrs. Grundy Say?: or, A Calamity on Two Legs (A Book for Men.). London: Simpkin, Marshall, 1891. 206 pp.
Narrator flies in balloon to planet with State control and euthanasia. Spirit separated from body. Slight.

Shelley, Mary Wollstonecraft. "The Mortal Immortal," in her Tales and Stories. London: Paterson, 1891, pp. 148-64.
Narrated by alchemist's apprentice who drank immortality potion three centuries ago, outlived all human ties, and has grown weary unto death.

Skorpios, Antares (pseud. of James William Barlow). History of a World of Immortals Without a God. Dublin: McGee, 1891. 177 pp.
Protagonist's fragmentary notes from 160 years ago with authorial persona's interpolations and explanations. Swiftian hatred of mankind led protagonist to learn light-speed jumping, came to Venus with shining city where 100 million people appeared 20,000 years ago from unknown where. No progeny, illness, or death, but alternate senescence and juvescence at 60 and 20. Complete socialism, universal language, synthetic food, anti-Christian deism. City on continent surrounded by impassable ocean, "joy and sorrow metronome" disintegrates people who suffer too much; submarine discovers all are reintegrated on second continent south of the ocean. Seek their Unknown Creator, open ending. All over the place but interesting, prefigures Stapledon. (Seen in identical London 1909 reprint with full name, titled The Immortals' Great Quest; 1891 edition not available.)

Strachey, [John] St. Loe. How England Became a Republic: A Romance of the Constitution. Bristol: Arrowsmith, and London: Simpkin, Marshall, [1891]. 71 pp.
Monarch with constitutional genius finds way for collective monarchy, allowing him to become Prime Minister.

Thomas, Chauncey. The Crystal Button: or, Adventures of Paul Prognosis in the Forty-Ninth Century. Edited by G.

Houghton. London: Routledge, 1891. 160 pp. (Another
edition London: Ward & Lock, 1891.)
After blow on head hero lives 10 years in trance during
which he is in classless, peaceful, affluent, engineering
future with new architecture, energy, means of locomotion,
also communication with more advanced Mars, observation of
other star systems, etc. Framed by Introduction and Conclusion, also Preface by author.

Verne, Jules. The Purchase of the North Pole: A Sequel
to "From the Earth to the Moon." London: Low, Marston,
1891. 182 pp. (French original Sens dessus dessous,
1889; US edition as Topsy-Turvy, 1890.)
In order to exploit polar minerals, Gun Club attempts to
shift Earth axis by building immense cannon on Kilimanjaro,
and is outlawed by world powers. Attempt fails because of
mathematical error. Somewhat strained farce substitutes
for the euphoria of the Moon novels (q.v., 1873).

X.Y.Z. (pseud.). The Vril Staff. London: Stott, 1891.
298 pp.
Incoherent narrative of young Anglo-Irishman, member of
secret society, using occult power to enforce right-wing
peace in Christian Europe. Marries perfect girl, founds
model settlement. When Europe relapses, his new warship
routs attack on America; unclear ending. Marginal.

1892

Besant, Walter. The Ivory Gate: A Novel. London: Chatto & Windus, 1892. 3 vols., 286+301+293 pp.
Involved intrigue based on the protagonist's dual personality because of brain sickness--one a solicitor, one a
socialist prophet. Superficial. Marginal.

Chilton, H[enry] Herman. Woman Unsexed: A Novel. London: Foulsham, 1892. 330 pp.
Plot moves between Dickensian lower depths and upper
class: in 1925, after new European war, workers' mob
uprising quelled by the army, hero blinded. Everything
solved by abolishing women's labor which rivaled men's,
happy ending. Indigestible.

Clowes, W[illiam] Laird. The Captain of the "Mary Rose":
A Tale of To-morrow. London: Tower, 1892. xvi+308 pp.
Naval war with France in 189-. Though outgunned, the
British eventually win, with decisive help from our hero
who commands privateer.

Donnelly, Ignatius [Loyola]. The Golden Bottle: or, The Story of Ephraim Benezet of Kansas. London: Low, Marston, 1892. 246 pp.
Mysteriously given bottle transmuting iron into gold, poor farmer protagonist rescues girl friend, is elected president, drives away bankers and politicians by means of cheap money, defeats aristocratic Europe. All was a dream, but spurs him to action. In final vision bottle identified as allegory for financial powers of government.

The Doom of the County Council of London. London: Allen, 1892. 38 pp.
In 1911 Progressist London municipality controls House of Commons, its mob attacks House of Lords, is dispersed by army, and London County Council abolished.

Farningham, Marianne (pseud. of Mary Ann Hearn). Nineteen Hundred?: A Forecast and a Story. London: Clarke, 1892. viii+318 pp.
Christian reforms and sentimental entanglements. Christian party stops anarchism by model colonies, youth movement, and domination of parliament.

Hyne, C[harles] J[ohn] Cutcliffe [Wright]. The New Eden. London and New York: Longmans, Green, 1892. 258 pp.
Archduke scientist conducts experiment on tropical island, having young man and woman start from zero. They invent art, alcohol, Sun worship.

J.A.C.K. (pseud. of J. MacCulloch?). Golf in the Year 2000: or, What We Are Coming To. London: Unwin, 1892. 159 pp.
Narrator awakens in 2000 to comic items and events, from depilatory lotion through female equality to new golf with automatic caddies and weather control.

Lach-Szyrma, W[ladislaw] S[omerville]. Under Other Conditions: A Tale. London and Edinburgh: Black, 1892. 229 pp.
Narrator meets Venusian, who liberates some Poles from Russians, saves woman twice by flying, mesmerism, and medicine. Narrator and wife fly in his electrical aircraft. Less coherent continuation of author's 1883 book (q.v.).

Lehmann, R[udolf] C[hambers]. Mr. Punch's Prize Novels: New Series. London: Bradbury, Agnew, 1892. 175 pp.
Brief imitations of popular novelists, including Kipling, Haggard, Besant, Jerome, and Verne (Through Space on a

Formula, by Rules Spurn, pp. 100-7), and Future Naval War
(Who'd Be a Sailor, [Anon.], pp, 166-75).

L'Estrange, Miles (pseud.). What We Are Coming To.   Edinburgh: Douglas, 1892. 124 pp.
   Satire on progress found by narrator returning from dark-
est Africa: 6 hours' daily work, female emancipation, secu-
larization, phonetic spelling, decimal currency, etc.

[Morris, Alfred.]   Looking Ahead: A Tale of Adventure.
   London: Henry, [1892?]. 264 pp.
   Shipwrecked in 1894 on Antarctic island, initial socialist republic fails. Life to 1958, return to UK devastated
after 1905 socialist seizure of power followed by looting,
hunger, terror, and cruel neofeudalism. Now UK is slowly
rebuilding. (Date and pagination from the only available,
second "corrected and revised" edition.)

Potter, Robert. The Germ Growers: The Strange Adventures
   of Robert Easterley and John Wilbraham. London: Hutchinson, 1892. 274 pp.
   Evil "ethereal" race recruits evil men, has telepathy and
control over will, air carriages, invisible paint, food
pills, can discorporate and reincorporate, grows germs in
remote places (here North Australia) to sow pestilences and
render people irreligious. Heroes defeat them with help of
second, good, ethereal race. History as occult battle of
the two races for humanity.

Strongi'th'arm, Charles (pseud. of Charles Wicksteed
   Armstrong). The Yorl of the Northmen: or, The Fate of
   the English Race: Being the Romance of a Monarchical
   Utopia. London: Reeves & Turner, 1892. 127 pp.
   Patriarchal dream-vision of transfer into 2000, using
Bellamy against socialism. Feudalism, eugenics, clean
race; fails.

Tincker, Mary Agnes. San Salvador. Boston and New York:
   Houghton Mifflin, 1892. 335 pp. EC 1892.
   Love and ethics in hidden ideal valley-city where Christ
is King.

1893

Anderson, Mary. A Son of Noah. London: Digby & Long,
   [1893]. 318 pp.
   Prehistoric and pre-Deluge story, mixing the Bible with
pterodactyls and a more advanced people. Marginal.

Bennett, Arthur. The Dream of an Englishman. London: Simpkin, Marshall and Warrington: "Sunrise" Publ., 1893. 190 pp.
Future political history to mid-20th century. Municipal ownership federating up to world scale, liberalism, ecumenicism, possibility of interplanetary exploration.

Bramston, M[ary]. "The Island of Progress," in her The Wild Lass of Estmere and Other Stories. London: Seeley, 1893, pp. 227-74.
After 500 years, woman wakes from unconsciousness to find "perfectly scientific Government" resulting in balloons, equality, 4-hours' work, prettiness, comfort, scientific inventions, but also listlessness, vulgar music, loss of imagination and history, and euthanasia. A rebellious youth yearning for "soul" is instructed by her in religion and old values, then tortured by authorities. All was a dream.

Clowes, W[illiam] Laird. The Great Peril and How It Was Averted. London: "Black & White," 1893. 133 pp.
US trust attempts to take over UK by means of drugs and scientific devices which destroy will. Foiled at last moment by English girls. More interesting than average.

Colomb, Philip H[oward], et al. The Great War of 189-: A Forecast. London: Heinemann, 1893. 308 pp.
Serious attempt by four collaborators to describe future war, in which UK is allied to central Europe, Russia defeated and deprived of Poland, stand-off in France.

An Ex-Revolutionist (pseud.). "England's Downfall": or, The Last Great Revolution. London: Digby & Long, [1893]. 175 pp.
Reactionary narrator observes future mob burn London, universal penury results. Tiresome.

Fawcett, Edward Douglas. Hartmann, the Anarchist: or, The Doom of the Great City. London: Arnold, 1893. 214 pp.
Narrator accompanies Vernean demonic inventor of light aircraft and anarchist leader who dynamite-bombs London in 1920s. Rising fails and repentant protagonist destroys his aircraft. Sensationalist gore and destruction.

Granville, Austyn [W.]. The Fallen Race. New York and Chicago: Neely, 1982. 352 pp. EC 1893.
Unknown race in Australia, cross-bred from kangaroo males and native females, has four classes (noble, warrior, labor-

er, slave) and white queen. Narrator slaughters enemies,
develops in 7 years civilization, money, taxes, printing,
Church. Battle with aborigines and conspirators. Happy
ending. Perfect example of bourgeois and imperialist wishdream.

Griffith, George (pseud. of George Chetwynd Griffith
    Jones). The Angel of the Revolution: A Tale of the Com-
    ing Terror. London: Tower, 1893. 393 pp.
Hero invents in 1903 airplanes combining principles of
Verne and Maxim, joins Terrorists under Natas against the
tsar and his dirigibles. Franco-Slavonic alliance with balloons, submarines, and poison gas occupy Germany, land in
UK. But the Terrorists gain power in US, eventually save
UK with torpedoes and better airships, set up world state
by racial groups and disarmament. Love story of inventor
with daughter of daimonic Terrorist leader. Strange, mainly sensationalist mixture of sympathy for avenging underground and chauvinism, with some crude but powerful elements. Very popular in its day.

Hayes, Frederick W[illiam]. The Great Revolution of 1905:
    or, The Story of the Phalanx. London: Forder, 1893.
    316 pp.
1930 account of 1905 collectivist revolution borne by
enlightened middle class with support of proletariat and
working through parliament and economic pressure. Detailed
organization of all public life, State socialism inspired
by Bellamy.

Hyne, Charles J[ohn Cutcliffe Wright]. The Recipe for
    Diamonds. London: Heinemann, 1893. 241 pp.
Lully's recipe found, after intrigue with anarchist
destroyed again.

L'Estrange, Henry. Platonia: A Tale of Other Worlds.
    Bristol: Arrowsmith, and London: Simpkin, Marshall,
    [1893?]. 190 pp.
Aerial vehicle based on old manuscript; narrator flies
first to the Moon with saurian monsters, then through
meteor shower to unknown planet Platonista, capital
Campanella, with scientific and unclear social progress.
Thick atmosphere slows down light so that astronomers see
Earth of 100 years ago. Love affair, flees with his
beloved from planet falling into Sun.

Maël, Pierre (pseud. of Charles Causse and Charles
    Vincent). Under the Sea to the North Pole. London:

Low, Marston, 1893. 244 pp. (French original Maël, Une Française au Pole Nord, 1893.)
Sub-Vernean trip in submarine and balloon with new combustible. Warm sea and island at North Pole with geyser in the middle and subterranean tunnel through which heroes escape finding ichthyosauruses etc. Intrigue with German saboteur.

Moffat, W. Graham, and John White. What's the World Coming To?: A Novel of the Twenty-first Century Founded on the Fads, Facts, and Fiction of the Nineteenth. London: Stock, 1893. 172 pp.
Discussions among a few characters in 2003 Boston, guying various aspects taken from Bellamy, Darwin, or 1890s articles: telephones, movies, aerial bombardments, equality of sexes and woman Prime Minister in UK, ghosts and clairvoyant visions used in crime detection, fourth dimension, emigration from socialism to Ireland, hypnotic cures of love.

Mr. Dick (pseud.). James Ingleton: The History of a Social State A.D. 2000. London: Blackwood, [1893]. 450 pp.
After civil war, Social State with equality of labor and women and republicanism leads to poverty and loss of individuality. Hero and his friends with new weapons and aircraft overthrow it, he restores monarchy and becomes prime minister, the villain in love triangle goes mad. Prolix and bad writing.

Nisbet, Hume. Valdmer the Viking: A Romance of the Eleventh Century by Sea and Land. London: Hutchinson, [1893]. xii+306 pp.
Included in this involved novel are a voyage around the world by way of North Pole, a narrator reincarnated from ancient Greece who revives his hibernating wife after 1,000 years, and priests who control Earth heat. Very marginal.

O'Flannagan, Phineas (pseud.). Ireland a Nation! The Diary of an Irish Cabinet Minister: Being the History of the First (and Only) Irish National Administration, 1894. . . . Belfast: Olley, 1893. 37 pp.
Diary of secretary of foreign affairs 1893-1894. Church rules Ireland, government left without money or army, riots and collapse. Satire from chauvinist Ulster viewpoint.

Pemberton, Max. The Iron Pirate: A Plain Tale of Strange

Happenings on the Sea. London: Cassell, 1893. vi+298
pp.
Melodrama of bloodthirsty pirate, very faintly also sub-
Vernean avenger. His ship has gas engines and phosphor-
bronze hull. Marginal.

Richter, Eugen. Pictures of the Socialistic Future (Freely Adapted From Bebel). London: Sonnenschein, 1893.
134 pp. (German original Sozialdemokratische Zukunftsbilder: frei nach Bebel, 1891.)
Socialism comes to power, ruins adherent, ends in famine,
workers' revolt, and war. Epistolary novel.

Rickett, J[oseph] Compton. The Quickening of Caliban: A
Modern Story of Evolution. London: Cassell, 1893. 275
pp.
Alternate branch of human evolution, more spontaneous and
nearer to nature, exists in Africa. Reactions of one of
its members in England, accessible to better spiritual
influences of a girl who is herself of "mixed blood," are
examined within a story of narrow caste morality versus
true religiousness.

Roberts, J.W. Looking Within: The Misleading Tendencies
of "Looking Backward" Made Manifest. New York: Barnes,
1893. 279 pp. EC 1893
Hero takes mysterious potion and sleeps to 1927, finds
world revolution and civil war in USA, airships. Another
sleep 1930-2000, visits Bellamy's Boston, finds horrors
ignored by West's guide; in final collapse West's fiancée
is disfigured but cured by another potion, plan for (literally) molding people into equality foiled, US renewed by
returning to private property and independence. Long
speeches, barely fictional and even less credible.

Stimson, F[rederick] J[esup]. "Dr. Materialismus: His
Hypothesis Worked Out," in his In the Three Zones. New
York: Scribner's Sons, 1893, pp. 1-40. EC 1893.
Relates friend's story: German professor in Maine college induces emotion by vibrations at the end of continuum
going from sound and light through gravity to emotions. He
uses it to seduce narrator's beloved.

Verne, Jules. The Castle of the Carpathians. London:
Low, Marston, 1893. 211 pp. (French original Le
Château des Carpathes, 1892.)
Gothic castle mysteries of calling up dead singer are
finally explained by new optical and acoustical inven-

tions based on electricity. Marginal.

Ward, Herbert D[ickinson]. A Republic Without a President
and Other Stories. New York: Tait & Sons, [1891]. 271
pp. EC 1893. Contains among others: "A Republic Without a President" (pp. 5–57), "Colonel Odminton" (pp. 245–
71), and "The Lost City" (pp. 59–141).
First two stories: in 1955 US president kidnapped for
ransom by supership; malefactor later repents and returns
ship and ransom. Third story: reporter in balloon saves
girl as sole survivor from city fused by overused electricity.

1894

Astor, John Jacob. A Journey in Other Worlds: A Romance
of the Future. London: Longmans, Green, 1894. 476 pp.
Antigravitation takes three friends to Jupiter, where
they find strange fauna and flora, then to Saturn, a kind
of purgatory with spirits of the dead and dragons. Earth
is ruled by Anglosaxons, with Vernean scientific advances.
Uncouth and badly written mixture of scientism, religious
preachments, spiritualist evolutionism, and upper-class
safari banalities. Well known in its time. Only partly
SF.

Barr, Robert. The Face & [sic] the Mask. London: Hutchinson, 1894. 304 pp. Contains among others: "The
Chemistry of Anarchy" (pp. 12–29), "The Doom of London"
(pp. 78–94), and "A New Explosive" (pp. 118–33).
First story: feeble satire of cowardly anarchists;
second: millions of Londoners killed in mid-20th century
by fog-cum-smoke; third: super-explosive and inventor
destroyed by appalled war minister. Very superficial.

Barrett, Frank. The Justification of Andrew Lebrun.
London: Heinemann, 1894. 277 pp.
Narrator's master Lebrun opens up 100-year old laboratory
and revives man. Love-intrigue and murder follow, with
happy ending.

[Berens, Lewis Henry, and Ignatius Singer.] The Story of
My Dictatorship: The Taxation of Land Values Clearly
Explained. London: Bliss, Sands, 1894. 221 pp.
Dream-vision of one year's reforms in dialogs with representative complainers--loafer, socialist, small merchant,
bishop, various capitalists and landowners, William Morris
(from whom the frame is borrowed). Interesting as being

halfway between Henry George tract and utopian dialog dealing with dynamic changes.

Bingham, Frederick. The Cap Becomes a Coronet: A Down-
stairs Romance. A.D. 19--. London: Simpkin, Marshall,
1894. 50 pp.
Comic account of dispossessed future aristocracy having
trouble paying servants. Lady goes into service to stewed-
eel billionaire, marries his son.

[Chamberlain, Henry Richardson.] 6000 Tons of Gold.
London: Innes, 1894. 317 pp.
Young American uses huge gold-find given him by Pata-
gonian Indians to destroy bear stockmarket of 1895, help
the needy, endow education and rapid transit, etc.--all
anonymously. The gold--and his new ship running on
carbonic acid--prevents European threat to Britain, but it
cannot stop economic chaos and unrest. Finally, international conference of powers-thst-be decides to sink most of
it in the ocean. Bland.

Clowes, W[illiam] Laird. The Double Emperor: A Story of
a Vagabond Cunarder. London: Arnold, [1894]. 238 pp.
Ruritanian emperor finds look-alike who covers up for
kidnap aboard ship. Marginal.

Danyers, Geoffrey. Blood Is Thicker Than Water: A Political Dream. London: Tower, 1894. 159 pp.
Federalization of British Empire with rights for whites
only. War at sea against France and Germany results in
Anglo-American Commonwealth enforcing free trade on both.

Doyle, Arthur Conan. Round the Red Lamp: Being Facts and
Fancies of Medical Life. London: Methuen, 1894.
Contains among others: "Lot No. 249" (pp. 220-80) and
"The Los Amigos Fiasco" (pp. 281-94).
First story: mummy revived and destroyed. Second story:
electric chair with too high tension makes criminal unkill-
able.

Fawcett, E[dward] D[ouglas]. Swallowed by an Earthquake.
London: Arnold, [1894]. 235 pp.
Narrator with scientist uncle and two companions navi-
gates underground waters finding Carboniferous age with
reptiles, Neanderthals, and savages. Nothing but imitation
Verne.

Flammarion, [Nicolas] Camille. Omega: The Last Days of

the World. New York [and London]: Cosmopolitan Publ.,
1894. 287 pp. (French original La Fin du Monde,
1893.)
First part comet scare in 25th century, with radio warnings from the Martians. Second part, in 10 million years,
ice-death of last human pair. Includes psychic messages
from planets and lots of details about the nearer future.
The most popular novel by Flammarion, influencing even
Wells and the last phase of Verne.

G.H.P. (pseud. of George Haven Putnam). The Artificial
Mother: A Marital Fantasy. New York and London:
Putnam, 1894. 31 pp.
Dummy with clockworks, etc., helps harassed mother of
large family. All was a dream.

Griffith, George (pseud. of George Chetwynd Griffith
Jones). Olga Romanoff: or, The Syren of the Skies.
London: Tower, 1894. vii+377 pp.
Sequel to author's 1893 novel (q.v.). In 2030 the terrorists retire to African stronghold, with airplanes
and vril, leaving a peaceful world with new technology
such as monorail trains and cheap power. Olga plots to
reestablish her dynasty, drugs hero and learns secrets of
airplanes and submarines, with new fleet and aid of sultan
battles for world power. At height of battle terrorists
withdraw having (as in Flammarion) heard from Mars of
coming comet, which incinerates surface of Earth. Emerging
from under a mountain, they repopulate globe. Boyish
heroes in halfway house from future-war tale to space
opera.

Harben, Will[iam] N[athaniel]. The Land of the Changing
Sun. New York: Merriam, 1894. 233 pp. EC 1894.
In huge cavern under Atlantic, our heroes lost in balloon
discover superscientific state with electricity, airplanes,
submarines, climate regulation, artificial sun, something
akin to TV, wicked (but finally converted) scientist-king,
and beautiful princess. Nature as instrument of God finally destroys it. Verne and Haggard fused with the horizon
of Christian romance.

Hertzka, Theodor. A Visit to Freeland: or, The New Paradise Regained. The Bellamy Library, no. 21. London:
Reeves, [1894]. vi+155 pp. (German original Eine Reise
nach Freiland, 1893.)
Sequel to author's 1891 book (q.v.). Guided tour with
lectures, barely fiction. Marginal.

[Hird, James Dennis.] Toddle Island: Being the Diary of
Lord Bottsford. London: Bentley, 1894. 406 pp.
Island in Pacific as vehicle of satire on customs, poli-
tics, religion, Oxbridge.

Howells, William Dean. A Traveler From Altruria: A Romance. Edinburgh: Douglas, 1894. 244 pp.
US seen by candid glance of visitor from utopian country,
explicated in final lecture as ethical socialism controlling   technology--for   example,   electricity,   changing
climate, rapid transit--for public good. Mostly genteel
conversations, of a piece with Altrurian ideal of middle-
class   craftsmen   and   its   ideal   parliamentary   genesis;
critical aspects interesting effort by major author.

Lazarus, Henry, "ed." (written by). The English Revolution of the Twentieth Century: A Prospective History.
London: Unwin, 1894. xi+463 pp.
Found manuscript describes democratic revolution in one
day leading to rule of small owners in welfare state.
Genuine indignation against starvation and want contrasted
to luxury of upper classes, but also imperialism strengthened   and   touches   of   ludicrous   puritanism.   Long   newspaper   quotes   and   arguments,   on   border   of   nonfiction.
Marginal.

McIver, G[eorge M.]. Neuroomia: A New Continent: A Manuscript Delivered by the Deep. London: Sonnenschein,
1894. 307 pp.
Narrator finds warm land in Antarctic. Advanced technology, people live 200 years, no wars, telescope sight of
inhabited Mars. Insipid banalities and love romance.

Miller, Joaquin (pseud. of Cincinnatus Hiner Miller). The
Building of the City Beautiful. London: Mathews and
Lane, 1894. iv+196 pp. (US original, 1893.)
Incoherent   Christian   rhapsodizing   about   two   utopian
cities, a failed one in California and a successful one in
Mexican desert founded by Jewish girl, with Christian
socialism, noble metals devalued, use of electric train
(polemic against Morris's disregard of machine).

Murphy, G[eorge] Read. Beyond the Ice: Being a Story of
the Newly Discovered Region Round the North Pole: Edited
From Dr. Frank Farleigh's Diary. London: Low, Marston,
1894. 326 pp.
Civilization with minor technological and social differences. State control and planning, early marriage, etc.,

on Bellamy's model. Sentimental complications, military and political adventures.

Shannon, J[ohn] C. "The Dream of Jacques, the Anarchist," in his Who Shall Condemn? and Other Stories. Walsall: Robinson, and London: Simpkin, Marshall, 1894, pp. 102-27.
Dream of future war similar to Griffith's in which resentful slum anarchist moves amid aircraft and new explosives.

Tucker, Horace [Finn]. The New Arcadia: An Australian Story. London: Sonnenschein, 1894. vi+31 pp.
Poor people resettled by philanthropist in valley. Model settlement with telephones, prohibition, etc. Much love and dastardry: communist villain kidnaps philanthropist, proclaims democracy and socialism, everything decays. After much bloodshed philanthropist rescued, a good cooperative develops. Very marginal.

1895

Allen, [Charles] Grant [Blairfindie]. The British Barbarians: A Hill-top Novel. London: Lane, 1895. xiii+202 pp.
Anthropological look by researcher from 25th century at English taboos of behavior and property, primarily in erotics. For his pains shot by jealous husband. Very good satire.

Carter, Tremlett. The People of the Moon. Artemis Library. London: "The Electrician" Publ., and Simpkin, Marshall, [1895]. 402 pp.
Narrator invents deciphering method and communicates with Moon interior, first by hypnotic thought-transference then by antigravity missile manuscript in third person. Prince Indra comes to Moon surface in flying machine, discovers stars. Intrigues, love melodrama, battles with giants and monsters, etc. Clumsy story but interesting historically and because it adopts the point of view of the rock-bound race.

Chambers, Robers W[illiam]. "The Mask," in his The King in Yellow. London: Chatto & Windus, 1895, pp. 57-82.
Solution of new elements solidifies living beings, but they revive.

Chetwode, R.D. The Marble City: Being the Strange Ad-

ventures of Three Boys. London: Low, Marston, 1895. 312 pp.
Lost city in Pacific tropics with yellow-brown race. No money, total regulation, children, women, and possessions held in common under privileged caste of high priests. Listlessness but still political factions. Boys flee, find treasure. Marginal dystopia.

[Constable, Frank Challice.] The Curse of Intellect. Edinburgh and London: Blackwood, 1895. 177 pp.
Written alternately by human narrator and intelligent monkey with estranged point of view. Intrigues and murders plus long essay on loss of happiness because of reason. Monkey commits suicide. Influenced Island of Dr. Moreau.

Cromie, Robert. The Crack of Doom. London: Digby & Long, 1895. 214 pp.
Incoherent narration around amoral scientist who knows secret of atomic energy, with lots of Victorian gentility, telepathy, hypnotism, a secret society, coincidences, and pseudophilosophy about cruelty of nature and existence being suffering which should be undone. Loves and intrigues at the end of 20th century, with happy ending for nice characters.

Dixon, Charles, "ed." (written by). Fifteen Hundred Miles an Hour. London: Bliss, Sands, 1895. 313 pp.
Manuscript found in meteor tells of flight by our heroes in electricity-run spacecraft to Mars, where they find monsters and giants, court and captivity, love intrigues. Extremely clumsy.

Eastwick, James. The New Centurion: A Tale of Automatic War. London and New York: Longmans, Green, 1895. 93 pp.
Sea fighting with automatic weapons in war against France.

Ellis, T. Mullett. Zalma. London: Tower, 1895. 438 pp.
Superbeautiful anarchist courtesan-conspiratrix versus the Vatican and UK secret service hero. She publishes Byronic poem, tries to scatter anthrax from balloons over main world cities, when foiled commits suicide. Feverishly escapist concoction out of Sue and outdoing Griffith, full of cardinals and princes, superscientist aristocrat as head of anarchists, hints of vampirism, even discreet pornography.

Fawcett, E[dward] Douglas. The Secret of the Desert: or, How We Crossed Arabia in the "Antelope." London and New York: Arnold, 1895. 246 pp.
Vernean voyage in large wheeled craft, finds lost Phoenician people in oasis. Marginal.

Geissler, L[udwig] A. Looking Beyond: A Sequel to "Looking Backward" by Edward Bellamy and an Answer to "Looking Forward" by Richard Michaelis. London: Reeves, 1895. 102 pp. (US original, 1891.)
Defense of Bellamy 1889 against Michaelis 1891 (q.v., both) by continuing their plots: Michaelis's depiction is either a dream or wrong, refuted in long discussions. West married to fiancée, sees aeronautics, electric railroads and industries (including agribusiness), and savage hermit who refused participation. Martians start communicating with Earth, answer by giant electric pictures planned.

Griffith, George (pseud. of George Chetwynd Griffith Jones). The Outlaws of the Air. London: Tower, 1895. 376 pp.
Anarchist intellectual and engineer with new gunboat, submarine, and flying ship have subverted South Sea utopian colony. Enter English gentleman, after various adventures the Aerial Navigation Syndicate saves England from them and from Franco-Russians. Hasty imitation of Verne plus feeble echoes of author's earlier novels.

Hinton, C[harles] H[oward]. "Stella," in his Stella, & An Unfinished Communication: Studies of the Unseen. London: Sonnenschein, 1895, pp. 1-107.
Transmitted manuscript of girl rendered invisible by a "higher matter" potion. She is kidnapped by spiritualists, defeats pirates, marries narrator. Her baby grows opaque from mundane food.

Jane, Fred[erick] T[homas]. Blake of the "Rattlesnake": or, The Man Who Saved England: A Story of Torpedo Warfare in 189-. London: Tower, 1895. 269 pp.
War against France and Russia in torpedo-carrying ships, with love melodrama around hero. He dies saving England, after her fleet has been destroyed because of coalminers' strike. Bloody-minded anticivilian militarism.

Lloyd, John Uri, and Llewellyn Drury (pseud. for same). Etidorhpa: or, The End of the Earth. London: Gay & Bird, 1895. 234 pp.
Occult journey narrated in manuscript given to "Drury."

Narrator taken by eyeless blue guide on tour of hollow
Earth where gravity diminishes, energy is equivalent to
spirit and serves to explain science, telepathy, and all
else. Semiallegorical, esoteric. Very marginal.

Mackay, Kenneth. The Yellow Wave: A Romance of the Asiat-
   ic Invasion of Australia. London: Bentley & Son, 1895.
   xii+435 pp.
   Russians invade India and Chinese Australia in 1954,
France helps. Defense of Queensland fort; love melodrama
between turncoat and Anglo-Saxon heroine ends in death with
war unresolved.

Mears, A[melia] Garland. Mercia, the Astronomer Royal.
   London: Simpkin, Marshall, 1895.   349 pp.
   In 2002 Europe dominated by Germanic peoples, women are
equal, some technological advances but also psychomagnetic
energy. Jejune love triangle with heroine and an emperor,
she becomes empress of India and marries a swami. Quite
indigestible.

Pemberton, Max. The Impregnable City: A Romance. London, Paris, and Melbourne: Cassell, 1895.   310 pp.
   Pacific island with submarine approach, ruler with fair
daughter. Love story, conspiracy, some trance-dreams.
Very marginal.

Suffling, E[rnest] R[ichard]. The Story Hunter: or,
   Tales of the Weird and Wild. London: Jarrold & Sons,
   1896 [1895]. Contains among others: "A Visitor From
   Mars" (pp. 88-104) and "Doctor Angus Sinclair" (pp. 184-
   210).
   Stories told to a hypnotist. First: spirit of Friar
Bacon from Mars hints at possible inventions. Second:
doctor reanimated after 90 years, commits suicide.
Marginal.

Wells, H[erbert] G[eorge]. The Stolen Bacillus and Other
   Incidents. London: Methuen, 1895.   275 pp. Contains
   among others: title story, "The Flowering of the Strange
   Orchid," "In the Avu Observatory," "The Diamond Maker,"
   "Aepyornis Island," "The Remarkable Case of Davidson's
   Eyes."
   For these well-known S-F stories see WMSF.

_____. The Time Machine: An Invention. London:
   Heinemann, 1895. 152 pp.
   In SF, kick-off of Wells's writing, culmination of 19th-

century, and historical turning point. First time-travel story with machine subject to guidance back and forth. (See for more on it MOSF.)

_____. The Wonderful Visit. London: Dent, 1895. 251 pp.
Angel-like being falls to Earth, gradually deteriorates in its poisonous air despite his innocence. Slight but deft parable; see WMSF.

X (pseud. of Frank Attfield Fawkes). Marmaduke, Emperor of Europe: Being a Record of Some Strange Adventures in the Remarkable Career of a Political and Social Reformer Who Was Famous at the Commencement of the Twentieth Century. Chelmsford: Durrant, and London: Simpkin, Marshall, 1895. 271 pp.
Manuscript from the future in which narrator for a moment found himself. Hero inaugurates social reforms against socialists and with help of German emperor, then hides and is proclaimed posthumous emperor of Europe. Clumsy.

1896

Acworth, Andrew. A New Eden. London: Ward, Lock, [1896]. vii+134 pp.
In 2096 Russian monarchy rules India, Germany Europe, and China East Asia while republican England has sadly deteriorated to barbarism. Two friends find Pacific island of egalitarianism with electrical factories, birth control, citizen-"numbers," no disease or poverty, total regulation up to euthanasia, and listless people. Lectures by its officials. Sexes look alike, but women more easily redeemable through love. One escapes with younger friend, another accompanies older friend into death.

Andreae, Percy. The Vanished Emperor. London, New York, and Melbourne: Ward, Lock, 1896. 310 pp.
European emperor vanishes amid political intrigue. Detective-story piecing together of clues. Marginal.

Anson, Captain [Charles Vernon], "ed." (written by). The Great Anglo-American War of 1900. London: Stanford, 1896. 88 pp.
Naval action on Pacific coast with destruction of San Francisco. When new invention secures US coasts, Canada surrenders, Ireland and England invaded. Peace treaty cedes UK possessions in North America and gives Ireland independence.

Aubrey, Frank (pseud. of Francis Henry Atkins). The Devil
Tree of El Dorado: A Romance of British Guiana. Lon-
don: Hutchinson, 1896. xx+392 pp.
Imperialist preface on importance of colonial possession.
Pair of friends with mysterious stranger find city of El
Dorado, stranger is king of lost race with usual political
intrigues. Longevity plant, also flesh-eating tree with
human sacrifices.

Cowan, James. Daybreak: A Romance of an Old World. New
York: Richmond, 1896. 399 pp. EC 1896.
Moon falls into Pacific, narrator drawn away with it,
meets last woman, visits giants with older civilization and
utopian society on Mars, where high technology and Christianity dispense with war and uncouth workers and swindlers.
Unclear love story. Very muddled.

Cromie, Robert. The Next Crusade. London: Hutchinson,
1896. v+240 pp.
Continuation of author's 1899 book (q.v.) as "the history
of the future." Love tangles, European war, Britain occu-
pies Constantinople.

Davidson, John. The Pilgrimage of Strongsoul and Other
Stories. London: Ward & Downey, 1896. 278 pp. Contains among others: "Eagle's Shadow" (pp. 213-41) and
"The Salvation of Nature" (pp. 243-78).
First story: boy from 8020 materializes in 1886, reads
to narrator fragments of history--future war with invasion
of England, saved by Yankees; diversion of Gulf Stream by
Nihilists. Second story: Scotland is turned into "natural-
ised," primitivist tourist reservation by demolishing all
post-1700 artifacts, importing Polynesian soil, and regu-
lating moisture by new invention; finally, new plague
leaves only one couple in the world. Scarcely coherent
attempts at comedy.

Glyn, [Alice] Coralie. A Woman of To-Morrow: A Tale of
the 20th Century. London: Women's Printing Soc.,
[1896]. 172 pp.
Diary of conservative woman who awakens in 1996. Female
equality in professions and politics, lack of "proper"
behavior, and better architecture are only changes. She
marries "archaeologist" who studies 19th century.

Grier, Sydney C[arlyon] (pseud. of Hilda Caroline Gregg).
An Uncrowned King: A Romance of High Politics. Edinburgh and London: Blackwood, 1896. 487 pp.

Sappy romance of love and politics in the Balkans. English aristocrat loses throne but gets girl.

Kinross, Albert. The Fearsome Island: Being a Modern Rendering of the Narrative of One Silas Fordred, Master Mariner of Hythe, Whose Shipwreck and Subsequent Adventures Are Herein Set Forth: Also an Appendix Accounting in a Rational Manner for the Seeming Marvels That Silas Fordred Encountered During His Sojourn on the Fearsome Island of Don Diego Rodriguez. Bristol: Arrowsmith, and London: Simpkin, Marshall, [1896]. 199 pp.
Mariner shipwrecked in South Sea in Elizabethan times, finds modern traps and boat made by old alchemist.

Laurie, André (pseud. of Paschal Grousset). The Crystal City Under the Sea. London: Low, Marston, 1896. 293 pp. (French original Atlantis, 1895.)
Greek Atlanteans in crystal dome reached by hero in diving bell, only old man and beautiful daughter left. Submarines, danger, love, rivals, Atlantis destroyed.

Markwick, Edward. The City of Gold: A Tale of Sport Travel, and Adventure in the Heart of the Dark Continent. London: Tower, 1896. 324 pp.
Hidden city of proto-Semites with matriarchal communism, black slaves, and gold. Sentimental and political melodrama around female ruler, destroyed by mysterious lightning force possibly akin to the telepathy some possessed. Hodgepodge. Marginal.

Pallander, Edwin. Across the Zodiac: A Story of Adventure. London: Digby & Long, [1896]. 306 pp.
English narrator-explorer with Yankee adventurer and German professor in balloon, saved by spaceship with Nemo-like captain. Nonsensical pseudoscientific explanations, visit to Moon with fauna and ruins underground, to prehistoric Saturn, to Venus with vampire plants. Mutiny by convict crew. Falling into Sun, saved by comet. Shameless and bad imitation of Verne with snatches of Flammarion.

Smythe, Alfred. A New Faust. London: Digby & Long, 1896. 399 pp.
Begins with letters on desire for flight and immortality. Professor discovers materialized electricity, and with devil's help a solvent to help it bring about rejuvenation.

From here on occult story, finally solvent destroyed,
professor dies. Marginal.

Sykes, Arthur A[lkin]. Without Permission: A Book of
    Dedications. London: Roxburghe, [1896]. Contains
    among others: "Trancemogrification" (pp. 145-47), "With
    the V.W.H. in 1945" (pp. 241-44), and "The New Bacillus"
    (pp. 309-13).
    Book of very brief parodies. First one: hypnotic hiber-
    nation à la Rip Van Winkle; second: robot foxes and
    hounds; third: epidemic of "amnesia bacillus" affects
    borrowers, women, burglars.

Tracy, Louis. The Final War: A Story of the Great Betray-
    al. London: Pearson, 1896. xi+372 pp.
    In 1898 superior race of Anglo-Saxons defeat Europe and
    impose disarmament. A new electric rifle helps.

Traill, H[enry] D[uff]. The Barbarous Britishers: A Tip-
    top Novel. London: Lane, 1896. 95 pp.
    Not very successful parody of Allen (q.v., 1895).

Verne, Jules. The Floating Island: or, Pearl of the
    Pacific. London: Low, Marston, 1896. vii+382 pp.
    (French original L'Ile à hélice, 1895.)
    Mechanical island with Milliard City populated by the
    rich travels across Pacific. Party political differences
    finally tear it (literally) apart. Satirical parable on
    American progress as power without harmony.

Waldo, Cedric Dane (pseud. of Cecil Drummond Wolfe). The
    Ban of the Gubbe: A Novel. Edinburgh and London:
    Blackwood & Sons, 1896. 195 pp.
    Amphibious men in North Sea, whose prophet cursed a
    traitor. Adventure and love story with traitor's female
    descendant.

Wells, H[erbert] G[eorge]. The Island of Dr. Moreau: A
    Possibility. London: Heinemann, 1896. 219 pp.
    Higher animals vivisected and educated into Beast Folk by
    ruthless scientist attempting to accelerate evolution; the
    experiment fails, bestiality returns. (For more see MOSF
    and bibliography therein.)

1897

Bellamy, Edward. Equality. London: Heinemann, 1897.
    x+365 pp.

Sequel to author's 1889 book (q.v.), plugging its gaps mainly by lectures, but also by some first-rate parables. More openness and participatory democracy than in earlier novel.

Druery, Cha[rle]s T[homas]. The New Gulliver: or, Travels in Athomia. [London]: Roxburghe, [1897?]. 160 pp.
Evolutionist Spirit of the Age shrinks narrator to small size and allows him to accelerate time to see growth of plants and insects. He explores garden, pond, air. Mainly ponderous popularization, marginally fiction.

Du Maurier, George [Louis Palmella Busson]. The Martian. London and New York: Harper, 1897. 477 pp.
The soul of female Martian with magnetic sense leads hero to become famous spiritual teacher, as Martians have always done. Finally she reincarnates in his daughter.

Flammarion, [Nicolas] Camille. Lumen, Experiences in the Infinite. London: Heinemann, 1897. vi+224 pp. (French original published as part of Récits de l'infini, 1872; US edition as Stories of Infinity, 1873; revised and enlarged as separate book 1887, US edition 1892.)
Dialogs with a being reincarnated on a number of worlds, with descriptions of alien life. History and evolution seen as reversed down to extinction of Earth. Portions of last chapter added for UK edition. A treasure trove of ideas pillaged by very many, probably including Wells, though barely fiction.

Gorst, Harold E[dward]. Without Bloodshed: A Probability of the Twentieth Century. London: Roxburghe, [1897]. 109 pp.
Satirical tale of US millionaires financing victory of socialism in England in order to get compensation for 4/5 of UK which they previously bought up. UK becomes a cooperative without the profit motive.

Griffith, George (pseud. of George Chetwynd Griffith Jones). Briton or Boer?: A Tale of the Fight for Africa. London: White, 1897. ix+296 pp.
After initial successes, Boers routed in final grand battle, Russian intrigues thwarted. Simple-minded military tale.

_____. The Romance of Golden Star. London: White, 1897. vii+284 pp.

Mummified Inca and sister revived, buried treasures used
for revolt in Peru to reestablish rule. Treacherous revivi-
fier dies, sister weds faithful Englishman.

Hendow, Z.S. The Future Power: or, The Great Revolution
of 190-. London: Roxburghe, 1897. 79 pp.
General strike by the people, joined by army. New order
with economic security set up in UK, being set up elsewhere.

Hervey, Maurice H. David Dimsdale, M.D.: A Story of Past
and Future. London: Redway, 1897. 344 pp.
Dimsdale succeeds in suspending animation 1895-1920, has
to relearn use of senses. Finds Britannic Confederation
established   in   1901   after   war   which   leaves   Russia
dominating Europe,   also   aircars,   electric   cabs,   color
photography. Marries daughter of old sweetheart and when
she dies, new niece-love. Habsburg duke also "hibernized"
to same recipe in order to miraculously resurrect when
needed.

Jane, Fred[erick] T[homas]. To Venus in Five Seconds: An
Account of the Strange Disappearance of Thomas Plummer,
Pillmaker. London: Innes, 1897. 130 pp.
Narrator abducted by Venusian lady-doctor by means of
instant transmission. Finds old Egyptians who control
energy, nullify weight, want to vivisect him. Battles,
electrical storm, Egyptians destroyed by monstrous looking
but more intelligent insectoid aboriginals. Hodgepodge.

Le Queux, William [Tufnell]. A Madonna of the Music
Halls: Being the Story of a Secret Sin. London:
White, 1897. viii+118 pp.
Scientist villain terrorizes beautiful Italian woman
through invention transferring brain qualities (talent,
hate, murder-lust) into potion she is made to drink. From
misleading title to happy ending shoddy. Marginal.

Munro, John. A Trip to Venus: A Novel. London: Jarrold & Sons, [1897]. 254 pp.
New force powers spacecraft to pastoral Venus with ideal
Hellenic-type long-lived people, love intrigue with beautiful maiden. Adventures on Mercury in "aerial locomotive." Banal.

Palmer, J[ohn] H[enry]. The Invasion of New York: or,
How Hawaii Was Annexed. London and New York: Neely,
[1897]. iv+248 pp.

US wins naval war against Spain and Japan in 1898. Vague populist invective at end.

Rosewater, Frank. Utopia, a Romance of Today: Presenting a Solution of the Labor Problem, a New God & a New Religion. Neely's Popular Library, no. 94. London and New York: Neely, 1897. 268 pp. (US original '96, 1894.)
Muddled story of two alternate countries where time and space are different from rest of the world. In first the injustice of capitalists and priests leads to bloody mob revolt, in second treating labor (i.e., labor-power) as property leads to Utopia, a guild socialism. Intercut with silly love story with double of US girl and melodrama of second wronged girl whose father leads revolt, and with a future history of USA which leads the world to peaceful socialism. All a dream in balloon flight, itself revealed as allegory. Narratively disjointed, but with some ingenious dialectics in the economic argument.

Spence, J.C. The Dawn of Civilization. London: Watts, [1897]. 176 pp.
Mediumistic communication with a Spencerian future allows critique of socialism and religion in chapters on politics, war, taxes, etc. Marginal.

Stockton, Frank R[ichard]. The Great Stone of Sardis: A Novel. London and New York: Harper & Bros., 1898 [1897]. xi+341 pp.
Super-X-ray discovers middle of Earth to be immense diamond, hero goes 14 miles down to it. In subsidiary plot hero's submarine takes possession of North Pole for United North America (extending to Panama), foiling Polish dastard. Finally discovery abandoned for love and quiet life. Chauvinist and insipid sub-Vernean tale by popular author.

Thorburn, S[eptimus] S[met]. His Majesty's Greatest Subject. Westminster: Constable, 1897. 324 pp.
Deathbed manuscript relating 20th-century story of Englishman who--impersonating the viceroy, his twin brother--saves India from seditious radicals "white and brown," agrarian revolts, and Franco-Russian invasion by wise reforms balancing various classes. Finally marries beautiful and mostly white Hindu princess.

Tracy, Louis, [and Matthew Phipps Shiel]. An American Emperor: The Story of the Fourth Empire of France. London: Pearson, 1897. viii+380 pp.
American millionaire brings about Vernean irrigation of

Sahara as part of plan to become emperor. Intrigues, gangsters, abandons his plan for love.

Verne, Jules. <u>For the Flag</u>. London: Low, Marston,
1897. 312 pp. (French original <u>Face au drapeau</u>,
1896.)
Antisocial mad inventor of superexplosive, joined to
pirate with electric submarine, repents when faced with
French flag and blows up pirate's island and himself.
Verne has declined into patriotic melodrama.

Waterloo, Stanley. <u>The Story of Ab: A Tale of the Time
of the Cave Man</u>. London: Black, 1897. ix+363 pp.
Caveman hero discovers use of bow and huts as paleolithic
evolves into neolithic. Love wins over friendship in triangle. Pioneering prehistoric tale.

Wells, H[erbert[G[eorge]. <u>The Invisible Man: A Grotesque Romance</u>. London: Pearson, 1897. 245 pp.
Amoral scientist discovers invisibility, but even this
fails in the face of invincible obtuseness and cruelty of
petty bourgeois England. Brilliant idea, memorable scenes,
and vigorous chase-plot in an ambiguous (and scientifically
impossible) tale.

_____. <u>The Plattner Story and Others</u>. London: Meth-
uen, 1897. 301 pp. Contains among others: title story,
"The Argonauts of the Air," "The Story of the Late Mr.
Elvesham," "In the Abyss," "Under the Knife," "The Sea
Raiders."
For these well-known stories see <u>WMSF</u>.

Windsor, William. <u>Loma: A Citizen of Venus</u>. St. Paul,
MI: Windsor & Lewis, 1897. 200 pp. EC 1897.
Electro-magnetic-gravitational-sexual force propagates
life-germs from Sun outwards, inner planets older. Therefore Venus prophet comes to Earth to save bastard child who
will become teacher of truth, like Jesus. Long lectures
for sexual freedom and phrenology, on Venus welfare state
with religion of love and similarities to Bellamy. Child
born, prophet disappears back to Venus.

1898

Augustinus (pseud.). <u>Two Brothers: A Story of the Twentieth Century</u>. Cardiff: Chapple & Kemp, 1898. 88 pp.
Exemplary Catholic, who converts Wales and becomes cardinal, opposed to spiritualist infidel brother who founds

settlement (extrapolated from Cardinal Newman and his brother). England split into Catholic and nonbelievers, Judgment Day comes. Mostly zealous tract, marginal.

Bellamy, Edward. The Blindman's World, and Other Sto-ries. London: Watt, 1898. 415 pp. Contains among others: title story (pp. 1-29), "With the Eyes Shut" (pp. 335-65), and "To Whom This May Come" (pp. 389-415). First story: narrator's soul transported to Mars where people have "foresight" of their lives. Earth is the only cosmic "Blindman's World" turned toward past. All emotions are modified accordingly. A minor classic. Second story: recorded-word world, ubiquitous use of phonographs in trains, etc.; all a dream. Third story: islands of tele-paths, making for true love; poignant.

Benham, Charles. The Fourth Napoleon: A Romance. Lon-don: Heinemann, 1898. 600 pp. (US original, 1897.) Cowardly Englishman, Napoleon's descendant, is raised to power and eventually killed in love imbroglio. Pallid.

Boussenard, Louis. 10,000 Years in a Block of Ice. New York and London: Neely, [1898]. 256 pp. (French original Dix mille ans dans un bloc de glace, 1890.) Future ruled by blend of Chinese and Negroes whose large heads and vital energy control force, including levitation; Europeans are degenerated servants, women have been arrested at smaller brain development. Hypnopedia, incipi-ent communication with Mars, incidental satire. Poor.

Buchanan, Robert [Williams]. The Rev. Annabel Lee: A Tale of Tomorrow. London: Pearson, 1898. 255 pp. In 21st century, charming young woman tries to lead pros-perous and peaceful but monotonous Humanism back to Christi-anity. Much sermonizing about life after death and beauty of suffering. Story breaks off with first "martyr" of persecutions. Axe grinding.

Chambers, Robert W[illiam]. "A Matter of Interest," in his The Mystery of Choice. London and New York: Harper & Bros., 1898, pp. 213-82. (US original, 1897.) One of a set of connected stories--giant lizards, marine and airborne, found off Long Island; love interest added.

Chesney, Weatherby (pseud. of Charles John Cutcliffe Wright Hyne). The Adventures of an Engineer. London: Bow-den, 1898. 295 pp. Contains among others: "The Ruler of the World" (pp. 41-55), "The Anarchist Plot" (pp. 85-

89), "Byng's Annihilator" (pp. 129-39), and "The Motor
Battle-Car" (pp. 167-77).
First story: airship used in bid to rule the world;
second: attempt to blow up Bank of England; third: man-
propelled torpedo; fourth: tank. All novelties destroyed
with the inventors.

_____. The Adventures of a Solicitor. London: Bow-
den, 1898. 268 pp. Contains among others (including
some marginal S-F stories): "The Mechanical Burglar" (pp.
37-47), "The Ghost of Farnley Abbey" (pp. 48-61), "A
Maker of Thumbs" (pp. 78-93), "The Rain Maker" (pp. 125-
39), "The Crimson Beast" (pp. 184-97), and "The Men From
Mars" (pp. 242-54).
First story: robot constructed by vengeful cripple;
second: compound renders man invisible; third: mad
scientist makes extra fingers; fifth: mutant prehistoric
saurian in underground cave; last: Martians with large
skulls visit Earth in flying machine, read thoughts, eat
pills. All novelties are destructive and end up destroyed.

Craig, Alexander. Ionia: Land of Wise Men and Fair Wom-
en. Chicago: Weeks, 1898. 301 pp. EC 1899 [1898?].
Amid poverty and discontent of East London, visitor from
ideal valley in Himalayas appears. Our hero visits it:
social utopia similar to More's, with strict eugenics:
artificial diamonds and balloon.

A Diplomat (pseud.). The Rise and Fall of the United
States: A Leaf From History, A.D. 2060. Neely's Popular Library. New York and London: Neely, 1898. 205 pp.
First 9 chapters overview of US past and of plutocratic
corruption of all institutions. During the decadence 1925-
2010 discontent of intellectuals, farmers, and workers
grows. Finally great labor leader allies them with "negroes" and nationalizes great corporations, but his lenien-
cy and popular inexperience result in US splitting into
several states, tyranny, and ruin. Future history, no
plot. Marginal.

Gerrare, Wirt (pseud. for William O. Greener). The War-
stock: A Tale of Tomorrow. London: Greener, 1898.
218 pp.
A plug for inventors: new community of Cristallia has
wireless telegraph and other inventions, notably magnetic
destruction of explosives, is warred upon by great powers.

Gleig, Charles. When All Men Starve: Showing How England

Hazarded Her Naval Supremacy, and the Horrors Which Followed the Interruption of Her Food Supply. New York and London: Lane/Bodley Head, 1898. 192 pp.
Brief opening with war against Boers and Europe and lost naval battles. Food shortage, unwillingness of capitalists to bear burdens, mob revolt, troops refuse to fight the people, police slaughtered, Buckingham Palace burned. Ends abruptly here. Sympathy for lower classes plus sensationalism.

Gorst, Harold E[dward]. "Sketches of the Future," in his Sketches of the Future. London: MacQueen, 1898, pp. 1-54.
Ludicrous events turning, for example, on women ministers and children's strike making for a topsy-turvy world.

Graves, C[harles] L[arcom], and E[dward] V[errall] Lucas. The War of the Wenuses: Translated from the Artesian of H.G. Pozzuoli. Arrowsmith's Bristol Library, vol. 78. Bristol: Arrowsmith, and London: Simpkin, Marshall, [1898]. 140 pp.
Superficial parody of War of the Worlds: women from Venus invade lovestruck mankind.

Grier, Sydney C[arlyon] (pseud. of Hilda Caroline Gregg). A Crowned Queen: The Romance of a Minister of State. Edinburgh and London: Blackwood & Sons, 1898. 590 pp.
Love and political intrigue set in same locale as author's 1896 work (q.v.).

Griffith, George (pseud. of George Chetwynd Griffith Jones). The Gold-Finder. London: White, [1898]. 312 pp.
Old scientist invents locator of gold and noble metals, which passes through many hands in melodramatic tale until virtue triumphs. Marginal.

Hannan, [Robert] Charles. The Betrothal of James: A Tale. London: Bliss, Sands, 1898. 243 pp.
Female cats' electricity used to obtain rejuvenation pill. S-F humor.

Jepson, Edgar [Alfred]. The Keepers of the People. London: Pearson, 1898. viii+358 pp.
English superdespot of country in Indian mountains beats off dastardly Russians and rebuffs political bleeding hearts from home. Apotheosis of male supremacy, eugenics, and racism.

Oppenheim, E[dward] Phillips. <u>Mysterious Mr. Sabin</u>. Lon-
   don: Ward, Lock, [1898]. 397 pp.
Malignant French aristocrat plans German invasion of
England with help of his electrical destruction machines.
Foiled by secret order of Nihilists, but happy ending for
him too.

Pemberton, Max. <u>The Phantom Army: Being the Story of a
   Man and a Mystery</u>. London: Pearson, 1898. viii+357
   pp.
Uchronia in 1893: Spanish Napoleonic rebel organizes
secret army and threatens Europe, love story of English
officer and rebel's fiancée with happy ending after the
plot's failure. Mediocre thriller.

Perry, Walter Copland. <u>The Revolt of the Horses</u>. London: Richards, 1898. 229 pp.
Englishman shipwrecked in 1950 on island of Houyhnhnms
and Yahoos, repulsed by them. Houyhnhnms in England, their
prince wins the Derby and organizes strike which precipi-
tates society into civil war. UK and USA defeat European
fleet, horses resolve to destroy our murderous race.

Reeve, B[enjamin]. <u>The Divines of Mugtown: or, The Story
   of the Romoanglicongrebaptimethodistical Church</u>. London: Stockwell, 1898. 30 pp.
Satirical account of test reunion of Christian churches
in small town in 1920s, which fails through personal
discord of priests.

Shiel, M[atthew] P[hipps]. <u>The Yellow Danger</u>. London:
   Richards, 1898. 348 pp.
Chinese plot intra-European war, malevolent master-mind
craves sexual revenge, English hero foils\ him. Cruel
Chinese surge westward; naval battles, 20 million of them
dumped into Maelstrom, others injected with cholera. Frenzied melodrama of repulsive racism.

Stead, W[illiam] T[homas]. <u>Blastus the King's Chamberlain: A Political Romance</u>. London: Richards, 1898.
   xvi+302 pp.
Near-future tale of international and national UK politics around B's (i.e., Joseph Chamberlain's) rise to power.
Imperialism with some mysticism and much melodrama. The
end sees English king in mega-Israel and women's suffrage.

Tracy, Louis. <u>The Lost Provinces</u>. London: Pearson,
   1898. viii+380 pp.

Sequel to author's 1897 book (q.v.). Germany attacks France with fifth column and assassinations. Battles and detections, communists in Paris. Fortified cars with cannons (i.e., tanks). Hero saves day, Germans surrender, Alsace and Lorraine halved.

Wells, H[erbert] G[eorge]. The War of the Worlds. London: Heinemann, 1898. viii+303 pp.
Perhaps Wells's most popular S-F romance because of the sensationalist action, with memorable scenes of social breakdown. Culmination of "future war" subgenre (and much other catastrophic SF, even horror-fantasy) but also reversal of its imperialist confidence; progenitor and standard for later alien invasions and catastrophes of SF. (For more on it see MOSF and bibliography therein.)

1899

Aubrey, Frank (pseud. of Francis Henry Atkins). A Queen of Atlantis: A Romance of the Caribbean Sea. London: Hutchinson, 1899. 391 pp.
Island of Atlantis found in Sargasso Sea, also giant cuttlefish and pirates. Civil war won by right side with help from European castaways. Also land of telepathic flying people (fallen angels?), savages. Battles, superweapons. Worthless.

Augustinus (pseud.). Paul Rees: A Story of the Coming Reformation. London: Simpkin, Marshall, [1899]. 125 pp.
In 1905 England forbids Catholic church, loses prosperity and war with France because of new weapon invented by English emigrant. Great miracles of Holywell, one cures child of Protestant leader who converts. Revolution in UK prevented by providential plague, curable only with Holywell water. Marginal.

Beale, Charles Willing. The Secret of the Earth. New York and London: Neely, 1899. 256 pp.
Airship with new fuel and antigravity flies through Symmesian hole from North to South Pole with fiery zone in the middle. Aeronauts find strange birds and animals, also lost race in Earthly Paradise of oriental splendor but which is not contacted.

Clark, Alfred. In a State of Nature. London: Low, Marston, 1899. 322 pp.
Descendants of Elizabethan sect near North Pole practice

polygamy, nudism, euthanasia, breed tall and beautiful but
amoral "White savages," brute force rules. Unnatural pursuits such as cooking, washing, and singing are sinful.
Modern Englishmen find them; lower-class harpooner is corrupted but two upper-class characters are not. Glacier
cataclysm wipes out settlement, our heroes escape with two
beautiful reformed girls on iceberg. Glimpses of interesting otherness if only as horrible warning. Marginal.

D'Argenteuil, Paul (pseudonym?). The Trembling of Bore-
    alis. London and New York: Neely, 1899. iv+316 pp.
Critique of dastardly and debauched plutocracy, with
transparent country names (Borealis=USA). After Cuban War,
in near future lower classes revolt against its total
power, force dissolution of trusts and disfranchising of
Negroes, introduce welfare state and general happiness,
including our heroes.

Douglass, Ellsworth. Pharaoh's Broker: Being the Very
    Remarkable Experiences in Another World of Isidor Werner
    (Written by Himself). London: Pearson, 1899. 316 pp.
German inventor and Jewish-American speculator-narrator
travel in antigravity vessel to Mars, which has developed
more slowly. Its history is now in phase analogous to
Egypt under Joseph, whom they meet in "bad vizier" variant.
Hero corners all wheat for coming famine. Strange
animals, weaker gravity, humans stronger in fights at
arrival and final escape. Influenced both by Verne and
Wells.

Griffith, George (pseud. of George Chetwynd Griffith
    Jones). Gambles With Destiny. London: White, 1899.
    Contains among others: "Hellville, U.S.A." (pp. 1-88),
    "The Great Crellin Comet" (pp. 89-147), "A Corner in
    Lightning" (pp. 149-80), and "A Genius for a Year" (pp.
    181-209).
First story: young idealist elected president of USA
against trusts and anarchists, violence and Chicago revolt
crushed, "hard cases" put into Arizona oasis, women missionaries massacred, Heaven destroys it with meteorites.
Second story: comet out of Flammarion destroyed by gun out
of Verne. Third story: capitalist uses inventor to store
all "electric fluid," causes epidemic, works destroyed by
accident. Fourth story: hashish gives man writing inspira-
tion, finally kills him; marginal.

_____. The Great Pirate Syndicate. London: White,
    1899. 302 pp.

Pirate syndicate of English capitalists fights rest of world with airplanes, torpedoes, energy obtained directly from coal and petroleum. Melodrama with splendid or inferior women, Society of Assassins, antisemitism. Imperialist struggle for China, finally the Syndicate with UK and USA win and annex all colonies. Bloodthirsty chauvinism.

Hale, Edward Everett. "The Brick Moon," in his The Brick Moon and Other Stories. Boston: Little, Brown, 1899. 369 pp. EC 1899. (US original in his His Level Best and Other Stories, 1872, pp. 30-124.)
Brick satellite is accidentally catapulted into orbit with people. Tame humor of little group not missing large cities, churches, and parties. They have own atmosphere, write books, communication with them is by catapult and light signals. Pioneering tale.

Hayes, William D. (pseud. of Edmund Downey). Mr. Boyton: Merchant, Millionaire, and King. London: Simpkin, Marshall, 1899. 266 pp.
Enterprising American becomes king of Poland and conqueror of Germany, 1900-1905, with help of old scientist and his electrical machine.

Jane, Fred[erick] T[homas]. The Violet Flame: A Story of Armageddon and After. London: Ward, Lock, 1899. vi+245 pp.
Armageddon is struggle between English and Jewish stockmarket. After it, sinister French professor establishes heavenly bodies are alive, gets superpowers by communicating with Earth, is killed after drawing down comet-brain of solar system. Floods, brutality, all annihilated save narrator and girl friend as new Adam and Eve.

Lawrence, Edmund. It May Happen Yet: A Tale of Bonaparte's Invasion of England. London: The Author, [1899]. 295 pp.
In 1805 the French invade East England but have to surrender. Mixed up with love and dastardry plot. Pretence at "forgotten history" rather than uchronia.

North, Franklin H. The Awakening of Noahville. New York: New York Publ., 1898. 383 pp. EC 1899.
Sub-Twainian comedy of two Yankees persuading somnolent rural country of medieval type to try modern civilization. After initial successes this causes capitalist class-conflicts, technology-caused flood, revolt, and flight of protagonists to USA.

Pereira Mendes, H[enry]. Looking Ahead: Twentieth Century Happenings. London, New York, and Chicago: Neely, and London: Gay & Bird, 1899. 381 pp.
Retrospective future history of series of international wars, revolts by dastardly socialists and anarchists, and Christian-Jewish near-theocracy solving it all by reform, State intervention, and killing all dissidents. Religious ethics established, Palestine returned to Jews as arbiters of world commerce and peace. Confused and overweening.

Slee, Richard, and Cornelia Atwood Pratt. Dr. Berkeley's Discovery. The Hudson Library, no. 40. New York and London: Putnam, 1899. 219 pp.
Liquid "develops" images from human brains when grafted upon living animals. Used to understand hero's murdered wife: love lost when he overdid his science. He dies, invention lost.

Wells, H[erbert] G[eorge]. Tales of Space and Time. London and New York: Harper & Bros., 1900 [1899]. 360 pp.
Contains: "The Crystal Egg," "The Star," "A Story of the Stone Age," "A Story of the Days to Come," and "The Man Who Could Work Miracles."
First two stories are minor S-F classics: interplanetary TV with glimpses of strange life on Mars opposed to dingy London; and "the epitome of the colliding worlds theme" (WMSF), lifting Flammarion to great fiction. Third story: variant on prehistoric tale with great inventions. Fourth long story: love set in megalopolis of When the Sleeper Wakes (q.v., 1899). Final story: fantasy miracles with S-F consequences, marginal.

_____. When the Sleeper Wakes. London: Harper & Bros., 1899. 328 pp.
Wells beginning to buckle down to relatively short-range extrapolation: a megalopolis about 2100 with mass sociopolitical struggles within a nightmarish corporate capitalism, belying both liberal and socialist (Bellamy's) optimism. Flying and mass media used for caste system and political control, competing police forces, demagogic leaders. Observer-hero waking into it moves within jerky plot as he vacillates between savior and liberal intellectual. Both such inconsistencies and brilliant details became the model for all subsequent antiutopian anticipation.

Wright, Henry. Depopulation: A Romance of the Unlikely. London: Allen, 1899. 166 pp.

Class struggles in emblematic mid-US city, hero forms
Depopulation League, decides not to marry. Helped by great
capitalist, becomes president and carries out full national-
ization. Capitalist assassinated, hero weds in freedom.
Genuine bitterness alongside wishdream.

1900

Bennett, Arthur. The Dream of a Warringtonian. Warrington: "Sunrise" Publ., 1900. xiv+245 pp.
Dream of town's history, with final chapter in 1950:
electrical ships, afforestation, aircars, ecumenic Christianity, municipally run companies, imperial Federation.
(See same author, 1893.)

Cole, Robert William. The Struggle for Empire: A Story
of the Year 2236. London: Stock, 1900. 213 pp.
Earth, run by Teutonic nations with advanced science (TV,
electrical antigravity, flying, no disease, new forces per-
mitting colonization of planets), wars with Sirius planet.
Insipid love story from Victorian-type high society. Space
war with new weapons and rays, moons of Jupiter and London
destroyed. Sinister Earth scientist invents new force and
wins war. Translates "future war" melodrama into first
interstellar war of space-opera type, is already perfunctory, bloodthirsty, and socially idiotic.

Grier, Sydney C[arlyon] (pseud. of Hilda Caroline Gregg).
The Kings of the East: A Romance of the Near Future.
Edinburgh and London: Blackwood, 1900. 363 pp.
Continuation of author's Balkan locale (q.v., 1896 and
1898). Englishman intrigues for return of Palestine to
Jews, as well as on Balkans. His scheming fails and he
marries happily. Marginal.

Hulme-Beaman, Emeric. The Experiment of Doctor Nevill: A
Novel. London: Long, 1900. 317 pp.
Portion of executed criminal's brain transplanted to
upper-class man turns him into "a Frankenstein," that is,
thief. Second operation rights everything.

Hyne, Charles J[ohn] Cutcliffe [Wright]. The Lost Continent. London: Hutchinson, 1900. 368 pp.
Manuscript found, narrated by Atlantean noble. Upstart
empress, giant saurians and animals, civil war, flood, he
escapes with wife.

Jones, Jingo, M.P. (pseud.). The Sack of London by the

Highland Host: A Romance of the Period. London: Simpkin, Marshall, 1900. 336 pp.
Semicomic, exaggeratedly "Scots" intrigue story, avowedly
parallel to contemplated invasions of London and uprisings
of the Irish: clan chieftains with 30,000 followers pretend to gather for Boer War, sack London to avenge old
wrongs and decentralize Empire. Special explosive (formula
lost) wrecks main city points, Highlanders defeat plunder-
ing mob but are tricked by Prince of Wales.

Kellett, E[rnest] E[dward]. A Corner in Sleep and Other
Impossibilities. London: Jarrold & Sons, [1900]. Contains among others: "A Corner in Sleep" (pp. 7-23) and
"The New Frankenstein" (pp. 74-113).
11 humorous stories, some of preposterous inventions, all
ending badly. Title story: sleep as form of energy, is
condensed as fluid, sleep-famine ensues. Second story:
talking doll-robot, poetry machine, "hedonometer" for
pleasure and pain, "liquefied memory" narrator gets rid of
is drunk by his wife.

Lafargue, Philip (pseud. of Joseph Henry Philpot). The
Forsaken Way: A Romance. London: Hurst & Blackett,
1900. 287 pp.
End of 20th century in ruined English countryside. Protagonist sets out from eugenic celibate monastery, meets
girl, love-story with mistaken identity and happy ending.

Linton, [Elizabeth] Lynn. The Second Youth of Theodora
Desanges. London: Hutchinson, 1900. vi+335 pp.
Narrator old woman who is spontaneously rejuvenated.
View on present from statelier past. Grandson of former
flame falls in love with her. She is disappointed by
politics, art, science, religion, and people.

Netterville, Luke (pseud. of Standish James O'Grady). The
Queen of the World: or, Under the Tyranny. London:
Lawrence & Bullen, 1900. 293 pp.
Manuscript of narrator with psychic powers, magically
transferred into 22nd century, when Russo-Mongolians dominate over Aryans. English resistance movement for racial
equality, battle in king's Antarctic hideout; narrator
awakes.

Newcomb, Simon. His Wisdom, the Defender: A Story. London and New York: Harper, 1900. 329 pp.
Future historians tell of establishment of their new
state by scientist with new matter and energy weapon (anti-

gravity) who defeats Germany and rest of Europe and rules justly ever after. Naive technocratic politics.

Peck, Bradford. The World a Department Store: A Story of Life Under a Coöperative System. London: Gay & Bird, 1900. viii+311 pp.
Businessman revives in cooperative world after Bellamy and George which has eliminated waste, smoking, etc. Very poor prose, raptures plus lectures.

Rogers, Lebbeus Harding. The Kite Trust: (A Romance of Wealth). New York: Kite Trust Publ., 1900. 475 pp. EC 1900.
Spirits instruct boy in Earth prehistory (which saw colonizers from Mars, Saturn, Moon, and Venus) and finances. He and friends proceed to become owners and rulers of both Americas; one of them invents new energy, underground railways, artificial diamonds. Chapter-length lectures on female suffrage, Darwin leading to spiritualism, above all on sublime virtues of monopoly capitalism fused with State. Boring. Marginal.

Serviss, Garrett P[utman]. The Moon Metal. New York and London: Harper Bros., 1900. 164 pp.
After discovery of Antarctic gold, villain saves currency standard by mysterious new metal of which he has monopoly. It is beamed down from Moon in atoms by proceeding similar to giant cathode ray. Young engineer unmasks him, currency collapses again but saved by states intervening. Occult ending, villain disappears possibly to the Moon. Inconsistent and marginal.

West, Julian (pseud. of Ernst Müller). My Afterdream: A Sequel to the Late Mr. Edward Bellamy's "Looking Backward." London: Unwin, 1900. 247 pp. (German original Ein Rückblick aus dem Jahre 2037 auf das Jahr 2000, 1891.)
Bellamy's hero recapitulates that story and resolves to tell whole truth; shows shady sides of future. Grotesque send-up. Wakes back in 19th century and weds his fiancée whom he now knows better.

Wetmore, Claude H[azeltine]. Sweepers of the Sea: The Story of a Strange Navy. Indianapolis: Bowen-Merrill, 1900. 349 pp. EC 1900.
Peruvian brothers--president and admiral--defeat UK and Chile with Inca treasure and superbattleships, found Incaland in alliance with USA.

White, Fred[erick] M[errick]. <u>The White Battalions</u>. London: Pearson, 1900. 341 pp.

France and Russia fight UK in 1900. New explosive cuts off Gulf Stream, inundation and rat invasion of London. Russia turns on France, fire of Paris.

Wilson, [John] Grosvenor. <u>The Monarch of Millions: or, The Rise and Fall of the American Empire</u>. New York, Chicago, and London: Neely, 1900. vi+204 pp.

In 1950 North America, ruled by plutocratic emperor, consists of very rich Nobles and very poor Plebeians. Electric agribusiness, weather control, household implements, walkie-talkie, power airships; China partitioned. Love between daughter of emperor and naive Alaskan, Demos, who finally appeals to the people's self-interest. Emperor wants to ruin highest henchmen and abets Demos in arousing public opinion but is overthrown in favor of republic with full business freedom. Cheerful satire of stock-market plutocracy and some literary clichés, including a ridiculous anarchist; slightly allegorical.

Wright, W[illiam] H[enry]. <u>The Great Bread Trust</u>. New York, London, and Montreal: Abbey, 1900. 54 pp.

Villainous capitalist corners all cereal, causes famine, is crowned king of US plutocracy. Satire.

Appendix: Books Dealing with Future War and Politics Only

(without social or technological changes)

I rely in this Appendix on Clarke, <u>Tales of the Future</u>— see "Sources" list.

<u>History of the Sudden and Terrible Invasion of England by the French. . . .</u> London: Bosworth, 1851. 23 pp.

<u>After the Battle of Dorking; or, What Became of the Invaders?</u> London: Maddick, 1871. 23 pp.

<u>The Battle of Dorking: A Myth</u>. London: Style, 1871. 31 pp.

<u>The Battle of the Ironclads; or, England and Her Foes in 1879</u>. London: Palmer, 1871. 32 pp.

J.W.M. <u>The Siege of London</u>. London: Hardwicke, 1871. 64 pp.

Moltruhn, M. (pseud.). The Other Side at the Battle of Dorking. London: Whittaker, 1871. 84 pp.

Our Hero: or, Who Wrote "The Battle of Dorking." London: Bradbury, Evans, 1871. 48 pp.

[Payn, James.] The Cruise of the Anti-Torpedo. London: Tinsley Bros., 1871. 48 pp.

[Stone, C.] What Happened After the Battle of Dorking: or, The Victory of Tunbridge Wells. London: Routledge, 1871. 60 pp.

An Octogenarian (pseud.). The British Federal Empire: How It Was Founded. A Speech. . . . London: Clarke, 1872. 32 pp.

Macaulay, C. (pseud. of W.M. Adams). The Carving of Turkey. London: Mead, [1874]. 80 pp.

The Battle of Pluck. London: Humphrey, 1875. 31 pp.

Cassandra (pseud.). The Channel Tunnel: or, England's Ruin. London: Clowes, 1876. 37 pp.

The Invasion of 1883. Glasgow: Maclehose, 1876. 62 pp.

Fifty Years Hence: An Old Soldier's Tale of England's Downfall. London: Bacon, 1877. 32 pp.

Dekhnewallah, A. (pseud.). The Great Russian Invasion of India. London: Harrison, 1879. 69 pp.

Budge (pseud.). The Eastern Question Solved. London: Allen, 1881. 82 pp.

[Butler, W.F.] The Invasion of England, Told Twenty Years Later. . . . London: Low, Marston, 1882. 190 pp.

The Demure One (pseud.). The Battle of Boulogne: or, How Calais Became English Again. London: Roworth, 1882. 51 pp.

Grip (pseud. of E.L. Welch). How John Bull Lost London: or, The Capture of the Channel Tunnel. London: Low, Marston, 1882. 127 pp.

The Battle of Port Said. London: Reprinted from "Engineering," 1883. 72 pp.

Forth, C. The Surprise of the Channel Tunnel. London: Wightman, 1883. 22 pp.

How Glasgow Ceased to Flourish: A Tale of 1890. Glasgow: Wilson & McCormick, 1884. 28 pp.

Posteritas (pseud.). The Siege of London. London: Wyman, 1885 [1884]. 68 pp.

A Landlord (pseud.). The Great Irish Rebellion of 1886. London: Harrison, 1886. 48 pp.

[Clowes, W.L., and A.H. Burgoyne.] The Great Naval War of 1887. London: Hatchards, [1887]. 60 pp.

Gopcevic, S. The Conquest of Britain in 1888, and the Sea Fights and Battles That Led To It. London: Griffith, 1887. 54 pp.

Hope, W. An Omitted Incident in "The Great Naval War of 1887." London: Redway, [1887]. 24 pp.

The "Russia's Hope"; or, Britannia No Longer Rules the Waves. London: Chapman & Hall, 1888. iv+175 pp.

Lester, H.F. The Taking of Dover. Bristol: Arrowsmith, 1888. 44 pp.

The Bombardment of Scarbro' by the Russian Fleet in 1891. London: Crown, [1889]. 36 pp.

England's Danger: or, Rifts Within the Lute: A Russian Plot. Portsmouth: Griffin, 1889. 98 pp.

Arnold-Forster, H.O. In A Conning Tower. London: Cassell, 1891. 54 pp.

Seaforth, A.N. (pseud. of G.S. Clarke). The Last Great Naval War. London: Cassell, [1892]. 120 pp.

1895: Under Home Rule. London: Simpkin, Marshall, 1893. 18 pp.

Eardley-Wilmot, S. The Next Naval War. London: Stanford, 1894. 175 pp.

Le Queux, William. <u>The Great War in England in 1897</u>. London: Tower, 1894. 330 pp.

Burton, F.G. <u>The Naval Engineer and the Command of the Sea</u>. London: Technical Publ., 1896. 231 pp.

Morris, J. <u>What Will Japan Do?</u> London: Lawrence & Bullen, 1898. xii+190 pp.

Wilson, H.W., and A. White. <u>When War Breaks Out</u>. London: Harper, 1898. 94 pp.

Stevenson, P.L. <u>How the Jubilee Fleet Escaped Destruction, and the Battle of Ushant</u>. London: Simpkin, Marshall, 1899. 68 pp.

Allen, F.M. (pseud. of E. Downey). <u>London's Peril</u>. London: Downey, 1900. 96 pp.

[Maude, F.N.] <u>The New Battle of Dorking</u>. London: Richards, 1900. 255 pp.

Offin, T.W. <u>How the Germans Took London</u>. London: Simpkin, Marshall, 1900. 64 pp.

3. On the Limits of the Genre

A) The Limits of the Genre:
An Annotated Checklist of Books Not to Be Regarded as SF, with an Introductory Essay on the Reasonable Reasons Thereof

1. On What Is and Is Not an S-F Narration

When establishing the list of S-F books published in the
United Kingdom in the period 1848-1900, I found that the
existing bibliographies deal only with such subgenres as
"the tale of the future" or "voyages in space." Therefore,
I had to supplement them with information from the more
general bibliographies of "fantasy," "utopias," "the novel
of science," etc. At the conclusion, I found that I had
read ca. 200 novels (many in three volumes) that could not
be regarded as SF. I offer the resulting list to future
researchers in hope that they will be able to avoid going
off on the same or similar tangents. After all, in research a negative result is sometimes as important as, or
even more important than, a positive one, for--as Spinoza
figured out for us all even before Hegelian dialectics--
"Omnis determinatio est negatio."

If any determination is also a negation, each negation is
also a determination. My list does not escape that general
law, for it was compiled on the basis of a determining and
excluding premise: that SF <u>is distinguished by the narrative dominance of a fictional novelty</u> (novum, innovation)
<u>validated both by being continuous with a body of already
existing cognitions and by being a "mental experiment"
based on cognitive logic</u> (see MOSF, chapters 1 to 4).
This is not only nor even primarily a matter of scientific
facts or hypotheses, and critics who protest against such
narrow conceptions of SF as the Verne-to-Gernsback ortho-
doxy are quite right to do so. But such critics are not
right when they throw out the baby with the bath by denying
that what differentiates SF from the "supernatural" genres
or fictional fantasy in the wider sense (including mythical

tales, fairy tales, etc., as well as horror and/or heroic fantasy in the narrower sense) is the presence of scientific cognition as the sign or correlative of a method (way, approach, atmosphere, worldview, sensibility) identical to that of a modern philosophy of science.

This is not the place to go into all the consequences that follow if one accepts some such determination of SF as the one stated above. Nonetheless, I shall try—proceeding from the general to the particular—to indicate a few categories or ensembles of writings that are excluded by it.

1.1. Nonfiction

The inclusion of a nonfictional work on science or pseudoscience in an S-F bibliography presumably arises most often from a sloppy bibliographer's listing a work on the basis of its title or of hearsay. We may find such errors amusing and even say that they have the value of indicating which kinds of writing are sufficiently near SF in the topology of literature for errors to be likely, but the confusion of science or pseudoscience with science fiction is not a trivial matter. For some of the most pernicious ideological impostures in or near SF are perpetrated exactly when the fundamental condition of "as if" is forgotten or wilfully violated. From Mr. Hubbard's Dianetics and Scientology to Mr. von Däniken's Chariots of the Gods, there are unfortunately many examples of the obscurantist fringe near or even in SF whose basic procedure is to blur the firm boundaries between imaginative literature and empirical reality. I do not, of course, argue in favor of art for art's sake; I do, however, argue that the contribution of art (literature, SF) to the human reality from which it springs and to which it returns can be useful, or even sane, only if one keeps firmly and continuously in mind that it is an imaginative construct. When any art—for example, S-F literature— sets itself up as a "real" ontological alternative rather than as a stimulus for understanding and changing our collective reality, it becomes a branch of the dope trade, an opium for the people. Hopefully, even the most fervent fans usually know that even the most "mind-expanding" wishdreams of a Clarke or Heinlein are only imaginatively and not ontologically real—but did Charles Manson?

This confusion between fact and fiction applies also, as I have argued elsewhere (MOSF, chapter 3), to the confusion of nonfictional political writings with utopian or sociopolitical SF, from Cabet to Skinner.

1.2. Nonrealistic Mode

A category that cannot be called SF consists of those works
for which the question of whether they possess a novelty
cannot even be posed, because they use novel worlds, characters, or relationships not as coherent, albeit provisional,
ends but instead as immediately transitive and narratively
nonautonomous means for direct and sustained reference to
the author's empirical world and some system of belief in
it. In other words, the question whether a writing is SF
is meaningless for works written in a nonrealistic mode
such as moral allegory, whimsy, satire, and the
lying tall tale ("Muenchhauseniade," as the Germans call
it). The moral allegory by "Lookup" in my list, for example, will use an allegorical character such as General
Power to bring justice to the USA and then the world in a
manner not too dissimilar--though dessicated and degener-
ated--from medieval allegories, only with reference to
Jeffersonian, Jacksonian, or Lincolnian politics rather
than to scholastic philosophy or troubador erotic casuistry. And though I am in favor of retroactive traditions in
culture, where each new significant work or genre rearran-
ges our perception of the past, it would seem rather absurd
to call the Roman de la Rose or Dante's Comedy SF.
Whimsy can well be exemplified by Delorme in my list, with
his seas of fried fish on the moon; the Munchausen-type
tall tale by Carruth; and the transparent satire with
contemporary allusions that prevent the narration from ever
developing an S-F novelty in its own right, by Burnand.
   Coming into the 20th century, this means that most of
Kafka, Borges, and a number of other writers around and
after them cannot be claimed for SF. No doubt, as in all
distinctions I am making here, there are borderline cases,
such as Barth's Giles Goat Boy and Kafka's Metamorphosis, as well as exceptions that use a predominantly
science-fictional narrative procedure of letting the novelty develop on its own and underlie in its turn the whole
narrative logic, as in Borges's Library of Babel, Kafka's
In the Penal Colony, or Book 3 of Gulliver's Travels.
But all such gray areas and exceptions should not prevent
us from employing our time better than in comparing incom-
mensurables--fiction in which novelty is used in the realistic mode with fiction in which it is used in the "transitive" mode, tenor with vehicle.

1.3. "Naturalistic" Fiction with Minor S-F Elements

Within fiction of the realistic mode it is of course necessary to distinguish between SF and such tales as possess no
innovation or novum that is unknown in the author's empiri-

cal environment: the events do not happen in a different space or time, nor with characters that are not Homines sapientes, nor with any significant and as yet unknown modification of basic relationships (as by the introduction of a startlingly new invention). This should be clear, for it is the usual watershed between SF and the naturalistic "mainstream." The difficulty here lies in borderline cases such as were mentioned in section 1.2 and will be mentioned in later sections. There are many writings--hundreds if not thousands in the 19th century alone--that contain one or even several minor elements or aspects of an S-F kind but still do not strike us as S-F stories. When SF--it seems so long ago!--was being defined as fiction about science and scientists, Sinclair Lewis's Arrowsmith was usually mentioned as being on the other side of the water-shed, dealing as it does with the ethics of present-day science. No doubt, this is correct; but on what basis do we erect the watershed? Clearly, on the basis of differen-tiating between part and whole, the peripheral and the central. Therefore, I would like to propose the concept of an S-F narration as an important tool in analysis. An S-F narration is not just a story that possesses this or that S-F element or aspect: utopian strivings, as with Lookup; visions of other worlds, better or worse than our own, as in Milton, Swedenborg, and thousands of their popu-lar imitators (of whom more in section 1.4); new technologi-cal gadgets; or anything else of the kind. An S-F narra-tion is a fiction in which the S-F element or aspect is hegemonic--that is, so central and significant that it determines the whole narrative logic, or at least the over-riding narrative logic, regardless of any impurities that might be present. For example, although Grant Allen's Recalled to Life has a new invention, an automatic elec-tric camera, whose existence becomes a factor in the search for its inventor's murderer, this strand in the story is quite minor and quite overwhelmed by Allen's usual sensa-tionalist melodrama, in this case a long account of how the inventor's daughter is shocked into amnesia and has dream-visions by which she is "recalled to life" and without which no one would have thought of using the new invention as a piece in the detection puzzle. Typically and confusingly enough, Allen's novel is a detective-cum-supernatural-fantasy tale with a subordinate S-F element. Similarly, Andrew Lang had five years earlier used a newly invented flying machine for the purpose of having its inventor witness a crime in one of the 16 chapters of The Mark of Cain, otherwise a standard detective-mystery novel, which to my mind can only be called a detective tale with one S-F element (tenuous at that, though no doubt there).

To claim for SF both those tales whose narrative logic is, and those whose narrative logic is not determined by the S-F novum, seems to me insensitive, confusing, and useless. This is my major objection to "thematic" studies of S-F elements and aspects. From J.O. Bailey's Pilgrims, which had of course an excuse in being a pioneering work, down to the present-day practitioners of S-F criticism in the atomistic and positivistic vein, strongly present in, for example, Extrapolation, these studies seem to me to ignore the basic and determining feature of what they are studying: the narrative logic of a fictional tale. (Correlatively, they also tend to become boring catalogs of raisins picked out of a narrative cake, and shriveled in the process.) Of course all this does not necessarily mean that a discussion of cameras or flying machines in fiction (whether SF or not) cannot be, for some strictly limited purposes, found useful; and for such limited purposes we should probably know where new cameras or satellites or creatures first appeared (a task facilitated by the delight it gives to squirrelly fact-gatherers, especially to "who was there first" collectors such as Mr. Moskowitz.) But we should not be lured by this very peripheral necessity into annexing any and every tale with a new invention or such into SF, as, for example, Bailey does with Bulwer-Lytton's A Strange Story, Wilkie Collins's Moonstone, and Thomas Hardy's Two on a Tower by putting them into his bibliography of "Scientific Romances" at the end of Pilgrims. S-F scholarship that does this (without the excuse that Bailey may have had) is sawing off the branch on which it is--on which we are--sitting; for if these three works are SF just like (are not radically different from), say, The Invisible Man, then in fact there is no such thing as SF.

1.4. Supernatural Fantasy

Within fiction whose narrative logic is determined by a novelty strange to the author's empirical reality, it is necessary, if we accept the italicized premise in the second paragraph of this essay, to distinguish between SF and fantastic fiction--that is, fiction in which the novelty is not validated by references to both existing cognitions and intrinsic cognitive logic. Of the two, the second--the intrinsic, culturally acquired cognitive logic--seems the crucial one to me. Though I would at the moment be hard put to cite an S-F tale whose novelty is not in fact directly continuous with (extrapolated from) or at least analo-

gous to existing "scientific" cognitions, I would be
disposed to accept theoretically a faint possibility of a
fictional novelty that would at least seem to be based on
quite new, imaginary cognitions, beyond all real possibilities known or dreamt of in the author's empirical reality.
(My doubts here are not so much formal as psychological,
for I do not see how any author could imagine something not
even dreamt of by anyone else before; but then, I don't
believe in individualistic originality.) But besides the
"real" possibilities there are also the much stricter
(though also much wider) limits of "ideal" possibility,
meaning any conceptual or thinkable possibility whose
premises and/or consequences are not internally contradictory. Any tale based on metaphysical wishdreams--for example, omnipotence--is "ideally impossible" (can an omnipotent god create a stone he won't be able to lift?, etc.)
according to the cognitive logic humanity has cumulatively
acquired in its culture from the beginnings to the present
day. It is this, and not positivistic scientism, which
separates boys from men, supernatural fantasy from SF. (I
cannot enter here into the important complications that
stem from the very different narrative role the supernatural or metaphysical elements may play according to whether
they are vehicle or tenor, signifier or signified; suffice
it to say that in the great majority of cases, and certainly in those discussed below, they are a muddled blend of
both.)

In my list of non-S-F books, allowing for both borderline
cases and the occasional skimpiness of my notes (since I
was not interested in whether a given tale was or was not
supernatural fantasy, but only in whether it was or was not
SF), the largest group, about 75 of the 197 books, is
constituted by tales of more or less supernatural fantasy.
This is not accidental, but is instead a result of the
ideological and commercial habit, stimulated by irrational
capitalist conditions of life and still very strong in our
field of research, of confusing SF and supernatural fantasy
on the purely negative basis that their imagined realities
are not identical with the author's empirical reality.
This habit has resulted not only in bibliographies such as
Bleiler's (1948) and Day's, but on a deeper and more pathological level in tales that incongruously mingle science-
fictional and fantastic narrative. A misshapen subgenre
born out of such mingling is "science fantasy," about which
I could only repeat the strictures of the late James Blish
in More Issues at Hand (Chicago, 1970, pp. 98-116). I
can add a historical point: the subgenre did not begin
with Merritt or such, but much earlier, and it is repre-

sented in my list, for example, by Chambers's The Maker of
Moons. Nonetheless, I would guess that the flowering of
"science fantasy" does come in our century, since the 19th
was much more straightforward about basing tales on ghosts,
occultism, and such, without the shamefaced alibi of a
superscience lurking in the background, which seems necessary for 20th-century readers.

In supernatural fantasy proper, the supposed novelty
(usually going back to 18th-century gothic novels or even
to Renaissance Neoplatonism) rejects cognitive logic and
claims for itself a higher "occult" logic--whether Christian, or a-Christian, or indeed atheistic (as will be the
case in Lovecraft), or, as is most usually the case, an
opportunistic blend of Christian and a-Christian, such as
Corelli's "Electric Christianity." This type of writing,
well known to Romantic poets and a number of cognoscenti
among earlier writers, was rediscovered for English 19th-
century prose by Edward Bulwer-Lytton in his tales Zanoni
(1842) and A Strange Story (1861), and all subsequent
writers have cribbed from and watered down these tales of
his. Recent research (Robert Lee Wolff, Strange Stories
[Boston, 1971]; Allan Conrad Christensen, Edward Bulwer-
Lytton [Athens, GA, 1976]) has shown how the central
postulate of this type of writing is the existence of a
"sympathetic" quasi-electric fluid pervading both Man and
Nature, so that an adept can--for good or evil--command
this Principle of Existence or "Soul" of the Universe
(these writings are much given to pseudoallegorical capital-
ization). The adept, trained in ancient Chaldean lore, can
thus command both Nature beyond "our mere science" (Bulwer)
and Man's mind (by mesmeric or other forms of hypnotic
will-control or by telepathy and such); since Time and
Space do not exist for the World Soul, the adept can
achieve clairvoyance and/or immortality (in such variants
as the Wandering Jew, the transmigration of souls, or the
posthumous spirit-life impinging on the "lower life").

The character system (or, more precisely, the system of
narrative agents) in such tales includes usually some
combination of an older adept-mentor, an evil adept abusing
his powers, our hero hesitating between the two, and a pure
woman taming or channeling the hero toward the Good. The
energies unleashed are clearly to be connected with sex--
openly in Bulwer, coyly and titillatingly in later
Victorian fiction, for example, Corelli, and the proper
analysis of these works would to my mind have to be a
Freudo-Marxist one. The Marxist aspect would follow up the
insights of the Bulwer research by going more thoroughly
into Bulwer's avowed association of Evil with Materialism,

the French Revolution, communism, and the Theory of Evolution. Bulwer is interesting and important, first because
he both knows and avows what he is doing, and second
because he is uneasily fascinated by his principle of Evil
(most clearly, of course in his S-F novel The Coming Race
--discussed in my essay--where vril-fluid is borne by emancipated females).

Among later writers, the most popular prolific practitioner, who might well be called the Haggard of the occult
tale, is Marie Corelli, represented in my list by half a
dozen entries. I think that her first, and probably most
developed, novel of this kind is A Romance of Two Worlds
(1886). In it a young woman musician narrates the story of
how she met a Chaldean wiseman who uses "human electricity," who gradually and fascinatingly teaches her the
existence of twin souls for each of us (her second soul is
off Earth, as it happens), and who in a trance shows her
life on other planets (Saturn, Venus, Jupiter--probably
from Flammarion). The inhabitants of Saturn can communicate directly with spirits, and they know no sickness or
aging because of the "electric belt" around their planet,
which is a Terrestrial Paradise, as are all the other
planets, except Earth, which is unique in having humans so
corrupt as to doubt God. The character of the Chaldean
wiseman obviously fuses the good adept with the sexually
fascinating young man, just as that of the woman musician
fuses the young protagonist (usually male) with the pure
girl, reminding us that the main readership of Corelli must
have been middle-class females. Among other matters in the
melodramatic plot, our narrator can in her vision do a
"Miniature Creation" to understand Christ better, and the
occult science propounded is finally revealed to be the
"Electric Principle of Christianity." Of course, the narration itself is much less coherent and much more boring (it
goes on for 500 pages!) than this résumé in which I have
loyally focused on the elements nearest to SF. Nonetheless, although a number of S-F writings, from J.J. Astor to
C.S. Lewis, have cribbed from Corelli, so that S-F
historians have to know that she existed, I hope it is
clear that her type of narration is not only fraudulent
(e.g., in reconciling a totally superordinated world with
all the Victorian sexual, religious, political, and ethical
taboos), is not only a proto-Fascist revulsion against
modern civilization, materialist rationalism, etc., is not
only a narration based on ideology unchecked by any cognitive logic, but is also (even in Bulwer, but much more so
in his followers) cobbled together from orts and scraps of
esoteric metaphysics, so that the narrative logic is simply

ideology plus Freudian erotic patterns. If SF exists at all
this is not it.

A limit-case of considerable importance which I have left
out of my list, is Stevenson's The Strange Case of Dr.
Jekyll and Mr. Hyde. Stevenson is, no doubt, a better
literary craftsman than any of the supernatural-fantasy
writers in my list after Bulwer; nonetheless, he is cheat-
ing in terms of his basic narrative logic. On the one
hand, his moral allegory of "good and evil" takes bodily
form with the help of a chemical concoction. On the other
hand, the transmogrification Jekyll-Hyde becomes not only
unrepeatable because the concoction contained unknown
impurities, but Hyde also begins "returning" without any
chemical stimulus, by force of desire and habit. This
unclear oscillation between science and fantasy, where
science is used for a partial justification or added alibi
for that part of the readership that would no longer be
disposed to swallow a straightforward fantasy or moral allegory, is to my mind the reason for the elaborate--clever
but finally not satisfying--exercise in detection from
various points of view, which naturalistically shelves but
does not explain the fuzziness of the narrative nucleus.
This marginal SF is therefore, in my opinion, an early
example of "science fantasy," with its force not stemming
from any cognitive logic, but rather from the anguish of
Jekyll over his loss of control and from the impact of the
underlying moral allegory (which is both so very cognate to
Victorian bourgeois repressions of the nonutilitarian or
nonofficial aspects of life, and holding out the unsubstantiated promise that the oscillation between SF and fantasy
does not matter anyway since we are dealing with an allegory).

1.5.   The Lost-Race Tale

The final set of writings discussed here is the one based
on a geographic or ethnographic novelty foreign to the
author's time, place, and social mores, which has for historical reasons evolved into a genre contiguous to and
sometimes overlapping SF, but still, in my opinion, to be
distinguished from it; that is, the lost-race tale. It is
true that a number of such tales--for example, H. Rider
Haggard's She, the most famous work by the codifier of
the genre, though probably not typical of the genre
itself--are dominated by a supernatural-fantasy element,
but that is not a necessary characteristic of the genre;
this would at worst prove that a number of important works
in it are "science fantasy" in the Blishian sense. Instead, my argument for sundering the lost-race tale from SF

is as follows: the formal framework of the lost-race
tale--that is, a fictional community whose history develops
in radical isolation from the author's known world--is
potentially quite orthodox SF, since it can be used to show
us a cognitively strange new relationship in sociopolitics
(as in More's Utopia), in technology (as in Bacon's New
Atlantis), in biology (as in Foigny's La Terre australe
connue or Paltock's Peter Wilkins), or in other matters,
and with the most significant works usually combining
several such headings (e.g., technology, biology, and politics in Book 3 of Gulliver's Travels). Nonetheless, the
very listing of the above titles makes it immediately
apparent that the lost-race tale, as it has been developed
in 19th-century English fiction, does not as a rule actual-
ize these potentialities. Only in exceptional cases is
there a sociopolitical (utopian-dystopian), technological,
or other novum present, and such cases are of course SF to
the extent that such a novum is narratively dominant. But
as a historical genre, the lost-race tale uses instead (and
on the contrary) uncouth combinations of tribal, slave-
owning, and feudal societies, usually with a beautiful
princess and wicked high priest in trio with the virtuous
white explorer-protagonist. This nostalgia of primitivism
has been highly influential in the historical development
of SF, but that does not make the lost-race tale SF. As
Professor Mullen has noted, in an unpublished MS, "the
lost-race concept is latently science-fictional in that it
raises a what-if question: what would happen to a civil-
ized society isolated for centuries from the Ekumene?" The
trouble is that in Haggard and his imitators "the community's economy is simply ignored [modern SF follows the lost-
race tale faithfully in this, DS]; its premodern technology
is simply taken for granted; and its politics appears only
in a hierarchy of royalty, nobility, priesthood, and common
people. In sum, the latent SF remains merely latent"--or,
I would add, preempted. These writings, then, should only
be investigated as SF in those exceptional cases where a
real novum is present, and I have used my sources (mainly
Teitler) only to check on such potential exceptions.

2. Two Hundred Victorian Books That Should Be
Excluded from S-F Bibliographies

2.1. Bibliographies Used to Compile Annotated Checklist
My inclusion of an item into the Checklist does not necessarily mean that a source was to my mind wrong; it can also
mean that the source was unclear as to the S-F status of a
title.

Bailey, J.O. <u>Pilgrims Through Space and Time: Trends and
Patterns in Scientific and Utopian Fiction</u>.   New York:
Argus, 1947; reprinted 1972.
This is a pioneering and still necessary research tool;
unlike the Bleiler <u>Checklist</u> in the next entry, it lists
only titles the author has actually read. Methodological-
ly, however, its insistence on thematic analysis leads to a
strong atomization, very rarely taking into account the narrative whole that determines the use of the themes, which
has aged it heavily. This is responsible for the strange
inclusion into "Scientific Romances" of the Bulwer-Lytton,
Collins, and Hardy items.

Bleiler, Everett F. <u>The Checklist of Fantastic Literature: A Bibliography of Fantasy, Weird, and Science Fiction Books Published in the English Language</u>.   Chicago:
Shasta, 1948; reprinted 1972.
Even before publication of the next entry, which only
partially corrects the original errors (e.g., in dates and
pseudonyms) it had aged greatly. Its main drawback for S-F
research is twofold: first, it did not set itself the goal
of distinguishing between S-F and supernatural fantasy;
second, within its own frame of reference, it succumbs from
time to time to the temptation of listing books (books that
turn out to be neither SF nor fantasy) simply on the basis
that the author had published in the field (as with some
titles by Haggard and Wells, and in my list titles by
Allen, Aubrey, Besant, Boothby, Chambers, Corelli, Cromie,
Hyne, Le Queux, Meade or Stables) or on the strength of
likely plots or even titles (as with Chamerovzow, Farjeon,
Hodgson, and Oliver in my list). Marked as "Bleiler."

Bleiler, E[verett] F. <u>The Checklist of Science-Fiction
and Supernatural Fiction</u>.   Glen Rock, NY: Firebell,
1978.
For a comment on it and the new edition of Clarke below,
see the judicious review by George Locke in <u>Science-
Fiction Studies</u>, no. 20 (1980). Both of these pioneering
and basic bibliographies have sometimes erroneous annotations (in Bleiler's case supplied through a system of
symbols which are a vast improvement on the unannotated
first edition but not always crystal-clear); the bulk of my
list has Bleiler as its source. Marked as "Bleiler CSS."

Botros Samaan, Angele. "The Novel of Utopianism and Prophecy From Lytton (1871) to Orwell (1949): With Special
Reference to Its Reception." Ph.D. dissertation, University of London, 1962.

A veritable treasure trove of material and data, in spite of not always inspired comments on them and some inclusions I disagree with. An enterprising reprint publisher should put it into book form.

Clarke, I.F. The Tale of the Future From the Beginning to the Present Day. . . . London: Library Assn., 1978, superseding the 1972 edition, in turn superseding first edition of 1961.
See Bleiler entry. Again a basic book, including a few items before 1900 that to my mind are not SF.

Day, Bradford M. The Supplemental Checklist of Fantastic Literature. Denver [NY]: S-F & F Publ., 1962.
A simplified supplement to Bleiler, with numerous mistakes, relatively few titles that are SF, and many that are not even fantasy.

Henkin, Leo J. "Problems and Digressions in the Victorian Novel (1860-1900), Part 13: Science." Bulletin of Bibliography 19 (1948), 156-59.
Can be a useful research tool only if its often one-sided and not wholly trustworthy annotations are rechecked.

Locke, George. "An Annotated Addendum to Bleiler and Day," in his Ferret Fantasy's Christmas Annual for 1972. London: Ferret Fantasy, 1972.
A useful tool, much better in its range than Bleiler or Day since the reliable annotations strive to differentiate SF from fantasy; I disagree in only a few cases. Marked as "Locke 72."

_____. "An Annotated Addendum to Bleiler and Day," in his Ferret Fantasy's Christmas Annual for 1973. London: Ferret Fantasy, 1974. Continuation of the identical title for 1972--from which it will be differentiated here by being abbreviated as "Locke 73." Again a very reliable tool; my rare disagreements are on matters of literary theory.

_____. A Spectrum of Fantasy. London: Ferret Fantasy, 1980.
A rich list of the author's personal holdings. Pleasingly idiosyncratic. Abbreviated as "Locke 80."

Messac, Régis. Esquisse d'une chrono-bibliographie des utopies. Lausanne: Club Futopia, 2962 [i.e., 1962].
A checklist of titles 1502-1940 called "utopias" by any

one of 38 sources. Left in MS by the author at the time of his death at the hands of the Gestapo, and published with notes by Pierre Versins. Very useful, especially for non-English titles, but subject to the vagaries of Messac's sources.

Newman, John. "America at War: Horror Stories for a Society." Extrapolation 16 (December 1974), 33-41 and 16 (May 1975), 164-72.
An admittedly incomplete bibliography of "Imaginary Wars" with US imprints. Neither selection criteria nor data are always reliable, so that some caution is needed. Nonetheless a useful supplement to I.F. Clarke's bibliographies in his Voices Prophesying War, 1763-1984 (1966) and to the Clarke item above.

Reginald, Robert. Science Fiction and Fantasy Literature 1700-1979, vol. I. Detroit: Gale Research, 1979.
Voluminous and generally reliable work, seriously marred by following the bad old habits of mingling fantasy and SF without any indication of which is which. This prevents it from superseding the revised edition of Bleiler, though its scope and thoroughness are superior to it.

Rooney, Charles J., Jr. "Utopian Literature as a Reflection of Social Forces in America, 1865-1917." Ph.D. dissertation, George Washington University, 1968.
Pages 249-81 contain a rich but, in spite of some annotations, very unclearly classified primary bibliography. The lack of clarity begins when utopian fiction is defined as works advocating extensive change in the status quo. Two sections relevant but exasperating to the S-F researcher are not annotated: "Romances," which throws together clearly S-F titles with those that are either fantasy (Chambers) or neither SF nor fantasy (Dement, Glasgow, Hillhouse, Prince, Webster, and Westcott in my list); "Science Fiction and Fantasy," which defines SF as "works of fantasy whose wonders violate present laws of nature" and lists at least one UK title that is neither.

Sargent, Lyman Tower. British and American Utopian Literature 1516-1975: An Annotated Bibliography. Boston: G.K. Hall, 1979.
Has immediately become a basic research tool, on the order of Bleiler's, Clarke's, and Locke's bibliographies. Apart from dire need for better proofreading, I would also carp at the exceedingly laconic and entirely socioideologically oriented annotations, and the attendant lack of clari-

ty as to whether the "literature" is fiction or not—a consequence of the latter being the two entries below that would not otherwise have been included.

Shurter, Robert L. "The Utopian Novel in America, 1865-1900." Ph.D. dissertation, Western Reserve University, 1936; in book form US 1973.
It is greatly to be regretted that this pioneering work was not printed at least when Bailey was: by now it is to a large extent superseded. It contains useful lists of utopias, including one of "English Utopias, 1859-1888" which is not fully reliable either as to its Englishness or as to its utopianness.

[Teitler, Stuart A.] Eureka!: A Survey of Archeological Fantasies and Terrestrial Utopias. Kaleidoscope Books Catalogue, no. 29 (1975).
An invaluable annotated list of lost-race tales. As explained above, I do not think such tales are SF unless they contain narratively important sociopolitical, technological, or other novelties of an S-F kind. I have listed from this source only those titles whose annotations suggest that they might be SF in my sense but which turned out not to be SF.

2.2. Annotated Checklist
Since full bibliographic data can be found in the preceding bibliographies, only the author's name, full title, and year have been retained here. A book of criticism which mentioned one title in terms that led me to suspect it was SF is given by full title in the checklist (see under Merriman). A large number of other titles, which were also found not to be SF, is not listed here because they were not clearly claimed for SF in the sources.

Adderley, James Granville. Stephen Remarx: The Story of a Venture in Ethics. 1893. Messac.
Ideal young nobleman-priest works and dies in Franciscan poverty to Christianize and better the lot of the lower classes.

Ainsworth, William Harrison. Auriol: or, The Elixir of Life. 1892. Bleiler CSS.
Alchemical and supernatural fantasy melodrama that includes longevity.

Al Arawiyah (pseud. of H.N. Crellin). Tales of the Caliph. 1887. Bleiler CSS, Locke 72.

Updated "Arabian Nights" fantasy.

Alldridge, Lizzie. The World She Awoke In: A Narrative.
1879. Henkin.
The world in which the heroine awakes (from illness) is
simply the everyday world. Though the main male characters
are scientists, this story has no S-F component.

Allen, F.M. (pseud. of Edmund Downey). The Little Green
Man. 1895. Bleiler CSS.
The little green man is a leprechaun.

Allen, Grant. Babylon. 1885. Henkin.
The lives and loves of artists in the US, England, and
Italy. There is no trace of the "utopian story" Henkin
finds in it.

_____. The Desire of the Eyes. 1895. Bleiler.
Short stories, love melodramas.

_____. The Great Taboo. 1890. Bleiler CSS.
English gentleman and pure white maiden shipwrecked on a
cannibal island in the Pacific, where they are faced with
a mysterious savage taboo that is finally revealed by a
parrot.

_____. Hilda Wade. 1900. Bleiler (as US and UK with
subtitle).
Medical shenanigans and dastardies.

_____. The Jaws of Death. 1889. Bleiler CSS.
Two stories: the first concerns a murdering Chinese in
San Francisco, the second an English poet gone native in
Jamaica, whose manuscript masterpiece is burned after his
death.

_____. Recalled to Life. n.d. [1891]. Henkin.
The minor S-F element is an automatic electric machine
that takes six photographs a minute, but it is smothered
by the melodrama of the inventor's daughter, who becomes
amnesiac, by the dream-visions by which she is "recalled
to life," and by the detective story. I do not find
Henkin's "chemicals powerful enough to reduce a man to
ashes."

Anstey, F. (pseud. of Thomas Anstey Guthrie). Vice Versâ:
or, A Lesson to Fathers. 1882. Bleiler CSS.
Father and schoolboy son exchange "spirits" or souls for

a time with help of Indian talisman and with comic results.

Arnold, Edwin Lester. The Wonderful Adventures of Phra the Phoenician. 1891. Bleiler (as US).
Metempsychosis of hero and heroine through the ages, but no S-F narration.

Ascher, Isidore G. A Social Upheaval: A Novel in Twelve Parts. 1898. Botros Samaan (as 1899).
Godawful melodrama of secret society which robs the wealthy to help the poor. Neither SF nor fantasy.

Aubrey, Frank. A Studio Mystery: A Novel. 1897. Bleiler CSS.
Detective story. Neither fantasy nor SF.

Badger, Joseph E., Jr. The Lost City: A Story of Adventure. The Boy's Own Authors Series. 1898. Reginald, Rooney, Teitler (all as US 1898).
Juvenile lost-race tale.

Bell, Mrs. Hugh [i.e., Florence Evelyn Eleanore Bell]. Miss Tod and the Prophets: A Sketch. 1898. Bleiler CSS.
Mousy spinster believes false prophecy of the end of the world. Neither fantasy nor SF.

Besant, Walter. All Sorts and Conditions of Men: An Impossible Story. 1882. Bleiler (as US, without subtitle, and with James Rice as coauthor).
Rich heroine lives incognito in poor district working for reform. Love and politics but no SF.

[Besant, Walter, and James Rice.] The Case of Mr. Lucraft; And Other Tales. 1876. Bleiler (as US).
Some supernatural fantasy but no SF.

Black, William. The Magic Ink and Other Stories. 1892. Bleiler (as US).
Three tales, two of them supernatural fantasy, but no SF.

_____. Strange Adventures of a Phaeton. 1878. Bleiler.
The "phaeton" is a coach implicated in strange adventures, but not S-F adventures.

Bloundelle-Burton, John [Edward]. The Desert Ship. n.d. [1893]. Bleiler CSS (as Burton).

Love and battles around buried galleon in Colorado.
Neither fantasy nor SF.

Boothby, Guy [Newell]. A Bid for Fortune: or, Dr, Nicola's Vendetta. 1895. Dr. Nicola. 1896. Dr. Nicola's Experiment. 1899. Bleiler.
A series with a mesmerizing villain in melodramatic
plots; no S-F narrations.

_____. The Lost Endeavour. 1985. Bleiler (as A Lost
Endeavour, US).
Colonial romance, with no S-F content.

_____. Pharos the Egyptian. 1899. Bleiler (as US).
Supernatural fantasy; ancient black magician and hypnotist, after being revived, loosens plague upon the world,
but is defeated by ancient gods.

Bourdillon, Francis William. Nephelé. 1896. Bleiler
(as US, with subtitle).
Ghost story.

[Braddon, Mary E., pseud. of Mary Maxwell.] Ralph the
Bailiff and Other Stories. London: Maxwell, n.d.
Bleiler (as different publisher, 1862).
Realistic criminal stories, and some supernatural
fantasy.

Brailsford, Henry Noel. The Broom of the War God: A
Novel. 1898. Newman.
"Real" war in Greece 1896-1897.

Brereton, C[loudesley] S[hovell] H[enry]. The Last Days
of Olympus: A Modern Myth. 1889. Bleiler CSS.
Though there is a Miltonic trip through the universe, a
moral allegory.

Bridgman-Metchim, D. Atlantis: The Book of the Angels.
1900. Bleiler CSS (as Metchim).
Confused science-fantasy bordering on fantasy.

Buchanan, Robert W., and Henry Murray. The Charlatan.
1895. Bleiler CSS.
Some psychic powers amid the charlatanry. Marginal
occult fantasy.

[Bulwer-] Lytton, Edward George. A Strange Story. 1861.
Bailey.

Occult supernatural fantasy with elixir of life and mesmerism. Bulwer's earlier tale Zanoni (1842) is also occult fantasy.

Burnand, F.C. Mokeanna!: A Treble Temptation, etc. 1873. Day.
Four satirical stories with contemporary allusions. In "Chikkin Hazard" (pp. 79-222), some strange races, but not developed as an S-F narration.

Canton, William. The Invisible Playmate: A Story of the Unseen. 1894. Bleiler.
Letter about a little girl and her "invisible playmate," a child who had died earlier.

Carnegie, James, Earl of Southesk. Suomiria: A Fantasy. 1899. Bleiler CSS (as Southesk).
Mainly occult fantasy of man-animals. Certainly not Bleiler's "ideal societies, utopias."

Carrel, Frederic. The Adventures of John Johns. 1897. Day.
Career of a philandering adventurer; no S-F elements.

Carruth, Hayden. The Adventures of Jones. 1895. Bleiler CSS (as US).
Munchausen-type tall tales.

Chambers, Robert W. In the Quarter. 1895. Bleiler (as US 1894).
Bohemian life in Paris during Franco-Prussian war, with love and crime.

_____. The Maker of Moons. 1896. Bleiler (as US).
Series of science-fantasy stories.

Chamerovzow, Louis Alexis. The Man of Destiny: A Romance of Modern History. 1860. Bleiler CSS.
About Napoleon III during and after 1848.

Chaytor, H[enry] J[ohn]. The Light of the Eye: A Novel. 1897. Locke 72, Reginald.
Horror fantasy.

Cheney, Walter T. An Apocalypse of Life. US 1893; imported 1894. Bleiler.
Christian spiritualism: in dream, the narrator flies through "celestial spheres," meeting Beings from various

stars and Christ.

Clarkson, L. (pseud. of Louise Clarkson Whitelock). The
  Shadow of John Wallace. US 1884; imported. Bleiler CSS.
  Sentimental story of a mysterious stranger with a vague
"magnetism"; there is occurrence of clairvoyance à la
Jane Eyre, but this novel is no more a supernatural
fantasy than Jane Eyre is.

Cloudesley, Hubert. Adventures of the Remarkable Twain.
  1899. Reginald.
  Whimsical fantasy about a father and young son.

Coleridge, Christabel. The Thought-Rope. 1898. Locke.
  Old woman with second-sight helps in love story.

Collins, W. Wilkie. The Moonstone. 1868. Bailey.
  The only novelties are the mysterious Brahmins and the
assumption that sleepwalking under the influence of opium
leads to a reenactment of past behavior. I do not know why
Bailey calls this assumption a "relatively scientific
theory"; it is not such, and even if it were, that would
not make the whole narration SF.

Conrad, Joseph. Tales of Unrest. 1898. Bleiler (as
  US).
  Adventure tales, one with a haunted Malay. Alas, one
ghost (illusory or real) doth not a fantasy make (not to
speak of SF).

Corbett, Julian [Stafford]. Kophetua the Thirteenth.
  1889. Locke 80.
  Christian kingdom in Africa. Ruritania rather than
SF.

Corelli, Marie. Ardath: The Story of a Dead Self.
  1889. Bleiler (as US 189?).
  Occult supernatural fantasy oscillating between horror
and redemption, including dream trips to the past, a woman-
angel incarnating, etc.

_____. A Romance of Two Worlds. 1886. Bleiler (as US
  1888).
  Occult supernatural fantasy of the "Electric Principle of
Christianity" and trance communication with spirits on
other planets, all earthly paradises, unlike our corrupt
Earth, where some humans doubt God (a theory better known
today from C.S. Lewis).

_____. The Sorrows of Satan: or, the Strange Experiences of One Geoffrey Tempest, Millionaire: A Romance. 1895. Bleiler (as US 1896).
The narrator, Tempest, meets sorrowful Satan.

_____. The Soul of Lilith. 1892. Bleiler (as US).
Occult supernatural fantasy, similar to A Romance of Two Worlds, but the trance shows the planet of a double sun with immortal happy people.

_____. Vendetta! or, The Story of One Forgotten. 1886. Bleiler (as US).
A Neapolitan nobleman buried alive during a plague takes a three-volume revenge on his wife. Neither fantasy nor SF.

_____. Ziska: The Problem of a Wicked Soul. 1897. Bleiler (as US).
Occult supernatural fantasy, with posthumous life, etc.

Cromie, Robert. The King's Oak and Other Stories. n.d. [1897]. Bleiler CSS.
Certainly not SF, and so far as my skimpy notes serve, not supernatural fantasy either.

_____. The Lost Liner. 1899. Bleiler.
A shipwreck story; neither SF nor supernatural fantasy.

Curtois, M[argaret] A[nne]. The Romance of a Country: A Masque. 1893. Henkin.
A proto-Tolkien fantasy.

Dail, C[harles] C[urtis]. The Stone Giant: A Story of the Mammoth Cave. n.d. [1898]. Bleiler CSS.
Predominantly occult or science-fantasy novel narrated by long-living visitor from pre-Atlantean and Atlantean ages.

Davidson, John. A Full and True Account of the Wonderful Mission of Earl Lavender, Which Lasted One Night and One Day: With a History of the Pursuit of Earl Lavender and Lord Brumm by Mrs. Scamler and Maud Emblem. 1895. Henkin.
Comic adventures include false discovery of missing link. Neither fantasy nor SF.

[Davis, Ellis J.] Coralia: A Plaint of Futurity. 1876. Botros Samaan, Shurter.
Immortal spirits underwater after death; Miltonic flight

into universe and reincarnation.

Dawe, W[illiam] Carlton L[anyon]. The Golden Lake.
   1890. Reginald.
   Adventure tale.

Delorme, Charles (pseud. of Charles Rumball). The Marvellous and Incredible Adventures of Charles Thunderbolt in
   the Moon. 1851. Bleiler.
   Whimsical tale; the hero finds a sea of fried fish,
dragons, etc.

Dement, R[ichmond] S[heffield]. Ronbar: A Counterfeit
   Presentment. US 1895. Rooney (with author's name given
   as Richard S.).
   Love intrigues and illegal coining of silver; at the end
free minting for all is foreshadowed, but that's not enough
to make the story SF.

Denison, Tho[ma]s S[tewart]. My Invisible Partner. n.d.
   [1898]. Bleiler (as US).
   Fantasy about an invisible second self.

Dering, Ross George (pseud. of Frederic H. Balfour). Dr.
   Mirabel's Theory: A Psychological Study. 1893.
   Bleiler (as US).
   Supernatural fantasy; hypnotism is used for murder, but
not in an S-F narration.

Diehl, Mrs. A[lice] M. Dr. Paull's Theory: A Romance.
   n.d. [1893]. Bleiler CSS [as US].
   Supernatural fantasy: the transmigration of souls.

[Downey, Edmund.] A House of Tears: An Original Story.
   1886. Bleiler CSS (under Anonymous).
   Horror fantasy about man with snake mouth born such
because of his father's interest in snakes.

Doyle, Arthur Conan. The Parasite. 1894. Bleiler (as
   US 1895).
   Criminal story about a professor and his mesmerico-
hypnotic medium; not an S-F narration.

Du Maurier, George. Trilby: A Novel. 1894. Bleiler.
   This well-known melodrama turns on Svengali's use of
mesmerism to make Trilby into a great singer; no S-F development is given to the premise of mesmerism, which thus
remains occult supernatural fantasy.

[Dyas, Richard H.] The Upas: A Vision of the Past, Present, and Future. 1877. Clarke.
Dream about Spirit of the Future taking narrator on tour of history. Only final segment allegorical vision of future.

Ellis, Henry Havelock. The Nineteenth Century: A Dialogue in Utopia. 1900. Messac (as The Twentieth Century, a title I was unable to verify).
A strong critique of the 19th century from a utopian perspective, but truly a dialogue and not a fictional story.

Ellis, T. Mullet. Reveries of World-History: From Earth's Nebulous Origin to Its Final Ruin: or The Romance of a Star. 1893. Bleiler CSS.
Not fiction.

Falkner, John Meade. The Lost Stradivarius. 1895. Bleiler.
Supernatural fantasy of music and deviltry.

Farjeon, B[enjamin] L[eopold]. The Last Tenant. 1893. Bleiler.
A "haunted" house turns out to harbor a banal crime mystery; neither SF nor supernatural fantasy.

Favenc, Ernest. Marooned on Australia: Being the Narration by Diedrich Buys of His Discoveries and Exploits in "Terra Australis Incognita," About the Year 1630. n.d. [1896]. Reginald.
Adventures, partly on a mixed "lost race."

_____. The Secret of the Australian Desert. 1896. Reginald.
Adventures with cannibals. Neither fantasy nor SF.

Fenn, Geo[rge] Manville. The Golden Magnet: A Tale of the Land of the Incas. 1884. Bleiler CSS.
Adventure story of search for Inca gold; neither SF nor supernatural fantasy.

_____. The Man With a Shadow. 1888. Bleiler.
Villains and occult secrets of nature in medical research, but with no S-F narration.

[Ferrar, William M.] Artabanzanus: The Dream of the Great Lake: An Allegorical Romance of Tasmania: Arranged from the Diary of the late Oliver Ubertus by

William M. Ferrar. 1896. Bleiler CSS, Teitler.
Religious fantasy visions of a subterranean land, mixing
balloons and fiends. Possibly allegorical; certainly not
SF.

Fogerty, J. Mr. Jocko: A Novel. 1891. Henkin (as
　Foggerty and Jacko).
Ape, vaguely suspected of being missing link, sacrifices
life to save girl.

Frith, Walter. The Sack of Monte Carlo: An Adventure of
　To-day. 1897. Day.
Robbery of the gambling casino; neither SF nor supernatu-
ral fantasy.

[Frost, Thomas.] The North Pole, and How Charlie Wilson
　Discovered It. 1876. Bleiler CSS.
Vernean juvenile adventure, with the discovery of the
North Pole as a minor S-F element.

Fryers, Austin (pseud. of William Edward Clery). The
　Devil and the Inventor. 1900. Bleiler CSS, Clarke.
Inventor makes pact with the devil, who is finally exor-
cized by prayer. Fantasy.

Galier, W.H. A Visit to Blestland. 1896. Bleiler CSS.
A dream of Blestland, simultaneously ideal society and
abode of deceased friends. Minor utopian elements only.

Glasgow, Ellen. Phases of an Inferior Planet. 1898.
　Rooney.
Love and religion in New York; the planet of the title is
simply Earth.

Godfrey, Hal (pseud. of Charlotte O'Connor Eccles). The
　Rejuvenation of Miss Semaphore: A Farcical Novel.
　1897. Bleiler CSS.
Water from Fountain of Youth devolves woman back to
baby.

Gordon, Lord Granville. Notes from Another World. 1886.
　Bleiler CSS.
Life after death; a satirical fantasy of sorts.

Gorst, H[arold] E[dward]. Farthest South: An Account of
　the Startling Discovery Made by the Wise Antarctic Expedi-
　tion. 1900. Reginald.
Comic story of bicycling adventures, not SF.

[Gray, Annabel, pseud. of Anne Cox.] 'Twixt Shade and Shine. 1883 [1882]. Bleiler CSS.
Mundane love-intrigue story. Neither fantasy nor SF.

Grey, Edward (pseud.). Concealed for Thirty Years: Being the Narrative of One E. Grey. 1890. Locke 72, Reginald.
Lost-colony tale.

Gunn, Edmund S. The Romance of Paradise. 1895. Locke 72, Reginald.
Dream of Miltonic spirit journey through universe. Religious fantasy.

Haes, Hubert. The Past Shewer. 1899. Bleiler CSS.
Invention showing the past used for moral disquisitions without any specific scenes from the past. Not really fiction.

Halliday, Andrew, ed. Savage Club Papers for 1868. Day (author's first name as Arthur).
A collection of stories and poems; none is SF.

Hamilton, Bernard. The Light?: A Romance. 1898. Reginald.
Love melodrama and religious discussions, with a hint of reincarnation. Marginal fantasy.

Hardy, Thomas. Two on a Tower. 1882. Bailey.
Love and astronomy; no SF or fantasy.

Harris, Thomas Lake. The Great Republic: A Poem of the Sun. 1867. Messac.
Verse preachments, exhortations, and prophecies with vague references to men on the Sun, mainly allegorical. Semivisionary didactic poem—not SF, only marginally fiction.

Hatch, Mary R. [Platt]. The Missing Man. US 1892?; imported 1893. Bleiler CSS, Reginald (as 1893).
The setting of the narration in 1917 is mentioned once in the first chapter and then promptly and totally forgotten. For the rest it is a melodramatic fantasy with magnetic mind-reading, unknown twins, amnesia, crime, dastardy, and love triumphant.

Hawtrey, George Procter. Caramella: A Story of the Lotus-Eaters Up To Date. n.d. [1899]. Henkin.

Whimsical spoof of Lotus-land with imperious females.

Heron-Allen, Edward [i.e., Allen, Edward Heron] (and Selina
     Delaro?). The Princess Daphne: A Novel. n.d. [1885].
     Locke 72, Reginald.
     Psychic horror fantasy.

Hildreth, Charles L[otin]. Oo: Adventures in Orbello
     Land. US 1889; imported 1890. Bleiler.
     Lost white race similar to ancient Greeks found in
     Australia.

Hillhouse, Mansfield Lovell. Iola, the Senator's Daugh-
     ter: A Story of Ancient Rome. 1894. Rooney.
     Life of the "Business classes" in ancient Rome, with
     clear parallels to 19th-century New York, but no S-F nar-
     ration.

Hocking, Joseph. The Weapons of Mystery. 1890.
     Bleiler CSS.
     Crime and mesmerism; no S-F narration.

Hocking, Silas K[itto]. The Strange Adventures of Israel
     Pendray. 1899. Reginald.
     Adventures with smugglers and a fake ghost. Neither SF
     nor fantasy.

Hodgson, William Earl. Haunted by Posterity. 1895.
     Bleiler.
     Spiritualist interviews.

_____. Unrest: or, The Newer Republic. 1887.
     Bleiler.
     Contains a little speculation on psychic research but
     neither SF nor supernatural fantasy.

Holland, Clive. Raymi: or, The Children of the Sun.
     1889. Teitler.
     Adventures on sea and land in the 18th century; hero
     finds Inca chief, his daughter Raymi, and their treasure.

Holmes, Oliver Wendell. Elsie Venner: A Romance of Des-
     tiny. 1861. Bailey.
     S-F element of psychophysical coldness caused by prenatal
     snake-bite is never developed.

Hood, Tom. From Nowhere to the North Pole: A Noah's Ark-
     aeological Narrative. 1875. Bleiler CSS.

Semiwhimsical juvenile fantasy.

Hooper, Albert E. Up the Moonstair: A Story For Children. 1890. Bleiler CSS (with author's given names as Albert W.).
Juvenile fairy-tale.

Horniman, Roy. The Sin of Atlantis. 1900. Bleiler CSS.
Occult fantasy.

Hort, [Richard]. The Embroidered Banner. 1850.
Reginald.
Adventure and some supernatural fantasy stories.

Hovenden, Robert. A Tract of Future Times: or, The Reflections of Posterity on the Excitement, Hypocrisy, and Idolatry of the Nineteenth Century. 1850.
Clarke.
Look backward at wicked 19th century from regenerated 21st century, without any particulars of the transition. Not fiction, though at places coming near to it.

How the World Came to an End in 1881. 1884. Shurter (as by Edward Maítland, a probable but unproven authorship).
Occultist argumentation, not fiction.

Howard, Charles F. Olympus. 1855. Bleiler CSS.
Philosophico-satirical dialogues with the dead on Olympus.

Howell, George Rogers. Noah's Log Book: How Two Americans Blasted the Ice on Mt. Ararat and Found Noah's Ark and Some Curious Relics. 1898. Bleiler CSS.
Exactly what it says: anti-evolution tale.

Hume, Fergus W. The Harlequin Opal: A Romance. 1893.
Day.
Love and political-adventure melodrama around abandoned Aztec-Maya city. Neither SF nor fantasy.

Hungerford, Margaret W. The Professor's Experiment: A Novel. 1895. Bleiler CSS.
Love story. Not SF except for the initial brief incident of new sleep-inducing "anaesthetic."

Hutchinson, Horace G[ordon]. That Fiddler Fellow. 1891.
Bleiler CSS, Henkin.
Gothic horror story.

Hyne, [Charles J.] C[utcliffe W.]. <u>The Adventures of Captain Kettle</u>. 1898. Bleiler (as US).
Outrageous nautical tall tales.

J.N. <u>Cuttings from "The Times" of 1900</u>. 1873. Bleiler.
Not fiction.

Jane, Fred[erick] T. <u>The Incubated Girl</u>. 1896. Bleiler.
Secret from Egyptian papyrus used by sinister professor in his lab for creating a new race of chaste women. His first sample, a girl constituted both chemically and with the help of supernatural influences, is also used as an innocent eye on London. Oscillates between satire and horror fantasy, with the small S-F element overridden by these two types of narration.

Johnstone, David Lawson. <u>The Paradise of the North</u>. 1890. Henkin.
Lost-race tale.

[Kendall, May, and Andrew Lang.] <u>"That Very Mab."</u> 1885. Clarke.
Fantasy and satire. Not SF (certainly not an anticipation tale).

[Kirk, Ellen Warner Olney.] <u>A Daughter of Eve</u>. 1889. Bleiler CSS.
Mundane melodrama with some mention of unusual educational scheme.

Lang, Andrew. <u>The Mark of Cain</u>. 1886. Locke.
A crime-mystery narration that uses SF for a moment (but only a moment) in the 11th of its 16 chapters with the appearance of a flying machine whose inventor witnesses the crime.

Le Queux, William [Tufnell]. <u>England's Peril: A Novel</u>. 1899. Bleiler.
In spite of the title exploiting the popularity of future-war SF, this is simply a spy story.

_____. <u>The Great White Queen: A Tale of Treasure and Treason</u>. 1896. Bleiler (as 1898).
Lost-race tale (or more precisely, as Mullen's unpublished MS suggests, a "forbidden world" tale).

Lockhart-Ross, H.S. <u>Hamtura: A Tale of an Unknown Land</u>.

1892? Day.
Unknown island in the Pacific contains treasure; a magic
prophecy comes true; perhaps supernatural fantasy but not
SF.

Lookup, Alexander (pseud.). Excelsior; or, The Heir Apparent. 1860. Bleiler.
Political allegory-drama about reform of US government.

_____. The Soldier of the People: Or, The World's
Deliverer. 1860. Bleiler.
Dramatic allegory of General Power bringing justice to
the world.

LWJS (pseud. of Valdemar Adolph Thisted). Letters from
Hell. 1884 (Danish original 1866). Bleiler CSS.
Religious fantasy. (See entry under Rowel.)

M'Crib, Theophilus (pseud. of Henry Boyle Lee). Kenna-
quhair: A Narrative of Utopian Travel. 1872 (1871?).
Bleiler.
Description of a world in which literary characters live
as long as people remember. Fantasy rather than utopian
fiction or SF.

[Mackay, Charles.] Baron Grimbosh: Doctor of Philosophy
and Sometime Governor of Barataria. A Record of His
Experience. 1872. Messac (as anonymous).
Whimsical political satire, with no utopian or S-F narration.

Mason, Eveleen Laura. Hiero-Salem: The Vision of Peace.
US 1889; imported 1890. Rooney.
Occult supernatural fantasy of spirits, religious salvation, metempsychosis, etc., in tandem with political
reform.

Mathew, Frank. At the Rising of the Moon: Irish Stories
and Studies. 1893. Bleiler.
No S-F stories included.

McKesson, Charles L. Under Pike's Peak: or, Mahalma,
Child of the Fire Father. 1898. Teitler.
Lost-race science-fantasy.

Meade, L.T. (peud. of Elizabeth Thomasina Meade Smith).
The Desire of Men: An Impossibility. 1899. Locke 72,
Reginald.

Fantasy—psychic vampirism.

Meade, L.T. (pseud. of Elizabeth Thomasina Meade Smith),
and Clifford Halifax. Stories From the Diary of a Doctor: First Series. 1894. Bleiler CSS.
Detective stories with medical discoveries a bit in
advance of the state of the art but not really SF (unknown
drug, hypnotism, somnambulism).

_____. Stories From the Diary of a Doctor: Second
Series. 1896. Bleiler CSS.
Stories of medical technology: operations,   poisons,
drugs, etc.

Meade, L.T. (pseud. of Elizabeth Thomasina Meade Smith),
and Robert Eustace. The Brotherhood of the Seven
Kings. 1899. Bleiler CSS.
Novel of secret brotherhood with scientific tricks, for
example, germs, explosives, magnets. Neither fantasy nor
SF.

_____. A Master of Mysteries. n.d. [1898]. Bleiler
CSS.
Detective stories with technological tricks (magnet,
carbonic acid, submarine boat, speaking tube).

_____. The Sanctuary Club. 1900. Bleiler CSS.
Scientifico-medical criminal cases; the final a brain
experiment, but too small SF element.

Mendum, Bedloe. The Barbarian and Other Stories. 1899.
Teitler.
Short short stories, one a satire on Vulgaria (i.e., USA)
as seen by a Chinese visitor, but without S-F narration.

Merriman, Henry Seton (pseud. of Hugh Stowell Scott).
With Edged Tools. 1894. Elwin, Old Gods Falling
(1939).
African drug strengthening life sought and lost in adventures. S-F element subordinated to upper-class melodrama.

Mervan, Rencelof Ermagine (pseud.). What is This? 1898.
Bleiler CSS.
Religious fantasy.

Miller, George Noyes. After the Strike of a Sex: or,
Zugassent's Discovery: With the Oneida Community and The
Perfectionists of Oneida and Wallingford. The Bellamy

Library, no. 26. n.d. [1896]. Clarke (with wrong annotation), Bleiler CSS (as US [1895]).
Though there is a hint at the beginning this will be fiction continuing The Strike of a Sex, it develops into a nonfictional defense of Oneida sexual technique that prevents pregnancy.

Moody, Dr. H.A.   The City Without a Name.   1898.
   Bleiler.
Lost-race story of a hidden Inca city, with only faint echoes of a better state.

My Great Grandson (pseud.).   1975: A Tradition.   n.d.
   [1876].   Clarke, Bleiler CSS (with subtitle as A Prediction).
Manuscript from 19th century "published" in 1975, dealing with a murder in 1870s. Only the framework is SF; not "set in the future" as Clarke has it.

[Newman, John Henry.]   Callista: A Sketch of the Third
   Century. n.d. [1855].   Day.
Historical story by the future cardinal about Christian martyrs.

Newnham-Davis, N[athaniel].   Jadoo.   1898.   Bleiler CSS
   (as Davis).
Anglo-Indian story of love and human sacrifice. Neither fantasy nor SF.

[Newton, Alex.]   Posterity: Its Verdicts and Its Methods:
   or, Democracy AD 2100.   1897.   Clarke, Locke 80.
S-F framework of protagonist awakening in future used for nonfictional exposition.

Nicholson, John H[enry].   The Adventures of Halek: An
   Autobiographical Fragment. 1882.   Reginald.
Religious-cum-ethical allegory.

[Nicholson, Joseph Shield.]   A Dreamer of Dreams: A
   Modern Romance. 1899.   Bleiler CSS.
Young man invents directed dreaming through music and drugs. Love, near-crime, and the devil--all was a dream. One small S-F element, a larger one of fantasy.

Nisbet, Hume.   The Great Secret: A Tale of Tomorrow.
   1895.   Clarke, Bleiler CSS.
Despite the subtitle, this is merely a confused tale of anarchists taking people to an island in the Indian Ocean

where they find the abode of dead spirits and the Garden of
Hesperides(!).

Norton, Seymour F. Ten Men of Money Island. The Bellamy
    Library, no. 27. n.d. [1895]. Sargent (as US 1891).
    Island in Pacific with ten allegorical people (e.g.,
Donothing, Discount) explains finances.

Oliver, J[ohn] A. Westwood. The Doomed Comet and the
    World's End. 1882. Bleiler, CSS.
    A real goof proving Bleiler did not read some of his
titles: not fiction but an introduction to "Cometic Astronomy" combating alarmism.

Oppenheim, E[dward] Phillips. A Daughter of Astraea.
    n.d. [1898]. Reginald, Teitler.
    Lost-race tale.

Orpen, Mrs. G.H. Perfection City. 1897. Bleiler CSS
    (as US).
    Utopian community in everyday Kansas.

Owen, Evelyn. Driven Home: A Tale of Destiny. 1886.
    Bleiler CSS.
    Crime and supernatural fantasy, villain punished by Prov-
idence.

Peek, Hedley. The Chariot of the Flesh. 1897. Locke
    72.
    The discovery of a MS by Descartes on thought-reading and
mesmeric "will-force." The initial pretence at rational
explanation, making for an S-F narration, is soon abandoned
for occult supernatural fantasy.

Phillips, L[undern] M. The Mind Reader. 1898. Day.
    Occult supernatural fantasy where hypnotism, clairvoy-
ance, mind-reading, and astral protection foil dastardly
capitalist swindlers.

Prince, Helen Choate. The Story of Christine Rochefort.
    1895. Rooney.
    Religious reformism in conflict of capital and labor.

Quilp, Jocelyn. Baron Verdigris: A Romance of the Re-
    versed Direction. 1894. Reginald.
    Whimsical fantasy mingling modern and medieval ages.

Rathborne, St. George. A Son of Mars (A Tale). 1897

(another edition without subtitle also 1897). Newman (as US 1897).
Except for a wicked hypnotist, mundane tale of love and war-adventure.

Reade, Compton. Under Which King? 1885. Shurter.
No trace of its having been published in or imported into UK.

Rowel, M. (pseud. of Valdemar Adolph Thisted). Letters from Hell. 1886 (Danish original 1866). Locke 72.
Religious fantasy.

Russell, W[illiam] Clarke. The Frozen Pirate. 1887. Bailey (as US).
The potential S-F element of a frozen pirate thawed out after 48 years is lost in an adventure-story narration.

Savile, Frank [A.]. Beyond the Great South Wall: Being Some Surprising Details of the Voyage of the S.Y. "Racoon". 1899. Bleiler CSS.
Geographic adventures, with Mayan refugee-colony remnants and dinosaurs found in Antarctic. Only minor elements of both lost-race and prehistoric SF.

Sewell, Elizabeth M[issing], "editor." Uncle Peter's Fairy Tale For the Nineteenth Century. 1869. Locke 72.
Fairy pills fulfilling wishes for improving the world; no S-F narration.

[Shorthouse, J. Henry.] John Inglesant: A Romance. 1880. Day.
Historical romance about 17th-century Catholic plots, etc., neither supernatural fantasy nor SF.

Sirius (pseud. of Edward Martyn). Morgante the Lesser: His Notorious Life and Wonderful Deeds. 1890. Bleiler CSS.
Satirical allegory.

Sketchley, Arthur (pseud. of G. Rose). Mrs. Brown on the Battle of Dorking. 1871. Clarke.
Humorous account of a woman's panic on reading invasion tales. Neither SF nor laid in the future.

Skunks, Major, B.T. of the Volunteers (pseud.). The Great Battle of Patchumup, Fought Off Cape Kerkumover, June 1st, in the Year of the Three Naughts: The Only Official

Report. n.d. [1865?]. Locke 73.
Shandean whimsy about various battles in past and present.

Slosson, Annie Trumbull. Seven Dreamers. 1899 (US 1891). Day.
Fantasy stories.

Smeaton, [William Henry] Oliphant. A Mystery of the Pacific. 1899. Teitler.
Lost-race story of a large island with ancient Romans, magic Atlanteans, etc., with Vernean adventure elements, but no SF.

Smith, Mrs. J. Gregory. Atla: A Story of the Lost Island. 1886. Bleiler (as US).
Love and intrigue in Atlantis up to its destruction; pseudohistorical romance but with all the clichés of the lost-race story.

Smith, James [Elishama]. The Coming Man. 1873. Shurter.
Religious fantasy.

Stables, William Gordon. The Cruise of the Crystal Boat: The Wild, the Weird, the Wonderful. 1891. Bleiler CSS.
Magical pseudo-Oriental geographic adventures.

_____. From Pole to Pole. 1886. Bleiler CSS.
Nautical adventures. Neither SF nor fantasy.

_____. Wild Adventures Around the Pole: or, The Cruise of the "Snowbird" Crew in the "Arandoon." 1883. Bleiler CSS.
Adventures in ship and balloon. Neither SF nor fantasy.

Stebbing, W[illiam], "edited by." Probable Tales. 1899. Teitler.
Grotesque and whimsical European Ruritanias; for example, Ipsiland, the land without comparisons. No S-F narration.

Steelnib, Jocundus (pseud.). Freaks of Imagination: or, A Batch of Original Tales, Chiefly Facetious. 1852. Bleiler CSS.
Stories, one of which ("A Visit to the Moon") is whimsy of balloon flight and visit to Luna, with some Swiftian elements.

Storke, Francis Eugene. <u>Mr. De Lacy's Double</u>. US 1898;
  imported 1899. Bleiler CSS.
Man weds ghost of dead bride with help of medium.

Taylor, U[na] Ashworth. <u>The City of Sarras</u>. 1887.
  Bleiler.
Fantasy of love and religion in Galahad's city for souls
of the elect.

Theosopho and Ellora (pseud. of Gideon Jasper Ouseley).
  <u>Palingenesia: or, The Earth's New Birth</u>. 1884.
  Clarke, Botros Samaan.
Religious visions beginning with 69th century, then
passing to straight descriptions of its state. S-F elements overridden by religious fantasy and even more so by
lack of fictional story.

Thompson, W[illiam] M[ort]. <u>A Very Odd Dream</u>. Privately
  Printed Opuscula, etc., no. 6. 1883. Bleiler CSS.
Whimsical dream using S-F motifs of rejuvenation and
future setting.

Vitu, Auguste [Charles Joseph]. <u>The Strange Phantasy of
  Doctor Trintzius</u>. Vizetelly's Sixpenny Series of
  Amusing and Entertaining Books, vol. 12. 1885. Bleiler
  CSS.
Stories oscillating between delusion and occult fantasy.

Wait, Frona Eunice [Smith Colburn]. <u>Yermah, the Dorado:
  The Story of a Lost Race</u>. 1897. Teitler (as US).
Adventure story of Atlantis colony in California 11,000
years ago, with no S-F narration.

Wallace, William. <u>After the Revolution and Other Holiday
  Fantasies</u>. 1893. Locke 80.
Pseudosatires about a future just like the present.

Webster, Henry K. <u>The Banker and the Bear</u>. 1900 (US
  1898). Rooney.
Muckraking social comment about a stock-market "corner."

Wedmore, Frederick. <u>Renunciations</u>. 1893. Bleiler CSS.
Three sentimental stories. Neither fantasy nor SF.

Westall, William [Bury]. <u>The Phantom City: A Volcano
  Romance</u>. 1886. Messac, Reginald (the latter as US
  1886).
Lost-race tale.

Westcott, Edward Noyes. David Harum: A Story of American
   Life. 1899. Rooney (as US 1898).
   This well-known story has really no S-F elements at all.

Whiteing, Richard. The Island: or, Adventures of a Person of Quality. Botros Samaan.
   Love and harmony on Pitcairn Island. Utopian overtones
only.

Wright, Henry. Mental Travels in Imagined Lands. 1878.
   Sargent, Shurter.
   Semiallegorical socioeconomic countries (e.g., "Labour-
land," "Nomuniburgh") described. Not fiction.

Wright, Thomas. The Blue Firedrake; or, The Wonderful and
   Strange Relation of the Life and Adventures of Nathan
   Souldrop. 1892. Day.
   Story of the last English witch in the 18th century, with
no S-F elements.

Zola, Emile. Fruitfulness. 1900 (French original 1899).
   Clarke.
   Brief rhapsodic vision, toward the end, of France's colonial future is the only S-F element in this very long
novel.

B) Presumed S-F Pamphlets

I have not checked the titles in this Appendix de visu;
all but two are from Clarke, Tale of the Future.

Democracy by Telephone. London: Taylor, 1878.

Donovan, A. The Irish Rebellion of 1898. London:
   Hodges, Figgis, 1893.

England in 1910. London: Willing, 1884.

Gortschakoff and Bismarck. London: Parker, 1878.

[Hayward, A.] The Second Armada. London: Harrison &
   Sons, 1871.

J.M. (pseud. of John MacGregor?). Popery in AD 1900.
   London: Seeley, [1851].

A Man From the Moon. London: Brown, [1870].

A Member of the Legitimist Club (pseud.). The Jacobite Doctors. London: Box & Gilham, 1896.

A Parallel Case. London: Bell, Darlington, 1876.

Parnell, J. Cromwell the Third. London: The Author, 1886.

Peddie, J. The Capture of London. London: General Publ., [1887].

Plus encore d'Angleterre. Bristol: Arrowsmith, 1888.

Pope Booth. London: Lucas, 1890.

Prophet (pseud.). The Wearing o' the Green in 1890. London: Stanford, 1881.

The Suggested Invasion of England by the Germans. London: Houlston, 1871.

Vindex (pseud.). England Crushed. London: King, 1882.

C) Titles Not Found

(The sources are indicated in parenthesis.)

The Angel and the Idiot. London: Stott, 1890. (Clarke, Henkin.)

Caine, Hall. The Mahdi. London: Clarke, 1894. (Locke 80.)

[Carr, Francis.] Archimago. London: Ward & Lock, and Newcastle: Wilson, 1864. (Locke 80.)

Cutter, R.H. Reached at Last. London: Griffith, Farran, 1886. (Locke 80.)

The Doom of the County Council in London. London: Allen, 1892. (Clarke.)

Hinton, C[harles] H. Science Notebook. London: Haddon, 1884.

The Island of Liberty. London: Masters, 1848. (Sargent.)

<u>King Bertie, A.D. 1900.</u>   London: Crown, 1883.   (Clarke--this may be a ghost.)

Petzler, Johann.   <u>Life   in   Utopia.</u>   London: Author's Co-operative Publ., 1890.   (Messac.)

Randolph, Mrs.   <u>Mostly   Fools.</u>   London: Low, Marston, 1886.   (Henkin.)

4. Nineteenth-Century SF and the Book Trade

by John Sutherland

Darko Suvin's taxonomy and commentary furnishes provocative evidence and conclusions about the production of SF in the nineteenth-century book-world (not least--of course--that it originates within that world and not as some kind of literary outlawry). And by concentrating on production rather than textual homology or variation (the more usual approach), he throws illumination outside the history of the genre. In the notes that follow I aim to supplement his material with some reflections from the book-trade point of view. It should be emphasized that the research here is entirely Professor Suvin's own.

1

The salient feature is the crescendo of production. To move through his main list decade by decade: 1848-1860 furnishes 9 items; 1861-1870, 8; 1871-1880, 39; 1881-1890, 110; 1891-1900, 219. One should not read this increment as something merely linear--more of the same. What one would seem to see here is the evolution of SF from a satirical device to a genre. To theorise somewhat impressionistically, a genre could be taken to need intertextuality, consolidation, and a joint stock of techniques--all of which presume a numerical threshold. Given the evidence of the Anglo-American book trade in our century, "genre" or category fiction is only feasible given a minimum quota of full-size items per year. Support can be furnished for this proposition by the page counts which Suvin usefully supplies. Of his first 50 novel items, 7 are less than 50 pages in length; 7 are from 50 to 100 pages in length; 6 are from 100 to 150 pages in length; 3 are from 150 to 200 pages in length. This is to say, two-fifths of the sample can scarcely be called "books." (And, naturally, a consolidated genre presumes book-length items--at least in nonmagazine form.) Working backwards, all but 7 of the last 50 novel items are book-length (i.e., 200 pp. plus).

Thinking chronologically, other features present themselves. The 1890s was a momentous decade in the British
book trade. It was clearly formative for SF. To take
the obvious features--America moved in at this date, to
dominate the field, as it was to do even more successfully
later on. Harper's--for instance--concentrate their attack
on the British market with no less than 7 S-F titles
between 1897 and 1900. In terms of number Harper is only
in the first ten as regards publishers of the genre between
1848 to 1900. But in terms of rate--with all but one of
its list coming out in three years--it is the most intense
and (nationally) the most prophetic of publishers.

Interesting too is the way in which long-established
English publishers (e.g., Longmans, 8 items; Macmillans, 1
item; Smith Elder, 1 item) fought shy of SF. Meanwhile,
progressive new English publishers, founded in the last
three decades of the century, seem to have embraced it
(e.g., Heinemann, 9 items in 6 years; Edward Arnold, 4
items in 2 years; Hutchinson, 8 items in 10 years; Chatto,
8 items in 11 years; Lane--the most fastidious--3 items in
3 years). Another practice typical for the genre is the
organization of the genre's activity in the 1890s around
certain charismatic figures: famously Wells. Wells, in
this decade, also emerges as the first author to play the
publishers (Arnold, Methuen, Dent). Oeuvre--something
hitherto lacking--becomes as S-F possibility.

In tracing its autonomic development, one should not forget that SF is the most contingently dependent of genres.
Suvin is surely right to stress the surges that occur
around 1870-1872 (the Franco-Prussian War) and 1886-1888
(the period of extremest working-class distress and near-
revolution in England). SF's founding figures have been--
on Suvin's evidence--in part identical with the founding
generation of British socialism (Morris, Wells, Bellamy).
As what was called in the 1890s "Literature of Ideas," a
part of SF was naturally caught up in the progressive
political ferment. At the same time, another part of it
was nostalgically looking backward, and a large part was
simply commercial exploitation of an interested readership.
Still, just why so much twentieth-century Anglo-American
SF should be so reactionary remains an interesting question, that arises out of a thorough look at the nineteenth
century.

2

To return to bibliometrics. The most significant statistic
which emerges, in terms of the standard production of high-

grade fiction, is <u>the absence of the multivolume novel</u>. As is well known, the "three-decker" was the standard outlet for the Victorian novelist. Between 150 and 200 were brought out a year from its installation in 1821 to its demise in 1894, when the circulating libraries cartelized to boycott it. Yet of the 360 books which Suvin catalogues, only 11 are three-volume, and only 9 two-volume affairs. From which one concludes, that SF flourished outside the circulating library structure, for which the multivolume novel principally catered. (Indeed, SF may have had a valuable boost in 1894 with the establishment of the single volume novel as the standard dominant form.) Clearly more work will have to be done in this area-- particularly with reference to the serialized fiction. But on the face of it, there would seem to be evidence that SF reached its public independent of the standard fiction- supply system (i.e., the library three-decker, the serial in magazines, and the cheap reprint designed for sale principally at railway stations). This is borne out by the fact that suppliers of the staple library commodity figure so slenderly (e.g.: Bentley have only 4 items in a quarter of a century; Hurst and Blackett have 3 items in 29 years; yet these two publishers, for all the meagerness of their S-F output, furnish a third of the three-deckers produced in it during the period). Given the conformity with the type of author in straight fiction which Suvin establishes, it would be feasible to hypothesize a deviant apparatus at work here. In support of this, one would cite not just the end-of-century American intrusion, but the fact that throughout the sample period publishers with a known connec- tion with Europe (e.g., Sonnenschein, 8 items in 12 years) were prominent.

Suvin's list names, by my count, 129 imprints (excluding anonymous or author-published work). Of these, the vast majority--78--were publishers with only one S-F title to their credit, or printers working to commission.

12 were publishers with 2 titles to their credit

12 were publishers with 3 titles to their credit

6 were publishers with 4 titles to their name

2 were publishers with 5 titles

4 were publishers with 6 titles

7 were publishers with 8 titles to their name

5 were publishers with 9 titles to their name (Cassell, Digby & Long, Heinemann, Pearson, and Reeves & Turner)

At the top of the pyramid, Blackwood had some 16 titles come out under their imprint; Simpkin and Marshall 19 under theirs; while Low, Marston (sometimes known as Sampson Low, Marston) wins out with 32 titles.

Before dealing with the top three, some points should be made about the chronological scatter of statistics. It is--for reasons which easily suggest themselves--mainly at the beginning of the period that SF is a one-off thing. Many of the "publishers" listed here were, surely, vanity publishers or commission printers, bringing the work out at an amateurish author's expense. At the end of the period (especially after 1885-1886) production tends to concentrate around various commercial houses, some of whom were already developing a specialism in the genre.

It is not hard to see why the top three are who they are. Blackwoods, through their Magazine, had a long connection with the Gothic tale. This clearly led to a spin-off in SF. Simpkin and Marshall were the largest of the book wholesalers in the Victorian book trade, as well as being publishers. Their sizeable presence is probably explained by the fact that they were able to distribute the items with their other wares. As for Low, Marston, they were well known as a publishing firm with international connections. Thus when Dickens wanted to find a publisher for Lytton's A Strange Story (first published in Dickens's magazine All the Year Round)' he recommended Low, Marston for their first-rate agency facilities in the United States. Looking at the large number of French (especially Verne) items they feature in Suvin's catalog, it is evident that they also recruited successfully in Europe. If SF is what the twentieth century has often liked to think it, an international kind of novel, that character would seem to have originated here, in the Victorian book trade.

Many interesting profiles can be extracted from Suvin's evidence. It is to be hoped that his initiative will lead to further usefully methodical investigation of the notorious tangle of the Victorian book trade.

B. Biographical Study

1. Biographical Sketches of S-F Writers, 1848–1900

This section contains brief biographical sketches for all the certainly or probably known writers of works listed in the Bibliography of Part I. When attributions of such works were uncertain, this is briefly discussed. For the following names: Acworth, Bland, Brown, Carter, Cole C., Craig, Danyers, D'Argenteuil, Fairfield, Folingsby, Forrest, Geissler, Grove, Hendow, Herbert, Lang H., L'Estrange H., L'Estrange M., Lisle, MacKay D., Moffat, Moore, Morgan, North D., North F.H., Oakhurst, Penrice, Rustoff, Ryan, Spence, Stewart R., Stewart S., Vetch, Walsh, Watlock, White J., Wolfe, Yelverton--no data at all have been found, beside the fact that they are on the title page of the SF listed in the Bibliography and are so recorded in the main bibliographic catalogs without further comment. Any of these names might therefore well be a pseudonym. When there is any internal evidence making such a status more or less probable, this too is briefly discussed in the entry; in cases of my strong leanings that way, they are followed by "pseudonym?" It is, of course, not quite certain that some names to which other inconclusive--for example, publication--data are attached might not also be pseudonyms; a few other attribution puzzles are tentatively resolved or at least discussed in the entries, but much work, largely of an archival nature, still remains to be done in this field.

Each item is divided into an entry and a listing of "Main secondary literature" (abbreviated as M.s.l., and beginning with autobiographical texts); should there be no M.s.l. list, the data in the entry stem from bibliographical handbooks, primarily AD, BMC, and NUC with their supplements (see the lists below). The sources for biographical information are threefold: first, some information was gathered from the items listed in the sources for the Bibliography of Part I; second, much came from articles and books wholly or partly dealing with the subject of a given biographical sketch; these two kinds of sources are listed

by brief title in <u>M.s.l.</u> Third, the bibliographical handbooks and books covering several biographical subjects,
identified in the list immediately following, proved quite
indispensable; they will be used in <u>M.s.l.</u> with the
abbreviations indicated. In almost all the better docu-
mented cases, the "main" of <u>M.s.l.</u> is the operative word,
as many more sources were identified than are listed.
Most, but not all of them were examined <u>de visu</u>; the
listing has been carried to the year 1980 inclusive.

The entries have been written with an eye to maximum
informativeness--in compressed form and leaving most drawing of inferences for other places. A number of inferences
can be found in the following essay, but avenues for
further exploration and evaluation remain open. The contents and organization should be self-explanatory; perhaps
it should be remarked that writers from the UK (England,
Scotland, Wales, and Ireland at that time) are as a rule
not especially marked as such.

The following lists of biographical sources (and a few
other frequently cited sources) are divided into UK, USA,
and Other; in cases of significant overlaps, items are
listed under UK.

UK

AC   <u>Alumni Cantabrigienses From 1752-1900.</u> 6 vols.
        Comp. J. A. Venn. Cambridge: University Press,
        1940-1954.

AD   <u>A Critical Dictionary of English Literature and
        British and American Authors Living and De-
        ceased: From the Earliest Accounts to the Lat-
        ter Half of the Nineteenth Century.</u> 3 vols.
        Ed. S. Austin Allibone. Philadelphia: Lippin-
        cott, 1874.

ADS   <u>Supplement to Allibone's Critical Dictionary of
        English Literature: British and American
        Authors.</u> 2 vols. Ed. John Foster Kirk. Phila-
        delphia and London: Lippincott, 1891.

AL   <u>The [Monthly] Army List for January 1851</u>ff.
        London: Parker, Furnival [later H.M.S.O.],
        1850ff.

AO   <u>Alumni Oxonienses . . . : 1715-1866.</u> 4 vols.
        Comp. Joseph Foster. Nendel: Kraus Reprint,
        1968.

BI　　　Biography Index: A Cumulative Index to Biographi-
　　　　cal Material in Books and Magazines. 9 vols.
　　　　Ed. Bea Joseph [later Rita Volmer Louis], et al.
　　　　New York: Wilson, 1949–1974.

BIQ　　Biography Index: A Quarterly Index to Biographi-
　　　　cal Material in Books and Magazines. Vols. 30
　　　　and 33, no. 1. New York: Wilson, 1976 and
　　　　1978.

BIY　　Biography Index: A Cumulative Index to Biographi-
　　　　cal Material in Books and Magazines. [5
　　　　parts]. New York: Wilson, 1975–1979.

BMC　　British Museum: General Catalogue of Printed
　　　　Books to 1955. 263 vols. London: The Trus-
　　　　tees of the British Museum, 1959–1966.

BM5　　British Museum: General Catalogue of Printed
　　　　Books: Five-Year Supplement 1966–1970. 26
　　　　vols. London: The Trustees of the British
　　　　Museum, 1971.

BM10　　British Museum: General Catalogue of Printed
　　　　Books: Ten-Year Supplement 1956–1965. 50
　　　　vols. London: The Trustees of the British
　　　　Museum, 1968.

CBEL3　The Cambridge Bibliography of English Litera-
　　　　ture. Vol. 3. Ed. F.W. Bateson. Cambridge:
　　　　Cambridge University Press, 1941.

CCD　　Crockford's Clerical Directory for 1858ff.
　　　　[:varying subtitles]. London: Cox [later
　　　　Oxford University Press], 1858ff.

CGUD　A Catalogue of Graduates [of . . .] the Universi-
　　　　ty of Dublin. 3 vols. Dublin: Hodges, Smith
　　　　[later Church of Ireland], 1869–1906.

DAP　　Dictionary of Anonymous and Pseudonymous English
　　　　Literature (Samuel Halkett and John Laing).
　　　　New and enl. ed. 9 vols. Eds. James Kennedy,
　　　　et al. Edinburgh and London: Oliver and Boyd,
　　　　1926–1934, 1956, and 1962.

DEA　　Farquharson Sharp, R. A Dictionary of English
　　　　Authors. London: Kegan Paul, Trench, 1904.

DIB   Buckland, C.E. Dictionary of Indian Biography. London: Sonnenschein, 1906.

DNB   Dictionary of National Biography. 22 vols. Eds. Leslie Stephen and Sidney Lee. London: Smith, Elder, 1908-1909.

DNB11   The Dictionary of National Biography. 2d supplement, Jan. 1901-Dec. 1911. Ed. Sir Sidney Lee. London: Oxford University Press, 1912.

DNB21   The Dictionary of National Biography: 1912-1921. Eds. H.W.C. Davis and J.R.H. Weaver. London: Oxford University Press, 1927.

DNB30   The Dictionary of National Biography: 1922-1930. Ed. J.R.H. Weaver. London: Oxford University Press, 1937.

DNB40   The Dictionary of National Biography: 1931-1940. Ed. L.G. Wickham Legg. London: Oxford University Press, 1949.

DNB50   The Dictionary of National Biography: 1941-1950. Eds. L.G. Wickham Legg and E.T. Williams. London: Oxford University Press, 1959.

DNB60   The Dictionary of National Biography: 1951-1960. Eds. E.T. Williams and Helen M. Palmer. London: Oxford University Press, 1971.

DNBC   Institute of Historical Research, London. Corrections and Additions to the Dictionary of National Biography . . . Covering the Years 1923-1963. Boston: G.K. Hall, 1966.

DSB   Dictionary of Scientific Biography. 13 vols. Ed. Charles Coulston Gillispie. New York: Scribner, 1970ff.

DUR   Dupont, V. L'Utopie et le Roman Utopique dans la Littérature Anglaise. Toulouse and Paris: Didier, 1941.

EB   The Encyclopaedia Britannica: A Dictionary of Arts, Sciences, Literature and General Information, 11th-12th ed., 32 vols. London and New

York: Encyclopaedia Britannica, 1910–1911 and
1922.

FMB   Foster,   Joseph.   Men-at-the-Bar.   London:
Reeves & Turner, 1885.

LL   The Law List [: varying subtitles]:   1841ff.
London: Stevens, 1841ff.

MBF   Lofts, W.O.G., and D.J. Adley. The Men Behind
Boys' Fiction. London: Baker, 1970.

MD   The Medical Directory [for] 1845ff.   London:
Churchill, 1845ff.

MDEA   McNamee, Lawrence F. Dissertations in English
and American Literature . . . 1865–1964. New
York and London: Bowker, 1968; idem. Supplement I 1964–1968. Ibidem, 1969; idem. Supplement II. Ibidem, 1974.

MEB   Boase, Frederick. Modern English Biography. 6
vols. London: Cass, 1965.

MR   The Medical Register: 1859ff.   London:
[General   Council   of   Medical   Education],
1859ff.

NCBEL3 The Cambridge Bibliography of English Literature. Vol. 3. Ed. George Watson. Cambridge:
Cambridge University Press, 1969.

NEB   The New Encyclopaedia Britannica in 30 Volumes.
19 vols. Chicago and London: Encyclopaedia
Britannica, 1974.

NL   The Navy List for January, 1880ff. London:
H.M.S.O., 1880ff.

NUC   The National Union Catalog--Pre-1956 Imprints.
685 vols. London and Chicago: Mansell, 1968–
1980.

P   Clarke, Joseph F. Pseudonyms. London: Elm
Tree Books/Hamilton, 1977.

PIU   Philmus, Robert M. Into the Unknown. Berkeley:
University of California Press, 1970.

SAIF   Singh, Bhupal. A Survey of Anglo-Indian Fic-
          tion. London: Oxford University Press/
          Milford, 1934.

SFE   The Science Fiction Encyclopedia. Ed. Peter
          Nicholls. Garden City, NY: Doubleday, 1979.

SFFL   Reginald, Robert. Science Fiction and Fantasy
          Literature 1700-1979. Vol. 1. Detroit: Gale
          Research, 1979.

SFS   Science-Fiction   Studies   (periodical;   Terre
          Haute, IN, USA, 1973-1977; Montreal, Qué.,
          Canada, 1978ff.).

UL   University of London: The Historical Record
          (1836-1926).   London: University of London
          Press, 1926.

WGT   Rock, James A. Who Goes There. Bloomington,
          IN: Rock, 1979.

WWCL   Doyle, Brian. Who is Who of Children's Litera-
          ture. New York: Schocken, 1968.

WWW   Who Was Who, [5 vols.]. London: Black, 1920-
          1964.

USA

AA   American Authors, 1600-1900: A Biographical
          Dictionary of American Literature. Ed. Stanley
          J. Kunitz and Howard Haycraft. New York:
          Crown, 1972.

AAB   Burke, William J., and Will D. Howe. American
          Authors and Books, 1640 to the Present Day.
          3d rev. ed. Rev. by Irving Weiss and Anne
          Weiss. New York: Crown, 1972.

ACAB   Appleton's Cyclopaedia of American Biography. 7
          vols. Ed. James Grant Wilson and John Fiske.
          New York: Appleton, 1894-1900; rpt. Detroit:
          Gale, 1968.

BAL   Blanck, Jacob N. Bibliography of American Litera-
          ture. 6 vols. New Haven: Yale University
          Press, 1955-1973.

BDA   The Twentieth Century Biographical Dictionary of Notable Americans. 10 vols. Ed. Rossiter Johnson. Boston: The Biographical Society, 1904.

CHAL   Cambridge History of American Literature. Ed. William Peterfield et al. New York: Putnam, 1917–1921.

DAB   Dictionary of American Biography. 25 vols. and Index. Ed. Allen Jackson et al. New York: Scribner's, and London: Milford, 1928–1977.

DNAA   A Dictionary of North American Authors Deceased Before 1950. Ed. W. Stewart Wallace. Toronto: Ryerson, 1951.

LC54   Library of Congress Catalog. Books: Subjects 1950-1954. 20 vols. New York: Rowman and Littlefield, 1966.

LC59   Library of Congress Catalog. Books: Subjects . . . 1955-1959. 22 vols. Totowa, NJ: Rowman and Littlefield, 1966.

LC64   Library of Congress Catalog. Books: Subjects . . . 1960-1964. 25 vols. Ann Arbor: Edwards, 1965.

LC69   Library of Congress Catalog. Books. Subjects . . . 1965-1969. 42 vols. Ann Arbor: Edwards, 1970.

LC70   Library of Congress Catalog. Books. Subjects . . . 1970. 9 vols. Washington: Library of Congress, 1971.

LC71   Library of Congress Catalog. Books. Subjects . . . 1971. 11 vols. Washington: Library of Congress, 1972.

LC72   Library of Congress Catalog. Books. Subjects . . . 1972. 15 vols. Washington: Library of Congress, 1973.

LC73   Library of Congress Catalog. Books. Subjects . . . 1973. 16 vols. Washington: Library of Congress, 1974.

LC74   Library of Congress Catalog. Books. Subjects.
        . . . 19 parts. Washington: Library of
        Congress, 1974-1975.

LC75   Library of Congress Catalogs: Subject Catalog,
        1975. 18 vols. Washington: Library of
        Congress, 1976.

LC76   Library of Congress Catalogs: Subject Catalog,
        1976. 17 vols. Washington: Library of
        Congress, 1977.

LC77   Library of Congress Catalogs: Subject Catalog.
        7 parts. Washington: Library of Congress, 1977.

LC78   Library of Congress Catalogs: Subject Catalog.
        7 parts. Washington: Library of Congress,
        1978.

LHUS   Literary History of the United States. 2 vols.
        3d ed. Ed. Robert E. Spiller et al. New York:
        Macmillan, 1963.

NAW   Notable American Women, 1607-1950: A Biographi-
        cal Dictionary. 3 vols. Ed. Edward T. James.
        Cambridge, MA: Belknap Press of Harvard Univer-
        sity Press, 1971.

NCAB   National Cyclopedia of American Biography. 53
        vols. New York: White, 1892-1971.

NUC   The National Union Catalog--Pre-1956 Imprints
        [see preceding UK section].

OCAL   The Oxford Companion to American Literature.
        Ed. James David Hart. New York: Oxford Univer-
        sity Press, 1965.

PAD   Parrington, Vernon Louis, Jr. American Dreams:
        A Study of American Utopias. Providence, RI:
        Brown University Press, 1947; rpt. New York:
        Russell & Russell, 1964.

REAL   The Reader's Encyclopedia of American Litera-
        ture. Ed. Max J. Herzberg et al. New York:
        Crowell, 1962.

RON   Roemer, Kenneth M. The Obsolete Necessity:

America in Utopian Writings, 1888-1900. [Kent, OH]: Kent State University Press, 1976.

WWWA   Who Was Who in America. 4 vols. Chicago: Marquis, 1943-1968.

Other (Australian, Canadian, French, German)

ADB   Allgemeine Deutsche Biographie. 56 vols. Leipzig: Duncker & Humblot, 1875-1912.

AuDB   Australian Dictionary of Biography. 5 vols. [Melbourne]: Melbourne University Press, 1966-1974.

BA   Bibliography of Australia. Vols. 5-7. Comp. John Alexander Ferguson. Sydney and London: Angus & Robertson, 1963-1969.

BE   Brockhaus Enzyklopädie. 20 vols. Wiesbaden: Brockhaus, 1966-1974.

BU   Biographie Universelle, Ancienne et Moderne. 45 vols. Ed. J. Fr. Michaud. Paris: Desplaces & Michaud, 1854ff.; rpt. Graz: Akademische Druck-u. Verlagsanstalt, 1966-1970.

CCB   A Cyclopaedia of Canadian Biography. Ed. Geo. Maclean Rose. Toronto: Rose, 1886.

DAuB   Dictionary of Australian Biography. 2 vols. Ed. Percival Serle. Sydney: Angus & Robertson, 1949.

DBF   Dictionnaire de Biographie Française. 13 vols. Paris: Letouzey, 1933ff.

DCBL   Dictionary of Canadian Biography, Vol. 10: 1871-1880. Ed. Marc LaTerreur. Toronto: University of Toronto Press, 1972.

DCBW   The Dictionary of Canadian Biography. Ed. W. Stewart Wallace. Toronto: Macmillan of Canada, 1945.

DEQ   Dictionnaire Encyclopédique Quillet. 8 vols. Paris: Quillet, 1968-1970.

DSAB   Dictionary of South African Biography. 3 vols.
          Ed. W.J. de Kock et al. Cape Town: Nasionale
          Boekhandel & Tafelberg, 1968-1977.

ECan   Encyclopedia Canadiana. 10 vols. Toronto,
          Ottawa, and Montreal: Grolier, 1972.

GE   La Grande Encyclopédie. 31 vols. Paris:
          Lamirault, n.d.

GHAL   Green, H.M. A History of Australian Literature,
          Pure, and Applied. Vol. 1. Sydney: Angus &
          Robertson, 1961.

L20S   Larousse de XXe Siècle. 6 vols. Paris:
          Larousse, 1928-1933; Supplement. Ibidem,
          1953.

MAL   Miller, E. Morris. Australian Literature From
          Its Beginnings to 1935. 2 vols. Sydney:
          Sydney University Press, 1975.

MEL   Meyers Enzyklopädisches Lexikon. 25 vols.
          Mannheim, Wien, and Zürich: Lexikonverlag,
          1971-1979.

MWT   Men and Women of the Time: A Hand-book of Canadi-
          an Biography. Ed. Henry James Morgan.
          Toronto: Briggs, 1898.

NBU   Nouvelle Biographie Universelle. 44 vols.
          Paris: Firmin Didot Frères, 1852-1864.

NDB   Neue Deutsche Biographie. 11 vols. Berlin:
          Duncker & Humblot, 1953-1977.

NZNB   New Zealand National Bibliography to the Year
          1960. Vols. 2-4. Ed. A.G. Bagnall. Welling-
          ton: Shearer, 1969-1975.

OCCHL   The Oxford Companion to Canadian History and Lit-
          erature. Ed. Norah Story. Toronto, London,
          and New York: Oxford University Press, 1967.

OCCS   Supplement to the Oxford Companion to Canadian
          History and Literature. Ed. William Toye.
          Toronto, London, and New York: Oxford
          University Press, 1973.

List of Name Entries in the Biography
(F=French, US=American, O=other non-UK)

Abbott, Edwin Abbott
About, Edmond François
  Valentin (F)
Acworth, Andrew
Allen, Charles Grant
  Blairfindie
Anderson, Mary
Andreae, Percy
Anson, Charles Vernon
Armstrong, Charles
  Wicksteed
Astor, John Jacob IV (US)
Atkins, Francis Henry
Barlow, James William
Barr, Robert
Barrett, Frank
Beale, Charles Willing (US)
Bellamy, Edward (US)
Benham, Charles (US)
Bennett, Arthur
Berens, Lewis Henry
Besant, Walter
Bingham, Frederick
Blair, Andrew
Bland, Charles Ashwold
Bleunard, Albert (F)
Boussenard, Louis Henri (F)
Bramston, Mary
Bridge, James Howard
Brookfield, Arthur Montagu
Brown, Charles R.
Buchanan, Robert Williams
Bulwer-Lytton, Edward
  George Earle Lytton
Burnaby, Frederick Gustavus
Butler, Samuel
Carne-Ross (or Ross),
  Joseph
Carter, Tremlett
Causse, Charles (F)
Chamberlain, Henry
  Richardson (US)
Chambers, Robert William
  (US)
Chatelain, Clara de

Chesney, George Tomkyns
Chetwode, R.D.
Chilton, Henry Herman
Clark, Alfred
Clark[e], Charles Heber
  (US)
Clarke, Percy
Clemens, Samuel Langhorne
Clowes, William Laird
Cobban, James MacLaren
Cobbe, Frances Power
Cole, Cyrus (US)
Cole, Robert William
Collens, Thomas Wharton
  (US)
Collins, Edward James
  Mortimer
Colomb, Philip Howard
(Comer, Cornelia
  Atwood--see Pratt)
Constable, Frank Challice
Corbett, "Mrs.
  George"=Elizabeth
Cowan, James (US)
Craig, Alexander (US)
Cromie, Robert
Curwen, Henry
Dalton, Henry Robert Samuel
Danyers, Geoffrey
D'Argenteuil, Paul (US)
Davidson, John
Davis, Ellis James
De Mille, James
Dering, Edward Heneage
Dixie, Florence Caroline
Dixon, Charles
Dodd, Anna Bowman (US)
Donnelly, Ignatius Loyola
  (US)
Douglass, Ellsworth (US?)
Downey, Edmund
Doyle, Arthur Conan
Druery, Charles Thomas
Dudgeon, Robert Ellis
Du Maurier, George Louis

Palmella Busson
Eastwick, James
Ellis, T. Mullett
Fairburn, Edwin
Fairfield, ?
Fawcett, Edward Douglas
Fawkes, Frank Attfield
Fiske, Amos Kidder (US)
Flammarion, Nicolas Camille
  (F)
Folingsby, Kenneth
Forrest, Henry J.
Fox, Samuel Middleton
Gale, Frederick
Geissler, Ludwig A. (US)
Gillmore, Parker
Gleig, Charles
Glynn (or Carr-Glyn), Alice
  Coralie
Gorst, Harold Edward
Gould, Frederick James
Grant, John King
Granville, Austyn W. (US)
Graves, Charles Larcom
Greener, William Oliver
Greer, Thomas
Greg, Percy
Gregg, Hilda Caroline
(Griffith, George--see
  Jones)
Grousset, Paschal (F)
Grove, W.
Hale, Edward Everett (US)
Hannan, Robert Charles
Harben, William Nathaniel
  (US)
Harting, Pieter (O)
Hay, William Delisle
Hayes, Frederick William
Hayward, William Stephens
Hearn, Mary Anne
Helps, Arthur
Hemyng, Samuel Bracebridge
Hendow, Z.S.
Herbert, William
Hertzka, Theodor (O)
Hervey, Maurice H.
Hinton, Charles Howard

Hird, James Dennis
Hoffmann, Ernst Theodor
  Wilhelm (O)
Howells, William Dean (US)
Hudson, William Henry
Hulme-Beaman, Emeric
Hume, Fergus William or
  Fergusson Wright
Hyne, Charles John
  Cutcliffe Wright
Jackson, Edward Payson (US)
Jane, Frederick Thomas
Jefferies, John Richard
Jenkins, John Edward
Jepson, Edgar Alfred
Jerome, Jerome Klapka
Jones, George Chetwynd
  Griffith
Jones, Jingo
Kellett, Ernest Edward
Kinross, Albert
Lach-Szyrma, Wladislaw
  Somerville
Lancaster, William Joseph
  Cosens
Lang, Andrew
Lang, Hermann
Lawrence, Edmund
Lazarus, Henry
Lee, Thomas
Lehmann, Rudolf Chambers
Le Queux, William Tufnell
Lester, Edward
L'Estrange, Henry
L'Estrange, Miles
Linton (or Lynn Linton),
  Eliza(beth)
Lisle, Charles Wentworth
Lloyd, John Uri (US)
Lucas, Edward Verrall
Lumley, Benjamin
Lyon, Edmund David
(Lytton, E.G.E.L. Bulwer--
  see Bulwer-Lytton)
M., J.W.
MacColl, Hugh
MacCulloch, J.
MacKay, Donald (US?)

Mackay, James Alexander
  Kenneth
Macnie, John (US)
Maguire, John Francis
Maitland, Edward
Markwick, Edward
McIver (or MacIver), George
  M.
(Marriott-Watson, Henry
  Brereton--see Watson,
  H.B.M.)
Mears, Amelia Garland
(Mendes, Henry Pereira--
  see Pereira Mendes, H.)
Michaelis, Richard C. (US)
Middleton, William H.
Miller, George Noyes (US)
Miller, "Joaquin" (US)
Minto, William
Mitchell, John Ames
Moffat, W. Graham
Moore, G.H.
Morgan, Arthur
Morris, Alfred
Morris, William
Müller, Ernst (O)
Munro, John
Murphy, George Read
Murray, George Gilbert
  Aimé
Newcomb, Simon (US)
Nicholson, Joseph Shield
Nisbet, Hume
North, Delaval
North, Franklin H. (US)
Norton, Philip
Oakhurst, William
O'Brien, Fitz-James (US)
O'Grady, Standish James
O'Neil, Henry Nelson
Oppenheim, Edward Phillips
Pallander, Edwin
Palmer, John Henry (US)
Payn, James
Peck, Bradford (US)
Pemberton, Max
Pemberton, Robert
Penrice, Arthur

Pereira Mendes, Henry (US)
Perry, Walter Copland
Philpot, Joseph Henry
Poe, Edgar Allan (US)
Potter, Robert
Pratt, Cornelia Atwood (US)
Putnam, George Haven (US)
Reeve, Benjamin
Richardson, Benjamin Ward
Richter, Eugen (O)
Rickett, Joseph Compton
Roberts, J.W. (US)
Robinson, Edward A. (US)
Robinson, Philip Stewart
Roe, William James (US)
Rogers, Lebbeus Harding
  (US)
Rosewater, Frank (US)
(Ross, Joseph Carne--see
  Carne-Ross, Joseph)
Rowcroft, Charles
Rustoff, Michael
Ryan, G.H.
Schofield, Alfred Taylor
Serviss, Garrett Putman
  (US)
Shannon, John C.
Shelley, Mary
  Wollstonecraft
Shiel, Matthew Phipps
Singer, Ignatius
Slee, Richard (US)
Smythe, Alfred
Soleman, William
Spence, J.C.
Stead, William Thomas
Stewart, Ritson
Stewart, Stanley
Stimson, Frederic Jesup
  (US)
Stockton, Frank Richard
  (US)
Strachey, John St. Loe
Suffling, Ernest Richard
Sykes, Arthur Alkin
Thomas, Chauncey (US)
Thorburn, Septimus Smet
Tincker, Mary Agnes (US)

Tourgée, Albion Winegar
(US)
Tracy, Louis
Traill, Henry Duff
Trollope, Anthony
Tucker, Horace Finn
Verne, Jules (F)
Vetch, Thomas
Vincent, Charles (F)
Vogel, Julius
Wall, George A. (US)
Walsh, Rupert
Ward, Herbert Dickinson
(US)
Waterhouse, Elizabeth
Waterloo, Stanley (US)
Watlock, W.A.
Watson, Henry Brereton
Marriott
Watson, Henry Crocker
Marriott

Welch, Edgar Luderne
Wells, Herbert George
Westall, William Bury
Wetmore, Claude Hazeltine
(US)
White, Frederick Merrick
White, John
Whiting, Sydney
Widnall, Samuel Page
Wilson, John Grosvenor (US)
Windsor, William (US)
Wise, Clement
Wolfe, Cecil Drummond
Wright, Henry
Wright, William Henry (US)
Yelverton, Christopher

Unresolved Pseudonyms

Unresolved Anonyms

Biographical Sketches

ABBOTT, Rev. Edwin Abbott (1839-1926), Doctor of Divinity, educator, Broad Church theologian, scholar. Born in London, son of headmaster, graduated from Cambridge in classics, elected fellow there in 1862; ordained in 1862. Distinguished educator of the Thomas Arnold type, 1865-1880 headmaster of City of London School, select preacher at Oxford and Cambridge, and Hulsean Lecturer at Cambridge. In 1870 began to publish textbooks on grammar, on the teaching of English and Latin, as well as works of literary and theological scholarship. Wrote a life of Francis Bacon, as well as the standard scholarly book against Cardinal Newman. Under the pseudonym "A Square" published the S-F romance listed (reprinted several times down to the present).
M.s.l.
AC, vol. 1.
Hipolito, Jane, and Roscoe Lee Browne. "Flatland," in
  Frank N. Magill, ed., Survey of Science Fiction Litera-
  ture, vol. 2. Englewood Cliffs: Salem Press, 1979.
PIU, pp. 66-69.

ABOUT, Edmond François Valentin (1828-1885), French drama-tist, novelist, journalist. Born at Dieuze, educated at Ecole Normale Supérieure and at French archeological school in Athens. Reporter during Franco-Prussian war, supported Thiers after armistice. In 1871 was cofounder and editor of anticlerical and antimonarchist periodical Le XIX Siècle, contributed articles on literature, art, political economics, and politics to Opinion Nationale, Figaro, and other publications from the 1850s, often in anticlerical vein. From 1854 published over a dozen novels and stories, a number of plays collected as Théâtre Impossible, two books on Greece and one on Egypt, and four works on social, political, and religious issues, including

his collected articles published as Causeries. In 1884
elected to Académie Française but died before taking
seat.
M.s.l.
[Citoleux, M.] Entry in DBF, vol. 1.
Columbia Dictionary of Modern European Literature. Ed.
  Horatio Smith. New York: Columbia University Press,
  1947.
Hobana, Ion. "The Man With the Broken Ear," in Frank N.
  Magill, ed. Survey of Science-Fiction Literature, vol.
  3. Englewood Cliffs: Salem Press, 1979.
Mullen, R.D. [Review of The Man With the Broken Ear.]
  SFS, no. 6 (1975), 192.
Thiébaut, Marcel. Edmond About. Paris: Gallimard,
  1936.

ACWORTH, Andrew (? - ?, fl. 1896). Perhaps Andrew Oswald
Acworth (1857 or 1858 - ?), son of clergyman, Oxford BA
1880 and MA 1884, barrister in London 1882-1895.
M.s.l.
FMB.
LL:1895, s.v. "Counsel."

ALLEN, Charles Grant Blairfindie (1848-1899), writer. Born
in Ontario, son of Protestant clergyman; educated at New
Haven, CT, Dieppe, Birmingham, and Oxford (BA 1870). For a
few years teacher in England and Jamaica, then prolific
writer in England, exponent of evolutionism, Spencerianism,
emancipation of women, member of Fabian Society. From 1877
published 14 books and essays on science, two on philosophy
and religion, 30 novels of mystery, adventure, romance,
society (including the famous The Woman Who Did, 1893),
and SF, five collections of short stories, one collection
of poems, as well as three biographical works and six historical guidebooks to Europe; six more books were published
posthumously to 1909, and Grant Allen's Historical Guides
in 12 volumes from 1897 to 1912. He also wrote three
novels, a collection of short stories, and a children's
book under the pseudonyms "Cecil Power," "Olive Pratt
Rayner," "J. Arbuthnot Wilson," and "Martin Leach
Warborough."
M.s.l.
Cazamian, Madeleine. Le Roman et les idées en Angleterre: L'Influence de la science (1860-1890). Publ. de
  la Faculté des Lettres de l'Univ. de Strasbourg, fasc.
  15. Strasbourg: Istra, 1923.
Clodd, Edward. Grant Allen: A Memoir. London:
  Richards, 1900.

DNB, vol. 22.
DUR, pp. 424–25.
Elwin, Malcolm. Old Gods Falling. London: Collins, 1939, pp. 64–65.
Historical Register of the University of Oxford. Oxford: Clarendon Press, 1900.

ANDERSON, Mary (1872– ?, fl. 1893–1898), writer. Published three novels and a book of short stories.

ANDREAE, Percy (? – ?, fl. 1888–1902). Son of merchant, educated at private school in England and Hanover Polytechnium, then studied literature. In 1888 published in Berlin an inaugural dissertation on Rolle's Pricke of Conscience in German, and from 1894 four mystery novels and one tale. Contributed theater and literary criticism to German and English periodicals.
M.s.l.
Bookman (London) 6 (Sept. 1894), 170.

ANSON, Charles Vernon (1841– ?, fl. 1859–1896), officer in the Royal Navy from 1859, retired as commander in 1896, when he also published the future-war SF listed. Saw service in all the oceans, won award for essay (written with E.H. Willett) on oyster culture in 1883, commanded ship engaged in suppressing slave trade in Persian Gulf and East Africa, obtained British protectorate over Socotra in 1886.
M.s.l.
The Active List . . . of the Royal Navy. Portsmouth: Griffin, [1876].
Lean's Royal Navy List, no. 73 (Jan. 1896).

ARMSTRONG, Charles Wicksteed (1871– ?, fl. 1892–1951). Published, beside the S-F novel listed (under the pseudonym "Strongi'th'arm"), from 1909 to 1951 five books on various subjects, mostly eccentric disquisitions on existence and happiness, including another eugenic utopian novel.

ASTOR, John Jacob IV (1864–1912), US capitalist, traveler, author, inventor: great-grandson of John Jacob I (founder of the Astor fortune). Graduated in science from Harvard in 1888, traveled in Europe, North and South America, hunted, managed family estate, was on board of various companies. Took out patents for various fanciful inventions about vehicles (rumored to have been bought from needy inventors), commissioned part of the Waldorf-Astoria hotel. Honorary colonel, was on US general staff in Cuba

during 1898 war; died in the Titanic disaster. Journey
in Other Worlds had a large sale in the USA, and was
republished in UK, France, and Germany.
M.s.l.
DAB, vol. 1.
NCAB, vol. 8.

ATKINS, Francis Henry (1840-1927), writer. Born in Oxford,
son of engineer, brought up in South Wales, studied to be
engineer, owned a small factory in London in the 1890s. In
early 1900s contributed stories and serials to pre-S-F
pulps and boys' magazines. Published from 1896 to 1903,
under the pseudonym of "Frank Aubrey," besides the two SF
listed, one more lost-world SF, and under his own name a
mystery and a book of short stories dealing with events in
hospitals. Involved in scandal at turn of century, after a
short gap reemerged as "Fenton Ash" and published from 1905
to 1915 five romances of SF and mystery (possibly in collaboration with his son Frank Howard Atkins), and one novel
under the pseudonym of "Fred Ashley." Died penniless in
London.
M.s.l.
[Eggeling, John.] Entry in SFE.
MBF.
Mullen, R.D. [Reviews of A Queen of Atlantis and A Trip
   to Mars.] SFS, no. 6 (1975), 183, 184.

BARLOW, James William (1826-1913), cleric, professor, and
writer. Son of clergyman, educated at Trinity College Dub-
lin, professor of modern history there, vice-provost 1899.
Beside the SF listed (published first under the pseudonym
"Skorpios Antares"), published six historical, theological,
and ethical studies, for example, on death and pessimism.
Not to be confused with James Barlow (1827-1887), cotton
manufacturer.
M.s.l.
WWW, vol. 1.

BARR, Robert (1850-1912), writer. Born in Glasgow, educated in Toronto, headmaster of public school in Windsor, Ontario, until 1876, then on editorial staff of Detroit Free
Press, came to Britain in 1881. With J.K. JEROME (q.v.)
coedited the Idler 1892ff. Popular author, published
about 40 books, mainly romance-type novels (one with S.
Crane) and short stories, but also some travel impressions;
in earliest works also used pseudonym "Luke Sharp."
M.s.l.
[Clute, John.] Entry in SFE.

WWW, vol. 1.

BARRETT, Frank (1848-1926), writer. Born in London, for a short time journalist then modeler in clay. From 1877 to 1914 published over 30 novels of society and popular romances, as well as one collection of short stories and a play.

BEALE, Charles Willing (1845-1932), US writer. Born in Washington, educated at University of Pennsylvania. Besides the SF listed, published in 1897 The Ghost of Guir House.
M.s.l.
DNAA.
WWWA, vol. 4.

BELLAMY, Edward (1850-1898), US writer and reformer. Born in Massachusetts, son of Baptist clergyman, studied briefly in Schenectady and Germany, admitted to bar but never practiced. Wrote for New York Evening Post, editor of Springfield Union, in 1880 founded with brother the Springfield Daily News. Contributed two dozen stories to various magazines. His first fiction, the highly interesting historical novel The Duke of Stockbridge, began to be serialized in 1873. Two of his early novels (Mrs. Ludington's Sister and Dr. Heidenhoff's Process) began the evolution from psychological analysis to greater concern with social problems. His socialist utopia Looking Backward was spectacularly successful, selling about one million copies in the first few years and provoking dozens of similar books all over the world. Its publication led to the founding of the Nationalist party advocating Bellamy's views, two journals, and various Bellamy Clubs. The sequel Equality was less successful. Published two more novels, as well as addresses, lectures, and pamphlets on various social issues (including the introduction to US edition of Socialism: The Fabian Essays), posthumously collected in three volumes. The Duke of Stockbridge and the short stories in The Blindman's World were also published in book form posthumously.
M.s.l.
Morgan, A.E. Edward Bellamy. New York: Columbia University Press, 1944.
Quint, Howard Henry. The Forging of American Socialism. Indianapolis: Bobbs-Merrill, 1964.
Suvin, Darko. Metamorphoses of Science Fiction. New Haven and London: Yale University Press, 1979 (with further bibliography).

BENHAM, Charles (? - ?, fl. 1897-1898), US writer. Beside
the SF listed, published one romance.

BENNETT, Arthur (1862- ?, fl. 1889-1930), chartered
accountant and justice of peace, probably in Warrington,
England. Published two political S-F books, a lecture and
two other books on British politics, as well as five books
of songs and poems, mostly printed as vanity publications.
Not to be confused with Arthur Bruce Bennett (1865-1948).

BERENS, Lewis--or Louis--Henry (? - ?, fl. 1890-1909),
follower of Henry George. Lived in the 1890s in Australia,
and in 1908 in London. Published (with Ignatius SINGER,
q.v.) in 1897 a book on physics, Government by the People, as well as the anonymous SF listed (The Story of My
Dictatorship), reissued in 1910, 1927, and 1934 by the
Henry George movement and translated into various
languages. From 1903 to 1909 published two books and a
pamphlet on social, economical, and ethical problems in the
17th and 19th centuries.
M.s.l.
See under SINGER, Ignatius.

BESANT, Sir Walter (1838-1901), novelist, historian, and
civic reformer. Born in Portsmouth, educated at University
of London and at Cambridge, intended for church but abandoned this career. Professor in Royal College of
Mauritius, secretary of Palestine Exploration Fund 1868-
1886, social reformer, helped found People's Palace in East
London, founder-member of the UK Society of Authors,
knighted. Published from 1882 35 novels (10 with James
Rice)--mostly dealing with social problems--which ran to
230 editions, 32 books of history, travel, and literary
studies, a book of plays with W.W. Pollock, and his auto-
biography. Edited books on Palestine, began a multivolume
Survey of London.
M.s.l.
Besant, Walter. Autobiography. Ed. S. Squire Sprigge.
  New York: Dodd, Mead, 1902.
Becker, Joseph Anthony. "Walter Besant: A Focal Point in
  the Art of Fiction." Ph.D. dissertation, Western Reserve
  University, 1955.
Boege, F.W. "Sir Walter Besant, Novelist." Nineteenth
  Century Fiction 10 (1956), 248-80; 11 (1956), 32-60.
Goode, John. "The Art of Fiction: Walter Besant and Henry
  James," in David Howard et al., eds., Tradition and Tol-
  erance in Nineteenth-Century Fiction. London: Rout-
  ledge & Kegan Paul, 1966, pp. 243-81.

BINGHAM, Frederick (? - ?, fl. 1894-1899), humorous writer. Beside the S-F novel listed, published a one-act play with a legal theme.

BLAIR, Andrew (? -1885, fl. 1870ff.), MD University of Edinburgh 1870, then medical officer of Tayport, Scotland, to his death. Not to be confused with three other Andrew Blairs in BI, NCAB, and NUC (one a physician 1896-1948, one a US chemist).
M.s.l.
MR: 1884 and MR: 1886.

BLAND, Charles Ashwold (? - ?, fl. 1891).

BLEUNARD, Albert (1852- ?, fl. in the 1890s), French professor at the lycée of Angers, writer, doctor of physics. The S-F book listed was translated in 1889-1890 in London and Philadelphia. Also published a history of industry, a book on biology, and lectures on physics and chemistry.

BOUSSENARD, Louis Henri (1847-1910), French novelist. Born in Escrennes, studied medicine, left it for journalism. From 1875 contributed to Corsaire, L'Eclipse, Petit Parisien, and from 1879 to Journal des Voyages. Visited Africa, South America, and southern US 1880-1881 as representative of French ministry of education. From 1879 published over 25 novels of adventure, travel, and SF, mostly for children; they were translated into many languages.
M.s.l.
[Clute, John.] Entry in SFE.
DBF, vol. 7.
L20S, vol. 1.

BRAMSTON, Mary (1841- ?, fl. 1869-1899), writer. Born in Essex, daughter of Dean of Winchester. Published over 50 works of fiction, including four collections of short stories, 7 historical novels, numerous girls' romances, society novels, a book of poems, and the SF listed. Also published a number of nonfiction works, including two textbooks of religion, and contributed to periodicals.

BRIDGE, James Howard (1856-1939), Anglo-American writer. Born in Manchester, England, educated in Marseilles. Journalist in England, private secretary to Herbert Spencer 1879-1884, came to US 1884, literary assistant to Andrew Carnegie 1884-1889, editor of Overland Monthly 1896-1900, editor of Commerce and Industry in New York 1902-1903,

curator of Frick Art Collection 1914-1928. Invented system
of water purification by electricity. Published in England, under the pseudonym of "Harold Brydges," the SF
listed and in 1888 a book on the USA. From 1902 to 1931
published in US under own name 7 books of nonfiction, mostly about public water supplies and the Carnegie Steel Co.,
and coedited one book.
M.s.l.
WWWA, vol. 1.

BROOKFIELD, Arthur Montagu (1853-1940), politician and
civil servant. Son of a chaplain to Queen Victoria.
Educated at Rugby and Cambridge, army career in India abandoned in 1881 in favor of politics. Unionist MP 1885-1902,
opposed Irish Home Rule, edited Hop Grower, served on
army committees, justice of peace for Sussex, colonel in
Boer War. Resigned from Parliament because of financial
difficulties, appointed UK consul in Danzig 1903-1910, in
Savannah 1910 on. Published from 1870 to 1892 five novels,
mostly anonymous, a Speaker's ABC, and in 1930 the autobiography adduced below.
M.s.l.
Brookfield, Arthur Montagu. Annals of a Chequered Life.
  London: Murray, 1930.

BROWN, Charles R. (? - ?, fl. 1891). Published with Arthur
MORGAN (q.v.) the SF listed. Not to be confused with
Charles Reynolds Brown, US clergyman.

BUCHANAN, Robert Williams (1841-1901), writer. Born in
Staffordshire, son of Robert Buchanan (Owenite journalist
and lecturer), from age 10 in Glasgow, educated in classics
at Glasgow University. In London 1860-1866, on staff of
Athenaeum, wrote reviews for Literary Gazette, poems
and articles for Temple Bar, Once a Week, St. James's
Magazine. Special correspondent in Germany for Morning
Star. From 1866 to 1873 lived in Scotland, 1874 to 1878
in Ireland, began career as novelist in 1874. Involved in
celebrated controversy with Rossetti and Swinburne against
the sensuality of Pre-Raphaelite poetry; from 1878 published and edited the weekly Light. Traveled to America
in 1884. From 1860 published about 20 books of poetry,
over 30 novels (of which one with Henry Murray), and over
25 popular plays, some in collaboration with other authors,
especially G.R. Sims and Harriett Jay, his sister-in-law,
as well as seven books of essays. Best known for editing
life of Audubon and works of Longfellow.
M.s.l.

Cassidy, John Albert. <u>Robert W. Buchanan</u>. New York: Twayne, 1974.

Jay, Harriett. <u>Robert Buchanan</u>. London: Unwin, 1903.

Murray, Henry. <u>Robert Buchanan: A Critical Apprecia-tion</u>. London: Welby, 1901.

BULWER-LYTTON, Edward George Earle Lytton (1803-1873), writer, editor, and politician. Born in London, youngest son of general. Educated at Cambridge, received MA in 1835 --and honorary LLDs from Oxford in 1853 and Cambridge in 1864. Edited <u>New Monthly Magazine</u> in 1831-1832 as follow-er of Bentham and <u>Monthly Chronicle</u> from 1841, 1831-1839 liberal member of Parliament in favor of Reform bill, helped reduce newspaper stamp duties, wrote influential pamphlet on the 1832 crisis. In 1852 reentered politics, this time as conservative, became colonial secretary in 1858, held seat till 1866. For the literary work of this, one of the most "biographized" authors of Victorian times, it is perhaps best to adapt the <u>Cambridge History of English Literature</u> (adduced below): In 1844, Bulwer assumed the name of Lytton, and in 1866 became Baron Lytton; early success confirmed him in the pose of <u>grand seigneur</u>. First book of verse published in 1820, first novel in 1827; amid social, editorial, and political con-cerns and disastrous matrimonial relations produced much fiction (collected as 43 volumes), eight dramas and comedies, a great mass of epic, satirical, and translated verse, much essay-writing and pamphleteering. His versatil-ity is not more remarkable than his anticipatory intuition for changes in public taste and the attendant swift popular-ity. Beside the SF listed, in a first phase wrote novels dealing with Wertherism, dandyism, and crime; in a second, historical romance; in a third, brought together English fairy lore and Teutonic legend; in a fourth, imported into fiction pseudophilosophic occultism; in a fifth, turned to comparatively staid "varieties of English life"; and final-ly, portrayed character and society transformed by the vulgarization of wealth.

M.s.l.

<u>The Cambridge History of English Literature</u>, vol. 13. Eds. A.W. Ward and A.R. Waller. Cambridge: Cambridge University Press, 1916.

<u>DUR</u>, pp. 406-16.

Lytton, Victor A.G.R., 2d Earl. <u>The Life of Edward Bulwer, First Lord Lytton</u>, 2 vols. London: Macmillan, 1913.

Oakley, John. "The Boundaries of Hegemony: Lytton," in Francis Barker et al., eds., <u>1848: The Sociology of</u>

Literature. [Colchester]: University of Essex, 1978, pp. 166-84.
Suvin, Darko. Metamorphoses of Science Fiction. New Haven and London: Yale University Press, 1979 (with further bibliography).
Wolff, Robert Lee. Strange Stories and Other Explorations in Victorian Fiction. New York and London: Garland, 1971.

BURNABY, Frederick Gustavus (1842-1885), officer and traveler. Born in Bedford as son of clergyman, educated at Harrow and in Dresden, in 1859 entered Royal Horse Guards. In 1868 together with T.G. Bowles launched the weekly magazine Vanity Fair; later correspondent of the Times in Spain, reporting from Carlist headquarters. In 1875/76 journeyed on horseback through Russian Asia. In Russo-Turkish war of 1877 acted as traveling agent to Red Cross committee. In politics, held extreme conservative and pro-Turkish views; in 1880 unsuccessfully ran at Birmingham for the Tory-Democrats. Interested in military ballooning, in 1882 crossed the English Channel in balloon. From 1868 to 1884 published three books about his travels and adventures, one book on the instruction of staff officers in foreign armies, an article on ballooning, and a series of letters under various pseudonyms to Vanity Fair, the Morning Post, and the Times (from Spain and the Sudan). He died in battle at Abu Klea and left the manuscript of the political S-F novel listed.
M.s.l.

Alexander, Michael. True Blue: The Life and Adventures of Colonel Fred Burnaby--1842-85. London: St. Martin's, 1958.
Duff, Louis B. Burnaby. Welland: Tribune-Telegraph Press, 1926.
Ware, James R., and R.K. Mann. The Life and Times of Colonel Fred Burnaby. London: Field & Tuer, 1885.
Wright, Thomas. The Life of Col. Fred Burnaby. London: Everett, 1908.

BUTLER, Samuel (1835-1902), writer. Born in Nottingham-shire, son of Anglican rector. Graduated from Cambridge in classics 1858, worked among the poor in London as lay assistant but gave up idea of ordination. In 1859 moved to New Zealand, where he managed a sheep-ranch; his letters home were printed as A First Year in a Canterbury Settlement in 1863. Returned to England in 1864 and lived a bachelor rentier's life. Studied painting, exhibited 1868-1876, composed (with H. Festing Jones) music in the style

of Handel, 1872–1884 worked intermittently on the autobiographical novel The Way of All Flesh. Contributed articles and letters on evolution and on art to the Press (Christchurch), Athenaeum, and Universal Review; traveled frequently to Italy. Attacked received opinion in religion, science, philology, and child-rearing, proposing unorthodox alternatives. Published from 1865 to 1901 the SF listed (at first anonymous) and its sequel Erewhon Revisited, a poem, an anonymous parody of Christian religion, four books on the evolution controversy, two on Italian art, four on philological controversies around Shakespeare and the Homeric texts, and a biography of his grandfather, Bishop Butler, headmaster of Shrewsbury school; translated The Odyssey and The Iliad into prose. His masterpiece The Way of All Flesh, a book of sonnets, two books of essays, a further book on religion, a translation of Hesiod, and several volumes of selections from notebooks and of correspondence were published posthumously.
M.s.l.

Dyson, A.E. "Samuel Butler," in his The Crazy Fabric. London and New York: Macmillan, 1965.
Furbank, P.N. Samuel Butler, 1835–1902. Cambridge: Cambridge University Press, 1948.
Henderson, Philip. Samuel Butler. London: Cohen & West, 1953.
Suvin, Darko. Metamorphoses of Science Fiction. New Haven and London: Yale University Press, 1979 (with further bibliography).
Wilson, Edmund. "The Satire of Samuel Butler," in his The Shores of Light. New York: Farrar, Straus, 1967.

CARNE-ROSS, Joseph--also as Joseph Carne ROSS--(? - ?, fl. 1880-1911), Scottish physician, MD Edinburgh 1882, worked in West Cornwall Infirmary, Penzance, then in Ancoats Hospital and in Manchester. Besides the SF listed published a medical book, two medical articles, and edited the letters of John Carne.
M.s.l.
MR: 1881-1911.

CARTER, Tremlett (? - ?, fl. 1895).

CAUSSE, Charles (1862-1905), French journalist and writer, born in Lorient. Left navy after an accident, became journalist, contributed articles--mostly on the navy--to Gazette de France. From 1886 published with Charles VINCENT (q.v.), under the collective pseudonym of "Pierre Maël," about 80 volumes of fiction, including novels of

travel, society, adventure, SF, and romance.
M.s.l.
[Prévost, M.] Entry in DBF, vol. 7.

CHAMBERLAIN, Henry Richardson (1859-1911), US journalist.
Born in Peoria, educated in Boston public schools, at 18 reporter for Boston Journal. Managing editor of New York
Press 1888, of Boston Journal 1891-1892, well-known European correspondent from 1892, expert commentator on European politics, predicted World War I. Wrote many short stories, a book on The Farmers' Alliance, and the S-F novel
listed (published in UK anonymously but in DAP--see list of
sources--entered under the pseudonym of "Kenzie Eaton Kirk-
wood" for reasons unknown).
M.s.l.
DAB, vol. 3.
WWWA, vol. 1.

CHAMBERS, Robert William (1865-1933), US illustrator and
writer, one of the most popular novelists of early 20th century. Born in Brooklyn, son of lawyer, studied at Brooklyn
Polytechnic Institute, Students' Art League, as well as at
the Ecole des Beaux-Arts and the Académie Julien in Paris.
In 1889 exhibited in Paris. In New York was illustrator for
various periodicals, friend of Charles Dana Gibson whom he
assisted in the creation of the "Gibson Girl." His successful science-fantasy short stories, The King in Yellow
(1895), were significant for US supernatural horror-tale.
Published over 70 novels and books of verse, in the first
decade mostly fantasies, then historical and romantic novels, as well as two stage and opera works; most of it appeared first in leading magazines in UK and US. Also wrote
articles on military matters for the New York Times. Not
to be confused with Robert and William Chambers of Chambers's Cyclopedia.
M.s.l.
Bleiler, E.F. Introduction to Robert W. Chambers, The
    King in Yellow and Other Horror Stories. New York:
    Dover, 1970.
[Clute, John.] Entry in SFE.
DAB, vol. 21.
Moskowitz, Sam. "The Light Fantastics of Robert W. Cham-
    bers," in Robert W. Chambers, In Search of the Unknown.
    Westport, CT: Hyperion, 1974.
M[ullen], R.D. [Reviews of In Search of the Unknown and
    The Gay Rebellion.] SFS, no. 4 (1974), 302, and no.
    6 (1975), 188.
WWWA, vol. 1.

CHATELAIN, Clara de, née de Pontigny (1801–1876), polygraph. Born in London of French father and English mother, first published some French poetry, from 1827 published in English, in 1843 married chevalier Ernest de Chatelain. Translated about 400 songs, stories, and operas from French and German, wrote about 140 stories, 50 fairy tales, also children's stories, novels (mainly juvenile), verse, articles in periodicals. Musician under pseudonym of "Leopoldine Ziska," wrote also 16 musical handbooks. Other pseudonyms used: "Leopold Wray," "Cornélie de B-," "Rosaria Santa Croce."
M.s.l.
Chatelain, J.B.F. Ernest de. In Memoriam. S.l.: privately printed, 1876.
DNB, vol. 4.
MEB, vol. 1.

CHESNEY, Sir George Tomkyns (1830–1895), officer and writer. Born at Tiverton, Devonshire, son of Anglo-Indian officer, educated at Tiverton and military college of East India Company. In 1848 entered Bengal Engineers, employed in public works department in India. From 1870 to 1880 president of Royal Indian Civil Engineering College, the next five years secretary to military department of Government of India, promoted general in 1882, in 1886 became member of Governor-General's Council, Conservative member of UK Parliament in 1892. Wrote a romance on Indian Mutiny and several works on the governing of India; his Indian Polity (1868) became a standing textbook. The Battle of Dorking created a sensation and was translated into Dutch, French, Swedish, and German. From 1868 to 1893 he also published the second SF listed, four novels (mostly anonymous) on political themes as well as studies on India, and was a frequent contributor to periodicals.
M.s.l.
Clarke, I.F. Voices Prophesying War 1763–1984. London: Oxford University Press, 1966.
DIB.
Eggeling, John. "The Battle of Dorking," in Frank N. Magill, ed., Survey of Science Fiction Literature, vol. 1. Englewood Cliffs: Salem Press, 1979.
SAIF, pp. 256–57, 315.
Times, 1 April 1895.
Vibart, Henry Meredith. Addiscombe, Its Heroes and Men of Note. Westminster: Constable, 1894.

CHETWODE, R.D. (? - ?, fl. 1892–1898), writer. Published the novel listed and five more novels of adventure and historical romances.

CHILTON, Henry Herman (1863- ?, fl. 1892-1943), manufacturer and writer. Born in Brussels, educated in Wolverton and
Milan, lock manufacturer and justice of peace in Staffordshire. Published nine books of mystery, romance, and SF
(the book listed and two more S-F novels), and one long
poem.
M.s.l.
The Authors' and Writers' Who's Who. Ed. Edward Martell.
   London: Shaw, 1934.

CLARK, Alfred (? - ?, fl. 1891-1912), writer. Published
the SF listed and five other novels. Probably identical
with the writer of boys' stories in The Captain.
M.s.l.
MBF.

CLARK--sometimes spelled CLARKE--, Charles Heber (1841-
1915), US businessman, journalist, and writer under
pseudonym of Max Adeler. Born in Maryland, son of Episcopal
clergyman with abolitionist sympathies, at 15 office boy in
Philadelphia commission-house, at 17 enlisted in Civil War.
Journalist in Pennsylvania, publisher of Textile Record
1882-1902 and various other journals. Wrote articles on
economic questions, defending protectionism. Businessman
1888-1905, president of a manufacture of surgical dress-
ings. Published in 1874 Out of the Hurly-Burly, humorous
sketches of suburban life which sold millions of copies,
and had many translations; also eight other novels and four
books of short stories from 1876 on, as well as contributions to US magazines.
M.s.l.
AA.
NCAB, vol. 35.
OCAL.
REAL.

CLARKE, Percy (? - ?, fl. 1886-1916), writer and artist.
Had a degree in law, was fellow of Royal Colonial Institute
1910-1916 when he resided in Surrey. Earlier probably
lived in Australia. Beside the SF listed published two
other novels of Australia and a biography.
M.s.l.
Royal Colonial Institute Year Book 1916. [London]:
   R.C.I., [1916].

CLEMENS, Samuel Langhorne (1835-1910), US writer under the

pseudonym of Mark Twain. See for this well-known author any history of US literature and the works below.
M.s.l.
Mark Twain. Autobiography. Ed. Charles Neider. New York: Harper, 1959.
Mark Twain in Eruption. Ed. Bernard De Voto. New York: Harper, 1940.
Brooks, Van Wyck. The Ordeal of Mark Twain. New York: Dutton, 1933.
Kaplan, Justin. Mr. Clemens and Mark Twain. New York: Simon & Schuster, 1966.
Suvin, Darko. Metamorphoses of Science Fiction. New Haven and London: Yale University Press, 1979 (with further bibliography).

CLOWES, Sir William Laird (1856–1905), naval critic and writer. Born at Hampstead, educated at King's College, London, and at Lincoln's Inn. Abandoning law for journalism, wrote for the Standard, Daily News, the Times, contributed to foreign magazines, was on staff of Army and Navy Gazette. Received various medals and awards from US and UK armed services, knighted in 1902. From 1897 to 1903 editor (with H.D. TRAILL, q.v.) and part-author of the six-volume Social England, advisory editor of The Unit Library from 1902 on. From 1875 to 1903 published, beside the SF listed, four books and articles on the navy (of which a collection of articles anonymously), four books of poetry, two books of adventure stories, a one-act comedy, a novel, and a book on Black America. Also translated from German A Distinguished Man by A. von Winterfeld.
M.s.l.
DNB11.
The New International Encyclopaedia, vol. 5. New York: Dodd, Mead, 1922.
Times, 16 August 1905.
Who's Who. London: Black, 1905.

COBBAN, James MacLaren (1849–1903), writer. Published from 1879 on 23 books of adventure, mystery, lost race, and SF, of which four mysteries posthumously.

COBBE, Frances Power (1822–1904), philanthropist and writer. Born in Dublin, daughter of magistrate and land-lord, educated at Brighton and at home. In 1857–1858 journeyed to Southern Europe and Middle East. Upon return helped in Ragged School reformatories and workhouses, introduced innovations to sick-wards. Founded antivivisection associations, also fought for women's rights, made promin-

ent acquaintances (Tennyson became vice-president of her
society). Was Italian correspondent for Daily News,
wrote for Echo and Standard, edited the Zoophilist,
contributed to most current periodicals. Published about
40 books, essays, and pamphlets on the education of women,
ethics, religion, and vivisection; edited and wrote introductions to books on these topics.
M.s.l.
[Atkinson, Blanche.] Life of Frances Power Cobbe as Told
   by Herself: With Additions by the Author. . . . London: Sonnenschein, 1904.
Chappell, Jennie. Women of Worth. London: Partridge,
   1908.
DNB11.
Times, 7 and 11 April 1904.

COLE, Cyrus (? - ?, fl. 1890), US writer, resident of
Garden City, KS.
M.s.l.
Fuson, Ben. "Three Kansas Utopian Novels of 1890."
   Extrapolation 12 (1970), 7-24 (variant rpt. as Ben W.
   Fuson. "Prairie Dreamers of 1890." Kansas Quarterly
   5, no. 4 [1973], 63-77).

COLE, Robert William (? - ?, fl. 1900-1908), writer.
Beside the SF listed published three inferior thrillers,
one of them marginal SF.
M.s.l.
Locke, George. Voyages in Space. London: Ferret Fan-
   tasy, 1975.

COLLENS, Thomas Wharton (1812-1879), US jurist and judge.
Born in New Orleans, trained as printer, studied law, admitted to New Orleans bar 1833, attorney then judge. In his
youth sympathized with Owen and Fourierist utopians, later
supported Secession, was Mason and devout Catholic. Contributed to newspapers articles on social problems, was
editor of True American. Besides the SF listed, published from 1837 a book of poems, a historical tragedy,
pamphlets on law and the labor movement, as well as three
books on humanitarianism.
M.s.l.
AA.
NCAB.
PAD, pp. 52-54.
Rand, Clayton. Stars in their Eyes: Dreamers and Builders in Louisiana. Gulfport, MS: Dixie Press, 1953, pp.
   116-17.

COLLINS, Edward James Mortimer (1827-1876), writer. Born at Plymouth, son of solicitor, educated at private schools. Mathematics master 1849-1856 at Guernsey, then journalist connected with various papers, in particular the London Globe, and freelance writer. Published 1848-1871 four books of poems, and from 1865 18 novels, mainly three-deckers (one under the pseudonym "R.T. Cotton"), also the verse-play The British Birds emulating Aristophanes, The Secret of Long Life, and many journalistic sketches on the British countryside and animals, on classical and English literature. Refuted Darwinism for religious reasons.
M.s.l.
Collins, Frances, ed. Mortimer Collins, His Letters and Friendships: With Some Account of His Life. 2 vols. London: Low, Marston, 1877.
DNB, vol. 4.
EB, vol. 6.
[Taylor, Tom, and Frances Collins]. "Mortimer Collins," in Mortimer Collins, Pen Sketches by a Vanished Hand. Ed. Tom Taylor and Frances Collins. London: Bentley & Son, 1879.

COLOMB, Philip Howard (1831-1899), naval officer, historian, critic, and inventor. Born in Scotland, son of general, entered navy in 1846. In 1855 devised system of flashing signals adopted by the Royal Navy. Was correspondent of the Times on naval subjects. After retiring as vice-admiral, devoted himself to history of naval warfare, published an important work on it in 1891. From 1870 to 1893 published 15 books and essays about the navy, especially about collisions and his experiences at sea, as well as participating in the S-F novel listed.
M.s.l.
Colomb, P.H. Fifteen Years of Naval Retirement. Portsmouth: Griffin, 1886.
DNB, vol.22.
Mullen, R.D. [Review of The Great War of 189-.] SFS, no. 6 (1975), 185.
Times, 16 October 1899.

COMER, Cornelia Atwood, married name of C.A. PRATT (q.v.).

CONSTABLE, Frank Challice (1846-1937), lawyer and writer, justice of peace. Educated at Cambridge, in India 1872-1892 as barrister, then public prosecutor. First to recognize Kipling's worth as writer, wrote Whims of the Week with him. Besides the anonymous SF listed, published from 1877 to 1928 four more novels (one under the pseudonym

"Colin Clout"), a book of sketches, five books of psychology and parapsychology, one against the notion of hereditary
genius, one about social success, a pamphlet on religion in
schools (also as "Colin Clout"), and with M.H. Starling
Indian Criminal Law.
M.s.l.
WWW, vol. 3.

CORBETT, "Mrs. George," née Elizabeth Burgoyne (1846- ?,
fl. 1881-1922), writer. Born in Lancashire, England,
educated in Germany. Was contributor to Newcastle Daily
Chronicle and other periodicals of the day. Published 15
novels and tales of mystery, adventure, society, as well as
the S-F novel listed.

COWAN, James (1870-1943), US writer.

CRAIG, Alexander (? - ?, fl. 1898), US reformer.
M.s.l.
DUR, pp. 806-09.
PAD, pp. 144-46.

CROMIE, Robert (1856-1907), Irish journalist and writer.
Born in County Down, son of surgeon and magistrate,
educated at Royal Academical Institution. Official in the
Ulster Bank, left it in the late 1890s to become man of
letters; contributed to Irish and English periodicals
primarily on engineering subjects, on staff of Northern
Whig (Belfast). Published 11 novels and tales (one with
T.S. Wilson), mostly SF, including the four listed.
M.s.l.
Brown, Stephen, S.J. Ireland in Fiction. Dublin and Lon-
    don: Maunsell, 1916.
Editorial note in Robert Cromie, The Crack of Doom. The
    Penny Library of Famous Books, no. 17. London: Newnes,
    [1896?].
Obituary in Weekly Northern Whig (Belfast), 13 April
    1907.
PIU, pp. 16-17, 32, 80-82.

CURWEN, Henry (1845-1892), Anglo-Indian journalist and
writer. Born in Cumberland, son of clergyman, educated
1858-1864 at Rossall School, settled in London. Worked for
John Camden Hotten, publisher, and compiled several books
bearing only publisher's name. Moved to India in 1876,
became assistant editor of the Times of India, chief
editor from 1880, proprietor from 1889 to death. In 1870
and 1871 selected and translated two anthologies of 19th-

century French poetry; from 1872 to 1890 published, besides
the prehistoric SF listed, two anonymous novels, a book of
tales, a book of poems under the pseudonym "Owen Christian," two books of biographical sketches of writers, and
A History of Booksellers. Also edited the works of Poe
and translated Baudelaire's article on him. Died aboard
ship.

M.s.l.

DIB.

DNB, vol. 22.

Henkin, Leo J. Darwinism in the English Novel 1860-1910.
New York: Corporate Press, 1940, pp. 174-75.

MEB, vol. 4.

DALTON, Henry Robert Samuel (1835- ?, fl. 1857-1889),
writer. Son of clergyman, Oxford BA 1857. Published five
books on women's movement, religion, priestcraft, and eschatology in relation to social revolution, including the SF
listed.

M.s.l.

AO, vol. 1.

DANYERS, Geoffrey, pseudonym? (? - ?, fl. 1894).

D'ARGENTEUIL, Paul, pseudonym? (fl. 1899), US writer.

DAVIDSON, John (1857-1909), poet and writer. Son of
Evangelist minister, worked from age 13 as chemical
analyst, clerk, and teacher in Scotland, moved to London
1890. In later years lived at Penzance in financial difficulties, ended by suicide. Best known for more than a
dozen books of lyrical and narrative verse, also wrote a
dozen plays and a dozen books of prose--novels (one with
C.J. Wills), essays, and stories (including the SF listed).
Translated or adapted plays by Hugo and Coppée and The
Persian Letters.

M.s.l.

DNB11.

Petzold, Gertrud von. John Davidson und sein geistiges
Werden unter dem Einfluss Nietzsches. Leipzig: Tauch-
nitz, 1928.

Townsend, James B. John Davidson, Poet of Armageddon.
New Haven: Yale University Press, 1961.

DAVIS, Ellis James (1847?-1935), barrister. Son of solicitor, student at London University 1867 and Middle Temple
1868, barrister 1871-1935 in London. Published six books
of fantasy and melodrama, of which two anonymous S-F works.

M.s.l.
DUR, pp. 435-46.
FMB.
LL: 1935, s.v. "Counsel."

DE MILLE, James (1833-1880), Canadian professor and writer.
Date of birth is contested: some authors use 1836; his
name was originally spelled as DeMill. Born in Saint John,
N.B., son of deeply religious merchant, shipowner, and
lumberman, educated at Acadia College, N.S., received MA
from Brown University in 1854, traveled in Europe. Professor of classics at Acadia College 1860-1864, professor
of English at Dalhousie College 1865-1880. Published about
30 books, mostly historical novels, adventure stories for
boys, mysteries--most of which first appeared serially in
US magazines--and one text-book. The anonymous SF listed
was published posthumously, as was a long mystical poem.
M.s.l.
ECan,vol. 3.
OCCHL.
Suvin, Darko. Metamorphoses of Science Fiction. New
   Haven and London: Yale University Press, 1979 (with
   further bibliography).
[Tracy, Minerva.] Entry in DCBL.

DERING, Edward Heneage (1827-1892), writer. Born in Pluck-
ley, son of Anglican parson. Invalidated out of army, studied theology, philosophy, music, history. With his wife,
well-known novelist Lady Georgiana Chatterton, received
into Catholic Church 1865, lived life of recluse in medieval country home, dressed in 17th-century costumes. From
1860 aired his views in seven novels republished 1890-1894
as The Atherstone Series. Besides the SF listed (published under the pseudonym of "Innominatus"), also wrote
one book on Esoteric Buddhism, a pamphlet on philosophy,
and a book of poems; edited his wife's memoirs, and translated from Italian two books on philosophy and one on
political science.
M.s.l.
Dering, E.H. The Ban of Maplethorpe: With a Memoir of
   the Author, 2 vols. London: Art & Book, 1894.
MEB, vol. 5.
Wolff, Robert Lee. Gains and Losses: Novels of Faith and
   Doubt in Victorian England. New York and London: Garland, 1977, pp. 88-91.

DIXIE, Lady Florence Caroline, née Douglas (1857-1905),
writer and traveler. Daughter of the seventh Marquis of

Queensberry, educated mostly at home, traveled extensively. In 1880 published an account of her explorations in Patagonia, in 1881 was war correspondent for the Morning Post during the Boer-Zulu war, in 1882 published two books on Zululand. Advocate of complete sex equality, expressed this in SF listed and in stories for children; supported Sinn Fein movement in Ireland. From 1877 to 1906, published seven other novels and tales of adventure, travel, society, mystery (of which two for children), also two verse-dramas (one of which SF), two books of poetry under the pseudonym "Darling," and articles attacking sports-- hunting in particular.

M.s.l.
DNB11.
Roberts, Brian. Ladies in the Veld. London: Murray, 1965.
_____. The Mad, Bad Line. London: Hamilton, 1981.
Times, 8 November 1905.
Who's Who. London: Black, 1902.

DIXON, Charles (1858-1926), naturalist. Besides the SF listed, from 1880 to 1909 published 23 books on ornithology, one book on nature, and one on evolution.

DODD, Anna Bowman, afterwards BLAKE (1855-1929), US writer. Between 1887 and 1927 published, besides the antiutopian SF listed, four guidebooks on southern England and France, five books of romance and adventure, a book on Talleyrand, as well as a comedy.

M.s.l.
PAD, pp. 61-64.
Pfaelzer, Jean. "Parody and Satire in American Dystopian Fiction of the Nineteenth Century." SFS, no. 20 (1980), 61-72.

DONNELLY, Ignatius Loyola (1831-1901), US writer, Populist political leader. Born in Philadelphia, studied law, founded Nininger City, in 1859 and 1861 elected lieutenant-governor of Minnesota, 1863 to 1869 Republican member of Congress, then independent journalist and writer, publisher of weekly Anti-Monopolist. In 1890s dominant figure in the New People's Party, involved in farm reforms; speaker, editor of propaganda pamphlets, writer of articles. In his youth published a book of poems, and from 1882 to 1892, besides the three SF listed, two novels (one under the pseudonym "Edmund Boisgilbert") and two books on Bacon's authorship of Shakespeare's plays; Donnelliana, a book of excerpts from Donnelly's writing, was edited by E.W. Fish.

M.s.1.

Abrahams, Edward H. "Ignatius Donnelly and the Apocalyptic
   Style." Minnesota History (Fall 1978), 102-11.
Anderson, David D. Ignatius Donnelly. Boston: Twayne,
   1980.
Jaher, Frederic Cople. Doubters and Dissenters. Glen-
   coe, IL: Free Press, 1964, pp. 108-23.
Martin, Jay. Harvests of Change. Englewood Cliffs, NJ:
   Prentice-Hall, 1967, pp. 231-34.
Rideout, Walter B. "Introduction" to Ignatius Donnelly,
   Caesar's Column. Cambridge, MA: Harvard University
   Press, 1960.
Ridge, Martin. Ignatius Donnelly. Chicago: University
   of Chicago Press, 1962.
RON, passim.
Saxton, Alexander. "Caesar's Column." American Quarterly
   19 (1967), 225-38.
Stableford, Brian. "Caesar's Column," in Frank N.
   Magill, ed. Survey of Science Fiction Literature, vol.
   1. Englewood Cliffs, NJ: Salem Press, 1979.
Ueda, Reed T. "Economic and Technological Evil in the
   Modern Apocalypse: Donnelly's Caesar's Column & The
   Golden Bottle." Journal of Popular Culture 14 (1980),
   1-9.

DOUGLASS, Ellsworth, probably pseudonym for US grain trader
Elmer DWIGGINS (? - ?, fl. 1899-1924). WGT has an "uncon-
firmed" identification misspelled "Dwiggens." L.W. Currey
(oral communication) has observed three presentation copies
of the S-F novel listed, signed--in Chicago, Des Moines,
and Buenos Aires 1900-1901--by Dwiggins as the author.
Together with the novel's content, this makes it probable
he was in the grain trade based in Chicago. Probably
identical with the author of a book on mah-jongg in 1924.
Under the "Douglass" name contributed to English magazines,
including an S-F story with E. PALLANDER (q.v.--reprinted
in George Locke, ed., Worlds Apart, London: Cornmarket,
1972).
M.s.1.
Lupoff, Richard A. "Introduction" to Ellsworth Douglass,
   Pharaoh's Broker. Boston: Gregg Press, 1976.
WGT.

DOWNEY, Edmund (1856-1937), writer and publisher. Born in
Waterford, Ireland, educated at St. John's College there.
From 1906 editor of Waterford News, founded London publishing firm of Ward & Downey, later Downey & Co. From
1883 to 1924 published 17 novels (one anonymously), four

books of stories, one fairy tale, a book on English history, two historical guides to Waterford, a book of literary anecdotes, two books of Irish humor and legends, and a biography. Till 1900 published mostly under the pseudonym of "F.M. Allen," also used "William D. Hayes."
M.s.l.
WWW, vol. 3.

DOYLE, Sir Arthur Conan (1859-1930), writer. Born in an upper clerk's family of Irish descent in Edinburgh, educated in Jesuit schools and Edinburgh University, took his MD in 1885, practiced medicine until 1891, began writing stories for magazines, became popular after 1887 with the Sherlock Holmes cycle of detective tales. Participated as doctor in war against the Boers, wrote books vindicating it, unsuccessful Unionist candidate for Parliament, knighted in 1902, engaged in judicial and tariff reforms and other public affairs. Active in Volunteer Corps, wrote a history of World War and several pamphlets supporting it. In 1917 converted to spiritualism and dedicated rest of life to its spread. Published over 60 titles--historical novels, detective and pirate fiction, fantasy, political history and exhortation, spiritualist propaganda, some poetry and plays, and a number of S-F stories (besides the three titles listed, three more novels and some stories after 1900).
M.s.l.
Doyle, A.C. Memories and Adventures. Boston: Little, Brown, 1924.
Brown, Ivor. Conan Doyle. London: Hamilton, 1972.
Carr, John Dickson. Life of Sir Arthur Conan Doyle. New York: Harper, 1949.
Hall, Trevor H. Sherlock Holmes and His Creator. London: Duckworth, 1978.
Higham, Charles. The Adventures of Conan Doyle. London: Hamilton, 1976.
Moskowitz, Sam. Explorers of the Infinite. Cleveland and New York: World, 1963, pp. 157-71.
[Stableford, Brian.] Entry in SFE.

DRUERY, Charles Thomas (1843-1917), naturalist and writer. Besides the SF listed, published from 1882 to 1914 three books on British plants, one book of poems, a book of stories, and translated from German a book on evolutionary theory.

DUDGEON, Robert Ellis (1820-1904), homeopath. Born at Leith, son of wealthy merchant and shipowner, educated in

medicine at Edinburgh and at Vienna, Berlin, and Dublin,
started practicing in 1843. From 1846 to 1884 coeditor of
the British Journal of Homeopathy, in 1850 helped to
found the Hahnemann Hospital and School of Homeopathy, was
president of the International Homeopathic Congress and of
the British Homeopathic Society. From 1847 published,
besides the anonymous SF listed, 11 medical books and lectures, mostly on homeopathy and optics, and a biographical
sketch on Hahnemann; edited the Pathogenetic Cyclopedia,
two collections of Hahnemann's works, three volumes of Homeopathic League Tracts, and Ameke's History of Homeopathy. Translated three of Hahnemann's works and two books
on optics. Constructed "Dudgeon's Pocket Sphygmograph," an
instrument for registering the pulse, and invented spec-
tacles for use under water.
M.s.l.
DNB11.
Homeopathic World, 1 October 1904, pp. 433-35 and 464-72.

DU MAURIER, George Louis Palmella Busson (1834-1896),
writer and one of the most eminent illustrators of his
time. Born in Paris, son of naturalized Englishman, studied chemistry in London, then art in Paris and Antwerp.
Lost sight in one eye 1859. Came to London 1860, contributed satirical drawings and illustrations to Punch, then
to Once A Week and Cornhill Magazine, wrote verse and
prose for Punch. Besides the SF listed, published from
1880 five books of illustrations, the fantastic romance
Trilby--the first modern English best seller--and a book
of poems. Illustrated about 20 books by other authors.
M.s.l.
Du Maurier, Daphne. The Du Mauriers. London: Gollancz,
    1937.
James, Henry. "George Du Maurier," in his Partial Por-
    traits. London: Macmillan, 1888.
MEB, vol. 5.
Ormond, Leonée. George Du Maurier. Pittsburgh: Univer-
    sity of Pittsburgh Press, 1969.
Rosenberg, Edgar. From Shylock to Svengali. Stanford:
    Stanford University Press, 1960.
Stevenson, Lionel. "George Du Maurier and the Romantic
    Novel." Essays by Divers Hands, n.s. 30 (1960), 36-54.
Whiteley, Derek Pepys. George Du Maurier. London:
    Pellegrini & Cudahy, 1948.
Wilson, Edmund. "The Jews," in his A Piece of My Mind.
    Garden City, NY: Doubleday, 1958.

EASTWICK, James (1851- ?, fl. 1895). Possibly James East-

wick, son of clergyman, Oxford BA 1873 and DCL 1876, barrister in London 1877-1935, who published on some legal
matters 1877-1896.
M.s.l.
LL: 1935, s.v. "Counsel."

ELLIS, T. Mullett (? - ?, fl. 1893-1916). From 1901 editor
of the Thrush, a poetry periodical. Published, besides
the SF listed, five novels of adventure, society, and
romance, one collection of tales about the Klondike reprinted from periodicals, and one story for children about Queen
Victoria.

FAIRBURN, Edwin (1827-1911). Lived in New Zealand. Be-
sides the SF listed, printed in 1867 but published in 1885
under the pseudonym "Mohoao," published a sequel to Sue's
Wandering Jew, and in 1908 a short essay on the Deluge of
Genesis.
M.s.l.
NZNB, vol. 2.

FAIRFIELD, ? ?, is the way Dupont and Clarke (see list of
sources for the Bibliography) tentatively identified the
pseudonym "An Eye-Witness," under which the 1884 SF listed
was published. The only Fairfield known at the time was
Edward Denny Fairfield (1845-1897), a liberal civil servant
in the Foreign Office, but neither the entry in MEB, vol.
5, nor his obituary in the Times, 29 April 1879, yield
any material for deciding.

FAWCETT, Edward Douglas (1866-1960), amateur religious and
mystical philosopher. Born in Hove, his father a Cambridge
graduate, on his mother's side from Indian Army family,
educated at Westminster College, lived after 1896 in Switz-
erland, apparently as wealthy rentier. For a while collaborator of Mrs. Blavatsky, later in contact with young
Stapledon's pantheist estheticism; also interested in
sport, motoring, and flying. Besides the three S-F works
listed, published from 1880 to 1939 two books of adventure
and travel, two poems, and six books expounding the idealist philosophy of "imaginism." Not to be confused with US
fantasy writer Edgar Fawcett (1847-1904).
M.s.l.
Fawcett, Douglas. "Imaginism," in Contemporary British
   Philosophy, Second Series. London: Allen & Unwin,
   1925, pp. 83-105.
Johnson, Raynor C. Nurslings of Immortality. London:
   Hodder & Stoughton, 1957.

Mullen, R.D. [Review of Hartmann the Anarchist.] SFS, no. 6 (1975), 186.
WWW, vol. 5.

FAWKES, Frank Attfield (? - ?, fl. 1881-1930), writer. Published--besides the SF listed, signed "X"--four books on architectural topics, a "philosophy of tools," a book of detective short stories, three "How To" books, four books on religious topics (of which one signed "F.A.F."), and one romance. The SF listed was adapted into German by noted pacifist Bertha von Suttner in 1897.
M.s.l.
Ritter, Claus. Start nach Utopolis. Frankfurt: Röderberg, 1978, pp. 235seqq.

FISKE, Amos Kidder (1842-1921), US journalist and writer. Son of Massachusetts farmer, as orphan worked in factories, put himself through Harvard, also studied law in New York City. From 1867 worked on the Annual Cyclopaedia, from 1869 on staff of various New York City and Boston newspapers. Beside the marginal SF listed, published from 1890 on a book of chatty essays, two on history, two on banking and business, and three on Hebrew literature.
M.s.l.
DAB, vol. 6.
RON, p. 190.

FLAMMARION, Nicolas Camille (1842-1925), French astronomer, scientific popularizer, and speculative writer. Born in peasant family, worked 1858-1866 in the Paris astronomical observatory and Bureau des longitudes. His first book, Pluralité des mondes habités in 1861, was an instant success, translated into most European languages--as were many of his later works. From 1864 science editor of several French magazines; simultaneously, deeply involved with spiritualism. In 1865 he published Mondes imaginaires et mondes réels, a survey of fictional and nonfictional writings on other worlds, thus one of the first books of S-F historiography. In 1866 started lecturing on popular astronomy and publishing scholarly articles on it, from 1867 voyaged in balloons studying atmosphere and meteorology. In 1873 started publishing the results of his pio- neering investigations on multiple stars, and somewhat later those on the planet Mars; in 1879 published his famous Astronomie populaire; founded the Revue mensuelle d'astronomie, de météorologie et de physique du globe, cofounded the French astronomical society. Published 43 books of astronomy, philosophy, general science, and SF.

M.s.l.

Boia, Lucian. "Le Roman astronomique." Synthesis (Bucharest) 7 (1980), 149-50.

Cuny, Hilaire. Camille Flammarion, 1842-1925. Paris: Seghers, 1964.

Hugo, Sylvio. Camille Flammarion, sa vie et son oeuvre. Paris: Marpon & Flammarion, [1891].

Lundwall, Sam J. "Omega: The Last Days of the World," in Frank N. Magill, ed., Survey of Science Fiction Literature, vol. 4. Englewood Cliffs, NJ: Salem Press, 1979.

Stableford, Brian. "Lumen," in idem, vol. 3.

FOLINGSBY, Kenneth, pseudonym? (? - ?, fl. 1891).

M.s.l.

DUR, pp. 487-90.

FORREST, Henry J. (? - ?, fl. 1848).

M.s.l.

DUR, pp. 399-401.

FOX, Samuel Middleton (1856-1941), writer. Son of barrister, Cambridge BA 1881, BL 1883, later lived in Cumberland. Besides the SF listed, published two stories (of which one anonymously), one book of poems, and three plays, of which the one on Goethe in collaboration with Miss C.S. Fox.

M.s.l.

AC, vol. 2.

GALE, Frederick (1823-1904), solicitor, cricketer, writer. Born in Wiltshire, studied at Winchester College 1836-1841, articled to a solicitor in London, practiced as parliamentary lawyer until 1886. Under the pseudonym of "The Old Buffer" contributed articles, mostly on cricket, to Globe, Punch, and other leading periodicals. From 1853 to 1867 published, besides the SF listed, two books about public schools and one on Ireland under the pseudonym of "a Wykehamist," as well as an anonymous novel and a political pamphlet. From 1871 published under his own name five books and an essay on cricket. Later lived in Canada for some years.

M.s.l.

DNB11.

GEISSLER, Ludwig A. (? - ?, fl. 1891-1895), US writer.

M.s.l.

RON, p. 191.

GILLMORE, Parker (? - ?, fl. 1868-1893), officer, then traveling hunter, naturalist, and writer. Besides the SF listed, published 19 books on travel, adventure, and life in the wilderness (two early ones under the pseudonym "Ubique"), edited two books on biology, and translated from the French a book on mammals.
M.s.l.
Ubique (pseud. of Parker Gillmore). Gun, Rod, and Saddle: Personal Experiences. London: Chapman & Hall, 1869.

GLEIG, Charles (1862- ?, fl. 1898-1927), writer. Besides the SF listed, published 11 novels, mostly of adventure, of which one with E.W. Pugh.

GLYN (or CARR-GLYN), Alice Coralie (186?-1928), writer. Daughter of admiral, sister of fourth Baron Wolverton. Founder of Sunday Institution for benefit of working women, wrote and lectured on social problems. Besides the SF listed, published in 1895 The Idyll of the Star-Flower, a mystic interpretation of the Sagas, and in 1897 A Drama in Dregs: Life Study.
M.s.l.
WWW, vol. 2.

GORST, Harold Edward (1868-1950), journalist and writer. Educated at Eton and at Leipzig Conservatory. Correspondent from House of Commons, parliamentary sketch writer on the Westminster Gazette, cofounder and editor of the Review of the Week, on staff of Saturday Review, editorial writer for Evening Standard. Studied problems of China, wrote articles and a book on it. Acted as father's (Sir John Gorst) assistant private secretary at Board of Education. Lectured on education, made one-year lecture tour of USA and Canada. Besides the S-F books listed, published from 1899 to 1936 seven more works--a biography, the book on China, one each on education, love, and Christianity, one based on the memories of his father, and a book on reminiscences. With Gertrude Jones published a masque in 1902 and a tale in 1905.
M.s.l.
Gorst, Harold E. Much of Life Is Laughter. London: Allen & Unwin, 1936.
New York Times, 15 August 1950, p. 30.

GOULD, Frederick James (1855-1938), educationist and lecturer. Born in Brighton, schoolteacher 1877-1896, active in the positivist and agnostic Ethical Movement and Secular Society, lectured widely on moral education and the League

of Nations in UK, US, and India, was secretary of the International Moral Education Congress 1919-1927 and 1930. Published over 40 books for adults and children on religion, ethics, education, history, the British Empire, and exemplary biographies (among others, a brief "chat" with E.L. LINTON, q.v.). Several of his books ran into many reprints, and he was translated into half a dozen languages.
M.s.l.
Gould, F.J. The Life-Story of a Humanist. London: Watts, 1923.
Hayward, Frank H., and Ebe M. White. The Last Years of a Great Educationist. Bungay: Clay, 1942.
Neumann, Henry. Spokesman for Ethical Religion. Boston: Beacon Press, 1951, pp. 115-17.
WWW, vol. 3.

GRANT, John King (? - ?, fl. 1887). Under the pseudonym "Bower Watten" published the S-F novel listed.

GRANVILLE, Austyn W. (? - ?, fl. 1890-1894), US writer, for some years lived in Australia. Before the SF listed, also published two other novels, and in 1894 a fantasy (with W. Wilson Knott).
M.s.l.
[Nicholls, Peter.] Entry in SFE.
RON, p. 124.

GRAVES, Charles Larcom (1856-1944), writer. Son of bishop, Oxford BA 1879, MA 1882. Besides the eight books (of which some are SF) written in collaboration with E.V. LUCAS (q.v.), published from 1888 to 1936 a dozen books of poetry, of which The Blarney Ballads is the best known, three books on music, and Mr. Punch's History of Modern England. Coedited with J.St.L. STRACHEY (q.v.) the Liberal Unionist Journal, 1886. Edited a book of poems by A.D. Godley, wrote introduction to a book by F. Anstey, translated the poems of Ronsard and Horace.
M.s.l.
AO, vol. 2
Mullen, R.D. [Review of The War of the Wenuses.] SFS, no. 6 (1975), 190.

GREENER, William Oliver (1862- ?, fl. 1895-1905), writer and secret agent. Times correspondent covering the Russo-Japanese war, in 1905 published one spy novel and a book about his intelligence experiences in Port Arthur. Under the pseudonym "Wirt Gerrare" published from 1895 to

1900, besides the SF listed, two books on Russia, one mundane and one theosophical novel, a book of short stories about an occult detective, and A Bibliography of Guns and Shooting; wrote introduction to W.W. Greener's Sharpshooting for Sport and War.

M.s.l.

Greener, William. A Secret Agent in Port Arthur. London: Constable, 1905.

GREER, Thomas (1846 or 1847-1904), Irish surgeon. Born in County Down in well-known Ulster family. MA Royal University Belfast 1868, MD Queen's College Belfast and London Hospital 1876. Surgeon in Inverary prison, in Zulu War 1879, then settled in Cambridge. Failed in bid for Parliament 1892 as Liberal Home Ruler.

M.s.l.

Brown, Stephen, S.J. Ireland in Fiction. Dublin and London: Maunsell, 1916.

MD for 1904 and MD for 1905.

Mullen, R.D. [Review of A Modern Daedalus.] SFS, no. 6 (1975), 185.

PIU, pp. 21-22.

GREG, Percy (1836-1889), writer. Born at Bury, son of W.R. Greg (businessman and prolific conservative but theologically skeptical social critic and essayist). Educated at Rugby and Cheltenham 1850-1854, journalist, later novelist and historian. Contributed copiously to the Manchester Guardian, the Standard, and the Saturday Review. Tending to exasperated positions, became champion of feudalism and absolutism and adversary of the American Union. From 1856 to 1859 published under the pseudonym "Lionel H. Holdreth" one book on atheism (with G.J. Holyoake) and two books of verse. From 1875 to 1887 published, besides the SF listed, four novels of romance, adventure, and history, one book of poems, one satirical philosophical dialogue, a book on ethics, and a two-volume History of the United States.

M.s.l.

AC, vol. 3.

[Clute, John.] Entry in SFE.

DNB, vol. 8.

DUR, pp. 416-21.

Henkin, Leo J. Darwinism in the English Novel 1860-1910. New York: Corporate Press, 1940, pp. 249-51.

Moskowitz, Sam. "Across the Zodiac: A Major Turning Point in Science Fiction," in Percy Greg, Across the Zodiac. Westport, CT: Hyperion Press, 1974.

Mullen, R.D. [Review of Across the Zodiac.] SFS, no.
  5 (1975), 95-96.
Stableford, Brian. "Across the Zodiac," in Frank N.
  Magill, ed., Survey of Science Fiction Literature, vol.
  1. Englewood Cliffs, NJ: Salem Press, 1979.

GREGG, Hilda Caroline (1868-1933), writer. Under the
pseudonym "Sydney C[arlyon] Grier" published from 1894 to
1925, besides the three SF listed, 31 novels of romance,
politics, and Indian history, one biography, the memoirs of
Mrs. Hester Ward, and edited the letters of Warren
Hastings.
M.s.l.
SAIF, pp. 247-50, 254-56.

GRIFFITH, George--see JONES, George Chetwynd Griffith.

GROUSSET, Paschal (1844-1909), French politician, journalist, and writer. Born in Corsica, son of college principal; abandoned study of medicine in Paris for journalism
and politics. Science editor of L'Etendard (founded by
Vitu) then of Le Figaro, politics editor of Marseil-
laise, founded or inspired five oppositional newspapers.
Loud opponent of the Bonapartes, imprisoned for "slandering
the dynasty." Director of a newspaper, Central Committee
and Executive member in Paris Commune 1871, after its crush-
ing deported to New Caledonia, escaped 1874, lived in USA,
London, and illegally in Paris, taught in English schools,
returned to France amnestied in 1881, from 1893 to death
socialist member of Parliament. From 1869 on published 65
books. He began with political works including a utopian
novel, also published a book defending Dreyfus, a play, and
a book about convicts in New Caledonia with F. Jourde. His
translations include works by Reid, Stevenson, and Haggard.
As "Philipe Daryl" wrote books on foreign customs and
mores, as "Tiburce Moray" a book about England, also wrote
as "Tommasi," "Blasius," "Leopold Virey." Founded the
French League for Physical Education, headed its journal
l'Education physique, edited Encyclopédie des sports.
From 1884 published as "André Laurie" over a dozen adventure novels, of which 10 are fantasy or SF (one with Jules
VERNE), a series of books about schoolboy life in various
countries, and many contributions to the Magazin d'éduca-
tion et de récréation.
M.s.l.
GE, vol. 19.
Lacassin, Francis. "Le Communard qui écrivit trois romans
  de Jules Verne." Europe, no. 595-596 (1978), 94-105.

L20S, vol. 3.2.

GROVE, W. (? - ?, fl. 1888-1889). It is faintly possible
this was Sir William Robert Grove (1811-1896), prominent
physicist and lawyer.

HALE, Edward Everett (1822-1909), US writer and Unitarian
minister. Born in Boston, educated at Harvard. Editor of
Boston edition of Lingard's History of England and of the
Christian Examiner, contributing editor of the Atlantic
Monthly, published many pamphlets on theological and political subjects, contributed to leading periodicals. In 1869
founded and edited, for the American Unitarian Association,
the monthly magazine Old and New (later merged into
Scribner's Monthly, then the Century), and in 1886
Lend a Hand, a journal of organized charity. Published
about 60 books of social and religious concern, portraits,
biographies, as well as SF and adventure novels and books
on language and literature, including a utopian book as
"Frederic Ingham"; best known for the story The Man With-
out a Country.
M.s.l.
Hale, E.E. A New England Boyhood. New York: Literature
    House, 1970.
[Clute, John.] Entry in SFE.
Holloway, Jean. Edward Everett Hale. Austin: Universi-
    ty of Texas Press, 1956.
Moskowitz, Sam. Explorers of the Infinite. Cleveland
    and New York: World, 1963, pp. 88-105.
PAD, pp. 43-47.
Pinkerton, Jan. "Backward Time Travel, Alternate
    Universes, and Edward Everett Hale." Extrapolation 20
    (1979), 168-75.

HANNAN, Robert Charles (? - ?, fl. 1887-1911), writer.
Fellow of the Royal Geographic Society 1887-1900, lived in
Sussex and Glasgow. Beside the SF listed, published eight
novels and tales of adventure and romance and nine plays,
mostly one-acters.
M.s.l.
Royal Geographic Society: List of Fellows: January
    1889. London: [R.G.S., 1889].
Royal Geographic Society: Year-Book and Record, 1900.
    London: [R.G.S., 1900].

HARBEN, William Nathaniel (1858-1919), US novelist. Born
in Georgia, claimed kinship with Daniel Boone, till age of
30 merchant in Georgia and Tennessee. Began writing in

1888 and moved to New York; in 1889 published a novel deal-
ing with Negro slavery, badly received in the South. From
1891 to 1919 published 22 books of mystery, adventure, and
Southern life, including at least one more S-F story, "In
the Year Ten Thousand."
M.s.l.
Curry, L.W. "Introduction" to Will. N. Harben, <u>The Land</u>
    <u>of the Changing Sun</u>. Boston: Gregg Press, 1975.
<u>Library of Southern Literature</u>, vol. 5. Eds. Edwin
    Anderson and Joel Chandler Harris. New Orleans and
    Atlanta: Martin & Hoyt, 1909.
M[ullen], R.D. Review of <u>The Land of the Changing Sun</u>.
    <u>SFS</u>, no. 7 (1975), 276.
Murphy, James K. <u>Will N. Harben</u>. Boston: Twayne, 1979.
<u>RON</u>, pp. 114-17, 178-79, 193.
Rutherford, Mildred Lewis. <u>The South in History and Liter-</u>
    <u>ature</u>. Atlanta: Franklin & Turner, 1907.

HARTING, Dr. Pieter (1812-1885), leading Dutch scientist
and public figure. Born in rich merchant family of Rotter-
dam, studied medicine and practiced in Oudewater. From
1843 to his death professor of natural science at University of Utrecht. Published a huge number of scholarly works
in biology, geology (drew up geological map of the Netherlands), human and animal medicine, photography, and various
social sciences, including two works of "popularization"--
as he characterized the SF listed. Also interested in
hypnotism and spiritualism. Active in international
affairs, as chairman of Netherlands-South Africa Society defended the Boers, protested against pogroms in
Russia, corresponded with fellow-liberal Gladstone on
such questions, and with Darwin and Lyell on scientific
matters.
M.s.l.
Harting, Pieter. <u>Mijne herinneringen: Autobiografie</u>.
    Eds. J.C. van Cittert-Eymers and P.J. Kipp. Amsterdam:
    Noordhollandsche Uitg., 1961.
Coolhaas, Willem P. "De Nisero-kwestie, professor Harting
    en Gladstone," in <u>Bijdragen en Mededelingen van het his-</u>
    <u>torisch Genootschap</u>, vol. 28. Groningen: Wolters,
    1964, pp. 271-325.

HAY, William Delisle (? - ?, fl. 1880-1893), Fellow of
Royal Geographic Society. Besides the two SF listed,
edited a book on South Sea Islanders and published one on
New Zealand, two on fungi, and a tragic tale.
M.s.l.
<u>DUR</u>, pp. 455-56.

HAYES, Frederick William (1848-1918), painter and writer.
Son of Liverpool painter, studied architecture and painting, exhibited at Royal Academy from 1871, illustrated at
least one book. Lived in London from 1880, member of Society for Psychical Research and of Fabian Society for which
he published a pamphlet. Also published, beside the SF
listed, 11 popular plays, four romances, three articles on
economics, and a political prospectus.
M.s.l.
Bookman (London) 18 (May 1900), 40.
DUR, pp. 593-603.
Grundy, Cecil R. Frederic William Hayes, 1848-1918.
   London: Walker's Galleries, 1922 [destroyed in World War
   2, not available].

HAYWARD, William Stephens (? - ?, fl. 1862-1886), writer.
Published 53 books of romance and adventure--beginning with
some novels on the condition of women--of which about a
dozen anonymously.

HEARN, Mary Anne (1834-1909), writer and lecturer under the
pseudonym of "Marianne Farningham." Born in very religious
Nonconformist family, teacher to 1867. Wrote for the
Christian World from 1857 on, first verse, then articles,
as of 1876 also biographies. Public speaker on religious
and educational matters, from 1855 edited Sunday School
Times, argued for temperance in drink and against vivisection. Published 34 titles from 1860 to 1906, including
books of verse and religious hymns, collected articles and
lectures, books for children, and fiction (including the SF
listed).
M.s.l.
Farningham, Marianne (pseud. of Mary Anne Hearn). A Working Woman's Life: An Autobiography. London: Clarke,
   1907.
DUR, pp. 540-41.

HELPS, Sir Arthur (1813-1875), civil servant. Born in
Surrey, educated at Eton and Cambridge, MA 1839. Was
private secretary to chancellor of the Exchequer, then to
chief secretary for Ireland, commissioner of French,
Danish, and Spanish claims, and from 1859 till his death
Clerk of the Privy Council. As advisor to Queen Victoria
was entrusted with revision of Prince Albert's speeches
(published in 1862) and the queen's notes (published in
1868 and 1869). Knighted in 1872. Besides the SF listed,
published from 1835 to 1875, mostly anonymously, 14 works
of nonfiction on social and political topics including the

popular book of cautious advice, Friends in Council, three historical books on Spain and Russia, three dramas, and a novel; parts of his Spanish-American histories were reissued as four biographies. Edited Brassey's Work and Wages and Humboldt's Thoughts and Opinions of a Statesman, coauthored a book on Anna E. Brentano. A selection from Helps's essays and a book on Columbus were published posthumously with introductions by his son E.A. Helps, who also edited his correspondence.
M.s.l.
AC, vol. 3.
The Cambridge History of English Literature, vol. 14.
   Eds. A.W. Ward and A.R. Waller. Cambridge: Cambridge University Press, 1964, pp. 98–99, 163–64.
DNB, vol. 9.
EB, vol. 13.
Times, 8, 9, 10 March 1875.

HEMYNG, Samuel Bracebridge (1841–1901), writer. Educated at Eton and as barrister at Middle Temple, never practiced law. Pseudonymous creator of the "Jack Harkaway" stories in Boys of England, wrote 11 of its serials 1871–1879. Beside that and the SF listed, from 1860 on published 38 books, mainly novels and stories of mystery and adventure, but also some nonfiction; contributed the survey of prostitution to Mayhew's London Labour and the London Poor (see bibliography to interpretive essay).
M.s.l.
An Old Etonian (pseud. of Bracebridge Hemyng). Eton School Days. London: Maxwell, 1863.
James, Louis. "Tom Brown's Imperialist Sons." Victorian Studies 17, no. 1 (1973), 94–96.
Johannsen, Albert. The House of Beadle and Adams. Norman OK: University of Oklahoma Press, 1962, II, 138–39.
WWCL.

HENDOW, Z.S. (? – ?, fl. 1897).
M.s.l.
DUR, pp. 479–80.

HERBERT, William, writer of The World Grown Young (1891). Since this is the name of the narrator of the story and since no data could be found on him, it is highly probable that this is a pseudonym. WGT has as a "totally unsubstantiated" possible identification Herbert David Croly (1869–1930), US editor and writer about the "promise of America"; given the anti-US tenor of the book, I strongly

doubt this.
M.s.l.
DUR, pp. 535-40.
WGT.

HERTZKA, Theodor (1845-1924), Hungarian economist and
journalist of Jewish origin. Born in Budapest, educated in
economics in Budapest and Vienna, wrote mostly in German.
Science and economics editor of Neue Freie Presse 1872-
1879, founder and editor of Wiener Allgemeine Zeitung
1880-1889, publisher of Zeitschrift für Staats- und
Volkswirtschaft, editor of Budapest daily Magyar
Hírlap. Published widely acclaimed treatises on economics, in 1874 founded Austrian Economics Society, strongly
influenced by Dühring and Henry George in ideas of quasi-
socialist cooperativism. In his four utopian S-F writings
proposed establishment of farming communes in Central
Africa; Freiland associations were formed in many
countries, and there was a failed attempt at realizing it
in 1893 in Kenya.
M.s.l.
Bloomfield, Paul. Imaginary Worlds. London: Hamilton,
    1932.
[Perliss-Kressel, I.] Entry in Encyclopaedia Judaica.
    Vol. 8. Jerusalem: Macmillan, 1971.
Pollak, Fred. L. The Image of the Future. Leyden:
    Sythoff, and New York: Oceana, 1961, I, 348-49.
Ross, Harry. Utopias Old and New. Darby PA: Folcroft
    Library, 1973, pp. 159-75.
[Stavenhagen, Gerhard.] Entry in NDB, vol. 8.

HERVEY, Maurice H. (? - ?, fl. 1891-1901), newspaperman.
Was special correspondent of the Times. Besides the SF
listed, published six novels of adventure, crime, and
romance, an account of the Chilean revolution, and a book
on trade.

HINTON, Charles Howard (1853-1907), mathematician. Born in
London in a surgeon's family, schooled at Rugby and Oxford,
BA 1877 and MA 1886, taught mathematics first in English
private schools, from 1886 in Japanese schools, 1893-1897
as instructor at Princeton where he invented a "baseball
gun," and 1897-1900 at University of Minnesota. From 1900
in Washington DC, first with the Naval Observatory, then
examiner at US Patent Office, member of Society of Philan-
thropic Inquiry. Edited a book by his father James Hinton
(a prolific writer on ethics and suffering) speculating
about pain. Published from 1880 magazine essays and from

1884 a number of pamphlets and nine books of mathematico-
physical speculation centered on the fourth dimension and
ethics, including the two SF listed and a posthumous book--
using Abbott's Flatland--which can also be considered SF.
Best known are A New Era of Thought, completed by A.
Boole and H.J. Falk, and The Fourth Dimension, with their
exercises for visualizing the hyper-cube or "tesseract."
Probably supplied the term of "scientific romances" and
some hints to H.G. Wells.
M.s.1.
Cazamian, Madeleine L. Le Roman et les idées en Angle-
    terre 1860-1914. Paris: Les Belles Lettres, 1923-1955,
    II, 22, and III, 300.
Chambers's Cyclopaedia of English Literature. Ed. David
    Patrick. London and Edinburgh: Chambers, 1903, III,
    s.v. "James Hinton."
Rucker, Rudy. "Life in the Fourth Dimension: C.H. Hinton
    and His Scientific Romances." Foundation, no. 18
    (1980), 12-18.

HIRD, James Dennis (1850-1920?, fl. 1890-1908), clergyman,
later rationalist writer and educationist. BA Oxford
University 1875, MA 1878, tutor of noncollege students at
Oxford 1878-1886, ordained in Church of England 1884,
curate in various places 1884-1887, organizing secretary of
Church of England Temperance Society for London, compelled
to resign this post for being a member of the Socialist
Society. Rector in South England 1894-1896, when he was
cast out of the Church for writing A Christian With Two
Wives. From 1899 warden of Ruskin Hall, Oxford. Published, besides the anonymous SF listed, three books for
the Church of England Temperance Society, six lectures and
novels on Christianity, mainly in relation to socialism and
marriage (one as "Walter James"), and three popularizations
of the evolution theory; from 1899 on rewrote and edited,
at times with W.H. Forbes, the Oxford University exams in
logic, republished in many editions until 1950.
M.s.1.
Blurb and prefatory matter in Dennis Hird, Was Jesus
    Christ a Ritualist? London: Watts, 1900.
CCD for 1898.

HOFFMANN, Ernst Theodor Wilhelm--later Amadeus--(1776-
1822), German writer and composer. See for this well-known
author any history of German literature and the works
below.
M.s.1.
Hoffmann, E.T.A. Tagebücher. Ed. Friedrich Schnapp.

München: Winkler, 1971.
Daemmrich, Horst S. The Shattered Self. Detroit: Wayne
     State University Press, 1973.
Harich, W. E.T.A. Hoffmann, 2 vols. Berlin: Reiss,
     1922.
Hewett-Thayer, Harvey W. Hoffmann: Author of the Tales.
     New York: Octagon Books, 1971.
Matt, Peter von. Die Augen der Automaten. Tübingen:
     Niemeyer, 1971.
Negus, Kenneth. Hoffmann's Other World. Philadelphia:
     University of Pennsylvania Press, 1965.
Segebrecht, W. Autobiografie und Dichtung. Stuttgart:
     Metzler, 1967.

HOWELLS, William Dean (1837-1920), US novelist, essayist,
and public figure, major proponent and practitioner of
realism. Born in Ohio, had little formal schooling, at
nine worked in father's typesetting office. On Ohio State
Journal as compositor and reporter 1856-1860. In 1860
wrote campaign biography of Lincoln, as reward appointed US
consul in Venice 1861-1865. Connected with New York
Times and Nation, subeditor of Atlantic Monthly, 1872-
1881 editor in chief, also conducted "Editor's Study"
department of Harper's Monthly, was editor of Cosmopolitan, first president of American Academy of Arts and
Letters. Published over 35 novels--including two utopian
S-F ones--, 35 plays, four books of poetry, six books of
criticism, over 30 miscellaneous volumes of sketches, criti-
cism, and travel, as well as autobiographical works (of
which one semifictional).
M.s.l.
Howells, William D. A Boy's Town. New York: Harper,
     1890.
_____. Years of My Youth. New York: Harper, 1916.
Woodress, James, and S.P. Anderson. "A Bibliography of
     Writings About W.D. Howells." American Literary
     Realism, special no. (1969), 1-133.
Kasson, J.F. Civilizing the Machine. New York: Gross-
     man, 1976.
Kirk, Clara, and Rudolf Kirk. W.D. Howells. New
     Brunswick NJ: Rutgers University Press, 1962.
Lynn, Kenneth S. William Dean Howells. New York: Har-
     court, Brace, 1971.
RON, pp. 24, 58, 62, and passim.
Underwood, John Curtis. "William Dean Howells and
     Altruria," in his Literature and Insurgency. New York:
     Biblo & Tannen, 1974.
Vanderbilt, Kermit. The Achievement of William Dean

Howells. Princeton: Princeton University Press, 1968.

HUDSON, William Henry (1841-1922), naturalist and writer.
Born near Buenos Aires of English father and American
mother. In youth collected bird skins for museums, eucated
privately, went to England 1874, began writing for magazines 1880. Instrumental in formation of Society for Protection of Birds, published many pamphlets in its support.
Besides the SF listed, published from 1883 four novels
(including one more SF), two books of stories, 12 books of
essays on nature (primarily on birds), two books of
ornithology (of which one with P.L. Sclater) and his autobi-
ography; two anthologies of his works were published post-
humously.
M.s.l.
Hudson, William Henry. Far Away and Long Ago. London:
  Dent, 1951.
DUR, pp. 482-87.
Frederick, John T. William Henry Hudson. New York:
  Twayne, 1972.
Hamilton, John Robert. W.H. Hudson. Port Jefferson NY:
  Kennikat, 1970.
Liandrat, F. W.H. Hudson, 1841-1922, naturaliste. Lyon:
  Audin, 1946.
Roberts, Morley. W.H. Hudson. London: Nash, 1924.
Tomalin, Ruth. W.H. Hudson. New York: Greenwood Press,
  1969.

HULME-BEAMAN, Emeric (? - ?, fl. 1898-1905). Published
four novels of mystery and SF, contributed to Chambers's
Journal.
M.s.l.
PIU, pp. 23-25.

HUME, Fergus William or Fergusson Wright (1859-1932),
writer. Some uncertainty concerning first names and date
of birth (either 1859 in Britain or 1860 in New Zealand).
Educated in New Zealand and admitted to bar there, moved to
Melbourne in mid-1880s. Started writing in imitation of
the popular novelist Gaboriau, had great success with The
Mystery of a Hansom Cab, 1886, which sold half a million
copies in his lifetime. Settled in England in 1886, lectured to clubs and societies, published 140 books--mainly
detective novels, but also lost-race novels, occult fantasy, romances, and the SF listed (as well as another S-F
novel The Mother of Emeralds, 1901).
M.s.l.
DAuB, vol. 1.

MAL.
Times, 14 July 1932.

HYNE, Charles John Cutcliffe Wright (1865 or 1866-1944), novelist and short story writer. Born in Gloucestershire, a vicar's son, as boy worked in coal pits, educated in natural sciences at Cambridge, MA 1891. Began writing for Dickens's periodical All the Year Round, also wrote pot-boilers, boys' books, and under the name "Aunt Ermyntrude" advice-column in a women's paper. His "Captain Kettle" humorous stories first appeared in serial form in maga-zines, then as book-series (10 books 1898-1938) popular both in USA and UK; the character appeared in a play, its author became wealthy. Besides this series, published from 1898 to 1940 about 50 books, mostly novels and short stories of adventure, romance, and mystery (including half a dozen S-F novels and some S-F stories), some under the pseudonym "Weatherby Chesney." Traveled extensively in Europe, Africa, and Latin America gathering material for adventure books. In latter part of life did research into causes of congenital deafness.
M.s.l.
Hyne, C.J.C.W.   My Joyful Life.   London: Hutchinson, 1935.
AC, vol. 3.
[Eggeling, John.] Entry in SFE.
Mullen, R.D. [Review of Empire of the World.]   SFS, no. 6 (1975), 187-88.
Twentieth Century Authors, 1st Suppl. Ed. Stanley J. Kunitz. New York: Wilson, 1961.

JACKSON, Edward Payson (1840-1905), US teacher and writer. Born at Erzerum, Turkey, where his parents were missionar-ies, returned to US at age five. Graduated in 1870 at Amherst, from 1877 on master in Boston Latin School. Besides the SF listed, published from 1873 to 1891 two manuals of geography and astronomy, and a book on character building (published in one volume with Nicholas P. Gilman's The Laws of Daily Conduct).

JANE, Frederick Thomas (1865 or 1870-1916), writer. Was on staff of Illustrated London News. Best known for his two reference books Jane's Fighting Ships (1889) and Jane's All the World's Aircraft (1909--followed by annual All the World's Air Ships), with many continuations and atten-dant compilations up to our time. Besides these and the three SF listed, published from 1896 to 1915 one satirical fantasy, 14 books on the navy, and four novels of naval

adventure and romance. Illustrated two books in the 1890s and wrote introduction to A.M. Laubeuf's Naval Supremacy (1908).
M.s.l.
Dempsey, D. "Jane's World." New York Times Book Review, 9 December 1951, p. 8.
Mullen, R.D. [Review of The Violet Flame.] SFS, no. 6 (1975), 190.

JEFFERIES, John Richard (1848–1887), naturalist, journalist, and writer. Born on his father's small dairy-farm in Wiltshire, descended on mother's side from London engravers' and printers' family, worked on provincial English newspapers 1866–1877, wrote in London press and magazines on farming and nature, later lived in southern England, died of tuberculosis. From 1874 on published eight novels (including the SF listed), an autobiography, collected his excellent and much admired rural sketches and essays from magazines into 10 books on country life; a dozen posthumously collected titles include his diaries and notebooks as well as his writings on nature and society.
M.s.l.
Jefferies, Richard. Story of My Heart. Ed. Samuel J. Looker. London: Constable, 1947.
Fowles, John. "Introduction" to After London. Oxford: Oxford University Press, 1980.
Keith, W.J. Richard Jefferies. Toronto: University of Toronto Press, 1965.
Leavis, Q.D. "Lives and Works of Richard Jefferies," in F.R. Leavis, ed., A Selection From Scrutiny. Cambridge: Cambridge University Press, 1968, II, 202–11.
Looker, Samuel J., and Crichton Porteous. Richard Jefferies, Man of the Fields. London: Baker, 1965.
Salt, H.S. Richard Jefferies. Port Washington NY: Kennikat, 1970.
Thomas, Edward. Richard Jefferies. London: Faber, 1978.
Williams, Raymond. The Country and the City. St. Albans: Paladin, 1975, pp. 232–38.

JENKINS, John Edward (1838–1910), politician and satirist. Born in India, son of Wesleyan missionary, educated at McGill College, Montreal, and University of Pennsylvania. Barrister in London from 1864, agent general for Canada 1874–1875, Liberal MP for Dundee 1874–1880. Editor of Overland Mail and Homeward Mail. From 1869 published over 20 books and essays of political topics and social and political satire, among others Lord Bantam, Ginx's

Baby, The Coolie; acted for protection of coolie labor
in British Guiana. Also published two legal handbooks for
architects.
M.s.l.
DNB11.
Dod's Parliamentary Companion, I, 249. London: 1880.
Times, 6 June 1910.

JEPSON, Edgar Alfred (1863-1938), writer. Born in London,
educated at Oxford, schoolmaster in England and Barbados
for some years, prolific writer without literary ambition.
Published from 1895, besides the SF listed, over 60 melodramatic and humorous romances, mysteries, and fantasies,
three of them in collaboration and some as "R. Edison
Page." Translated seven novels from the French, wrote the
two autobiographies adduced below.
M.s.l.
Jepson, Edgar. Memories of a Victorian. London:
    Gollancz, 1933.
_____. Memories of an Edwardian and Neo-Georgian.
    London: Richards, 1937.

JEROME, Jerome Klapka (1859-1927), journalist and writer.
Born in Staffordshire of Nonconformist parents, educated at
Philological School in London. Was clerk, actor, and
schoolmaster before becoming journalist, coeditor of the
Idler, and editor of To-day. From 1886 published five
novels, 20 volumes of humor, short stories, and essays, 25
plays, an anonymous handbook on playwriting, and his memoir
adduced below.
M.s.l.
Jerome, J.K. My Life and Times. London: Harper, 1926.
DNB30.
EB, vol. 15.
Faurot, Ruth Marie. Jerome K. Jerome. New York:
    Twayne, 1974 (with further bibliography).
Stenbock-Fermor, Elizabeth. "A Neglected Source of
    Zamiatin's Novel We." Russian R. 32 (1973), 187-88.
Tuzinski, Konrad. Das Individuum in der englischen
    devolutionistischen Utopie. Tübingen: Niemeyer, 1965,
    pp. 32-45.

JONES, George Chetwynd Griffith--probably adopted his
pseudonym of George [Chetwynd] GRIFFITH as his legal name--
(1857-1906), journalist and writer. Born at Plymouth, son
of clergyman, educated in private school at Southport, went
to sea as ship apprentice, traveled around the world, studied one year in Germany, was teacher until 1887 when he
turned journalist. Apparently involved with freemasonry,

wrote actively for their movement and secularist causes. Became editor of a local London paper which was bankrupted by libel actions arising out of Griffith's political journalism, turned free-lance journalist, globe-trotter, and writer for Pearson periodicals. From 1893 published 43 books of crime, adventure, fantasy, romance, social melodrama, and historical novels, as well as four books of nonfiction, mostly travelogs (two books of poems under the pseudonym "Lara" and a novel on prostitution as "Stanton Morich"); also published short stories and articles as "Levin Carnac." This includes 21 books of or in the margins of SF (the eight published by 1900 are listed), one a collection of short stories.

M.s.1.
Moorcock, Michael. "Introduction" to his Before Armageddon. London: Allen, 1975, I, 10–13.
Moskowitz, Sam. "George Griffith--The Warrior of If"; Locke, George. "Additional Notes" and "Bibliography"; both in [George Locke, ed.,] The Raid of "Le Vengeur." London: Ferret Fantasy, 1974.
M[ullen], R.D. Reviews of The Angel of the Revolution and Honeymoon in Space. SFS, no. 4 (1974), 301; no. 6 (1975), 183–84.
PIU, pp. 25–27.
Stableford, Brian. "The Angel of the Revolution," in Frank N. Magill, ed., Survey of Science Fiction Literature, vol. 1. Englewood Cliffs NJ: Salem Press, 1979.

JONES, Jingo (fl. 1900), pseudonym, most probably of a 1900 member of UK Parliament.

KELLETT, Ernest Edward (1864-1950), literary critic and writer. Son of clergyman, educated at Oxford, BA 1886. Senior English Master in Cambridge until 1924. From 1897 to 1940 published, besides the SF listed, two books of verse, a historical saga, over 15 books of nonfiction, mostly on history, religion, aesthetics, and literature, as well as his reminiscences. Edited various literary and historical works, most notably the Book of Cambridge Verse, contributed articles to Encyclopaedia Britannica and Dictionary of Religion and Ethics, and translated two books of nonfiction from German.

M.s.1.
Kellett, Ernest Edward. As I Remember. London: Gollancz, 1936.
WWW, vol. 4.

KINROSS, Albert (1870-1928), novelist, journalist, cricketer. Born in South Hampstead, son of West Indies merchant,

educated at boarding schools, worked as junior clerk, then
as clerk for father's business. From 1888 to 1892 worked
at assorted jobs (e.g., selling glass eyes) in Europe.
Upon return to England began to write for papers and to
play cricket, associate editor of Outlook, drama critic
for Morning Post, art critic for Academy, contributor
to leading periodicals. Sent to Greece by the Tribune,
and to Russia by Daily Mail to cover the Russo-Japanese
war. From 1896 on published over a dozen novels and tales
of SF, humor, and adventure as well as the reminiscences
adduced below.
M.s.l.
Kinross, Albert. An Unconventional Cricketer. London:
   Shaylor, 1930.

LACH-SZYRMA, Wladislaw Somerville (1841-1915), clergyman,
writer, fellow of the Royal Historical Society. Born in
Polish émigré family at Devonport, BA Oxford University
1862, MA 1865, Church of England clergyman in Cornwall and
South England, vice-president of British Archeological Society in 1907. Beside the two SF listed, published 16 books,
mostly on religious topics, but also on geography, history,
and culture of Cornwall, and a book of poems on Franklin
and Garibaldi. Another S-F series in Cassell's Magazine
1887-1893 saw book publication only in 1972 in George
Locke, ed., Worlds Apart.
M.s.l.
CCD for 1915.

LANCASTER, William Joseph Cosens (1843 or 1851-1922),
writer. Born at Weymouth, son of naval officer, educated at
Royal Naval School, midshipman in navy, then civil
engineer. Traveled extensively, lived eight years in South
Africa. Besides the SF listed (the first novel of a marginally S-F trilogy), published from 1878 under the pseudonym
of "Harry Collingwood" over 40 historical, travel, lost-
race, and adventure (especially naval) novels, and with
Percival Lancaster In the Power of the Enemy.
M.s.l.
WWCL, p. 55.

LANG, Andrew (1844-1912), journalist, poet, critic, and
historian. Born at Selkirk, son of lawyer, educated at St.
Andrew's and Oxford, afterwards became a fellow there.
Extremely prolific writer, wrote articles in various
journals, literary editor of Longman's Magazine for many
years. Interested in folklore, myth, and religion, involved in controversy with Max Müller, was one of the
founders of "psychic research." From 1863 on published (at

times together with various other writers, including R. Haggard) over 120 pamphlets and books of poetry, translations from French and Greek (including Homer), essays, works on myth and folklore, literary criticism, children's fantasy, biography, legends, and history (including a seven-volume History of Scotland), about 100 introductions to various books, as well as some editions of writers such as Burns. One of the most influential literary critics of the age, now deservedly forgotten.
M.s.l.
[Clute, John.] Entry in SFE.
DNB21.
EB, vol. 16.
Gordon, G.S., et al. Concerning Andrew Lang. Oxford: Oxford University Press, 1949.
Green, R.L. Andrew Lang. Leicester: Ward, 1946.
Gross, John. The Rise and Fall of the Man of Letters. London: Weidenfeld & Nicolson, [1969], pp. 132-39.
Mullen, R.D. [Review of "The Romance of the First Radical."] SFS, no. 6 (1975), 194.
NCBEL3.

LANG, Herrmann, writer of The Air Battle (1859). Internal evidence all but rules out the identification as a German professor of chemistry accepted by Gibbs-Smith (adduced below). He was clearly a native of the British Isles (possibly a Scotsman), the German name is probably a pseudonym, and he might have been living in Dawlish, South Devon, where the preface to his work is signed as from 1858.
M.s.l.
Gibbs-Smith, Charles H. Introduction to Herrmann Lang, The Air Battle. London: Cornmarket Rpts., 1972.

LAWRENCE, Edmund (? - ?, fl. 1884-1902), political writer. Beside the SF listed published one political and one theological book, edited a historical memoir.

LAZARUS, Henry (? - ?, fl. 1892-1897). Published in 1892 a short book against the slums and landlords of London; both it and the SF listed provoked violent discussions. Probably not the same as Henry Lazarus (1815-1894), musician.
M.s.l.
DUR, pp. 570-93.

LEE, Thomas (? - ?, fl. 1886-1890), London plasterer, later probably publican of Old Bull Inn at Edmonton, Middlesex. Published, beside the SF listed, three novels there.

M.s.1.
The Edmonton and Tottenham Weekly Guardian, 16 August
    1889.
Title page and reviews in the back of Thomas Lee, The Old
    Bull Inn of Silver Street, Edmonton. Edmonton: Lee,
    1887.

LEHMANN, Rudolf Chambers (1856-1929), journalist and
writer. Son of London merchant, educated at Cambridge (MA
1881) and Harvard, barrister of Inner Temple 1880, member
of staff and then editor of Punch 1890-1919, editor of
Daily News 1901, high sheriff of Buckinghamshire 1901,
Liberal member of Parliament 1906-1910 after several unsuccessful attempts in previous elections. Coauthored in 1887
a legal digest, from 1890 published about 20 books on
sports, literature, and miscellaneous subjects, as well as
some fiction including the book of parodies listed.
M.s.1.
Lehmann, R.C., ed. Memories of Half a Century. London:
    Smith & Elder, 1908.
AC, vol. 4.
Who's Who of British Members of Parliament, vol. 2. Eds.
    Michael Stenton and Stephen Lees. Hassocks: Harvester
    Press, 1978.
WWW, vol. 3.

LE QUEUX, William Tufnell (1864-1927), novelist, journal-
ist, traveler, possibly Secret Service agent. Born in
London of French draper's assistant and English mother,
educated privately in London and Italy, studied art in
Paris. Was reporter for English paper in Paris, clerk in
Italy, then reporter for, and later editor of, various
papers in England; from 1891 to 1893 foreign editor of
Globe. Traveled extensively all over Europe and North
Africa, acquainted with European royalty. Special
correspondent of the Times, Daily Mail, New York
Herald, and Le Journal, consul of Republic of San
Marino. In 1893 gave up journalism and wrote pot-boilers
(more than 150 exotical, lost-race, political, occult
suspense, and spy novels) to support his travel and
unofficial Secret Service activities, including the two SF
listed and four more after 1900. Claimed to have
discovered German spy network in UK; in his forecast The
Invasion of 1910 (1906) appealed to England to prepare for
war and fifth-column activities. Was a chief exponent of
the new genre of spy adventures, where the villains were
foreign Jews, and of aristocratic memoirs; also interested
in wireless broadcasting and admired Fascism.
M.s.1.

Le Queux, William. Things I Know About Kings, Celebri-
ties, and Crooks. London: Nash, 1923.
Sladen, Norman St. Barbe. The Real Le Queux: The Offi-
cial Biography of William Le Queux. London: Nicholson
& Watson, 1938.
MacCormick, Donald. Who's Who in Spy Fiction. London:
Elm Tree Books, 1977, pp. 112–16.
WWW, vol. 2.

LESTER, Edward (1831–1905), clergyman. Son of landowner,
at Cambridge University 1850–1853 but did not graduate,
ordained in Church of England 1856, served in South England
then in Lancashire. Published three religious pamphlets
and the SF listed.
M.s.l.
AC, vol. 4.
CCD for 1904.

L'ESTRANGE, Henry, pseudonym (? – ?, fl. 1893).

L'ESTRANGE, Miles (? – ?, fl. 1892). The total lack of
data, and the "speaking name"--Franco-Latin for "a strange
(or unknown) soldier"--indicate that this is probably a
pseudonym for an officer.
M.s.l.
Connes, Georges. Etude sur la pensée de Wells. Paris:
Hachette, 1926, passim.

LINTON (or LYNN LINTON), Mrs. Eliza(beth), née Lynn (1822–
1898), essayist and novelist. Born at Crosthwaite vicar-
age, lived in London 1845-1851, in Paris 1851-1854. From
1848 to 1851 wrote in Morning Chronicle, contributed
regularly to Dickens's Household Words. In 1858 married the Chartist engraver and writer W.J. Linton,
separated in 1867. Won fame with the antifeminist
articles, "The Girl of the Period," in Saturday Review
from 1866, often reprinted; also had great success with
the anonymous novel The True History of Joshua Davidson,
portraying Christ as a communist (1872). From 1846
published about 30 books, including two historical novels,
a number of antifeminist novels, as well as a veiled
autobiography which traces her theological and ideological
doubts and developments.
M.s.l.
Lynn Linton, Eliza. The Autobiography of Christopher Kirk-
land. New York and London: Garland, 1976.
_____. My Literary Life. London: Hodder & Stoughton,
1899.
Colby, Vineta. The Singular Anomaly: Women Novelists of

the Nineteenth Century. New York: New York University Press, 1970, pp. 15-45.
DNB, vol. 22.
Layard, G.S. Eliza Lynn Linton. London: Methuen, 1901.
Thal, Herbert van. Eliza Lynn Linton. London: Allen & Unwin, 1979.
Wolff, Robert Lee. Gains and Losses: Novels of Faith and Doubt in Victorian England. New York and London: Garland, 1977, pp. 378-88.

LISLE, Charles Wentworth (? - ?, fl. 1886).

LLOYD, John Uri (1849-1936), US pharmacist, plant chemist, drug manufacturer, and novelist. Born in New Jersey, son of teachers, educated at home and then apprenticed to a druggist. With his two brothers formed drug manufacturing firm. President of the American Pharmaceutical Association, of the National Eclectic Medical Association, and of the Eclectic Medical Institute. From 1878 to 1907 professor of chemistry at the latter, 1883-1887 taught pharmacy at Cincinnati College of Pharmacy. Produced drugs for use of Eclectics (physicians advocating use of plant extracts in treatment), began campaign against adulteration in medicine, invented numerous apparati, received a number of honorary degrees and a medal from the American Pharmaceutical Association. Besides the very popular occult SF listed (which seems to have gone through 18 editions in his lifetime and is now again in print), published till 1934 seven novels, mostly about northern Kentucky, a collection of pharmaceutical formulas, a comprehensive survey of vegetable pharmacopeia, and coauthored with his brother two volumes of Drugs and Medicines of North America. Also published 35 bulletins on little-known plants, three volumes of bibliography, edited and coedited a number of periodical publications. Many of his works became standard texts in college of pharmacy.
M.s.l.
DAB, vol. 22.
RON, pp. 80-81.
Wilgus, Neal. "Down to Earth." Samisdat, no. 20 (1976), 25-27.

LUCAS, Edward Verrall (1868-1938), journalist, essayist, critic. Born in Kent, son of insurance agent, at 16 apprenticed to Brighton bookseller, joined staff of Sussex Daily News, studied at University of London. Began journalistic career 1893 on Globe, published light and sentimental essays on art, literature, life in the city. On staff of

Punch, chairman of Methuen & Co., Publishers, from 1924,
from 1928 member of Royal Commission on Historical Monu-
ments. Published eight books (some SF) in collaboration
with Charles Larcom GRAVES (q.v.), about 30 collections of
essays on varied subjects, a dozen books on travel, a book
of reminiscences, as well as short books on painters and a
few novels. Also edited many anthologies and the standard
seven-volume edition of The Works of Charles and Mary
Lamb.
M.s.l.
Lucas, E.V. Reading, Writing, and Remembering. London:
    Methuen, 1939.
DNB40.
Lucas, Audrey. E.V.L.: A Portrait. Port Washington NY:
    Kennikat, 1969.
WWW, vol. 3.

LUMLEY, Benjamin--born LEVY--(1812-1875), lawyer and opera
manager. Son of Jewish merchant from Canada, educated
at University of Birmingham, assumed name of Lumley.
Solicitor in London 1832, parliamentary agent, studied
for bar, employed from 1835 at Her Majesty's Theatre,
home of Italian opera. Manager of that theater 1841-
1859, introduced a number of Italian operas to England,
1850-1851 managed also the Paris Italian Opera House.
Later returned to practice of law. Published, besides
the SF listed (under the pseudonym "Hermes"), two
books on the opera, one on parliamentary practices, and
the-anonymous Sirenia; or, Recollections of a Past Existence.
M.s.l.
DNB30.
DUR, pp. 428-29.
MEB, vol. 2.

LYON, Edmund David (? - ?, fl. 1870-1888), infantry captain. Besides the SF listed supplied notes to accompany
photographs in a book on Indian architecture and published
one novel. Not to be confused with Edmund Lyon (1855-
1920), humanitarian.

LYTTON, E.G.E.L. Bulwer--see BULWER-LYTTON, Edward G.E.L.

M., J.W. (? - ?, fl. 1871-1891). Besides the two SF listed, published from 1876 to 1891 two more novels, a pamphlet
on missionary work, and one on financial matters. Not to
be confused with John William Mackail, the biographer of W.
Morris.

MacCOLL, Hugh (? - ?, fl. 1889-1891). Besides the SF listed, published a novel.

MacCULLOCH, J. (? - ?, fl. 1892). Under the pseudonym J.A.C.K. published the SF listed.

MacKAY, Donald (? - ?, fl. 1888). Perhaps Ian Donald Mackay, BA University of Dublin 1883, and/or an Irish-American.
M.s.l.
CGUD, vol. 2.

MACKAY, James Alexander Kenneth (1859-1935), Australian public figure and writer. Born at Wallendbeen, served in Boer War, vice-president of the New South Wales Executive Council. Besides the SF listed, published from 1887 to 1901 one more novel about Australia, three books of poems, and a book of travel in Papua.
M.s.l.
MAL.

MACNIE, John (1836-1909), US college teacher. Born in Stirling, Scotland, moved to US. Traveled in Europe in the late sixties, professor of French and German at the University of North Dakota from 1884. Beside the SF listed (published under the pseudonym of "Ismar Thiusen"), published two books on mathematics.
M.s.l.
Carlson, William A. "Professor Macnie as a Novelist." The [University of North Dakota] Alumni Review (December 1934), 4 and 16.
DNAA.
Morgan, A.E. Plagiarism in Utopia. Yellow Springs, OH: The Author, 1944.
PAD, pp. 57-61.
Suvin, Darko. Metamorphoses of Science Fiction. New Haven and London: Yale University Press, 1979.

MAGUIRE, John Francis (1815-1872), Irish journalist, politician, and writer. Born in Cork, MA University of Dublin 1832, called to Irish bar 1843, but became journalist. Founded and edited Cork Examiner in 1841 in support of O'Connell. Member of Parliament from 1852 to 1872, mayor of Cork. In favor of Home Rule, advocated improvements in system of public education in Ireland and other reforms, in 1866 traveled through Canada and US. Besides the SF listed, published The Industrial Movement in Ireland, a biography, a book in defense of the papacy, one on The

Irish in America, and a book of fairy tales (posthumous).
M.s.l.
CGUD, vol. 1.
DNB, vol. 12.
Illustrated London News 61 (9 November 1872).
MEB, vol. 2.

MAITLAND, Edward (1824-1897), occultist. Born at Ipswich
as son of curate and popular Evangelical preacher, BA
Cambridge 1847, was forty-niner in California gold rush,
traveled through the Pacific to Australia where he lived
for some years, returned to England 1857. Brought up in
strictest Evangelical sect, studied to be minister but did
not get ordained, devoted his life to reconciling religion
and "higher" knowledge, combating materialism, vivisection,
and liberalism (including Gladstone's anti-Turkish policy).
From the 1870s on ever more deeply involved in mystic
visions, spiritualist sessions, contact with astral entities and demons, esoteric studies, and the internal politics of occult sects throughout Britain and Europe. Beside
the SF listed and The Pilgrim and the Shrine--his first,
transparently autobiographical novel--wrote about 20
religious and occultist works 1868-1893 (some together with
Anna Kingsford, most notably The Keys of the Creeds and
The Perfect Way), founded first the Hermetic Society
then--"in response to astral intimations"--the Esoteric
Christian Union whose doctrine he wrote in 1892. In later
years claimed to remember his past lives as Marcus
Aurelius, St. John the Evangelist, etc.
M.s.l.
Maitland, Edward. Anna Kingsford, 2 vols. London: Red-
　　way, 1896.
　　　　　. The Pilgrim and the Shrine, 3 vols. London:
　　Tinsley, 1868.
AC, vol. 4.
DNB30.
DUR,pp. 429-35.
EB, vol. 17.

MARKWICK, Edward, originally Edward Markwick JOHNSON (? -
?, fl. 1873-1898), political leader-writer and barrister.
Son of Royal Navy man, practiced in London 1883-1898. Pub-
lished the SF listed and assisted James Williams in The
Schoolmaster and the Law, collaborated in London peri-
odicals.
M.s.l.
FMB.
LL: 1898, s.v. "Counsel."

McIVER (or MacIVER), George M. (? - ?, fl. 1894-1943).
Resided in New South Wales. Besides the SF listed, pub-
lished a book on reminiscences of life in the interior of
Australia, and a book of verse.

MARRIOTT-WATSON, Henry Brereton--see WATSON, H.B.M.

MEARS, Amelia Garland (? ?, fl. 1890-1895). Published the
S-F romance listed, two books of tales, and one of Idylls,
Legends and Lyrics.

MENDES, Henry Pereira--see PEREIRA MENDES, H.

MICHAELIS, Richard C. (1839-1909), German-American journal-
ist. Born in Germany, studied and lived there for the
first part of his life, fought in the Prusso-Austrian war
of 1866. Moved to USA where he edited the German-language
newspapers Chicago Freie Presse and Illinois Staats-
Zeitung and was manager of the papers' publishing company.
The utopian SF listed was first published in USA both in
German and English.
M.s.1.
DUR, pp. 790-95.
WWWA, vol. 1.

MIDDLETON, William H. (1825-1911), planter. Born in
Manchester, England, came to South Africa in 1842 and went
into business, later into plantations of various kinds.
Prominent Anglican, supported Colenso in the religious
debates. Traveler, went around the world twice. Published
two books on coffee planting, two on South African
politics, one in defense of Christianity, and the SF
listed.
M.s.1.
DSAB, vol. 3.

MILLER, George Noyes (1845-1904), US businessman and propa-
gandist. Nephew of Oneida Community founder John Humphrey
Noyes and its business representative. Born at the Putney
Community in Vermont, educated at Oneida, graduated from
Yale in 1872. Head of New York office of the joint-stock
company that was formed in 1881 after the dissolution of
the Oneida commune. Besides the anonymous SF listed,
published a book about the Oneida Community in 1893, one
about its sexual attitudes in 1895, and in 1875 coedited
Noyes's Home Talks.
M.s.1.
Carden, Maren Lockwood. Oneida: Utopian Community to

Modern Corporation. Baltimore: Johns Hopkins Press, 1969.
WWWA, vol. 1.

MILLER, "Joaquin"--i.e, Cincinnatus Hiner or Heine--(ca. 1837-1913), US poet, novelist, and dramatist. There is much disagreement on his early data, partly due to his exaggerations and fabrications; date of birth may be as late as 1841. Born in Indiana as son of Quaker school teacher and preacher, 1850 traveled to Oregon with family, ran away to California gold mines, lived with Digger Indians, married an Indian woman, planned to establish Indian republic at base of Mount Shasta. Imprisoned for horse-thieving in 1859, escaped; claimed to have lived also among Modoc Indians, wrote an autobiographical protest-novel on it. Studied at Columbia College in Oregon, taught school, 1861 admitted to the bar there. Established, with another man, pony express between Washington Territory and Idaho, 1862 purchased and edited proslavery weekly. Judge 1866-1870, published pamphlet in defense of Mexican bandit Joaquin Murieta, took up his first name. Having published two books of poems, traveled to Europe, found favor with Rossetti, gained English recognition. Later returned to USA,, traveled extensively. From 1868 published, besides the two SF listed, 26 books--mostly poetry, but also novels, plays, and a history of Montana--as well as a six-volume edition of his poems; his autobiography was published posthumously.
M.s.1.
Miller, Joaquin. Unwritten History: Life Among the Modocs. Boston: Gregg Press, 1968.
_____. Overland in a Covered Wagon: An Autobiography. Ed. Sidney G.G. Firman. New York and London: Appleton, 1930.
Frost, Orcutt William. Joaquin Miller. New York: Twayne, 1967.
Marberry, M.M. Splendid Poseur. New York: Crowell, 1953.
PAD, pp. 161-63.
RON, pp. 68-74, 129, 159.
Taylor, Walter Fuller. The Economic Novel in America. New York: Octagon Books, 1964.

MINTO, William (1845-1893), professor and man of letters. Born in Aberdeenshire, studied at Aberdeen where he received MA in classics, mathematics, and philosophy, and at Oxford 1866-1867. Assistant for logic and English literature in Aberdeen 1867-1873 and then professor 1880 on, after an interlude in London as editor of the Examiner

and <u>London Opinion</u>. Contributed to leading English
reviews and to <u>Encyclopaedia Britannica</u> on literary subjects. Besides the SF listed, published from 1869 two more
novels, five well-argued books on literary topics, a manual
of logic, two books on Defoe and one on Byron, as well as a
one-act farce. Also edited three books by Sir Walter Scott
and an autobiography of W.B. Scott.
<u>M.s.l.</u>
<u>Athenaeum</u>, 4 March 1893, p. 282.
<u>DNB</u>, vol. 13.
<u>EB</u>, vol. 18.
<u>MEB</u>, vol. 2.

MITCHELL, John Ames (1845-1918), US editor, novelist,
artist. Born in New York, educated at Harvard, studied art
and architecture in Boston and Paris. In 1883 founded the
humorous weekly <u>Life</u>, known for its biting political
satire and cartoons. Outspoken opponent and derider of modern medicine. From 1881 published, besides the SF listed,
nine novels (including another SF, <u>Drowsy</u>, 1917), two collections of stories, mostly fantasy, a book of poems, and a
book of illustrations.
<u>M.s.l.</u>
<u>AA</u>.
[Clute, John.] Entry in <u>SFE</u>.
<u>DAB</u>, vol. 13.

MOFFAT, W. Graham (? - ?, fl. 1893). Published the SF
listed, with John WHITE (q.v.).

MOORE, G.H. (? - ?, fl. 1886). Not to be confused with any
other UK George or G.H. Moores on which there are data.
Internal evidence from the anonymously published comic SF
faintly suggests he might have been living in Ireland.

MORGAN, Arthur (? - ?, fl. 1891). Published with Charles
R. BROWN (q.v.) the SF listed. Not to be confused with
Arthur Morgan, premier of Queensland (1856-1916), nor with
A.E. Morgan, US college president and utopian scholar.

MORRIS, Alfred (? - ?, fl. 1892-1893). Was provincial secretary to the conservative Primrose League for the metropol-
itan boroughs, toured Ireland propagating Unionism. Besides the SF listed, published <u>Discussions on Labour</u>
<u>Questions</u>. Not to be confused with various US persons,
for example, Alfred Hennen Morris (1864-1959).
<u>M.s.l.</u>
<u>DUR</u>,pp. 526-31.

Robb, Janet Henderson. <u>The Primrose League 1883-1906</u>. New York: AMS Press, 1968, p. 199.

MORRIS, William (1834-1896), poet, writer, designer, later printer, socialist political leader, and lecturer. See for this well-known author any history of English literature and the works below.
<u>M.s.l.</u>
Bradley, Ian. <u>William Morris and His World</u>. New York: Scribner's, 1978.
Henderson, Philip. <u>William Morris</u>. London: Thames & Hudson, 1957.
Kirchhoff, Frederick. <u>William Morris</u>. Boston: Twayne, 1979.
Mackail, J.W. <u>The Life of William Morris</u>. New York: Blom, 1968.
Morris, May. <u>The Introduction to The Collected Works of William Morris</u>. New York: Oriole, [1973].
_____ . <u>William Morris, Artist, Writer, Socialist</u>. New York: Russell & Russell, 1966.
Suvin, Darko. <u>Metamorphoses of Science Fiction</u>. New Haven and London: Yale University Press, 1979 (with further bibliography).
Thompson, Paul. <u>The Work of William Morris</u>. London: Heinemann, 1967.

MÜLLER, Ernst (? - ?, fl. 1891-1892), German political satirist. Besides the SF listed (translated into English as by "Julian West"), published two booklets on taxes and socialism.

MUNRO, John (1849-1930), civil engineer, professor of mechanical engineering at Bristol. Beside the SF listed, published seven books popularizing electricity and the telegraph, the biography of Thomson, Lord Kelvin, the tale <u>The Downfall of Dover</u>, and an autobiographical study, as well as contributions to periodicals (including two S-F stories).
<u>M.s.l.</u>
[Eggeling, John.] Entry in <u>SFE</u>.

MURPHY, George Read (1856-1925), Australian magistrate and writer. Lived in Sydney, warden for Victoria goldfields, later police magistrate and chairman of the City Court Bench. Beside the SF listed, published a book on prison reform, one on peace, two novels, and a history of Australia in fictional form.
<u>M.s.l.</u>

MAL.
Obituary in the Argus (Melbourne), 16 September 1925, p.
25.

MURRAY, George Gilbert Aimé (1866-1957),classicist.   Born
in Sydney to prominent Irish family, left Australia at 11,
educated in England with studies at Oxford where he won
numerous scholarships and prizes.   Fellow at Oxford 1888,
at age of 23 professor of Greek at Glasgow, 1907-1936 at
Oxford.   Became one of the central figures of British
cultural life as lecturer and writer, primarily of epoch-
making and still authoritative books on Hellenic epic and
drama, as well as verse translator of drama which G.B. Shaw
(who, with some distortion, modeled his Cusins in Major
Barbara on him) hailed as original plays.   Liberal and
utopian in the wake of Mill and Shelley, speaker and worker
for causes such as women's suffrage, pacifism, and education for world citizenship.   Founder--and chairman of the
executive council, 1923-1938--of the League of Nations
Union, president (1945-1957) of the United Nations' Association.   Broadcaster, editor of Home University Library;
besides nonfiction published the S-F novel listed, two
original plays, and the unfinished autobiography adduced
below.   His tablet in the Westminster Abbey reads: "Verae
humanitatis exemplar/Quo vivente Graecorum veterum litterae
revixerunt/Nec de concordia gentium fas erat desperare."
M.s.l.
Smith, Jean, and Arnold Toynbee, eds. Gilbert Murray: An
    Unfinished Autobiography: With Contributions by His
    Friends. London: Allen & Unwin, 1960.
DNB60.
EB, vol. 31.

NEWCOMB, Simon (1835-1909), US astronomer and mathematician.   Born in Nova Scotia, son of country-school teacher,
at 16 apprentice to physician in New Brunswick, then
teacher in county schools in New England.   Worked as
mathematician while putting himself through a study of
mathematics and astronomy at Harvard.   From 1861 professor
of mathematics at US Naval University, in charge of various
congressional activities in astronomy such as telescope
construction and observation of transit of Venus.   His most
notable achievements were the theory and tables for the
motions of all of the Sun's planets and the Moon.   For many
years director of US Nautical Almanac and editor of
American Journal of Mathematics, received numerous awards
and honorary degrees.   Published over 500 books, articles,
and lectures, mainly on astronomy and mathematics, but also

on popular science, economics, and other subjects. The SF listed is his only venture into book-length fiction, but he wrote at least one more S-F story.
M.s.l.
Newcomb, Simon. Reminiscences of an Astronomer. London and New York: Harper, 1903.
Asimov, Isaac. Asimov's Biographical Encyclopedia of Science and Technology. New York: Avon, 1972.
Campbell, W.W. Biographical Memoir Simon Newcomb 1835–1909. Washington DC: Government Printing Office, 1924.
Mullen, R.D. [Reviews of His Wisdom, the Defender and "The End of the World."] SFS, no. 6 (1975), 186, and no. 10 (1976), 298.

NICHOLSON, Joseph Shield (1850-1927), professor of economics, writer. Born in Lincolnshire, son of Independent minister, received BA in philosophy at London 1870, studied mathematics and philosophy at Edinburgh and Cambridge, received MA from London in 1877, also listened to law lectures in Heidelberg with fellow-student J.G. Frazer. Tutor in political economy and history at Cambridge, 1880-1925 professor of political economy and mercantile law in Edinburgh. Follower of Adam Smith, supporter of a federated British Empire and World War I, and opponent of socialism, "economic utopias," and Marxism, published a profusion of lectures, essays, and books on economic theory and its political application. Contributed to Encyclopaedia Britannica and Chambers's Encyclopaedia, wrote introduction and notes to an edition of Smith's Wealth of Nations, and a chess column in the Times. Received honorary LLDs from the universities of St. Andrews and Edinburgh. Besides the two anonymously published S-F romances listed--of which Thoth had success and was published in the US and Germany--published another romance and several books on literature, mainly Greek and Italian, including two on Ariosto as the father of modern romance.
M.s.l.
DNB30.
Scott, W.R. "Joseph Shield Nicholson 1850-1927." Offprint from Proceedings of the British Academy, vol. 14. London: Milford, [1928].

NISBET, Hume (1849-1921), writer and artist. Born in Scotland, lived in Australia 1865-1872, theatrical experience in Melbourne. Returned to England 1872, no success as artist in London. Associate of John Ruskin, influenced by his social and political views. Art master at college in Edinburgh to 1883, illustrated books, exhibited at Royal

Scottish Academy. In mid-1880s returned to Australia. Went to New Guinea to sketch natives, recorded strong views on treatment of aborigines in his first Australian romance The Land of the Hibiscus Blossom. Wrote chapters for Cassell's Picturesque Australasia and five books on art. His fiction includes four volumes of verse, two books of travel, and 46 novels and romances published 1888-1905, some with S-F elements or lost-race romances, including the marginal SF listed. Illustrated 11 books.
M.s.l.
DAuB, vol. 2.
MAL.

NORTH, Delaval, pseudonym? (? - ?, fl. 1887).

NORTH, Franklin H. (? - ?, fl. 1898), US writer.
M.s.l.
RON, passim.

NORTON, Philip (? - ?, fl. 1866-1924), clergyman and author. Graduated from University of London 1866, minister of splinter Protestant sects 1871-1879, of Church of England 1879-1924. Published three books on religious topics, a biography, a book of verse, I See Through Mr. Britling--a reply to WELLS's Mr. Britling Sees It Through--and under the pseudonym Artegall Smith the SF listed. Also published two books of prayers with H.L. Harkness.
M.s.l.
CCD for 1924.

OAKHURST, William (? - ?, fl. 1891).

O'BRIEN, Fitz-James (1828-1862), British and US writer. Born in Limerick, Ireland, son of well-to-do lawyer, published in Irish, Scottish, and English magazines, came to New York in 1852. Contributed stories influenced by POE, Hawthorne, and HOFFMANN, but especially poetry, to numerous magazines; the SF listed first appeared in the Atlantic Monthly. The S-F story "How I Overcame My Gravity" was published anonymously and posthumously in Harper's Monthly. Three collections of his works were published in the 1880s, and one in 1925.
M.s.l.
Franklin, H. Bruce. Future Perfect. New York: Oxford University Press, 1978.
Moskowitz, Sam. Explorers of the Infinite. Cleveland and New York: World, 1963, pp. 62-72.
OCAL.

Wolle, Francis. _Fitz-James O'Brien_. Colorado University
   Studies series B. Studies in Humanities, vol, 2, no. 2.
   Boulder, CO: University of Colorado Press, 1944.

O'GRADY, Standish James (1846-1928), Irish folklorist and
antiquarian. Born in County Cork, son of Protestant clergyman and small landowner, educated at University of Dublin,
called to bar in 1872, never practiced. Contributed literary articles to _Gentlemen's Magazine_, lead-writer for
Daily Express (Dublin), editor of _Kilkenny Moderator_
from 1898, in 1900 founded and edited to 1907 _All Ireland
Review_. Besides the pseudonymous SF listed, published
seven books on early Irish history, legends, and politics,
five literary reworkings of Irish legends, a volume of
short stories, three novels, one historical romance, one
historical play, a book on Irish bardic literature, and
three other books of nonfiction, some as "Arthur Clive."
Influenced the writers of the Irish revival.
M.s.l.
Marcus, Phillip L. _Standish O'Grady_. Lewisburg: Bucknell University Press, 1970.

O'NEIL, Henry Nelson (1817-1881), painter, later musician
and author. Born in St. Petersburg, brought to England at
age 6, in 1837-1842 member of student painters' group "The
Clique." Associate of Royal Academy 1860, exhibited about
100 paintings there. Later shifted interests to violin
playing and writing. Published, besides the SF listed, two
books on art and two satires. Not to be confused with
Henry O'Neill, Irish writer.
M.s.l.
DUR, pp. 404-06.
Forbes, Christopher Charles. _Royal Academy (1837-1901),
   Revisited_. [New York: Forbes Magazine, 1975], pp. 114,
   152.
Trollope, Anthony. Obituary in the _Times_, 15 March 1880,
   p. 6.

OPPENHEIM, Edward Phillips (1866-1946), novelist. Born in
London, son of merchant. Wrote serial stories for _Weekly
Telegraph_ (Sheffield); from 1887 published about 160 popu-
lar novels, mostly spy thrillers, mysteries (some as
"Anthony Partridge"), and romantic fantasies, including the
SF listed (and some more SF after 1900), and his autobiogra-
phy. After World War I earned large sums, especially from
US magazine serialization, lived on the Riviera.
M.s.l.
Oppenheim, Edward Phillips. _The Pool of Memory_. Boston:

Little, Brown, 1942.
[Clute, John.] Entry in SFE.
DNB50.
Standish, Robert (pseud. of Digby George Gerahty). The
  Prince of Storytellers. London: Davies, 1957.
WGT.

PALLANDER, Edwin (? - ?, fl. 1896-1902). Published two S-F
novels, the one listed and The Adventures of a Micro-Man,
as well as a Pacific travelog; wrote an S-F story with E.
DOUGLASS (q.v.).

PALMER, John Henry (? - ?, fl. 1875-1897), US writer.
Besides the SF listed, published Individual, Family, and
National Poverty.

PAYN, James (1830-1898), writer. Son of civil servant,
born in Cheltenham, educated at Eton and Cambridge, as
student wrote verse and articles in journals and published
a volume of poetry in 1852. Lived 1858-1861 in Edinburgh,
later in London. Influential editor of Chambers's
Journal 1859-1874, of Cornhill Magazine 1883-1896, from
1888 wrote weekly column in Illustrated London News.
Regular contributor to Dickens's publication Household
Words, under Dickens's influence to some extent. Pub-
lished more than 100 volumes of sketches, essays, and
novels of adventure, society, and sentimental melodrama.
M.s.l.
Payn, James. Gleams of Memory. London: Smith, Elder,
  1894.
_____. Some Literary Recollections. London: Smith,
  Elder, 1884.
DNB30.
EB, vol. 21.
MEB, vol. 6.
Stephen, Leslie. "Introduction," in James Payn, The Back-
  water of Life. London: Smith, Elder, 1899.
Tinsley, William. Random Recollections of an Old Publish-
  er. London: Simpkin, Marshall, 1900.

PECK, Bradford (1853-1935), US businessman and utopianist.
Born in Lewiston, ME, after working his way up through a
department store in Boston while attending night school
established in 1880 own store in Lewiston which became the
largest one in New England outside Boston. Also president
of B. Peck Real Estate and vice-president of Joliet (IL)
Dry Goods. Devout Christian, founded in 1899 cooperative
association, turned his store over to it 1902-1912, attempt-

ed a nation-wide movement which failed. Besides the utopi-
an SF listed, published under the pseudonym "Truth" a book
on cooperation.
M.s.l.
Cary, Francine C. "The World a Department Store:
  Bradford Peck. . . ." American Quarterly 29 (1977),
  370-84.
Davies, Wallace Evan. "A Collectivist Experiment Down
  East." New England Quarterly 20 (1947), 471-91.
DUR, pp. 810-14.

PEMBERTON, Sir Max (1863-1950), novelist, journalist, play-
wright. Born in Birmingham, son of merchant, BA Cambridge
1884, first editor of boys' magazine Chums 1892-1893, is
best known for juvenile SF. From 1896 to 1906 editor of
Cassell's Magazine, where many of his stories appeared;
frequent contributor to Vanity Fair, Standard, and
other periodicals; later a director of Northcliffe Newspapers and justice of peace, in 1920 founded the London
School of Journalism, knighted in 1928. From 1891 to 1936
published over 60 novels and short story collections of
adventure, romance, and sea-oriented Sf for adults and
children (the SF includes, beside the books listed, Pro
Patria, The Giant's Gate, The House Under the Sea,
White Walls, and Captain Black, all 1901-1910), also
stage plays, revues, two biographies, a handbook for ama-
teur motorists, and a book of reminiscences. Edited Cas-
sell's Pocket Library and with B.F. Robinson The Isthmian
Library. Was one of the first people to drive a car in
Britain.
M.s.l.
Pemberton, Max. Sixty Years Ago and After. London:
  Hutchinson, 1936.
AC, vol. 5.
[Eggeling, John]. Entry in SFE.
DEA.
New York Times, 23 February 1950.
WWCL.

PEMBERTON, Robert (? - ?, fl. 1849-1859), Fellow of the
Royal Society of Literature, educator. Besides the SF list-
ed, published eight books, lectures, and letters on educa-
tion, and An Address to the Bishops and Clergy . . . on
Robert Owen's Proclamation of the Millennial State. . . .
M.s.l.
DUR, pp. 385-86.

PENRICE, Arthur. This name of the narrator of Skyward

and Earthward (1875) is in all probability a pseudonym.

PEREIRA MENDES, Henry--sometimes listed as MENDES, Henry
Pereira--(1852-1937), US rabbi, teacher, and writer. Born
in England of prominent Spanish-Jewish family, educated at
University College, London, and Northwick College, rabbi in
Manchester 1874-1877, came to US in 1877, rabbi of Seph-
ardic synagogue in New York City to 1920. Received MD from
New York University (but did not practice), doctorate in
divinity from New York Jewish Theological Seminary. Active
in numerous caritative, educational, and ecumenic causes, a
leader in US Jewish and world Zionist organizations,
involved in liberalizing immigration laws, first Jew to
become grand chaplain of Masonic Lodge of New York State,
founded the American Hebrew magazine. Professor of
history at Jewish Theological Seminary and of homiletics at
Rabbinical College of America. 1892 wounded for undiv-
ulged reasons by a man he was helping. Composer of litur-
gic music, prolific writer of historical articles, pamphlets, poems, hymns, plays for religious schools, children's
books, Jewish educational and religious books, including
the utopian SF listed.
M.s.l.
DAB, vol. 22.
NCAB, vol. 39.
Pool, D. de Sola. "H. Pereira Mendes." American Jewish
   Year Book 40 (1938), 41-60.
WWWA, vol. 1.

PERRY, Walter Copland (1814-1911), schoolmaster and
archeologist. Born in Norwich, son of clergyman and schoolmaster, educated in Manchester, York, and Göttingen.
Classical tutor in York, minister in Exeter 1838-1844,
became Anglican in 1844, studied at Middle Temple, called
to bar 1851, schoolmaster in Germany, returned to England
1875. Besides the SF listed, published from 1843 to 1908
two novels (one under the pseudonym of "John Copland"),
children's versions of the Iliad and the Odyssey, a
book and a catalog on art of antiquity, a book of French
history, one on German universities, a book of addresses
and reflections, The Women of Homer, and a book about
Sicily. Translated from German von Sybel's History of the
French Revolution.
M.s.l.
DNB11.
Times, 1 and 3 January 1912.

PHILPOT, Joseph Henry (1850-1939), physician. MD Universi-

ty of London 1875, doctor in fashionable quarter of London. Was sub-dean and house physician at King's College Hospital and some other London hospitals, editor of the Medical Times. Retired in the 1920s, awarded MBE. Under the pseudonym "Philip Lafargue" published three novels, including the SF listed, and a book of stories. Under his own name published a book on Wace and wrote introduction to a book by J.C. Philpot and W. Tiptaft.
M.s.l.
MR: 1925 and MR:1939.

POE, Edgar Allan (1809-1849), US poet, short-story writer, essayist, and critic. See for this well-known author any history of US literature and the works below.
M.s.l.
Allen, Hervey. Israfel. New York: Farrar & Rinehart, 1934.
Barthes, Roland. "Analyse textuelle d'un conte d'Edgar Poe," in Claude Chabrol, ed., Sémiotique narrative et textuelle. Paris: Larousse, 1973.
Bittner, William P. Poe. Boston: Little,Brown, 1962.
Ketterer, David. The Rationale of Deception in Poe. Baton Rouge: Louisiana State University Press, 1979.
Quinn, Arthur H. Edgar Allan Poe. New York: Appleton-Century, 1941.
Sinclair, David. Edgar Allan Poe. London: Dent, 1977.
Suvin, Darko. Metamorphoses of Science Fiction. New Haven and London: Yale University Press, 1979 (with further bibliography).
Symons, Julian. The Tell-tale Heart. London: Faber & Faber, 1978.

POTTER, Robert (? - ?, fl. 1856-1908), Australian Anglican clergyman. BA from Trinity College Dublin 1856, ordained 1864, lecturer in theology at Trinity College Melbourne 1878, canon of Melbourne cathedral 1883, chaplain to the bishop of Melbourne 1903. Published three books on religious topics, a book of poems, and the SF listed--remaindered copies of which were subsequently given to pupils as Divinity prizes.
M.s.l.
CCD for 1908.
MAL.
[Nicholls, Peter.] Entry in SFE.
Sussex, Lucy. "The Germ Growers." Science Fiction (Nedlands, W. Australia) (1980), 229-33.
Turner, George. "Science Fiction in Australia." SF Commentary (January-October 1979), 7.

PRATT, Cornelia Atwood, later COMER (? -1929, fl. 1896-1912), US journalist. From 1896 published two books of stories, the novel A Daughter of a Stoic, and with Richard Slee the SF listed.
M.s.1.
DNAA.

PUTNAM, George Haven (1844-1930), US publisher. Born in England, son of the publisher George Palmer Putnam, brought to US at age three. Studied at Sorbonne and Berlin, did scientific work at Göttingen, served in Union army during Civil War. President of G.P. Putnam's Sons, director of Knickerbocker Press, carried on father's fight for international copyright, organized American Publishers' Copyright League in 1886, responsible for copyright acts of 1891 and 1909. Founded American branch of the English-Speaking Union, served on grand jury 1879-1914. Wrote on publishing, copyright, and censorship, also two books about his war experiences, two more autobiographical works, biographies of his father and of Lincoln, a foreword to Jefferson's autobiography, as well as a story for children and the SF listed (under the pseudonym G.H.P.).
M.s.1.
Putnam, George Haven. Memories of My Youth, 1844-1865. New York and London: Putnam's, 1914.
_____. Memories of a Publisher, 1865-1915. New York and London: Putnam's, 1915.
DAB, vol. 15.
REAL.
WWWA, vol. 1.

REEVE, Benjamin (? - ?, fl. 1898-1920). Besides the SF listed, published to 1920 three books on religious topics --of which two biographies--and a history pamphlet for the Protestant Truth Society. Most probably not the same person as Arthur Benjamin Reeve (1880-1936), US Catholic author of the "scientific detective" Craig Kennedy series.

RICHARDSON, Sir Benjamin Ward (1828-1896), physician and author. MD from St. Andrew's University 1854, also honorary MA and LLD 1877, practiced at Barnes, in London from 1855, became lecturer, made medical discoveries in heart disease, started Journal of Public Health, 1855-1856, Social Science Review, 1862, Asclepiad, 1884-1896, which he wrote entirely by himself, planned city of health "Hygieiopolis," president of British Medical Temperance Association, knighted 1893. Published from 1858

about 70 publications, mainly numerous medical works on blood and heart disease but also works promoting health through exercise and hygiene, combating tobacco and alcohol; his two nonmedical books include the partial SF listed.
M.s.l.
Richardson, B.W. Vita Medica. London: Longmans, Green, 1897.
DNB, vol. 22.
MEB, vol. 3.
MacNalty, Arthur S. A Biography of Sir Benjamin W. Richardson. London: Harvey & Blythe, 1950.

RICHTER, Eugen (1839-1906), German politician. Born in Düsseldorf, son of army physician, studied at Bonn, Berlin, and Heidelberg, entered government service. Elected member of Reichstag 1867, of Prussian Parliament 1869, one of the most influential politicians in Germany. Member of Progressive party, advocate of laissez-faire, vehement opponent both of socialism and of Bismarck's colonial policy, state socialism, and increase of army. Budget expert, promoted free trade, participated in consumer cooperatives' movement. Party journalist, founded weekly Reichsfreund, in 1855 established daily Freisinnige Zeitung. From 1867-1896 published, besides the satirical SF listed, five books and pamphlets on economics and the memories adduced below.
M.s.l.
Richter, Eugen. Jugenderinnerungen. Berlin: Fortschritt, 1893.
_____. Im alten Reichstag, 2 vols. Berlin: Fortschritt, 1894-1896.
[Bellamy, Edward.] "Some Account of Eugen Richter's Anti-Socialist Romance." New Nation 3 (3 June 1893), 273-75.
EB, vol. 23.
Ein Freisinniger (pseud.). Eugen Richters Sprengbombe und ihre Wirkung. Berlin: Wilhelmi, 1893.
Hirsch, Felix E. "Bismarck's Enemy." Forum 105 (1946), 873-79.
MEL, vol. 20.
Ullstein, Leopold. Eugen Richter als Publizist und Herausgeber.
WWW, vol. 1.

RICKETT, Sir Joseph Compton (1847-1919), businessman, re' - gious and political leader. Chairman of an industrial fi.m to 1902, perhaps the most prominent lay Nonconformist (a moderate Evangelical) of his time, Liberal MP 1895-1919,

minister in the 1916 government. Preached, wrote many articles on religious, political, and societal subjects. Wrote
verse, mostly religious, collected after 1876 in two books
of poems under the pseudonym of Maurice Baxter, which he
also used for the semiautobiographical novel James
Strathgeld. Knighted in 1907, changed the name Rickett to
"Compton-Rickett" in 1908. Published also, beside the SF
listed, four books on Christianity 1893-1917.
M.s.l.
Baxter, Maurice (pseud. of Joseph Compton-Rickett). James
    Strathgeld, 2 vols. London: Guilford, 1873.
Compton-Rickett, Arthur, ed. Joseph Compton-Rickett: A
    Memoir. Bournemouth: Cooper, 1922.

ROBERTS, J.W. (? - ?, fl. 1893), US writer. Besides the SF
listed, published Laws of the Mind.

ROBINSON, Edward A. (? - ?, fl. 1884-1894), US writer.
With G.A. WALL (q.v.) published the SF listed and one other
novel in 1894.

ROBINSON, Philip Stewart (1847-1902), naturalist and
author. Born at Chunar, India, son of army chaplain and
journal editor. Educated at Marlborough College 1860-1865,
librarian at Cardiff 1866-1868. Went to India 1869, assisted father in editing of Pioneer. Editor of Revenue
Archives of Benares province 1872, professor of literature,
logic, and metaphysics in Allahabad 1873, censor of vernacu-
lar press. Returned to England 1877; correspondent in
Afghanistan and South Africa and leader writer for Daily
Telegraph. Publisher's reader for Sampson Low and Co.
1878-1893, edited and prepared for press Stanley's Through
the Dark Continent 1878. Correspondent of various
journals and periodicals in USA and Egypt 1881-1882,
lectured throughout US and Australia, correspondent of
Pall Mall Gazette and Associated Press in Spanish-
American war. During last years of his life wrote articles
for Contemporary Review and Good Words. Besides the SF
listed, published from 1871 10 books of natural history and
of sketches about India, a book on Cyprus, one on the US,
and pamphlets on India and Afghanistan; also four novels--
mostly about India--and two books of stories (of which one
in collaboration with his brothers).
M.s.l.
The Cambridge History of English Literature, vol. 14.
    Eds. A.W. Ward and A.R. Waller. Cambridge: Cambridge
    University Press, 1964, p. 341.
DIB.

DNB11.
SAIF, pp. 58-61.

ROE, William James (1843-1915), US writer. Graduated from West Point 1867. Published 10 books including some verse and defense of free thought, but mostly novels under the pseudonyms of "Genone Hudor" and "G.I. Cervus."

ROGERS, Lebbeus Harding (1847-1932), US businessman. Born in Cincinnati, educated at Woodward College there, president and director of Rogers Manifold and Carbon Paper Company in New York, died in Portland, OR. Besides the SF listed, published two biographical sketches and a volume of information for businessmen.
M.s.l.
Ohio Authors and Their Books. Ed. William Coyle. Cleveland and New York: World, 1962.
WWWA, vol. 4.

ROSEWATER, Frank (1856-19??, fl. 1882-1925), US reformer. Published four utopian S-F novels (the last under the pseudonym "Marian & Franklin Mayoe"), an adventure story, a pamphlet about the future, as well as a book and a pamphlet about industry and trade.

ROSS, Joseph Carne--see CARNE-ROSS, Joseph.

ROWCROFT, Charles (179?-1856). Educated at Eton 1809-1810, in Tasmania from 1821 to 1825, sheep-breeder, justice of the peace from 1822, in 1825 went to Brazil, later returned to England, 1852-1856 UK consul at Cincinnati. Besides the SF listed, published from 1844 eleven novels (of which two posthumously) dealing with public schools, Australian adventures (in Australia known for his pioneering Tales of the Colonies--first series published anonymously in 1843), life among the London poor, the condition of women, etc.; also one book on the railway system and one exposing the penal system.
M.s.l.
The Cambridge History of English Literature, vol. 14. Eds. A.W. Ward and A.R. Waller. Cambridge: Cambridge University Press, 1964, pp. 369-70.
GHAL, pp. 86-90.
MAL, vols. 1 and 2.
MEB, vol. 3.

RUSTOFF, Michael, pseudonym? (? - ?, fl. 1891).

RYAN, G.H. (? - ?, fl. 1880).

SCHOFIELD, Alfred Taylor (1846-1929), doctor and writer.
Born in Lancashire, studied medicine in London and Brussels, MD 1884. Practiced in London, officer in many health
and educational associations, also religious popularizer,
vice-president of Prophecy Investigation Society. Published nearly 50 titles, either of medicine and medical
popularization (including the marginal SF listed), especially on nervous diseases, the mind, hygiene, and eugenics,
and/or on Christianity, arguing for supernaturalism and
against materialism (including the nonfiction Another
World using ABBOTT's [q.v.] Flatland and HINTON's [q.v.]
Scientific Romances I-II).
M.s.l.
Locke, George. A Spectrum of Fantasy. London: Ferret
    Fantasy, 1980.
WWW, vol. 3.

SERVISS, Garrett Putman (1851-1929), US journalist, writer,
and science popularizer. Born in Sharon Springs, NY,
studied science at Cornell and law at Columbia, became
journalist. Editorial writer on the New York Sun until
1892 under Albert Page Mitchell and Charles Dana, specialized in astronomy; lectured on travel, history, and astronomy, was editor of Collier's Popular Science Library; in
1897 wrote Edison's Conquest of Mars as journal serial,
published in book form in 1947. Published the SF listed
and four more S-F novels and stories after 1900; also over
a dozen books on popular astronomy (of which three with
Leon Barrett), a work on the Shakespeare-Bacon controversy,
one on public speaking, and a series of lectures on "great
men."
M.s.l.
[Edwards, Malcolm J.] Entry in SFE.
Searles, A. Langley. "Introduction" to G.P. Serviss,
    Edison's Conquest of Mars. Los Angeles: Carcosa
    House, 1947 (variant rpt. as "Introduction" to idem, A
    Columbus of Space. Westport, CT: Hyperion Press,
    1974).
WWWA, vol. 1.

SHANNON, John C. (? - ?, fl. 1894-1901). Published two
books of stories and D'Aubisé: A Reminiscence; wrote
for the Walsall Advertiser.

SHELLEY, Mary Wollstonecraft, née Godwin (1797-1851),
writer. See for this well-known author most histories of

SF and 19th-century English literature as well as the works below.

M.s.1.

Grylls, R. Glynn. Mary Shelley. London: Oxford University Press, 1938.

Ketterer, David. "Mary Shelley and Science Fiction." SFS, no. 15 (1978), 172-78 (bibliography).

Levine, George, and Ulrich Knoepflmacher, eds. The Endurance of "Frankenstein." Berkeley: University of California Press, 1979.

Nitchie, Elizabeth. Mary Shelley. New Brunswick, NJ: Rutgers University Press, 1953.

Sterrenburg, Lee. "The Last Man." Nineteenth Century Fiction 33 (1978), 324-47.

Suvin, Darko. Metamorphoses of Science Fiction. New Haven and London: Yale University Press, 1979 (with further bibliography).

SHEIL, Matthew Phipps (1865-1947), novelist. Born in West Indies as son of Irish Methodist preacher, studied medicine at University of London but did not graduate, taught school for a short time, worked as interpreter. From 1895 published 26 novels, a book of poems, and four volumes of short stories--to 1913 mostly weird fiction, detective novels, and SF (of which several in collaboration with Louis TRACY as "Gordon Holmes," and one with W.T. STEAD, q.v., both), and from 1923 mostly ones dealing with his Nietzschean theory of "Overman" and other philosophical and political beliefs, including the posthumous Science, Life and Literature. Translated from German H. Smitt's The Hungarian Revolution.

M.s.1.

Shiel, M.P. "About Myself," in A. Reynolds Morse, The Works of M.P. Shiel Updated (see below).

Brophy, Brigid. "Rare Books." New Statesman 14 (June 1963), 904-05.

[Eggeling, John.] Entry in SFE.

"Fantastica." Times Literary Supplement (5 July 1963), 497.

Morse, A. Reynolds. The Works of M.P. Shiel Updated. Los Angeles: FPCI, 1980.

Moskowitz, Sam. Explorers of the Infinite. Cleveland and New York: World, 1963, pp. 142-56.

Mullen, R.D. [Review of The Lord of the Sea.] SFS, no. 6 (1975), 186-87.

Stableford, Brian. "The Yellow Danger," in Frank N. Magill, ed., Survey of Science Fiction Literature, vol. 5. Englewood Cliffs NY: Salem, 1979.

Stevenson, Lionel. "Purveyors of Myth and Magic," in his
  Yesterday and After. New York: Barnes & Noble, 1967.
WWW, vol. 3.

SINGER, Ignatius (? - ?, fl. 1882-1919), chemist and poly-
math of Hungarian origin. Around 1890 lived in Australia,
in 1908 worked in Bradford, UK, where he held a high post
in chemical industry. From 1882 to 1919 published three
theological books, a Simplified Grammar of the Hungarian
Language, and--with L.H. BERENS (q.v.)--a book on physics
Government by the People, as well as the anonymous SF
listed, which was after its 1894 edition reissued in 1910,
1927, and 1934 by the Henry George movement, as well as
translated into various languages including Hungarian and
Japanese.
M.s.l.
BA, vol. 6.
Braun, Robert. "A Fordító Elöszava"; and Jászi,
  Oszkár, "Elöszó"; both in Anon., Kormányzóságom
  Története. Budapest: Athenaeum, [1912], pp. 3-10.
Kretzoi, Charlotte. "Dimensions of Space and Time: Late
  Nineteenth Century American Utopias." Acta Litteraria
  Acad. Scientiarum Hungaricae 20, no. 1-2 (1978), 65-80.

SLEE, Richard (? - ?, fl. 1892-1899), US writer. Published
around the turn of the century two medical pamphlets, and
with C.A. PRATT (q.v.) the SF listed.

SMYTHE, Alfred (? - ?, fl. 1893-1931). Published two books
of poems, the SF listed, a comedy opera, and A New National Anthem.

SOLEMAN, William (? - ?. fl. 1863-1876). Published a book
of love poems, a story, and the satirical SF listed.

SPENCE, J.C. (? - ?, fl. 1897). No data available. Since
he was a Spencerian, the name may be an honorific pseudonym; on the other hand, it is not impossible it might be a
variant form of James Lewis Thomas Chalmers SPENCE, known
as Lewis Spence (1874-1955), UK author of a book of fantasy
stories.

STEAD, William Thomas (1849-1912), journalist and writer.
Born in Northumberland, son of Congregationalist minister,
at 14 apprenticed to merchant's office. Editor of liberal
daily Northern Echo from 1871, moved to London 1880,
assistant editor then editor of Pall Mall Gazette. Under
his editorship the journal initiated new social and politi-

cal movements, had great influence on politics and journalism, introduced the "interview." Champion of women,
achieved notoriety and sat in prison three months for
exposé on prostitution. Imperialist, had great influence
on Cecil Rhodes, later supporter of Boers and peace movement, went down with the Titanic. Founded the monthly
Review of Reviews in 1890 (US edition founded 1891,
Australian edition 1892), edited Borderland (1893-1897),
a periodical on psychic phenomena. Began cheap reprints.
Besides the SF listed, published from 1885 over 25 books
and pamphlets on political and social issues, numerous char-
acter sketches, two stories, a passion play, and Letters
from Julia, a book about automatic writing.
M.s.l.
DNB21.
Schults, Raymond L. Crusader in Babylon. Lincoln, NE:
    University of Nebraska Press, 1972.
Smith, Warren Sylvester. The London Heretics, 1870-1914.
    London: Constable, 1967.
Whyte, Frederic. The Life of W.T. Stead, 2 vols. New
    York and London: Garland, 1971.

STEWART, Ritson (? - ?, fl. 1888). With Stanley STEWART
published the S-F novel listed.

STEWART, Stanley (? - ?, fl. 1888). With Ritson STEWART
published the S-F novel listed.

STIMSON, Frederic Jesup (1855-1943), US lawyer, professor,
diplomat, author. Born in Dedham, MA, educated at Harvard,
professor of law there, assistant attorney-general of Massachusetts 1884-85, ambassador to Argentina and Brazil. From
1879 published 11 books and numerous lectures, articles,
and pamphlets on social and political issues, mostly on
labor law, also 12 novels--the first one with John T. Wheel-
wright, and another SF with him and some others--two books
of stories, a book of odes and verses, and a historical
verse-drama. Most of his fiction was published under the
pseudonym of "J.S. of Dale." Translated José Enrique
Rodo's Ariel, and with F.A. Korbay texts of Hungarian
melodies.
M.s.l.
Mullen, R.D. [Review of The King's Men.] SFS, no. 6
    (1975), 185.
NCAB, vol. 44.
REAL.

STOCKTON, Frank--Francis--Richard (1834-1902), US writer.

Born in Philadelphia, became wood engraver, then journalist
on Philadelphia and New York papers, in the 1870s editor of
Hearth and Home, on staff of Scribner's Monthly, assistant editor of St. Nicholas. Lived in New York and after
1899 in West Virginia. Very popular contributor to magazines and best-selling writer, from 1870 published over 45
novels (including the two SF listed) and collections of
short stories (at least half a dozen stories being SF).
Wrote tales for children, genteel comedy, and successful
fantasy (e.g., Rudder Grange, 1879), sometimes under the
pseudonym of "Paul Fort" and "John Lewees." A collected
edition of his works was published 1899-1904 in 23 volumes.
M.s.l.
[Eggeling, John.] Entry in SFE.
Griffin, Martin I.J. Frank R. Stockton. Port Washington
   NY: Kennikat Press, 1965.
M[ullen], R.D. [Review of The Science Fiction of Frank R.
   Stockton.] SFS, no. 10 (1976), 296-97.
Powers, Richard Gid. "Introduction" to The Science
   Fiction of Frank R. Stockton. Boston: Gregg Press,
   1975.
Suvin, Darko. Metamorphoses of Science Fiction. New
   Haven and London: Yale University Press, 1979.

STRACHEY, John St. Loe (1860-1927), journalist and political writer. Born in prominent upper-class Whig family,
educated at home and at Cannes, graduated from Oxford,
called to the bar but adopted journalism, coedited with
C.L. GRAVES (q.v.) the Liberal Unionist--organ of the
eponymous party--in 1886, wrote for various journals, on
staff of Spectator, in 1896-1897 edited Cornhill Magazine, 1898 became proprietor of Spectator. Ardent free
trader (see the SF listed written as "S.L.S.", reissued
1903), specially interested in rural housing, pauperism,
and local government, also in rifle-shooting in view of the
coming world war. Published a dozen books, mostly on politics and society, but also two autobiography titles (one
adduced below) and two works of fiction.
M.s.l.
Strachey, John St. Loe. The Adventure of Living. Lon-
   don: Hodder & Stoughton, 1922.
DNB30.
DUR, pp. 476-78.
NEB, vol. 32.
Strachey, Mrs. [Amy S.]. St. Loe Strachey. London:
   Gollancz, 1930.
Williams-Ellis, A. "St. Loe Strachey." Spectator (24
   August 1963).

SUFFLING, Ernest Richard (? - ?, fl. 1887-1910). Besides the SF listed, published seven novels, mostly of adventure and travel, one book of stories, four books on crafts, antiques, and decoration, four guidebooks on travel in Norfolk and the text to a collection of photographs of it, and a collection of British epitaphs.

SYKES--until 1884 SIKES--, Arthur Alkin (1861-1939), humorist. Born in Kent as vicar's son, Cambridge BA 1884 and MA 1919. Schoolmaster 1884-1886, then army and university coach, civil service examiner, special correspondent abroad, editor of art handbooks, head of statistics for Central Control Board 1915-1921. Published, besides the book of parodies listed, three books of articles, verse, and sketches reprinted from Punch, a travelog to Russia, and under the pseudonym "Zelotes Zigzag" Astonished at America; translated Gogol's The Inspector General.
M.s.l.
AC, vol. 5.

THOMAS, Chauncey (1822-1898), Boston mechanic and carriage builder, reformer. Besides the SF listed, published for the Nautical Almanac Office two works on astronomy--one under the direction of Simon NEWCOMB (q.v.)--, and a book of poems. Not to be confused with Chauncey Thomas (1872-1941), the "Sage of the Rockies."
M.s.l.
PAD, pp. 64-68.
RON, passim.

THORBURN, Septimus Smet (1844-1913?), civil servant in India. Educated at Cheltenham, in Bengal Civil Service 1865-1899, lastly financial commissioner for Punjab; fellow of Royal Geographic and Royal Asian societies. Published to 1913 five nonfictional works on India and five novels (including the SF listed) also mainly on India.
M.s.l.
DIB.
SAIF, pp. 58-61.

TINCKER, Mary Agnes (1833-1907), US writer. Born in Maine, began teaching at age 13, wrote anonymously from age 15. Converted to Roman Catholicism in 1863, nurse in military hospital in Washington during latter part of Civil War, lived 1873-1887 in Italy. Contributed short stories, sketches, and serials to US periodicals. From 1872 to 1898 published, besides the SF listed, eight novels of romance and adventure and one book of sketches.

M.s.l.
WWWA, vol. 1.

TOURGÉE, Albion Winegar (1838-1905), US journalist,
jurist, carpetbagger, writer. Born in Ohio of French and
German parentage, educated at University of Rochester 1859-
1861. In 1861 officer in Union army, wounded, studied law
in Ohio, reentered army 1862, discharged in 1864, admitted
to bar of Ohio, taught briefly, wrote for newspaper. Moved
to North Carolina 1865, practiced law, became one of the
most controversial figures in that state. In 1866 entered
politics, helped organize pro-Black Loyal Reconstruction
League; founded the radical weekly Union Register, active
in North Carolina "carpetbag" convention. From 1868 to
1870 wrote political essays under the pseudonym "Wenckar,"
his life constantly threatened by the Ku Klux Klan. Judge
of superior court 1868 to 1874, in 1878 published the anonymous "C" letters, an important contribution to Southern
political literature. Editor and chief contributor of weekly Our Continent, contributor to Chicago Daily Inter
Ocean. After 1882 lived in Philadelphia. In 1895 established in Buffalo The Basis: A Journal of Citizenship.
US consul to Bordeaux 1897-1903, appointed consul to
Halifax, Nova Scotia, but never held the post. Contributed
to numerous newspapers and magazines of the day. From 1868
published, besides the SF listed (under the pseudonym of
"Edgar Henry"), 17 novels, mostly on the Reconstruction
period (one as "Henry Churton"), two books of stories, two
on law and finance, a book on the Ku Klux Klan, and one on
education.
M.s.l.
DAB, vol. 18.
Dibble, Roy F. Albion W. Tourgée. Port Washington, NY:
    Kennikat Press, 1968.
Gross, Theodore L. Albion W. Tourgée. New York:
    Twayne, 1963.

TRACY, Louis (1863-1928), writer. Born in Liverpool,
educated privately in Yorkshire, then in France. Contributed articles to Northern Echo, spent some years in
India, visited USA. Officer in World War I, lectured and
wrote extensively on it, 1917 joined staff of British War
Mission in USA, liquidator of British Bureau of Information, temporarily attached to Foreign Office 1919. On
editorial staff of Times and Daily Mail, member of Westminster Abbey Restoration Fund. Besides the three SF
listed, from 1891 on published over 60 books, mostly novels
of mystery and romance but also a book about India and at

least two more SF after 1900; 6 books (mostly written with
M.P. SHIEL, q.v.) used the pseudonym of "Gordon Holmes."
M.s.l.
WGT.
WWW, vol. 2.

TRAILL, Henry Duff (1842-1900), journalist, editor, and
author. Born in Kent, son of magistrate. Educated in Oxford, BA 1865, called to bar 1868, barrister in London from
1869, inspector of returns under Education Act of 1870,
doctor of civil law 1873. On staff of Pall Mall Gazette
1873-1880, St. James Gazette 1880-1882, Daily Telegraph
1882-1896, Saturday Review 1883-1894, and of other leading periodicals of the day. Editor of the Observer 1889-
1891, of Literature from 1896. Political satirist in
verse, caricatured the Rossettian sonnet. Besides the SF
listed, published from 1882 five books of verse (of which
three satirical), four books on history and politics, two
books of essays on literary topics, eight biographies and
monographs, three books of fiction, and some travelogs.
Wrote introductions to a number of works, including his
standard edition of Carlyle's Works. Edited translations, essays, and the six-volume Social England with
various coeditors including W.L. CLOWES (q.v.).
M.s.l.
[Beeching, Henry Charles.] "Mr. H.D. Traill," in his
    Conferences on Books and Men. London: Smith, Elder,
    1900.
The Cambridge History of English Literature, XIII, 166
    and 510, XIV, 146-47. Eds. A.W. Ward and A.R. Walker.
    Cambridge: Cambridge University Press, 1964.
MEB, vol. 6.
Observer, no. 409 (25 February 1900).
WWW, vol. 1.

TROLLOPE, Anthony (1815-1882), civil servant and writer.
Born in barrister's family, educated at Harrow and Winchester, civil servant at the Post Office in Ireland and
England 1834-1867, introduced the pillar-box. Contributed
frequently to magazines, edited St. Paul's Magazine 1867-
1871, stood unsuccessfully for Parliament as Liberal 1868.
Possibly the most prolific of well-known English novelists,
from 1847 on published about 70 titles--over 50 novels
including the SF listed, but also 9 travelogs in British
colonies and the Americas, four biographies, and the autobiography adduced below--which enjoyed great success in his
time.
M.s.l.

Trollope, Anthony. Autobiography, 2 vols. Ed. F. Page.
   London and New York: Oxford University Press, 1950.
Booth, Bradford A. Anthony Trollope. Bloomington:
   Indiana University Press, 1958.
Briggs, Asa. Victorian People. London: Odhams, 1954.
Burn, W.L. "Anthony Trollope's Politics." Nineteenth
   Century and After 143 (1948), 161-71.
Cockshut, A.O.J. Anthony Trollope. New York: New York
   University Press, 1968.
Halperin, John. Trollope and Politics. London: Macmil-
   lan, 1977.
James, Henry. "Anthony Trollope," in his The Future of
   the Novel. New York: Vintage, 1956.
Skilton, David. "The Fixed Period." Studies in the
   Literary Imagination 6, no. 2 (1973), 39-50.
Snow, C.P. Trollope. London: Macmillan, 1975.

TUCKER, Horace Finn (? - ?, fl. 1873-1911), Anglican clergyman. Graduated from Moore College, New South Wales, in
1873, served in Australia to 1911. Rector of Melbourne
Cathedral 1894. Beside the marginal SF listed, published
one book of sermons and one of poems, and contributed to a
volume in aid of the cathedral building fund.
M.s.l.
CCD for 1911.
MAL.

VERNE, Jules (1828-1905), French adventure and S-F writer.
See for this well-known author the works below.
M.s.l.
Angenot, Marc. "Jules Verne, the Last Happy Utopianist,"
   in Patrick Parrinder, ed., Science Fiction. London and
   New York: Longman, 1979.
Raymond, François. Le Développement des études sur
   Jules Verne. Paris: Minard, 1976.
   _____, and Simone Vierne, eds. Jules Verne et les sci-
   ences humaines. Paris: UGE, 1979.
Soriano, Marc. Jules Verne. Paris: Julliard, 1978.
Suvin, Darko. Metamorphoses of Science Fiction. New
   Haven and London: Yale University Press, 1979 (with
   further bibliography).

VETCH, Thomas, pseudonym? (? - ?, fl. 1888).

VINCENT, Charles (1851-1920), French novelist. From 1891
to 1895 published two books on the French national epic, a
verse drama, and one novel. With Charles CAUSSE (q.v.) published from 1889 to 1907, under the pseudonym "Pierre

Maël," 41 books of mystery, adventure, romance, and SF.

VOGEL, Sir Julius (1835-1899), British colonial statesman. Born in London, educated at University of London. Went to Victoria 1852-1861 and edited newspapers, to New Zealand 1862, started Otago Daily Times, first daily in New Zealand; member and then head of Otago provincial government 1866-1869. Member of House of Representatives, colonial treasurer, headed various ministries 1869-1876, including two stints as prime minister, introduced a famous public works scheme, government life insurance, and public trust office. Knighted 1875, agent general in London for New Zealand 1876-1881, then again minister in New Zealand, secured second reading of Women's Franchise Bill. Spent last 11 years of his life in London as pioneer of Imperial Federation. Besides the SF listed, published from 1865 two books and one pamphlet on the colonies, an anonymous satire in verse, and an anonymous burlesque novel, edited The Official Handbook of New Zealand.
M.s.l.
Burdon, Randal M. The Life and Times of Sir Julius Vogel. Christchurch: Caxton, 1948.
Dalziel, Raewyn. Sir Julius Vogel. Wellington, New Zealand: Reed, 1968.
DUR, pp. 480-81.
EB, vol. 28.
MAL.
MEB, vol. 3.

WALL, George A. (? - ?, fl. 1884-1894), US writer. With Edward A. ROBINSON (q.v.) published the SF listed and another novel, as well as another novel with G.B. Heckel and a book on Vermont politics.

WALSH, Rupert (? - ?, fl. 1890).

WARD, Herbert Dickinson (1861-1932), US writer. Published the book of stories listed, six more romance and adventure books (including one more S-F novel), one political treatise, and with his wife, the popular writer Elizabeth Stuart Phelps Ward, two biblical tales.

WATERHOUSE, Elizabeth (? - ?, fl. 1887-1912), Catholic religious writer. Besides the anonymous SF listed, published two books of homilies, one book of poems, and Thoughts of a Tertiary. Also selected and arranged three books of prayers and moralizing writing.

WATERLOO, Stanley (1846-1913), US writer. From 1888 pub-
lished four novels and tales of SF, fantasy, and adventure
(one posthumously) and three books of drawings (one post-
humously). His first S-F novel The Story of Ab (1897)
was one of the earliest romances of anthropology.
M.s.l.
[Clute, John.] Entry in SFE.
Henkin, Leo J. Darwinism in the English Novel, 1860-
    1910. New York: Corporate Press, 1940, chapter 9.
M[ullen], R.D. [Reviews of The Story of Ab and Armaged-
    don.] SFS, no. 6 (1975), 192; no. 10 (1976), 297.
Powers, Richard Gid. "Introduction" to Stanley Waterloo,
    Armageddon. Boston: Gregg Press, 1975.

WATLOCK, W.A. (? - ?, fl. 1886).

WATSON, Henry Brereton Marriott--also as H.B. MARRIOTT-
WATSON--(1863-1921), journalist and writer. Son of H.C.M.
WATSON (q.v.), born in Melbourne, as boy taken to New
Zealand, educated at Canterbury College. Came to England
1885, assistant editor of Black and White and Pall Mall
Gazette, on staff of National Observer. Besides the SF
listed published from 1890 over 40 novels and 9 books of
stories, essays, and sketches, an introduction to a book on
highwaymen, and a play with J.M. Barrie.
M.s.l.
Hind, C. Lewis. More Authors and I. London: Lane/
    Bodley Head, 1922, pp. 217-22.
NZNB, vol. 4.
WWW, vol. 2.

WATSON, Henry Crocker Marriott (1835- ?, fl. 1858-1890),
clergyman. Born and educated in Tasmania, went to
Australia 1858, ordained in 1860, migrated to New Zealand
1873. Published from 1875 to 1890 two SF listed, under the
pseudonym "H.C.M.W.," and Adventures in New Guinea.
M.s.l.
MAL.

WELCH, Edgar Luderne (1855- ?, fl. 1876-1905), writer.
Besides the four SF listed (one anonymous, one under the
pseudonym of "J. Drew Gay," and two under "Grip"), published from 1876 to 1887, under the pseudonym of "J. Drew
Gay," a book about the Prince of Wales's visit to India,
one about the Russo-Turkish war, and under the pseudonym of
"Grip," a series (over a dozen) of historical guidebooks.
The utopian-socialist elements in the 1883 novel contrast
strongly with his other SF and lead me to query Sargent's

identification (see in list of sources for the Bibliography) of him as its author. Moved to USA, wrote 17 volumes
of "historical souvenirs" on places in New York State from
1894 to 1905.

WELLS, Herbert George (1866-1946), writer, utopianist, and
controversialist. See for this well-known author any
history of English literature and the works below.
M.s.l.
Wells, H.G. Experiment in Autobiography. New York:
  Macmillan, 1934.
Hughes, David Y. "Criticism in English of H.G. Wells," in
  Patrick Parrinder, ed., Science Fiction. London and
  New York: Longman, 1979.
Lodge, David. "Utopia and Criticism," in his The Novelist
  at the Crossroads. Ithaca: Cornell University Press,
  1971.
Suvin, Darko. Metamorphoses of Science Fiction. New
  Haven and London: Yale University Press, 1979 (with
  further bibliography).
_____, with Robert M. Philmus, eds. H.G. Wells and
  Modern Science Fiction. Lewisburg, PA: Bucknell Univer-
  sity Press, and London: Associated University Presses,
  1977 (with further bibliography).

WESTALL, William Bury (1834-1903), novelist and journalist.
Born in Lancashire, engaged in father's cotton-spinning
business. From 1870 foreign correspondent for the Times,
Spectator, and Daily News. In Geneva became acquainted
with Russian revolutionaries, collaborated with Stepniak in
translation of contemporary Russian literature and of Stepniak's Russia under the Czars. Traveled extensively on
American continent and in West Indies. Beside the SF
listed, published 11 novels--including several lost-race
novels--, a book of tales, and a book on Anglo-Continental
journalism in Geneva.
M.s.l.
DNB11.
[Eggeling, John.] Entry in SFE.

WETMORE, Claude Hazeltine (1862-1944), US newspaperman,
traveler and writer. Born in Cuyahoga Falls, OH, studied
at Western Reserve University and in Lausanne, editor of
Wetmore's Weekly and The Valley Magazine 1902-1907.
Besides the SF listed, published nine books, of which four
nonfiction and five fiction, including fairy tales and
Latin-American adventures.
M.s.l.

DNAA.
<u>Ohio Authors and Their Books</u>.   Ed. William Coyle.   Cleve-
    land and New York: World, 1962.

WHITE, Frederick Merrick (1859-19?, fl. 1888-1930), writer.
Wrote   SF   and   adventure   stories   in   magazines   such   as
<u>Pearson's</u>   and   <u>Strand</u>.   In   1888   published,   as   "F.M.W.,"
an attack on DONNELLY's (q.v.) idea of the cryptogram in
Shakespeare's plays.   From 1896 published over 75 novels
(including the one SF listed), mainly detective stories and
romances.
M.s.l.
[Eggeling, John.] Entry in <u>SFE</u>.

WHITE, John (? - ?, fl. 1893). Published with W.G. MOFFAT
the SF listed.

WHITING, Sydney (? -1875, fl. 1846-1873), barrister in London from 1847.   Besides the SF listed and <u>Memoirs of a
Stomach</u> (both translated into German), published two books
of poems and two tales of romance--some of them anonymously.   Edited the official catalog of the Industrial Department of the International Exhibition of 1862.
M.s.l.
<u>DUR</u>, pp. 426-27.
<u>Law Times</u>, 23 October 1875, p. 412.
<u>LL</u>: 1849, s.v. "Counsel."
<u>MEB</u>, vol. 3.

WIDNALL, Samuel Page (? - ?, fl. 1871-1889).   Besides the
SF listed, published two books on histories of English
towns and a book of fiction.

WILSON, John Grosvenor (1866- ?, fl. 1886-1900), US writer.
Published <u>Lyrics of Life</u> and the SF listed.

WINDSOR, William (1857- ?, fl. 1889-1921), US phrenologist,
self-styled "professor."   Besides the SF listed, published
two books on phrenology and two on health and happiness.
M.s.l.
<u>RON</u>, passim.

WISE, Clement (? - ?, fl. 1884-1911).   Besides the anonymous SF listed, published a book on Puritanism and <u>The New
Life of St. Paul</u>.   The initials "P.C." for him in <u>DUR</u>
(see below) are an error.
M.s.l.
<u>DUR</u>, pp. 474-76.

WOLFE, Cecil Drummond (? - ?, fl. 1896-1897). Lived in Dublin in 1897. According to a signature in a copy of his book, his name might be WOLFF, but no confirmation was found for this.
M.s.1.
Locke, George. A Spectrum of Fantasy. London: Ferret Fantasy, 1980.

WRIGHT, Henry (? - ?, fl. 1878-1938). Lived in London. Published, besides the SF listed, Eighty-Six Years Young and the semiallegorical Mental Travels in Imagined Lands, edited a book of plays, and translated Eugen RICHTER's Sozialdemokratische Zukunftsbilder (also listed).

WRIGHT, William Henry (186?- ?, fl. 1885-1900), US journalist and writer. Left home at age of 15, became schoolmaster at 16, speaker at 19, studied law in Minnesota but left it for journalism. Traveled for a newspaper syndicate throughout Europe, including Russia and the Caucasus, interviewed many prominent politicians and writers including Ibsen, Tolstoy, and Debs. Interested in problems of workers and mining. By 1900 had published two books on travel and two of fiction in London, including the SF listed.
M.s.1.
Publishers' note in W.H. Wright, The Great Bread Trust. New York, London, and Montreal: Abbey, 1900, pp. 3-4.

YELVERTON, Christopher (? - ?, fl. 1899).

Clearly Pseudonymous But Unresolved Names
Augustinus.
    See Two Brothers, 1898, and Paul Rees, 1899.

A Captain of the Royal Navy.
    See The Battle off Worthing, 1887.

Coverdale, Henry Standish.
    See The Fall of the Great Republic, 1885.

A Diplomat.
    See The Rise and Fall of the United States, 1898.

An Ex-M.P.
    See A Radical Nightmare.

An Ex-Revolutionist.
    See "England's Downfall," 1893.

An Eye-Witness.
See The Socialist Revolution of 1888, 1884, and the biographical note under "Fairfield."

J.W.M.
See The Coming Cromwell, 1871, and the biographical note under "M., J.W."

Lang-Tung.
See The Decline and Fall of the British Empire, 1881. Not to be confused with a different S-F book with the same title in 1890.

Mammoth Martinet, His Royal Highness, alias Moho-Yoho-Me-Oo-Oo.
See The Gorilla Origin of Man, 1871.

McCauley, Motley Ranke.
See Chapters From Future History, 1871.

Mr. Dick.
See James Ingleton, 1893.

Green, Nunsowe.
See A Thousand Years Hence, 1882.

Heliomanes.
See A Journey to the Sun, 1866.

Jones, Jingo, M.P.
See The Sack of London by the Highland Host, 1900.

One Who Was There.
See The Great Irish "Wake", 1888.

Pee, M.
See Hibernia's House . . ., 1881.

Trueman, Chrysostom.
See The History of a Voyage to the Moon, 1864.

Ulidia.
See The Battle of Newry, 1883.

X. Y. Z. (or Z., X.Y.)
See The Vril Staff, 1891.

Unresolved Anonymous Titles
Back Again, 1874.

The Battle of To-Morrow, 1885.

The Battle of the Moy, 1883.

The Dawn of the 20th Century: A Novel, Social and Political, 1882.

The Dawn of the Twentieth Century: 1st January 1901, 1888.

The Doom of the County Council of London, 1892.

"Down with England!", 1888.

Etymonia, 1875.
  M.s.l.
  DUR, pp. 446-55.

France and England, 1848.
  Attribution to Lamartine not verified.

The Great Irish Rebellion of 1886, 1886.

Imaginary History of the Next Thirty Years, 1857.

In the Future, 1875.
  M.s.l.
  Mullen, R.D. [Review.] SFS, no. 6 (1975), 185.

In the Year One . . ., 1886.

The Ingathering, 1891.

The Island of Atlantis, 1871.

John Haile, 1885.

The Last Peer, 1851.

Man Abroad, 1887.
  M.s.l.
  M[ullen], R.D. [Review.] SFS, no. 10 (1976), 296.
  Sargent, Lyman Tower. "Introduction" to Man Abroad.
  Boston: Gregg Press, 1975.

The New Democracy, 1885.

Politics and Life in Mars, 1883.
  Attribution to Welch seems dubious to me; see the annota-

tion to the book in the Bibilography and the biographical
note on him.

The Swoop of the Eagles, 1889.

2. The Social Classification of S-F Writers, 1848–1900

0. What do we know or can reasonably infer about the writers of the titles in the Bibliography? Not enough-- certainly not all the significant facts--yet quite a bit, at any rate enough for some first conclusions.

0.1. However, before marshaling the data from the pre- ceding "Biographical Sketches of S-F Authors" for the titles published in the UK from 1848 to 1900 (further referred to as Biographies), it might be well to clarify what is meant by "writer." The term is used here in prefer- ence to the pseudotheological connotations of "author" in order to distantiate this study from--

> the figure of the individual author . . . as a charac- teristic form of bourgeois thought. No man is the author of himself, in the absolute sense. . . . To be a writer in English is to be already socially speci- fied. But the argument moves beyond this: at one level to an emphasis on socially inherited forms, in the generic sense; at another level to an emphasis on socially inherited and still active notations and conventions; at a final level to an emphasis on a continuing process in which not only the forms but the contents of consciousness are socially produced (1).

Thus the biography and even psychology of "the author(s)" is not an end of these investigations, but strictly a means. Yet, for anyone committed to an historical under- standing, the opposite extreme of some formalist and techno- cratic tendencies in literary and cultural criticism, that wipe the author completely out in order to consider only the simon-pure texts in a vacuum (which then turns out not to be a vacuum at all but a medium filled with the critics' own ideology), is equally unacceptable. If the writers are only mediations between the socially general and the discur- sively or aesthetically unique, they are crucial media- tions. They are the most important particular "forms" that

blend the general and the singular, the inherited and the
innovative, convention and novum, in both unrepeatable and
at least partly reconstructible ways. The writer is, after
all, the "sender of the literary message . . . the first
pole in the communication circuit . . . the link between
the linguistic and stylistic conventions . . . to which he
has had access and our interpretation; if a work is in some
measure intelligible it is thanks to the codes author and
reader have in common" (2). It is, then, analytically convenient, and in the present case to my mind indispensable,
to single out from such a communication circuit the segment
sender-message, just as in the interpretive essay of the
following Part II the segment message-receiver will be
singled out.

My methodology will, then, be to use in this study the
data from the Biographies in order to describe "significant
groups which include, in a fundamental way, those personal
realities which [would] otherwise be relegated to a quite
separate area." This should provide ways of seeing groups
"in and through individual differences: that specificity
of individuals, and of their individual creations, which
does not deny but is the necessary way of affirming their
real social identities," and indeed of affirming "the inter-
penetration, in a final sense the unity, of the most
individual and the most social forms of actual life"
(Williams PMC 28-29). It is the necessary condition for a
full understanding of the circuit of literary communication.

0.2. The Biographies in this book contain--beside the
anonymous titles and 20 unresolved pseudonyms printed in an
appendix to them--270 names of authors. Not counting the
quite unidentified and probably pseudonymous Herbert,
Herrmann Lang (whom I.F. Clarke wrongly identifies as a
German), J.W.M., and Penrice, nor the mysterious Fairfield,
there are 265 names to be considered. Of these, 11--
Forrest, Rowcroft, Poe, R. Pemberton, Whiting, Hayward,
Chatelain, Gale, Fairburn, Helps, and O'Neil--are writers
of titles published 1848-1868, before S-F books became a
significant public phenomenon, and will not be used in the
considerations of this study. Finally, Mary Shelley, and
E.T.A. Hoffmann, authors of a single S-F story each printed
for the first time in book form (very belatedly) in the
period after 1870, will also not be considered. This
leaves a corpus of 252 names as a basis for discussion.
Of these 252 writers, 186 are British and 66 foreign (with
three or four uncertainties as to British or US provenience
for unknowns such as Douglass and D. MacKay, and disregarding also the fact that a few people such as Bridge and

Welch moved from UK to US in midcareer). Alas, sliced
another way, for 35 of the 252 there are no data at all
except that their names are on the title page of the S-F
book in the Bibliography, while even the basic data for
many others are only partly available.

It is unfortunately impossible to compare the overall
number of S-F writers from the UK--here, counting the appendix on future wars to the Bibliography, about 200 plus the
pseudonymous and anonymous ones--to the overall number of
fiction writers, since nobody knows how many of these there
were. The number of "authors" in England and Wales was,
according to the census in 1881, 3,400 and in 1901 11,000
(Reader 208-11), but this included editors and journalists
and in 1901 also shorthand writers(!). The actual writers
in that number were overwhelmingly "totally obscure penny-
a-liners" (Gross 200). More than 400 novelists are cited
in Brightfield's four-volume compilation (3), and it is
sometimes assumed that about 40,000 novels were produced in
Victorian times (without the penny-serials, cheap paperback
romances, and periodical serials not republished in book
form). If that is correct, the SF constituted less than 1
percent of book-length fiction, and its significance ex-
ceeds its quantity.

1. To begin with, the basic "bio-historical" data of
year of birth (generation), length of life, and median
date will be established for the corpus of UK writers, and
checked by means of the corpus of foreign writers.

Following Raymond Williams, it would be useful to distinguish the writers born before and after 1830 as belonging to different generations (Williams LR 255, 260-61).
Besides Mary Shelley and the 10 UK writers listed above as
having published before 1870, there are 15 more (one of
them by inference only) born before 1830. Half of their
S-F titles were published by 1877 (Bulwer, Maguire,
Dudgeon, Maitland, Lumley, Collins, Soleman, Cobbe). The
other half, published after 1882, were works of old age,
sometimes influenced by fear of death (Trollope) and
elegiac looks backward (Linton). Moreover, already the
1870s' group, and especially the post-1882 group (including
Dering, Richardson, Barlow, Perry) was as a rule quite
eccentric for the times: theirs were works not written for
the new, enlarged, bourgeois-dominated social addressees.
Not only do they all--when they go into social matters at
all--take an anticommercial stance, but they also use the
old genres and the related structures of feeling, situated
somewhere between whimsy and gentlemanly or nonconformist
satire. In other words, they hark back to the 18th-century
(openly in Perry's continuation of Swift) or early 19th-

century (Collins, Maguire) traditions, and attempt to con-
tinue them in unfriendly times. In tone, this can range
from the uncomfortable compromise of trying nonetheless to
safeguard the general middle-class verisimilitudes
(Trollope) to an exhilaratingly uncompromising and robust
opinionatedness, an eccentricity in the best sense of the
word (Barlow). In brief, this can be ranged under
Williams's "residual" structure of feeling (Williams ML
122ff., and see my discussion in Part II).

Williams's division of generations is borne out by the
fact that I cannot discover any age-based particularities
within the generation born 1830-1880, say in the post-1865
age group. The undoubtedly new tone of some writers from
the mid-1890s on is more a matter of social origin and orientation than of generation: Wells has most probably more
in common with Griffith Jones or Lee than with Fawcett or
Lucas.

The above is confirmed by the birthdate groups of the
foreign writers. About the pre-1830 group--with due modifications for national characteristics--some similar observa-
tions of hearkening back to a diluted romanticism and/or
rationalism might be made. This certainly applies to the
grotesques of About and O'Brien, the utopias of Collens and
Harting, and Hale's blend of both. The successful mechanic
and carriage-builder Thomas and the successful supplier of
reading-matter for bourgeois families Verne, though, escape
the residual structure of feeling: social position proves
in their case stronger than the Zeitgeist of their youth.

For the investigation into length of life there are
data for 112 UK writers, full data being known for 97.
Their average life-span is almost exactly 70 years. For
15 writers partial data have been found: dates of "floruit"
--that is, date of first and last mention in publishing,
university, and other records--as well as in many cases
either the date of birth or the date of death; the date of
birth has been--when missing--supplied by me by extrapolat-
ing backward 26 years from the first mention (this is the
halfway or median point between the university-leaving age
of 22 and a frequent first-publication age of 30, both
recurring as first mentions of a writer; the number of 26
has been confirmed by checking with 7 cases where both
birth and "floruit" data exist). For these 16, then, the
average length of life up to the last mention found--
usually a book-publication date--was 63 years, which, on
the assumption that for the last 5-10 years of their lives
they would have published no more, accords quite closely
with the 70 years' average from the larger sample with full
data.

For the 11 _female writers_ among these 112, the average
length of life is exactly the same--also 70 years. There
are 14 women in my corpus of 252 writers, and--to antici-
pate--the only statistical difference from males I can
discover is a concentration on both ends of the social
origin and social position scales--in the uppermost class
or the middle and lowest professionals--at the expense of
participation in the top professionals' group and, of
course, in university education. Their overall proportion
(about 6 percent) is very low, giving a particular point to
J.S. Mill's parallel between women and oppressed colonial
peoples (an even better parallel could be drawn, on the
strength of the writer statistics, between women and the
manual laborer classes). It is low not only in relation to
the proportion of women in the UK population (52 percent)
but even in relation to women "authors" in general (145 out
of 1,673 or 9 percent in 1865--Reader 173). Thus, the
impossibility of saying much about them on the basis of
these statistics is itself a very significant absence.

Among the 74 UK writers for whom we do not know nor can
we reasonably infer the length of life, and who would
almost always be from the lower, inglorious social classes,
the life-span was most probably lower. The average for all
186 would thus almost certainly be below 70. However, in
order to equate it to the average life expectation of that
period, which was about 60-65 years, the average for all
these unknowns would have to be 55 years or less, which is
not very likely. On the other hand, 53 out of 112 (or 47
percent) lived to 70 or over, which is twice as many as
among the rich at the period (23.5 percent of the rich, but
only 6.5 percent of the poor, survived to age 70--see
Mulhall 283 and 285). These writers were a hardy breed:
Perry lived to 97, Fawcett to 94, Davis at least to 86,
Constable and Murray to 91, Abbott, Atkins, Barlow,
Brookfield, Fox, Graves, Kellett, Middleton, and M.
Pemberton to their high 80s, Armstrong, Bridge, Chilton,
Cobbe, Downey, Dudgeon, Gorst, Gould, Hudson, Munro,
O'Grady, Oppenheimer, Schofield, Shiel, and Wells to their
low 80s, and 24 more into their 70s (including Bulwer,
Doyle, Hyne, and Maitland). Only 16 of them were certainly
and 2 more possibly under 55 when they died, including
Burnaby (killed in battle), Davidson (suicide), Griffith
Jones (drink), Jefferies (tuberculosis, i.e., poverty),
Allen, Greg, Hinton, and Jane--plus, of course, more from
among the 74 people about whom we cannot tell.

The _median_ date, or midpoint of life, is the one datum
available for all the writers: where we do not possess
dates of birth and death, we still know the midpoint of

their "floruit" period, from which the median date can be
calculated by subtracting 13 years, as explained above.
This median date turns out to be the year 1881. Taking
the average length of life of 70 years, a "robot-portrait"
of the average S-F writer in this corpus would have him
live from 1846 to 1916. No doubt, this is only a statistical construct. As an example, the latest writers whose
date of death is known died in fact as follows: Fawcett in
1960 or even later, Wells, Shiel, Murray, and 7 others
after World War II, and 23 more between 1930 and 1945. Yet
even if--as noted earlier--the full data would make for a
somewhat shorter life span, it is clear that the great
majority was formed in the years of covert tensions constituting the somewhat stifling mid-Victorian "equipoise"
(Burn) of 1855-1870.

The foreign writers confirm the above conclusions. Their
average life-span is also exactly 70 years, 7 of them
(including Hale and Lloyd) dying in their high 80s, and no
less than 19 in their 70s (including Clemens-Twain,
Donnelly, J. Miller, Newcomb, Serviss, and Verne). Thus 30
out of 53 for which data exist, or more than half, lived to
70 or over, but this is counterbalanced by 6 who died
before the age of 55 (including Astor in shipwreck, O'Brien
in the Civil War, Bellamy, and De Mille). These extraordinary lengths of life mean that 10 of them lived to the
1930-1945 period, including Chambers, Putnam, Stimson, and
Ward. As to the median date, it is 1879/80, a statistically insignificant deviation, readily accounted for by the
lag in republishing (which in fact for 90 works of the
identified foreign authors is exactly as much as the pre-
cession of the foreign median, i.e., 1.7 years).

2. I shall proceed further by adopting the fairly
self-evident categories from Raymond Williams's overview of
the social history of English writers--that is, social
origin; kind of education; and main source of income--while
modifying his further subdivisions for my purposes
(Williams LR 254-55).

For social origin, I shall in place of Williams's subcategories employ those from my investigation into the
social addressees of Victorian fiction in Part II, namely:

1. Upper class: nobility, gentry, upper officers
2. Rich bourgeoisie: industrialists, businessmen,
   bankers, brokers, etc.
3. Professional gentlemen: Church of England clergymen, barristers and law officers, physicians and top
   surgeons, civil servants, top educators, top men of
   letters

4. <u>Professional men</u>: other clergymen and doctors, solicitors, upper engineers, accountants, well-known educators and men of letters, etc.
5. <u>Middle bourgeoisie</u>: merchants and upper clerks
6. <u>"Unacknowledged" professionals</u>: nurses, teachers, artists, journalists, lower men of letters, etc.
7. <u>Nonprofessional petty-bourgeoisie</u>: tradesmen, junior clerks and other employees, foremen, etc.
8. <u>Manual laborers</u>: artisans, farmers, servants, other workers.

Much of the above is unavoidably tentative. If somebody's father is referred to as a landlord, did he own one small house in a provincial slum, or a country estate and/or tracts of London? Further, the direct or indirect source of most of such data in various biographical handbooks (all listed in the Biographies) is the writer himself, who would in Victorian times very frequently put the best possible construction on (not to say--fudge) his social origin for reasons of prestige and snobbery. Just for example, the father of our writer Markwick--originally named Johnson--is referred to as a "Royal Navy man"; since he is not referred to as an officer I take this litote as meaning he was a common seaman or at best an NCO. Or Conan Doyle's father is in various places referred to as an upper clerk or a civil servant (which is not at all the same "rank"--one would belong to class 5 and the other to class 3 above). In all such cases, unless other data were available, I have taken the lower alternative. A few decisions about categorization are circumstantial guesses: for example, I have assumed that as a rule education abroad indicated affluence, or that Navy officers were of upper-class (my class 1) origin. Guesses I am hesitant about are indicated by question mark, with the alternative class number sometimes also supplied.

Furthermore, even assuming most of my categorizations are reasonably correct, they are not sufficient. The above grid would have to be complemented with such other ones as geographic-cum-ethnic-cum-religious distribution (London versus the rest, to begin with--I have taken this into account when deciding between my classes 3-4-6 and 2-5). To return to Doyle, the fact that he was of Irish Catholic descent and educated at a Jesuit school in Victorian Scotland, when Catholics were still in a marginal and bleak position, probably had as much influence on his horizon and structure of feeling as his father's profession. One would also have to take into account such important groups as the Anglo-Indians or "nabobs"--"English families whose heads

had acquired wealth and social standing as administrators,
businessmen, professional men, or military officers in
India and then returned home to form a closely knit social
community of their own" (Altick VPI 30)--and to whom a
probably disproportionate number of S-F authors belonged
(and one can only speculate why): Brookfield, Chesney,
Constable, Curwen, Gregg, Jenkins, P.S. Robinson, Thorburn,
and probably a few more. It is also quite striking how
many UK S-F writers lived for long stretches abroad, primarily in Australia, but also in Canada, South Africa, South
America, etc., or were indefatigable travelers.

In spite of all this, my categorization is somewhat more
articulated than Banks's, Baxter's, or Williams's, and I
trust it might be found useful as a first further step. As
in subsection 1, the UK natives will be analyzed first:

1. Anson, Bulwer-Lytton, Chesney, Cobbe, Colomb, Dixie,
   Glyn, Lancaster, Lester, Strachey = 10.
2. Dudgeon, Fawcett (?), Gorst, Greg, Lehmann, W.
   Morris, Oppenheim, Westall = 8.
3. Acworth (?), Barlow, Bramston, Brookfield, Burnaby,
   Butler, Cromie, Curwen, Dalton, Dering, Eastwick
   (?), Fox, Graves, Hinton, Hyne, Griffith Jones,
   Kellett, Linton, Maitland, Payn, Perry, P.S.
   Robinson, Sykes, Traill, Trollope, H.B.M. Watson =
   26.
4. Abbott (3?), Allen, Atkins (6?), Collins, Davidson,
   Davis, Jenkins, A. Lang, Nicholson, O'Grady, Shiel,
   Stead = 12.
5. Andreae (2?), Corbett, Doyle, Greer (?), Kinross,
   Lumley, Murray (?), M. Pemberton (2?), Schofield
   (2?), Tracy (?) = 10.
6. Buchanan, Greener (?), Hayes = 3.
7. Lucas, Wells = 2.
8. Jefferies, Lee (?), Markwick (?) = 3.

In all, I found sufficient data on social origin for 74
UK writers out of 186. In class 1, of the 10 names 5 are
officers' sons, and it also comprises 3 of the 6 women in
all. A glance at the names will reveal that the sons of
the uppermost class wrote some of the most heavily and openly ideological narratives in my corpus. In class 2
(whose number might be swollen by a few more from class 5),
on the contrary, it would be tempting to postulate a clash
between the original democratic impulse of the bourgeoisie
and its English compromise-consensus with the older ruling
class. The resulting ideological dispossession of the
affluent and power-sharing bourgeoisie might explain both

its "soft core"--some of its sons turning openly to evasion in mass commercialized writing and/or eccentricity (Dudgeon, Fawcett, Lehmann, Oppenheim)--and its "hard edges"--the exasperated search for new flags on the right (Greg) or on the left (W. Morris). Gorst--son of a Liberal cabinet member--would be in the interesting position of spanning the hard edge and the soft core, or of having moved from one to the other. But it is more prudent to wait for any such conclusions until further discussion, if not until further basic research.

Class 3 is the largest one by far, so that the 24 sons and 2 daughters of the highest professionals comprise more than a third of this sample. Of them, 20 (including Butler, Griffith Jones, and Maitland) are descended from Anglican clergymen, and in strictly economic terms it would be mandatory to put the offspring of poor vicars and curates (half of the latter earned less than £80 a year, and a third of all Anglican clergymen less than £150-- Altick VPI 206) into a lower class, as different from the offspring of deans (Bramston), queen's chaplains (Brook-field) or the immensely rich bishops (Graves). However, as explained in the interpretive essay of Part II, I am primar-ily interested in ideological horizons and structures of feeling, which are certainly codetermined but not necessari-ly solely determined by financial status. The others are sons of barristers or law magistrates (Fox, Traill, Trollope), prominent surgeons (Cromie, Hinton) or civil servants (Payn). Adding class 4 (among whom there are 7 ministers' and 3 solicitors' sons) and class 6, the second-generation "intelligentsia" accounts for distinctly more than half the sample.

With class 5 the region of statistical uncertainty is entered, as a number of them could be in classes 2 or 6-7, according to the father's affluence. Classes 7 and 8 have extremely few representatives when compared to their 90 percent share of the population at large. This must be partly due to lack of data. Nonetheless, it is startling to see among their 5 writers 3 of the most interesting ones --Wells, Jefferies, and Lee--while the other two are, under-standably enough, among the most snobbish ones. Thus, when Lucas (son of an insurance agent who passed through Punch to the chairmanship of Methuen Publishers) wrote his upper-class whimsical parody aiming to defuse Wells's War of the Worlds, he was fulfilling the typical function of what Brecht (following Kipling, i.e., British practice) calls "the tame elephant"--the one employed to dragoon his untamed brethren. It is also highly interesting that his collaborator on The War of the Wenuses, Graves, was also

the collaborator of the quintessential upper-class writer
St. Loe Strachey: Graves's pivotal social origin of high
clergyman's son was best fitted to hold together both ends
of the social origin scale with a view to cementing and
reaffirming the dominant ideological consensus. Finally
(to step just a bit beyond the 19th century), when Lehmann
protested in Parliament against Le Queux's The Invasion of
1910 (1906) as warmongering, this was not simply the
Liberal S-F writer attacking the Tory one, or pacifist
ideology at odds with militarism (4). It was the typical
Establishment man--son of a prominent cosmopolitan and London business family which had "arrived" several generations
ago, barrister, Cantabrigian oarsman, editor of Punch,
High Sheriff of Buckinghamshire, genteel parodist, and
amateur author--acting upon the ideology of a social group
different from and at odds with that of a typical semire-
spectable arriviste--hack writer for Harmsworth, of
ethnically and socially obscure origins and of obscure
education, hired pen, rabid jingoist, and shady figure in
the half-world of political journalism, propaganda, and
spying as well as of sensationalist publishing at the rate
of half a dozen books per year.
     It might be instructive to see which S-F writers from
this list have survived until today, taking as criterion
the presence of both reprints and modern critical interest.
The full verdict may not be in, as the future might rediscover some still neglected names, but today this is the
case for Bulwer, Chesney (class 1), Greg, W. Morris (class
2), Butler, Griffith Jones, Trollope (class 3), Abbott,
Shiel (class 4), Doyle (class 5), Wells (class 7), and
Jefferies (class 8). This immediately shows the necessity
for not applying social origin in a mechanistic way: certainly Morris and Butler, and then Griffith Jones and
Wells, are significant because of their negative reaction
to the values and ideas of their social class. Nonetheless, even a negative reaction (usually blended with a
hearkening back to the pristine but lost ideals of that
social class) is a significant fact, codetermined by what
one is reacting against.
     I assume that the 112 UK writers with unknown social
origin, unless there are some indications to the contrary
in other data, belong to class 6, 7 or 8. The indications
from schooling (private, abroad, Oxbridge, or some other
major universities) rule out 18, and other indications of
income or social group probably 8 more. How to divide the
remaining 86 is even more difficult and must be openly
acknowledged as my guess. I suspect they belong overwhelmingly to the "unacknowledged professionals" (class 6).

Some but not many might also belong to the employees–cum–tradesmen class 7, and a fortiori still fewer to class 8 (workers', farmers', servants' offspring). If, then, the proportions 5:2:1 for these three classes are adopted, so that of the 86 unknowns 54 are allotted to class 6, 21 to class 7, and 11 to class 8 (as well as 13 each to classes 4 and 5), the result is as shown in table 1.

Table 1.
Social Origin of UK S-F Writers

Class	Unadjusted	%	Adjusted	%
1–Upper	10	13.5	10	5
2–Rich bourgeoisie	8	11	8	4
3–Professional gentlemen	26	35	26	14
4–Professional men	12	16	25	14
5–Middle bourgeoisie	10	13.5	23	12
6–Unacknowledged professionals	3	4	57	31
7–Petty bourgeoisie	2	3	23	12
8–Manual labor classes	3	4	14	8
Sum Total	74	100	186	100

If one wished to compare this with the data by Williams (LR 260-62), one would have to take his 1830-1880 generation and add to it the same proportion of the 1780-1830 generation as in my corpus, that is, 25:186 or about 13 percent. One would then have to translate my categories into his, and put for my class 1 his Nobility and Gentry, for my classes 3, 4, and 6 his Professionals, for my classes 2 and 5 his Merchants, for my class 7 and a part of 8 his Tradesmen and Craftsmen, and for the rest of my class 8 his Farmers and Laborers. Table 2 shows this comparison.

If it is recalled that Williams's statistics are based on the Oxford Introduction to English Literature, that is, on "high lit" writers, it will be seen that the results arrived at here are quite commensurate with his. The writers of largely popular literature, such as my corpus, would be more likely to come from Grub Street, that is, to be of lower social origin, and somewhat less likely to come from the uppermost class. Nonetheless, the coincidences for three quarters of all writers--of Professional and Tradesmen-plus-craftsmen origin--are quite astounding. But again, a caution must be entered, due to the need for much more biographical investigation in places such as archives

Table 2
Social Origins of UK Writers, Compared

Classes	Williams (general)	%	Suvin (SF)	%
Nobility & gentry	8	14	10	5
Professionals	34	57	108	58
Merchants	7	12	31	17
Tradesmen & craftsmen	11	17	30	16
Farmers & laborers	--	--	7	4
Sum Total	**60**	**100**	**186**	**100**

and contemporary periodicals. Yet even as general indications, these data tell us that SF was at the time written
--with the correction noted above--by people of much the
same social origin as the writers of "high" literature.
No amount of minor errors of judgment in my guesses would,
I believe, statistically invalidate this fairly surprising
conclusion. It indicates that what we today call SF was at
the time perhaps somewhat lower on the ladder of cultural
prestige than "high lit," but that it was not separated
into a special enclave by the writers' social origin. A
further discussion of S-F prestige will be attempted after
the writers' actual social position has been examined.

An even more important related point, however, can be
deduced from these data. It is excellently put in the following argument, which it confirms and indeed gives broader
empirical support to:

One reason for the broad similarities of outlook among
Victorian men of letters was that most of them were
children of the business and professional class, with
little if any first-hand knowledge of working-class
life or of the industrial regions. . . . It is of
course simple-minded to suppose that a writer's opinion
can be directly accounted for in terms of his social
origins; yet it would be hard to imagine a critic with
a working-class background writing in the style of,
say, Lang, or playing down politics quite as much as
Mackail does in his otherwise admirable life of William
Morris.--Not that there were many Victorian critics
with a working-class background in the first place.
Under nineteenth-century conditions an occasional
genius might overcome extreme poverty, but for mere

talent the obstacles were immense (Gross 164).

This is, of course, applicable not only to critics--we have
clear parallels at hand in SF with the genius of H.G. Wells
and the mutely eloquent absence of my classes 7 and 8. It
also explains many of the most intimate features of the
writers' texts, for example--as Gross implies--the overwhelming absence from them of industrial settings and working people. "At a rough guess," noted Altick, "90 per cent
of the characters in the Victorian fiction which is read
today belong to the middle class and the gentry" (Altick
VPI 33). At a rough guess, except possibly for a little
dip toward the lower professionals and déclassé intellectuals, this holds true for the characters in this S-F
corpus too.
    3. However, the importance of social origin was sup-
plemented for the middle reaches of the social scale--where
around four fifths of all writers belonged--with the often
different social position which they achieved towards the
middle or end of their career. With the growing dominance
of social relationships based on industrial and financial
capitalism, "the newly respectable integration . . .
offered to be self-recruiting; it was socially inclusive,
at a given level of price, taste and behaviour, rather than
categorically exclusive, as in an older kind of society"--
that is, one based on "gentlemanly" land-ownership
(Williams PMC 133). In spite of ideologically very important residual pieties carried over from the degree hierarchy, the new social integration of the last third of the
19th century was based on money hierarchy. This allowed
for a rise and/or fall in social position primarily (though
by no means exclusively) according to success on the
market.
    How is that social position to be determined? First,
even where we have shorter or longer biographies, they very
rarely give income figures; in very many cases, even the
main source of income is not clear. In the context of a
relative dearth of data, the category of main source of
income will be here treated together with the kind of
education for mutual illumination. It must also be borne
in mind that a good number of writers knew ups and downs in
their social position, and my classification takes into
account both what they had achieved at the time of publishing their S-F text(s) and the central tendency in their
lives. Furthermore, just as for social origin, other grids
supplementing these two categories have to be used for any
full account. Nonetheless, such biographical data can provide a good or approximate account of 144 UK writers,

double the number of those identified by social origin.

Concerning education, the extremely expensive frequenta-
tion of "public"--that is, private--schools (£140-180 a
year) and/or of Oxford/Cambridge (£100 and upward a year)
is a standard criterion of upper or upper-middle class position, though of course there were some black sheep and
quite a few very interesting ideological renegades or near-
renegades (for example, Allen, Butler, Hird, Maitland).
The annual intake of Oxford and Cambridge together was
about 700 students in 1860 and about 1,300 in 1880, with a
predominant social origin of landowners and Anglican clergymen (Clark 256-57). The higher number was roughly 1 per
mille of its male age-group and 0.5 per mille of the whole
population age-group, and it constituted the core of the
actually ruling elite. Thus, writers who had not frequent-
ed "public" school and Oxbridge (e.g., George Eliot, Hardy,
Gissing, or Wells) were in a way--together with some other
top professionals and working-class organizers--the only
alternative public "thinkers" or societal model-builders.

The grid of classes induced from the Biographies' data on
source of income and education turns out to be different
from and simpler than the grid employed for the writers'
social origins:

1) The landowning aristocracy and the rich bourgeoisie
fused in the second half of the century into a new wealthy
dominant group. As in the other following classes, two
subgroups can be distinguished: a) not directly dependent on the market--aristocrats, top officers, politicians, and civil servants (and their spouses): Anson (?),
Brookfield, Bulwer-Lytton, Burnaby, Chesney, Colomb,
Dering, Dixie, Fawcett (?), Glyn, M. L'Estrange (?), Vogel;
b) directly dependent on the market--industrialists,
businessmen, planters, newspaper or publishing-house
owners, rentiers: Butler, Chilton, Corbett (?), Curwen,
Downey, Hannan (?), Lehmann, Lucas, Middleton, W. Morris,
Rickett, Strachey; in all 24. Almost all of them went
either to "public" schools or to Oxbridge (or some equivalent thereof such as Trinity College Dublin, St. Andrews,
officers' academies, Inns of Court), usually to both.

2) Top professionals, divided into: a) top men of
letters (editors, the most successful writers): Barr,
Besant, Clowes, Doyle, Du Maurier, Gorst, Graves, Hudson,
Hume, Hyne, Jane, Jerome, A. Lang, O'Grady, Oppenheim,
Payn, Pemberton, Stead, Sykes, Traill, H.B.M. Watson,
Wells; b) others, including barristers, civil servants,
members of Parliament, Anglican clergymen, top educators
and medical men: Abbott, Acworth (?), Barlow, Bennett,
Constable, Davis, Eastwick (?), Gould, Hird, Jenkins,

"Jingo Jones" (?), Kellett, Lach-Szyrma, Lancaster, Lester, Lyon (?), J.A.K. Mackay, Maguire, Markwick, Minto, Munro, Murphy, Murray, Nicholson, Philpot, Potter, Richardson, Schofield, Thorburn, Trollope, Tucker; in all 53. A number of them went to Oxbridge, most to some university, but some (e.g., Barr, Du Maurier, Jane, Mackay) seem to have been without higher education. In this class one also encounters major oscillations of status: for example, Jane entered it only late in his career, while Gorst seems to have declined from it.

3) Middle professionals, divided into: "middle" men and women of letters: Allen, Andreae (?), Barrett, Bramston, Buchanan, Bridge, Cobbe, Collins, Cromie, Dalton, Davidson, Ellis (5?), Greg, Gregg (5?), Hayes, Hearn, Hemyng, Jefferies, Jepson, Griffith Jones, Kinross, Le Queux, Linton, Maitland, Nisbet, P.S. Robinson, Shiel, Tracy, Welch, Westall; b) other "middle" professionals, including general practitioners in medicine, solicitors, higher teachers, naturalists, Protestant ministers: Blair, Carne-Ross, Dixon, Druery, Dudgeon, Fox, Gillmore, Greer, Hay (?), Hinton, Lumley, Norton, Perry, Reeve (?), H.C.M. Watson; in all 45. Less than a quarter of them were educated at "public" school or Oxbridge, while almost half had no university-level education, and for a number of these there are no educational data at all.

4) Lower professionals, as a rule without much bio-graphical information, so that a question-mark might be put against most of these names: a) the lowest rung of journalists, men of letters, etc., often penny-a-liners: A. Clark, Cobban, R.W. Cole, Fawkes, Gleig, Greener, Hannan, Hervey (3?), Hulme-Beaman, Lawrence, Pallander, Shannon, Suffling, Waterhouse, F.M. White; b) other "unack-nowledged" professionals: Atkins, Carter, P. Clarke (3?), McIver (?), A. Morris, Singer; in all 21. Educational data are as a rule lacking; a few seem to have been engin-eering apprentices.

5) Tradesmen, employees: Lee was a plasterer by trade and seems also to have become publican; in all 1.

Though a number of people were earlier seen to have originated in families either of merchants and upper clerks or of farmers and laborers, both of these categories are conspicuously absent here. When people became writers, as far as we know they moved out of these classes and into the professional classes.

To recapitulate: 1) wealthy dominant group, mostly "pub-lic" school and Oxbridge = 24; 2) top professionals, mostly with Oxbridge or other university education = 53; 3) middle professionals, with non-Oxbridge university or secondary

education = 45; 4) lower professionals, with secondary
education, apprenticeship or lower = 21; 5) tradesmen = 1;
in all = 144. For 42 UK writers there are no data permit-
ting even a guess at their main source of income and education, and thus at their social position, except that it
must have been as a rule in the categories 4 or 5 (except
for 10 percent or 4 I shall allot to middle professionals).

Of the non-UK writers, 7 were independently wealthy, all
from the USA (Astor, C.H. Clarke, Lloyd, G.N. Miller, Peck,
Putnam, Rogers); 28 were top professionals--men of letters
as About, Chambers, Clemens, Harben, Hertzka, Howells,
Michaelis, J. Miller, Mitchell, Serviss, Stockton, Verne,
lawyers, politicians, clergymen, academics, scientists as
Collens, De Mille, Flammarion, Hale, Newcomb, Stimson, or
both as Bellamy, Donnelly, Grousset, Tourgée; 16 were middle professionals, as a rule men or women of letters (e.g.,
Dodd, O'Brien); 7 were lower professionals, as a rule men
or women of letters; and for 9 there are no data (I shall
allot 1 to middle professionals).

Tabulated, the UK and foreign writers give the results
shown in table 3.

Table 3
Social Position of S-F Writers

	UK	%	Foreign	%
Wealthy dominant group	24	12	7	10
Upper professionals	53	29	28	42
Middle professionals	50	27	16	25
Lower professionals	21	11 ⎫	8	12 ⎫
Tradesmen, employees	1	1 ⎬ 32	--	-- ⎬ 23
Unknown lower class	37	20 ⎭	7	11 ⎭
Sum Total	186	100	66	100

The only significant, and rather large, deviation in foreign writers is the preference given to the upper professionals at the expense of the lower classes. I do not have
a full explanation for this: it is partly due to the
better known writers having a better chance of being published outside of their own country, and perhaps partly to
their ideological horizons.

If one were to look at the social position of the writers
whose S-F works have survived until today (following the
criteria mentioned earlier), the UK names would be divided

absolutely equally (4 each) among the first three classes:
Bulwer-Lytton, Chesney, Butler, and W. Morris in class 1;
Doyle, Wells, Abbott, and Trollope in class 2; and Greg,
Jefferies, Griffith Jones, and Shiel in class 3. A conclusion that might be drawn from this is that the lower
classes in this scale (lower professionals, tradesmen,
employees, unknown) have rightly or wrongly, and I suspect
at least in the case of Lee wrongly, not (or not yet?) been
rehabilitated by the judgment of the intervening century.
But then, for a neglected genre and type of social discourse, in which reevaluation has gathered momentum only in
this last decade, a century is not that long. As for the
foreigners--the lack of data for whom precluded a comparison based on social origin--their division is rather different: 2 in class 1 (Lloyd and Peck); 12 in class 2
(Bellamy, Chambers, Clemens-Twain, Grousset, Harben,
Howells, Serviss, Stockton, Verne, De Mille, Donnelly,
Hale); and 3 in class 3 (Dodd, O'Brien, Waterloo). In this
case, the clear UK preponderance of the wealthy dominant
group has been replaced by an even clearer, indeed overwhelming preponderance of the upper professionals. Since
all the surviving foreigners are from the USA, except for
the Canadian De Mille and the Frenchmen Grousset and Verne,
this can be ascribed both to the different general class
structure in the United States, which lacked a traditionally ensconced upper class, and to a greater interest there
in sociopolitical and technological alternatives among top
writers, who account for exactly half of the foreign names.
A full comparison with Williams's sample is not possible
here as he does not use the same grid. However, from his
data, and with the correction explained à propos of
table 2, it is clear that Oxbridge and the "public" schools
were incomparably more important for his "high lit" sample,
with 45 percent as against my 23 percent. It might also be
inferred that his list is much more top-heavy in favor of
the wealthy dominant class, at the expense of partly the upper but mostly the middle and lower professionals. In that
light, the indication from table 2, that is, that SF was
written by people of not radically dissimilar social origin from the "high lit" writers, needs to be complemented, and leads to the following very tentative conclusion.
First, SF was not--as it would become in the 20th
century--a separate commercial genre (in the trade sense)
nor a fully separate readers' ghetto or subculture. It
was a recognized and legitimate, though clearly not central, part of literature's social discourse, addressed--at
least in the first place--to the same system of social addressees as general fiction.

Yet, at the same time, the actual social position of the writers of parts of this discourse was, so to speak, schizophrenic--disproportionately large at the top and at the bottom of the social position scale (see table 3). The top (my uppermost two classes, which can be compared to Williams's top categories), was appreciably smaller than in Williams's "high lit" sample, but still two fifths--a quite large proportion. The bottom (my nethermost three classes) was one third--quite disproportionately large in comparison to "high lit" writers. The reason for this bipolar concentration and split are complex; they would have to be considered further in connection with the subgenres of SF, and with possible subgroups of social addressees having a special interest in them, as subsystems within the hegemonic system of Victorian social addressees of fiction. Here it should be noted that this large bipolar split begins at a precise juncture, namely with the sudden quantitative outpouring of SF after 1886 (see the Bibliography). That outpour was accompanied by a sudden downward shift in the writers' social position. Quite dramatically, in that year the S-F book publication jumps from an 1871-1885 average of 6 to an 1886-1900 average of 21 new titles a year. At the same time, 54 out of the 59 UK writers in my three lower classes of Lower professionals, Tradesmen, and Unknown (i.e., all except for 5 aberrant Unknowns before 1855--E.A. Robinson, Ryan, Soleman, Wall, Wise--most or all of whom, I suspect, can be explained as amateur writers from the upper class) begin to appear in the S-F field; and this holds also for <u>all</u> the 15 "low class" foreign writers.

Up to 1886, then--except for a significantly smaller participation of the "wealthy dominant group"--S-F writers had the same social position as "high lit" ones. After 1886, the dramatic increase of publication brings an influx of lower-class or Grub Street writers, and changes the overall social status of S-F writers. Yet, paradoxically, the status of SF as a socially acceptable cluster of subgenres or variant of discourse is at the same time, I think, raised. It is significant that almost all the writers from my two highest classes who published before 1886 withheld their name (Besant, Brookfield, Bulwer-Lytton, Butler, Chesney, Strachey, Abbott, Lach-Szyrma), as did the middle professionals with pretensions to impeccable respectability (Blair, Cobbe, Dudgeon, Lumley, H.C.M. Watson, Welch). It is still more significant that roughly after 1886 it was not only other people from the same classes who started using their full name on the book title-page, but so did the "bell-wethers" among the just named writers who contin-

ued to publish S-F books after 1886--Besant (writer),
Strachey (journal editor), and Lach-Szyrma (clergyman).
This does not mean that there were no pseudonyms after
1886, but that their proportion decreased and that they
tended to be equally used by writers of high and low social
position, that is, more for personal than public reasons.
The new social acceptability of SF, which brought it both
the Grub Street professionals and a new group of upper-
class amateurs, is due to its becoming a forum for discourse about the heightened social tensions from the
mid-80s on.

   4. The three middle classes are divided into men of
letters and others. The fact that I have not disjoined
men of letters into entirely separate classes is due to an
osmosis prevailing at the same level of social position--
which also means the same level of income--between them and
other professionals. Indeed, the differentiation itself is
in some cases difficult: I shall take examples from class
2. Abbott was primarily a prominent educator, but also for
50 years a writer of significant works on language and its
teaching, on literature and theology; Minto was professor
of logic and literature in Aberdeen after having been
editor of two London periodicals, but also a prolific
contributor to leading British reviews on literary subjects, author or editor of 9 books of criticism or manuals
and of 7 works of fiction; Trollope was a civil servant in
the Post Office, but also frequent contributor to periodicals, for a while editor of one, and above all a man of
letters who published over 50 novels and almost 20 other
titles in 35 years. Their social position at the time was
probably primarily determined by their main professional
base, but I put them into the "other" instead of into the
"men of letters" subcategory with increasing reluctance.
Obversely, Traill began as a barrister and civil servant,
Conan Doyle as a doctor; Besant was the archetypal Establishment man of letters but also for a while college
teacher, then secretary of the Palestine Exploration Fund
and a public figure prominent in causes such as reform in
London's East End or organizing the Society of Authors; and
Sykes was a Punch-school humorist, journalist, author,
and editor, but at various stages of his life also educator
and civil servant. An increasingly stronger case could be
made to shift these names out of the men of letters
category.

   This osmosis was not only professional, it was also ideological. Yet while being determines consciousness, it
would be too crude to say that economic being alone
determines it. No doubt, this was the case with very many

writers in the Biographies.   Nonetheless, the case for a
special social group and ideological interest-group based
on status rather than finances, and consisting of either
the professionals as a whole or (more dubiously) the men of
letters by themselves has to be briefly examined.

The latter argument (which would mean fusing the men-of-
letters subcategories from classes 2, 3, and 4 into one new
class) can be disposed of by drawing attention to the huge
disparities in social position between their upper and
lower reaches.   Writers with the top incomes of a Thackeray
(paid £2,000 a year as editor of Cornhill in 1862) or a
Trollope (who according to his autobiography earned from
writing up to 1879 an average of over £2,000 a year--a
number significantly higher in his middle and later years)
were in the income range of an average industrialist or
businessman.   Indeed, some of them were also businessmen,
proprietors, or chairmen of journals such as Times of
India and Spectator, publishing houses such as Downey
and Methuen, etc. (Curwen, Strachey, Downey, Lucas, W.
Morris).   Their social position was thus equal or superior
to the businessman, and they could hobnob with the cream of
British society and with its power elite (Besant, Clowes,
Doyle, and Pemberton were knighted).   At the other end, we
do not know the yearly income of the totally obscure penny-
a-liners, but the trajectories of both fictional (e.g.,
Gissing's) and factual figures ethically unwilling to make
the necessary accommodations yet not (as Wells) talents of
the very first order are eloquent enough. For about one
third of the 186 UK writers we do not even have basic biographical data, and it is fair to ascribe this overwhelmingly (I would say in 90 percent of cases) to their financial
indigence, and resulting social obscurity, within what
already Defoe had called a branch of English commerce:

> Writing . . . is become a very considerable Branch of
> English commerce. The Booksellers are the Master Manu-
> facturers or Employers. The several Writers, Authors,
> Copyers, Sub-Writers and all other operators with Pen
> and Ink are the workmen employed by the said Master-
> Manufacturers (Williams LR 183).

This industrial and commercial branch expanded strongly
after 1850.   The yearly output of book-titles rose from
about 2,600 to about 8,400 in the 1880s and then started
falling, but by the end of the century it had still more
than doubled as against midcentury (5).   By then there were
over 400 publishing houses in London, while the periodicals
and newspapers had soared from about 550 in 1851 to about
5,000 (Gross 199, Saunders 201).   All this gave work to

more "authors" than ever before--perhaps 20 times as many
in 1901 as in 1851, that is, 11,000 versus 550 (Reader 207-
11--let it be remembered however that the census category
"authors" comprised in 1901 not only journalists and
editors but also shorthand writers). The average writers'
fee also rose in the last two decades of the century
(TLS-CEL 338-39, Hepburn passim). Yet paradoxically--
--but in line with the general economic argument which
will be developed about the UK lower classes in Part II,
section 1 of this work--of the approximately 110 men and
women of letters among the S-F writers almost precisely
half (in class 4 and among the Unknowns) were on the lowest
rung of obscurity, that is, in constant threat of indigence.

On the middle rung of what Besant in his writers' manual
called a "steady man of letters," neither indigent nor popular author, there were the 26 men and 5 women of my class
3. If one is to believe Besant, they could by writing
reviews and readers' opinions, contributions to encyclo-
pedias and periodicals, factual books such as biographies,
and perhaps an occasional novel, live regularly and com-
fortably--which I take to mean in the lower half of the
£300-1,000 a year bracket of the middle-class merchant, a
status that Besant evidently thought highly of--and
"educate [their] children properly." Besant added there is
no fear of work lacking "as soon as the writer has made
himself known as a trustworthy and attentive workman" (6).
But this bland optimism of Sir Walter's is factually not
correct--or perhaps it is only correct if we take the
ominous ideological implications of "trustworthy" and
"attentive" at their full value. Some quite well-known
names from my class 3, such as Buchanan and Davidson, got
into serious financial difficulties; indeed Davidson committed suicide for which this was at least one of the reasons.
As Grant Allen--more aboveboard about his difficulties
than usual among these writers--remarked bitterly when
explaining why he wrote his pot-boilers that could be
serialized without offending anybody (a state of affairs
discussed at length in the study on the social addressees
of Victorian fiction, in Part II of this work), the professional novelist "in order to write . . . must first eat"
(Allen x). At the other end within this "middle" class of
writers, Carlyle in 1854 had an income of about £400.
This kept him modestly comfortable if not affluent "in a
house where the rent was only £30 a year and the housekeep-
ing totalled £230" (Saunders 192)--including the keeping
of two woefully exploited servants and a brougham--but it
was scarcely what one would expect for a prophet-writer
honored in his day.

The argument about professionals as a whole is stronger,
though if put in any strict form—that is, that professionals constituted a homogeneous and separate social class—it
is subject to the same strictures as the one about the men
of letters. The great differences among the—roughly speaking—three strata of professionals (e.g., Anglican bishop
or law lord: general practitioner of medicine or civil
engineer: teacher of the poor) will also be rehearsed at
length in the first section of Part II to follow. Nonetheless, this argument has been put in a striking and
pertinent form by Hofstadter's hypothesis of the "status
revolution" within the upper classes of late 19th and early
20th-century USA. At that time, the "changed pattern in
the distribution and deference of power" profited the mush-
rooming new money-power at the expense of the small-town
professionals (lawyers, clergymen, physicians, editors) and
the local merchants. Feeling threatened both by the new
plutocracy and by the working classes growing restive under
its more oppressive rule, the older leading group—which
provided practically all the leaders for the reform
movement—proposed a public regulation of power that would
forestall mass plebeian violence (7). Now obviously, the
British social antecedents were different. The intelligentsia had here never participated in wielding power. It had
always been overshadowed by a firmly ensconced and ruthless
upper class—it is enough to recall the fate of the Godwin-
Shelley and similar circles from the time of the French
Revolution. Yet Hofstadter also speaks of some rising
professional groups, such as the academics. It would be
possible, thus, to adapt his thesis by drawing a parallel
between their growth in numbers and confidence and the
general growth of the British intelligentsia, at least a
fraction of which can reasonably be supposed to have been
searching for alternative social models of human relationships.
This has been done in a somewhat extreme form by Perkin
who proposes "lawyers, doctors, public officials, journalists, professors" and similar professionals as a separate
19th-century English class, the "non-capitalist or professional middle class." Its incomes were neither rent,
profit nor wage, they were "not the direct result of
bargaining in the market" but the result of a tacit
societal evaluation. These professions were "characterized
by expert, esoteric service demanding integrity in the
purveyor and trust in the client and the community, and by
non-competitive reward in the form of a fixed salary or
standard and unquestioned fee" (Perkin 252-54). "Their
ideal society was a functional one based on expertise and

selection by merit," and in the 19th century "their increasing professionalism led many of them increasingly to differentiate themselves from the business class and to play an
important part in criticizing the entrepreneurial policy of
laissez-faire and replacing it by collectivism" (Perkin
258 and 429). While the confrontation between the ideologies of laissez-faire and collectivism is obviously
important, I would like to enter a demurrer against basing
a social class (at least in the "strong" or Marxist sense)
on ideal, unspoken assumptions which sometimes turn out to
be themselves simply nostalgic ideologies: the post-
Victorian history of "a fixed salary or standard and unquestioned fee" has shown them to be intrinsically also based
on competition and bargaining. But this does not necessarily invalidate Perkin's point about the professionals'
possibly different social ideals and ideal society as
opposed to "the emerging plutocracy" (Perkin 428)--and of
course to the emerging working class--since these differential oppositions pertain precisely to the sphere of
ideology. As long as it is kept in mind that this is not a
social class in the "strong" sense of having totally different interests from the bourgeoisie, but a social group
hesitating between its "professionalist" ideals and its
economic status, and moreover that it is not a single group
but an internally layered and sometimes clearly antagonistic grouping (see, for example, the Wells-Lucas and
Lehmann-Le Queux oppositions in subsection 2 above!), it
seems to me the thesis of a separate "professionalist"
ideology could be a useful differential tool in discussing
pieces of social discourse--and especially so in the case
of an S-F corpus. It is possible that segments of the
middle-to-upper professionals after, say, the mid-1880s
might turn out to be (as their 20th-century Bloomsbury
successors):

> . . . a true fraction of the existing English upper
> class. They were at once against its dominant ideals
> and values and still willingly, in all immediate ways,
> part of it. It is a very complex and delicate posi-
> tion, but the significance of such fractions has been
> very generally underestimated. It is not only a ques-
> tion of this problematic relationship within any partic-
> ular section of time. It is also a question of the
> function of such relationships and such groups in the
> development and adaptation, through time, of the class
> as a whole (Williams PMC 156-57).

Other segments of the professionals certainly occupied a

different, less alienated position. However, the "professionalism"--consisting both of a precise social position
and (in the case of doctors, engineers, and even artists
and writers) of a systematic practice of cognizing or
reasoning, even if only about one more or less alienated
domain of the social world--can in my opinion be taken if
not as the central determinant of social group then as
one among the important determinants of all such people's
social being. The proof of the pudding will be, as always,
in the texts themselves.

However one explains it, a clear picture emerges, from
the statistics of social position as well as of social
origin, that various groups of professionals in general and
men/women of letters in particular were the principal
social addressors of Victorian fiction in general and my
S-F corpus in particular. In social origin, about 55 percent of my writers come from families of "professionals."
In social position, the tripling of numbers in all professions in the second half of the century is largely caught
up in the 10-to-20-fold multiplication of writers, so that
professionals account for 67 to 87 percent of all my UK
writers, and men/women of letters alone for 37 to 59
percent. The margin of uncertainty, due to the unknowns,
is in my opinion to be largely resolved in favor of the
higher percentage: it can be safely assumed that more than
four fifths of the UK S-F writers were professionals, of
which about two thirds--or more than half of all the S-F
writers--were men/women of letters. Obversely, the over 80
percent of UK population composed of manual workers and
paupers remained for all statistical purposes unrepresented
among the UK S-F writers. A remark about the Victorian
"novels of faith and doubt" stands thus for this corpus
too: "novel-readers and novel-writers are our subject, and
that fact distorts our sample . . . away from the laboring class and towards readers, intellectuals, would-be
intellectuals, and half-baked intellectuals" (8). This too
should be kept in mind when approaching S-F texts.

5. It might perhaps have been interesting to undertake
other quarrying of my biographical data. As mentioned
earlier, for example, an ethno-geographical division--by
provenience from and/or domicile in, say, Ireland,
Scotland, Wales, English provinces, London, India, other
venues abroad--would certainly give further elements for
understanding the subtle gradations of social rank and
ideology. Or, social origin is always counted by father,
but the mother is in many cases (e.g., Wells, Jefferies) as
important for a full understanding, and the grandparents
are not much less important. Or, it would be interesting

to see the results of division by writers of subgenres and
themes (future war, extraordinary voyage, alternative
history, position of women, etc.) combined with further
chronological subdivision. For 1848 to 1885, some results
of such investigations will be deployed in the conclusion
to this work, but for most of them much further data would
be necessary first.

Notes

1. Williams ML, p. 193. This work will be found in the
secondary Selected Bibliography at the end of these notes;
as with a number of other important titles, it will be
further cited by abbreviation and page number within the
text itself.--"The manner in which literary criticism once
. . . constructed the author . . . is directly derived from
the manner in which Christian tradition authenticated (or
rejected) the texts at its disposal," observes Michel
Foucault in his essay "What Is an Author," in Josué V.
Harari, ed., Textual Strategies (Ithaca NY, 1979), p. 141
ff. Foucault goes on to analyze how the author's monolith-
ic saintliness was in tight ideological feedback with the
construction of four "unities" in order that his opus might
be in turn admitted to the status of a significant unit(y):
the unity of value, of conceptualized doctrine, of style,
and of historical chronology.

2. Cesare Segre, Semiotics and Literary Criticism (The
Hague, 1973), p. 74. See also the essays by Gérard Klein
and Charles Elkins in, and my introduction to, "The Sociology of Science Fiction," in R.D. Mullen and Darko Suvin,
eds., Science-Fiction Studies: Second Series (Boston,
1978), p. 238ff.

3. Myron F. Brightfield, Victorian England in Its
Novels (Los Angeles, 1968).

4. See Samuel Hynes, The Edwardian Turn of Mind
(Princeton, 1968), p. 42.

5. Calculated by me from data in Sampson Low's introduction to The English Catalogue of Books, 5 vols. (all rpt.
Milwood, NY, 1971). This accords well with data in Plant,
pp. 446-47, but not with Saunders, p. 202. The whole area
of book-publishing in 19th-century UK is in some considerable statistical disarray and urgently requires fundamental
investigation based on archives and periodicals of the
time: for example, nobody knows how many titles were published for the first time in a given year or decade, nor

what their breakdown into categories (such as fiction) would be. My attempts to reach a reasonable degree of certainty based on sources such as the English Catalogue, the Publishers' Circular, the British Museum annual returns, and various editions of Mulhall, proved fruitless.

6. Besant, passim; see also the useful comments of Gross, pp. 199-200.

7. Richard Hofstadter, The Age of Reform (New York, 1955), pp. 135-64, 215-26, quote from p. 135; cf. also The Education of Henry Adams (New York, 1931), p. 32. Kenneth M. Roemer briefly comments on the imperfect applicability of Hofstadter's hypothesis to writers of US utopias in his "America as Utopia, 1889-1900," Ph.D. dissertation, University of Pennsylvania, 1971, pp. 74-76, portions of which he kindly sent to me. However, he does not pursue Hofstadter's larger argument either here or in his very useful, modified book The Obsolete Necessity ([Kent, OH], 1976) that resulted from the dissertation, which I have often consulted for comparison.

8. Robert Lee Wolff, Gains and Losses (New York and London, 1977), p. 419.

Selected Bibliography

Standard bibliographies, histories, and surveys of society, politics, culture, and literature have as a rule not been retained.

Allen=Allen, Grant. "Introduction" to his The British Barbarians. London, 1895.

Altick VPI=Altick, Richard D. Victorian People and Ideas. New York, 1973.

Banks=Banks, J.A. "The Challenge of Popular Culture: Introduction," in Philip Appleman et al., eds., 1859: Entering an Age of Crisis. Bloomington IN, 1959, pp. 199-214.

Baxter=Baxter, R. Dudley. National Income: United Kingdom. London, 1868.

Besant=Besant, Walter. The Pen and the Book. London, 1900.

Burn=Burn, W.L. *The Age of Equipoise*. New York, 1965.

Clark=Clark, G. Kitson. *The Making of Victorian England*. London, 1965.

Gross=Gross, John. *The Rise and Fall of the Man of Letters*. London, [1969].

Hepburn=Hepburn, James. *The Author's Empty Purse*. London, 1968.

Mulhall=[Mulhall, Michael G.] *Mulhall's Dictionary of Statistics*. London, 1884.

Perkin=Perkin, Harold. *The Origins of Modern English Society 1780-1880*. London and Toronto, 1969.

Plant=Plant, Marjorie. *The English Book Trade*. London, 1939.

Reader=Reader, W.J. *Professional Men*. London, 1966.

Saunders=Saunders, J.W. *The Profession of English Letters*. London, 1964.

TLS-CEL=*Times Literary Supplement*, 1 May 1937: "A Century of English Letters" (special issue).

Williams LR=Williams, Raymond. *The Long Revolution*. Harmondsworth, 1971.

Williams ML=Williams, Raymond. *Marxism and Literature*. Oxford, 1977.

Williams PMC=Williams, Raymond. *Problems in Materialism and Culture*. London, 1980.

Part II:
The Social Discourse of Victorian Science Fiction:
An Interpretive Essay

A. Introduction

> To collect facts about
> the past, and to leave
> the social application of
> this information for any
> one or no one to give it
> a philosophical meaning,
> is merely to encumber the
> future with useless
> rubbish.
>
> Frederic Harrison, <u>Auto-
> biographic Memoirs</u>

One of the foremost scholars in the field of Victorian literature—and the reading of popular literature in particular—prefaced a book about the historical context of the time by a warning that "it mercilessly simplifies topics which every well-informed student of the period recognizes to be extremely complicated; it makes broad statements which are, in reality, subject to all manner of qualifications" (1). In this, much briefer, essay with a much more modest function, I must not only repeat such a statement but also add that I was forced to pass under silence all those topics or aspects which were not seen as absolutely indispensable for my much narrower field.

This interpretive essay is part and parcel of that continuing interest of mine in SF to which I have referred in the Preface. I pointed out there how this book is, however, also designed as an experiment in dealing with or at least approaching a large body of paraliterature. If in <u>Metamorphoses of Science Fiction</u> it had proved just barely possible to deal with Wells—or Morris, or even Verne and Bellamy—by a methodology which only somewhat adapted and bent the tried approaches to "high lit," this was from the outset evidently impossible in this endeavor. Yet I was willing to accept the easy way out of using the 430-odd

255

titles identified in the Bibliography as "Victorian SF"
simply as sociological or ideological documents--in other
words, to forget their basic generic nature as fiction. I
believe this would have been merely the obverse of the
ruling-class or elitist (in the last two centuries mainly
bourgeois) ideology which holds that only a rather restricted group of "masterpieces" is really Art or Literature.
It would mean, among other things, subscribing to a tacit
division within fictional discourse into a body and soul,
or inert matter and quintessence, a division that validates
the pyramid with a few masterpieces on its top by claiming
that they "embody" the soul or quintessence, while the
plebeian great bulk of fiction and culture is soulless,
brute, etc. On the contrary, I hold that all discourse is
a material body, web, or texture, and fictional discourse a
particularly dense one: there is no kernel to it whose
extraction would then permit us to discard the husk. Furthermore, the split into "high" versus "low" literature
would mean using my texts as a starting point but not truly
as a convergence point of my investigation. Now, this
study might abundantly show that I am extremely skeptical
about any Great Walls of China not only within literature
but also between literary and other socioeconomic domains
(since they are all different facets of the same history of
human groups, their strivings, practices, beliefs, and discourses). Yet at the same time the specific pleasures and
values of a fictional corpus are slighted, or indeed
destroyed, unless it is treated as sovereign within its own
field of investigations. This means that the fascinating
and quite indispensable ways of understanding its context
are subservient to the final understanding of the texts
themselves as a specific organon of cognition (though the
spiral then winds on to what is being cognized). Thus, I
had to set about finding, if not a full-blown methodology,
then at least some useful methods for economically presenting my corpus. The only course that seemed open was to
treat this corpus as an example of fictional social discourse. More precisely, preferring plural to singular
abstractions, this meant treating my texts as specific
instances of value-sets of given social groups or classes,
sets developed into parables and exempla, as more or less
alternative "possible worlds"--in a sense that felicitously
fuses modern logic and narratology with the tradition of
SF.

In that view, any literary work, whatever else it may be,
always presents a set of interests and values, of dominant,
alternative, or oppositional subcultural or class norms.
True, this set might be hidden, parabolically transposed,

or indeed confused. Further, the transposing is usually easier to decipher in nonfiction, while fictional litera- ture requires more complex analysis. Most important, any literary text in its hidden or overt dialog continues and at the same time necessarily refashions or <u>reconstitutes</u> a set of interests and values, of class norms: each narra- tive is, clearly, both an echo of some existing set or system and (by the very fact of its difference from previous texts) its anamorphic distortion and reelabora- tion. The set of values and norms is thereby perpetuated but also more or less inflected. This could be treated as analogous to the relationship of individual versus class in the biological and social sciences, but in that case the potency of the individual and variability of the class, due to the artificial or artefactual nature of the texts, would have to be stressed.

In this light, the first two questions for the paraliter- ary, S-F corpus at hand should be: what normative systems are being reconstituted in it, that is--1) which ideal readers (addressees) are implied in it? 2) how are their normative systems continued and refashioned? The first question, about the ideal readers or addressees, seems most usefully approached by asking two subquestions: a) what do we know or can infer about the readers of our corpus?; and b) what do we know or can infer about its writers? The discussions of these two ancillary questions require some- what different methods--in the first case somewhat more deductive and in the second somewhat more inductive--and they are therefore treated in two separate sections. The section on writers is to be found in Part I of this book, so that this interpretive essay will begin with an overview of the readers as social addressees of fiction. This should sketch in a context for the two final sections, where an attempt will be made, on the basis of the S-F works published in the UK from 1848 to 1886, to provide some answers to the question about normative sets in fic- tion, that is, to indicate how these are molded and recon- stituted in various works or groups of works at hand.

B. The Social Addressees of Victorian Fiction

1. The Concept of Social Addressee

> It will be obvious to any-
> one who reads this book
> that I have made excur-
> sions into fields which I
> knew (and, for that mat-
> ter, know) imperfectly.
> But if we allowed modesty
> and prudence to have
> things all their own way
> and ourselves to be
> deflected by signs that
> say, "Sociology (or Art,
> or Literature, or Theolo-
> gy)—Keep Out," it would
> be a dull world for his-
> torians. . . . It must
> also be plain that
> neither my sympathies nor
> my interests are compre-
> hensive.
>
> W.L. Burn, <u>The Age of</u>
> <u>Equipoise</u>

What do we know or what can we reasonably infer about the original British readers of the approximately 430 S-F titles in the Bibliography? Paradoxically, not much, yet not so little either.

1.1. Not much: if there are any firsthand testimoni-als, statistical analyses, or inductive secondary investiga-tions about the readers or kinds of readers who had in 19th-century Britain actually read the S-F corpus at hand or subsets thereof (e.g., the utopias), I do not know of them. It is, of course, quite possible that some such tes-timonials—perhaps about readers of some comparable large set of texts--might be found, especially in the copious 19th-century periodicals which I confess to having perused unsystematically. But I trust that any important and general data of that kind would have been mentioned in the abundant and not rarely excellent discussions in the modern secondary literature, so that whatever I might have missed would not have been central to my purpose.

Not so little: for we have in the last decade or two acquired or refurbished some interesting instruments for inferring the implied, ideal reader from the texts themselves, when these are placed in the proper context of sociohistorical semantics and value-systems (thus avoiding the vicious circle of explaining texts by explanations solely from within the texts). This process of inference goes by way of a horizon of expectation, in order to arrive at the text's postulated ideal reader or social addressee.

The horizon of expectation(s) has been defined as the "specific predisposition on which the author of a given work counts in his audience" (2). It is sometimes directly evoked in a text--for example, the chivalry novels read by the protagonist of Don Quijote--but it can be indirectly reconstituted in three complementary ways from the postulatable generic, intertextual, and semantic contexts of any given work: that is, from the norms of the literary genre the text belongs to; from the text's relationships to other "printed matter" coexisting with it in a given historical moment; and most generally from the relationship of the text as a part of social discourse to nondiscursive practice and the accepted models thereof. All three of these ways are based upon our independent knowledge of the cultural conventions, ways of seeing, and ideologies a given precise social group of readers--or a cluster of such groups--can be expected to share. These normative structures are then refracted (and, as noted above, partly refashioned) through the more or less adequate structure of feeling in the literary work--which, of course, also can, and in SF often does, anticipate not yet realized possibilities of human relationships, not only conforming to existing values and desires but also defining partly new desires, formulating and thus stimulating new horizons of expectation. One could then imagine a hierarchy of horizons of expectation, from that of a single work through those of a coherent set of works such as a literary opus, a literary genre, a school, a generation, etc., to encompassing horizons of espectation of a given age's dominant social group.

The term of social group is crucial to this essay, and

perhaps this is the place to clarify how it will be used.
As a rule--and especially in 19th-century Britain--the
precise term to be used is that of a social class in Marx's
sense. However, at some points the precise term would be
segment or fraction of a class, and at other points I
simply do not know whether the group in question is a fully
fledged social class; in all such cases "social group" will
be used for the sake of convenience. The pedantry may be
excused if it draws attention to a crucial point. It is a
point which seems self-evident but which has evaporated
from a number of studies on what one might call "The
Victorian This or That" (e.g., The Victorian Culture, Literature, or Values):   namely, that the key to understanding
the society and culture of the time--including very much
its fictional discourse and the S-F corpus at hand--is <u>the
existence of fairly distinct, though interacting, social
classes and groups with specific sets of norms and values
or specific structures of feeling</u> (3). To put it bluntly,
it is misleading to speak of "Victorian" values etc., unless one clarifies that there was a hegemonic set within
the differing social group and class values in England--or
Britain--during the reign of Victoria (should we wish to
retain this monarchist chronology). As one of the most
lucid scholars in the social history of art wrote:

> the public is by no means unanimous in its outlook on
> life, and this divergence of outlook among its various
> sections explains the coexistence of different styles
> in the same period. Such divergence is, in its turn,
> due to the fact that what we call the public is not a
> homogeneous body, but is split up into various often
> antagonist groupings. Since the public is merely
> another word for society in its capacity as recipient
> of art, what is required next is to examine the struc-
> ture of society and the relationship between its
> various sections (4).

This quite basic methodological warning means that the
social addressees of the texts dealt with will not be iden-
tifiable without some initial delimitation of British socio-
economic classes after 1848.
   It might be objected that literature sold as a commodity
on the market is intended for all, so that its addressee is
every man, not to say Everyman. But while this may or may
not be true for the mid-20th century, with its more homogen-
ized "mass tastes" largely streamlined by the market
(though even this would have to be significantly qualified), and while I shall argue that turning fiction into

commodity is a crucial factor in its development under
capitalism (in France and the USA from the 1830s, in the
more conservative UK from the 1870s on)--this mass commodi-
fication had not fully conquered what turns out to be a
very peculiar UK literary market, clearly limited both by
penury economics and hierarchical ideology. The social
addressees of 19th-century fiction in general thus remain
to be ascertained by using the different expectation horizons of different social groups, based on their different--
complementary and/or competing--needs, interests, and structures of feeling.

How are, then, the addressees of a piece of social discourse, in this case a fictional text, to be identified?
First, one should distinguish the _receiver_ or actual
empirical reader from the _addressee_ or postulated typical
audience. The latter is _the image that the author of the
text has of an ideal, imaginary reader_, who is characterized by a horizon of expectation; that image can be recon-
structed from an interaction of the text with the contexts
mentioned above, and it has therefore also been identified
as "the act-character of the reading as it is traced out
(_vorgezeichnet_) in the text." It has further been shown
that any utterance or set of utterances is addressed to an
immanent societal receiver "whom the author himself takes
into account, the one toward whom the work is oriented and
who, consequently, intrinsically determines the work's
structure" while remaining quite distinct from the actual
reading public (5). Thus, the reconstruction of the textu-
ally implicit reader can do without the often unavailable
quantitative data on such an actual audience. In a further
stage, one should find out if not yet who the addressees of
various texts in my corpus were (which has to be discussed
at hand of the texts themselves), at least who were the
possible addressees of the whole spectrum of horizons
traced out in the fiction of the period.

1.2. At this point, the rather arbitrary term of
"Victorian age" needs to be scrutinized. Could it be
broken down into several historical periods within which
the constellation of possible addressees would be at least
somewhat, and perhaps significantly, different? I have
approached this question elsewhere (6), and indicated that
most social and economic historians believe a major break
is to be identified with the waning of "the sense of
imminent social explosion" (Hobsbawm 94) around 1848--which
is, then, my _terminus a quo_. This is the beginning of
the "Age of Equipoise" (Burn; cf. also Hobsbawm, Best,
Ensor, Ashworth, and Perkin) between landowners and industrialists, in which the permanently smoldering lower-class

discontent abated and was contained at the level of isolated individuals or gangs. The social stabilization
manifested itself in such momentous changes for the development of literature as free trade in books, the setting up
of W.H. Smith's railway book-stalls and of Mudie's Circulating Library in central London (the English had just become
the first people in human history to have a majority of
town-dwellers), and the beginning of Cassell's immensely
popular cheap educational--later also fictional--publica-
tions. The great turning point in general politicoeconomic
history revealed itself also as "the great turning-point in
the history of the English book trade's relations with the
mass public" (Altick ECR 294). In fact, the whole system
of British social discourse underwent a decisive sea-
change, which can be seen equally in such phenomena as the
introduction of the science degree at Oxbridge, the beginning of the Christian Socialists and (more importantly) the
Pre-Raphaelites, or the shift of _Punch_ from bitter
radicalism to safe oddball conservatism.

The second main break, my _terminus ad quem_, is still
disputed and could be put into the early 1890s, around
1900, or around 1914. Perhaps this date is still too near
to be decided, so that the best we can do is to take a cue
from the particular material at hand and leave a final
judgment to the future. The S-F corpus here clearly
culminates in the opus of Wells from 1894 to 1901, so that
I shall range myself with those who plump for the beginning
of the 20th century (though for other purposes a different
diachronic slicing might be equally, or more, legitimate).
At any rate, the turn of the century is not marked simply
by a new AD number or UK monarch. Parallel to international and national economic developments, at that time had
come into being those patterns of both bourgeois and
working-class life which were to characterize Britain until
the 1960s. This included a jelling of dominant structures
of feeling in culture at large, or at least in popular and
mass culture: "By 1900 the English reading public had
attained substantially the size and character it possesses
today [i.e., 1957, note DS]" (Altick ECR 365).

However, the 1848-1900 period saw too many changes to be
treated as a homogeneous whole, and for meaningful comment
to become possible it must be subdivided. I shall again
follow my material: it is quite unmistakable--as will be
argued at more length in section C--that Victorian SF is
constituted as a consistent social discourse in 1871/72,
with Bulwer, Chesney, Butler, and the first translations of
Verne. In that light, the years from 1848 to 1871 are its
phase of inception, while 1871-1885 is the phase of its

constitution. A new phase of heightened virulence clearly ensues in the mid-80s, comprising the "future Civil War in Ireland" tales, the catastrophe utopias of Jefferies and Hudson, and the works of Hinton, Bellamy, Morris, Twain, and Flammarion; and a final phase runs from about 1893 to 1901, embracing the best SF of Griffith and Wells.

In other words, British SF only finds its addressee(s) around 1871. This was the time, on the one hand, of a still strong self-confidence of the English upper and middle classes, which finally reposed on the unbroken economic boom of the 1850s and 1860s. Yet on the other hand, it was also a time pregnant with so many old and new contradictions: prosperity versus poverty, religion versus science, liberalism versus empire, Barbarians and Philistines versus Culture, the constant sore of Ireland, and so forth--all capped by the 1870/71 war, bringing the rise of Germany and a renewed Red Scare, or Hope, after the bloodily suppressed Paris Commune. It is my working hypothesis that, in this shifting situation, at least some segments of the dominant classes and/or the intelligentsia felt the need to sound the alarm and look at the wider context; and precisely because they wrote in a situation not only of gathering threat but also of relative political security and intraclass freedom of speech, they found ways to do it in written discourse. A number of instruments were at hand for that purpose, but such social groups also created a new one--the predominantly fictional form set in an estranged environment, SF. In other words: the writers of the early 1870s were not simply sensitive seismographs of a general Zeitgeist, catching the first tremors of a longer and deeper crisis of confidence (which was to be fed by the prices' and profits' depression of 1873-1896 and by later economico-ideological depressions). More particularly, they were addressing definite and definable groups whom they hoped to influence. My hypothesis, then, can be tested by an investigation that would confront evidence from both their texts and their contexts in a useful procedure of feedback and mutual validation. For practical reasons, my testing will in this book be confined to the first clear, full, and self-contained period of SF in the UK, the years 1871-1885 inclusive.

2. The Social Addressees 1867–1900: Eliminatory Delimitations

After the identification of the historical phase at hand--
roughly 1848-1900, with three subdivisions (around 1871,
the mid-80s, and the mid-90s) to be discussed in the following sections--the question of the possible social addressees for the horizons traced out in the fiction (and the SF)
of this phase can perhaps be posed with some hope for
provisional and approximate answers. First of all, one can
hope to find who were <u>not</u> its addressees. However, any
such delimitation requires a brief overview of the social
groups existing at the time.

   <u>2.1.</u> The UK population rose from 31.5 million in 1871
to 41.5 million in 1901, of which the over-10 population
rose from 23.5 to 32.5 million (Mitchell-Deane 6-15). In
contrast to some investigators today, nobody at that time--
from Disraeli to Marx--had any doubts that it was divided
into classes, mainly on the basis of income either from
ownership of property or from labor. British society of
the period, "it is hardly too much to say, was obsessed by
class, and riddled with class-consciousness . . ." (Best
xv). Any division into classes which would provide a
convenient overview is bound to simplify the "infinite
gradations" of social groups, of which one of our authors,
Charles Rowcroft, speaks perhaps as eloquently as anybody:

> The gradations of rank in this country are infinite;
> among the middle classes especially. There are the
> great merchants, and the little merchants, and the
> less; and the great shopkeepers, and the little shop-
> keepers, and the less in endless degrees. There are
> those who live in large houses, and those who live in
> small ones; and then again there are those who live in
> apartments in fashionable, or respectable, or incon-
> siderable streets; and these are divided into classes
> of greater or less consideration according to the
> particular floor which they occupy in the house. Thus
> a first-floor lodger would die rather than speak to a

ground-floor one; and the ground-floor would consider
his social position compromised by association with the
second-floor; and all would regard with horror any
approach towards intercourse from the inhabitant of the
attic, whatever might be in other respects his education or acquirements. Then there are the numerous
classes of carriage people varying in rank according to
the character of their equipages, from the occupant of
the close carriage with a footman behind it down to the
one-horse chaise. And nothing short of a general
conflagration would induce a member of any one of these
numberless classes knowingly to enter into social intercourse with a member of the class which he considers
beneath his own (7).

Nonetheless, the overview is indispensable: "the book-
reading public was largely defined by social and economic
class, and continued to be so even as literacy was becoming
universal" (Williams IP 21-22). Fortunately, the national
system of social classes was memorably analyzed for England
and Wales in 1867 by R.D. Baxter. His data can be tabulated as seen in table 1 (8).
The poverty line—defined as the "minimum necessary
expenditure for the maintenance of merely physical
health" (9) (i.e., not a penny being spent on matters such
as reading)—was at the time around £60 per family (Perkin
422-23). Subtracting from column five, for all the
working-class groups, 20 percent for unemployment (see note
8), it becomes clear that in all but the best years not
only were the 40 percent of the population from the bottom
two groups (paupers and unskilled labor) under the poverty
line, but so were also the lower skilled workers and many
servants. Even if we allow for this last group having hidden perks—such as reading their masters' discarded matter
—this first rough survey already indicates that around
1867 between one half and two thirds of the total population were below this extremely frugally defined poverty
line—and thus prevented from practically any reading.
This horrifying economic situation was worse in Scotland
and much worse in Ireland.
No doubt, the general prospering of the UK in the second
half of the century meant not only that inequality of
income between the capitalist and the working class was
increasing, but also that the latter received some real
benefits. The average wage increase, combined with a shift
toward higher paid occupations, can for 1867-1900 be calculated at over 50 percent (10). However, the benefits were
concentrated in the upper reaches of the working class,

Table 1

1867 Distribution of National Income

	Income per year per person in £	Number of recipients in 000s	% of all income recipients	Average income per year per family in £	% of total national income
UPPER CLASS (landowning aristocracy)	over 5,000 (large capital investors)	8	0.07	24,700 (keep large retinue)	16.2
UPPER MIDDLE CLASS (rich bourgeoisie—industrialists, businessmen, bankers, & upper professionals)	1,000–5,000 (middle to large capital investors)	42	0.37	2,800 (keep over four servants)	10.1
MIDDLE CLASS (upper merchants & clerks, lower professionals)	300–1,000 (small investors)	150	1.29	800 (keep 2 to 4 servants)	10.6
LOWER MIDDLE CLASS I (middle tradesmen, junior clerks, stationmasters, etc.)	100–300 (no capital for investment)	850	7.27	180 (struggling to keep one servant)	13.7
LOWER MIDDLE CLASS II	under			75	

				(wives work in home, shop, etc)	
(all non-manual workers irrespective of income, e.g. office workers, shop assistants, foremen, small shopkeepers)	100	1,003	8.58		10.3
Total Upper & Middle Classes:		**2,053**	**17.6**		**60.9**
MOST HIGHLY SKILLED LABOR CLASS	70–100	56	0.48	83	⎱ 10.5
HIGHLY SKILLED LABOR CLASS	60–80	1,067	9.1		⎰
LOWER SKILLED LABOR CLASS	35–52	2,591	22.2	70	⎱ 16.3
DOMESTIC SERVANTS	10–55	1,230	10.5		⎰
UNSKILLED AND AGRI-CULTURAL LABOR CLASS	15–52	2,840	24.3	45	10.3
Total Manual Labor Classes:		**7,784**	**66.7**		**37.1**
WAGELESS PERSONS (paupers)	7.5	1,832	15.7	22.5	2.0
Grand Total:		**11,669**	**100.0**		**100.0**

among the (male) higher skilled workers. Thus, toward the
end of the 19th century "painful poverty" still afflicted
around 30 percent of the population of England and Wales
and 40 percent of the working class (Best 124, Clark 139,
Lynd 52-53). At the other pole, the percentage of income
earners who earned more than £100 yearly remained static
at 11 percent--though doubling in absolute numbers together
with the population--and only 4 percent of the population
left property worth more than £300 when they died (Mulhall
747, Hobsbawm 167).

The increase in national wealth and the spread of "popularity" of fiction should not, therefore, make us forget
what the compact nonworking-class public opinion of Victorian Britain meant by "the people." The supposed democrat Brougham formulated this precisely, if somewhat rhap-
sodically, earlier in the century: "By the people I mean
the middle class, the wealth and intelligence of the
country, the glory of the British name" (Cole-Postgate
389). What is usually known in literary studies as "the
Victorian frame of mind" entails, in the as precise words
of one of its foremost practitioners, investigating the
spread of "ideas and attitudes . . . in the upper and
middle classes. . . . (The working class as such is not
here under consideration.)" (Houghton xvi). In fact, this
bourgeois-cum-aristocratic "frame of mind" held--in
accordance with the whole practice and theory from the
Tudors through Hobbes and Locke right down to the last
third of the 19th century--that the working class was
outside civil society: "That it cannot at present have a
sufficiency of light which comes by culture,--that is, by
reading, observing, and thinking--is clear from the very
nature of its condition," observed Arnold rather condescend-
ingly, and failing to address the reasons for that condition, in 1868; and he repeated it in 1882 (Arnold 93; see
MacPherson, passim).

2.2. Economics and ideology embrace in a number of
further barriers to genuine "mass"--never mind "democratic"
--reading of book fiction in 19th-century Britain. True,
exceptionally they combined to foster elementary education, since this was indispensable both for higher produc-
tivity and obligatory socialization of the lower classes by
their betters. Literacy rose in England and Wales from the
1871 level of 77 percent to 97 percent in 1900, while the
average school attendance progressed from two years in 1851
to over six years in 1900, and from competence in reading a
newspaper paragraph to extracts from poems, Defoe, or
Macaulay (Altick ECR 141-72, Williams LR 156-58 and 161-62,
Webb VRP 214). But only qualitatively and quantitatively

inadequate reforms were instituted in secondary and university schooling. In sum: "The poor got their elementary schooling; but the caste system in English education remained, and was even intensified. . . ." (Cole-Postgate 365); "Knowledge, especially scientific knowledge, therefore took second place in the new British educational system, to the maintenance of rigid division between the classes. In 1897 less than 7 percent of grammar-school pupils came from the working class" (Hobsbawm 169). Thus, past elementary school, educational opportunity for working-class children declined in the second half of the 19th century (Perkin 291ff. and 426–27, Reader 194–99).

This may in part explain a very curious, and crucial, phenomenon: that "the book-reading public increased only slowly and unevenly" (Williams IP 21). Its increase was real but very much smaller than the jump of literates in 1870–1900 from 20 to 30 million or the ninefold expansion of circulation for English dailies from 1855 to 1890 (Williams LR 222ff., also 188, 198–200, and 221–26, Williams IP 22–23). The most important obstacles for the formation of a popular or mass book-reading public were the general living standards, the distribution of "leisure" time, the availability of given types of printed matter and themes, and last not least, the cost of book reading.

The vastly different <u>standards of living</u> at the two ends of the social hierarchy have been suggested earlier on in this section. One of the most important aspects were the extremely long working hours for the lower classes. Even at the end of the century, they still averaged for the working class 50 to 70 hours weekly, and for many (e.g., servants, landworkers, shop assistants--as well as shopkeepers, the bulk of the "lower middle class II" from table 1) 12 hours daily if not more (Altick ECR 85–87, Best 117–18, Ashworth 193–94). Only the middle and upper classes, and the higher groups of Baxter's "lower middle class I," could spend evenings and full weekends at leisure. In both of his panoramas of the context to Victorian reading, Altick has pointed out how this led on the one hand to the governing classes' reading of dailies and "serious" items in reviews and the middle class family's evening reading of books and the more entertaining items in reviews, and on the other to the workmen's Sunday newspaper reading (often bought by and read in his pub). This confirmation of the gap between the "two nations" (if not more?) is important enough. However, one must add to the radically different incomes and hours of work also the shockingly bad working and housing conditions of the lower classes. Perhaps half the UK families were huddled six in a room, in squalid tene-

ments amid filthy and smoggy cities, where the indifferent
eyesight due to undernourishment combined with poor light-
ing into an actual physiological barrier to reading except
when in direct light (Altick ECR 90-94, Lynd 53-54, Altick
VPI 42-48). All of this brought about a fundamental difference of horizons that the main addressees enforced in the
subject-matter and indeed in the approach or basic tone of
their reading—that is, in the whole structure of feeling
involved. The working class, when it had leisure, turned
to the pub, the dancing saloon, the music hall, the brass
band, the football match; the bourgeoisie turned to private
entertainment, the singing class, the spoken (and censored)
theater, the piano, huntin', shootin', and fishin' (11).

This does not, of course, mean that working people did
not read, and in some cases buy, thousands of cheap books.
However, beyond the rising and superficially impressive
statistics it carries two very important implications: (a)
quantitatively, that the working classes' reading was a
very small proportion of the hundreds of millions of
volumes printed; (b) qualitatively, that this reading was
of a different nature as to its social frame, circuit of
discourse, and dominant reading matter.

As to the first point, only a relatively significant but
numerically small segment of working people became habitual
book-readers, and a still smaller number also became book-
buyers. It seems to have embraced two groups. First, the
few radicals—from the Chartist leaders to O'Casey, from
Alton Locke to Jude the Obscure—as well as some other stubborn self-improvers of whom we know that they frequently
went hungry in order to lay their hands on a book. Second,
a sizable proportion of the highly skilled "privileged
minority of the workers" (Engels, in Marx-Engels 29), often
early on organized into trade unions—builders, engineers,
tool and instrument makers, carpenters, joiners, etc. They
were estimated (at Baxter's over-£70 yearly income if
constantly employed) as being 840,000 adult men, of whom
42,000 had a yearly income of over £80 (see also Best
95-96, and Marx-Engels OB, passim). One might have to add
to them an unknown—probably for book-reading purposes not
too large—number of apprentices and increasingly of
office-boys. (However, the whole matter of juvenile
reading presents special problems of rapid change and
cannot be treated in this essay.) But the average English
yearly expenditure for books and papers around 1880 was
107d. (pence) per person. Given the data in table 1, this
means that the average working person's expenditure could
not have been more than 20d., or 120d. per a working-class
family of six (12). Given further the heavy preference for

papers, this would leave no more than 3 to 4s. (shillings) for yearly book-buying—an amount that would not go far even at the low prices in secondhand sales. Once bought, though, books accumulate and can be handed down.

As to the second and even more important point, mention has been made that the working classes had been until the 1867 reform—and in many respects later too—traditionally read out of English civil society. They had therefore developed reading traditions different from the upper and middle classes. Decisive for the argument of this essay is that even those who did become habitual readers were "[not inducted] into the fold of a common national culture" (13) but went one of two ways, neither of which is pertinent to new book-length fiction. Either they (and especially the doubly oppressed female workers, who made up about 30 percent of the whole working force as well as of the whole female population) went in for compensatory sensationalism, for distraction or what one of our authors—the noted editor and popular writer James Payn—called "the blessed chloroform of the mind" (Altick ECR 370). Such reading-matter was as a rule not read in book-length volumes but in serialized "numbers," of which more below. Or, the worker-readers who did go in for full-length books read primarily elementary science, history, biography, and informative sociopolitical works. Though they had occasional, if rare, fiction favorites based on ideologico-political interest (e.g., The Mysteries of Paris and Uncle Tom's Cabin), their nonfactual reading was oriented toward classical drama and poetry (e.g., Shakespeare and Shelley). Thus, Louis James's conclusion that the fiction "bought by the middle and the working classes during [the early Victorian] period differed in appearance, style, and content" is applicable after 1848 too (14).

The conclusion seems inescapable that, as a social-addressee group for new fiction in book-form being published in Britain from 1848 to 1900, the working classes can be left out of consideration. They were engaged in different circuits of social discourse—those of cheap serialized fiction, of nonfiction, of Sunday papers, and of the submerged, informal oral tradition. At this precise moment, the bourgeoisie had the economic leisure and ideological inclination to blend, in the uniquely flexible and durable form of fictional narrative, individualistic psychology and a serious consideration of social relationships, heavily stressing religious or quasi-religious dutifulness and uplift in compensation for avoiding radical politics and sex. An alternative (though still largely outnumbered and not prevalently working-class) addressee

for "serious" social matters will not arise until the 1890s-
--in terms of our corpus, until <u>News From Nowhere</u>, <u>The
Angel of the Revolution</u>, and <u>The Time Machine</u>. This
alternative is, clearly, correlative to a changing book-
market, that is, to a more regular presence of books aimed
at people who could pay 1 to 6s. but not 31s.6. per title.
As Dr. Sutherland's contribution in Part I of this book
indicates, such a different book-circuit was already being
formed earlier--not least, on the evidence of my corpus, in
this genre of alternative possibilities.

The lower classes' distinct structure of feeling and
reading circuit is strikingly evident in the fiction that
they really read when they read--the penny "numbers." These
sensational serials were much the cheapest source of
fiction and reached, according to one estimate in 1883,
over 5 million readers, overwhelmingly women (Wright CUP
279; see also Altick ECR 308). However--even though this
is a field whose investigation is particularly difficult
and particularly recent (James, Neuberg, Vicinus; though
see Mayhew and Wright CUP and GU)--it seems that, at the
time considered, most of the penny-serials' reading public
was not necessarily from the working classes (though it
undoubtedly embraced well-to-do artisans' wives, servants,
and in particular seamstresses) but from "the lower,
middle, or let-us-be-genteel-or-die classes, the classes
whose young ladies can . . .

    Sing or dance
    And parlez-vous France
    And play on the grand piano." (Wright CUP 283-84)

These dressmakers, milliners, shop-girls, or wives and
daughters of clerks and shopkeepers (and of course some of
their male counterparts) could and would spend a penny or
two weekly on this kind of reading, which also circulated
briskly among them. They were "great readers while, speaking broadly, they [were] neither book-buyers nor subscribers to libraries" (Wright CUP 288; see also Neuburg
186-90 et passim). Since my S-F corpus does not comprise
penny serials, the subject will not be pursued further
here. (It would, however, be fascinating to know whether
this absence is real--thus confirming the narrowness of the
social addressee of my corpus--or due to our ignorance of
the specific forms of SF in this largely unexplored field
[15].)

2.3. Returning, then, to fiction in book-form it is
apparent that economics and ideology, in intricate interaction, also determined the widening, in the field of daily

politics relatively liberalized, but still fairly clear
boundaries of subject-matter available to the reading
public. The ideological component can be called taste or
censorship, one of the powerful "social disciplines" of the
age, "more important than legal disciplines, if only
because in some spheres they were much more strictly
enforced" (Burn 232, and see the whole following chapter
with that title). In print, "taste" was most overtly
applied to sexual propriety, but the deeply implanted
general notion of respectability--the absolute precondition
for upward social mobility--also applied to matters radically subversive of the politicoeconomic system. A rare con-
junction of both author and publisher powerful enough to
resist snobbery, ostracism from one's "betters," fear of
financial failure, and finally, in some cases, fear of
legal prosecution, was needed to get such matters into
print, particularly into cheaper forms of print. Another
of our authors, Grant Allen, casting a retrospective glance
in the somewhat looser climate of 1895 on writing novels
for the past 20 years, went as far as to affirm that:

> it has seldom happened that writers of exceptional aims
> have been able to proclaim to the world at large the
> things which they conceived to be best worth their tell-
> ing it. . . . Most novels nowadays have to run as
> serials through magazines and newspapers; and the
> editors of these periodicals are timid to a degree
> which outsiders would hardly believe. . . . This story
> or episode would annoy their Catholic readers; that one
> would repel their Wesleyan Methodist subscribers: such
> an incident is unfit for the perusal of the young
> person; such another would drive away the offended
> British matron (Allen vii-viii).

Noting that "the serial rights of a novel at the present
day are three times as valuable, in money worth, as the
final book rights," thus making periodical serialization an
economic necessity, he concluded that it is "almost impossible" to achieve serialization unless the novel contains
"nothing at all" objectionable on "religious, political,
social, moral, or aesthetic [grounds]" (Allen ix-x) (16).
This sounds somewhat hyperbolic, but the subsequent discussion around his more iconoclastic S-F novel The British
Barbarians (from whose introduction the above quotation
stems) seems to justify it. A propos of the resulting
outcry, it has been observed that at least the professional
writer "in return for his bread-and-butter . . . had to
supply the milk-and-water required by the public" (17).

This is confirmed by the prevention or suspension of the
publication of (to stop at the most famous) stories by
Trollope, Ruskin's "Unto This Last" and Munera Pul-
veris, or Hardy's Far From the Madding Crowd in such
liberal reviews as Cornhill and Fraser's and under
editors such as Thackeray, Froude, or Leslie Stephen. The
historian surveying the Victorian "respectable reading
public" concluded that "many of them, including some highly
intelligent people," were "limited, insular, . . . shocked
by the licence and 'crudities' of George Eliot, Meredith,
and even Dickens, tending to prefer writers who today are
nearly forgotten" (Webb VRP 207). Possibly the most compe-
tent opinion we can find, Thomas Hardy's, is even more
decided:

> The popular vehicles for the introduction of a novel to
> the public have grown to be . . . the magazine and the
> circulating library. . . . [T]he magazine in particu-
> lar and the circulating library in general do not
> foster the growth of a novel which reflects and reveals
> life. They tend directly to exterminate it by monopo-
> lising all literary space. Cause and effect were never
> more clearly conjoined. . . ." ("Candour in English
> Fiction," 1890, in Hardy 128-29).

No doubt, legal prosecution was applicable only to the
distribution of religious blasphemy and obscenity. Yet the
latter in particular was an elastic term. It was applied
to the works of Robert Dale Owen on family and property, to
a pamphlet sold by Bradlaugh and Annie Besant (the wayward
ex-sister-in-law of our writer Sir Walter Besant, himself a
pillar of respectability) containing pages on birth control, and to Vizetelly, the publisher of Zola, who died
after jail as a ruined man (18). Even a peril of prosecution was enough to cause bowdlerizing of some titles, withdrawal of others (e.g., Swinburne's Poems and Ballads),
and surely a sizably greater number of refusals to publish
or indeed failures to write. The semiovert--"social"
rather than "legal"--censorship in its turn could not
absolutely prevent book publication of any non-"obscene"
title; however, it not only could cut off periodical publication, it also could easily frighten off publishers from
reprints and especially from cheaper editions. A similar
effect was obtained by a barrage of negative reviews or
refusals to review on grounds which often--for example, in
the case of Winwood Reade's Martyrdom of Man, a banner
for iconoclasts such as H.G. Wells--translated ideological
bias into slogans of taste and value.

Most important and pervasive for all "respectable" (i.e., three-decker) fiction was the internal censorship of such large scale book-buyers as W.H. Smith's bookstalls, whose withdrawal of Jude the Obscure precipitated the end of Hardy's novel-writing, or Mudie's Circulating Library, who refused to circulate Reade's Cream, Meredith, and George Moore, never mind Zola, Swinburne, or Shelley. Their demands, relayed by the publishers, were decisive for the writers' earnings and their entire careers. At a time when publishers were not at all averse from pressing quite specific textual demands upon the writer, his/her independence was entirely dependent upon and directly proportional to her/his books' financial success. The writers who achieved artistic autonomy could be counted on the fingers of one's hands (or hand?): Dickens and George Eliot did so early in their careers, Thackeray and Trollope late; "most novelists never achieved it at all" (Sutherland 78). Mudie in particular exercised a veritable ideological dictatorship over novels, down to the inflection not only of their overt ideas toward gentility and uplift but also of intimate writing technicalities such as plot length (19). In all fairness one should say, first, that as a rule the social disciplines were the result not simply of individual decisions but of substantial pressures by the bourgeois readership as well as by the public ideologists—churchmen, critics, et hoc genus omne; and second, that Victorian Britain was certainly neither the first nor the worst instance of the dominant taste being the taste of the dominant social classes and groups, understandably anxious about the survival of their interests and values.

As important as this rather efficient range of social constraints on the subject-matter, attitudes, and even metonymies in fiction was the constraint of price. That differed strongly as between first publications and reprints. The standard price for the great majority of first publications, which was 31s.6d.--among the highest in the world (Sutherland 19)--collapsed together with the three-volume novel in the 1890s, when the 10s.6d. one-volume novel descended to 6s. or even 5s. Though the picture is complex and much too little investigated, it seems that some novels (and collections of stories) first appeared in cheap series, down to 1s. railway "yellow-backs," but that, in most cases, cheaper contemporary fiction in book-form was until the 90s purchasable only in reprints. Thus, the hierarchy of cheaper reprints and serials looks like a fiction-market transposition of the British class situation. The expensive three-decker for the bourgeois readership functioned as a tone-setter and as a gate-keeper: only those novels were reprinted which had proved successful with the original, very restricted reader- ship of the 500-1,250 first-edition copies (Altick ECR 264, Locke in Mullen-Suvin 60)--including, of course, the gate- keeping ideologists. Again, economics and ideology were inextricably intertwined. (Novels often also ran in period- icals; the readership of periodicals, however, came at the latest after the 1860s roughly from the same upper economic classes as that of the first publication in volume form.) The price of reprinted books was usually around 5s. or lower, down to as little as 3d. for classics, while in the 1890s even popular "copyrighted" authors slid to 6d. (Altick ECR 313-15). Even so, I would agree with the conclusion that until the passing of the three-decker "books could be bought only by comparatively wealthy readers, though they were read by a wider circle . . ." (TLS-CEL 345). From what we know about prices and incomes, I would hold that, at least until the mid-90s, volume- length fiction was available for purchase to no more than about 5-15 percent of the UK families. Perhaps 10-25 percent bought the penny parts and the cheapest reprints (there was, of course, some overlap at the edges of all these categories of buyers), while rather more than half of the population did not buy fiction at all (20). As to the free public libraries, their borrowers seem to have made up about 5-6 percent of the local population. Though this may have by the end of the century meant that around one million people were library borrowers, so that with their families and servants perhaps four million people were at least occasional readers of borrowed books, it would still at the very best represent one eighth of the literate (over- ten) population (21). The largest segment of these readers was probably constituted--just as in the libraries of the Mechanics' Institutes--by the lower middle class (Gattie 312, Webb VRP, Altick ECR 196 and 236-39); certainly the bulk came from fin-de-siècle versions of Baxter's "lower middle class II" and "highly skilled labor class," with smaller groups from the classes immediately above and below them. One might reasonably speculate that--as distinct from the book-buying public--this would make for the total UK fiction-reading public (counting everybody who read, say, two novels or four penny parts monthly) in- creasing from the "tiny minority" at midcentury (Williams LR 188) to perhaps as many as one fifth to two fifths of the literate population around 1900. This accords well with the data of about 30 percent of the people in England (or certainly at least one third in the whole of UK) being below the poverty line. The 60-80 percent nonreaders are the paupers, almost all the unskilled, agricultural, and lower skilled laborers, the great bulk of the male upper classes and of the highly skilled laborers, as well as the confirmed readers of nonfiction only and the devotees of other leisure pursuits (possibly to call them Philistines and Barbarians would not bend Arnold's basic insight too far) from other classes.

3. The Actual Social Addressees: Three Clusters

It might now be possible--above and beyond the negative or eliminatory delimitations of subsection 2--to attempt some tentative positive or identificatory determinations of the main social addressees of volume-length new fiction in Victorian Britain. It should be stressed that this attempt does not deal with the larger "general reading public" but with that "literary public" about which Raymond Williams, establishing this crucial distinction, immediately noted that its "disparity in actual figures [from the general reading public] was now becoming startling" (Williams LR 189). For the purposes of this essay, it might be more precisely called the "fiction-reading public." It has been seen that for penny serials, the public consisted mainly of "lower middle class II" women, with smaller segments of women from "lower middle class I," "highly skilled labor class," and "domestic servants," and with still smaller segments of men from these three classes. The borrowers from the free (public) libraries seem to have come from-- possibly in part different strata of--the same classes, with a preponderance of men. But neither of these audiences can be regarded as a dominant social addressee kept in mind by the authors and middlemen (publishers, periodical editors, libraries) of new three-decker fiction, since the latter did not either financially or ideologically depend on these audiences.

At the very outset of determining the fictional public that was the social addressee of the new book-length fiction, the absence from it of the great bulk of the "manual labor classes" has to be insisted upon. For this specific elimination is in fact (together with the absence of the powerful but "Barbarian"--and anyway increasingly capitalist--landowning aristocracy) what constitutes the general ideological profile or structure of feeling of the reading public as bourgeois rather than popular (plebeian, democratic). This comports an almost absolute hegemony of certain taboos or "unsayables," well suggested by the Victorian keywords of gentility, respectability, etc. The social discourse, the textual universe of Victorian book-length fiction is appropriated by propriety, obsessed by possession, shaped and haunted by an all-pervasive, tacit but constitutive, split between the high-proper-gentlemanly and the low-improper-vulgar. The "low" is best represented by the body, the working class, women, and non-European "races" as subjects in their own right, that is, not reified, fragmented, or sentimentalized by repression but possessing legitimate specific claims on the property/propriety of the higher gentlemen. Among other consequences, this axiomatic structure of textual presuppositions will be of basic importance for the S-F corpus of this investigation. Further, this very strong ideological hegemony means that even those working-class groups which were a part of the literary public did not on the whole develop an alternative horizon of expectations:

> Throughout the period [of 1830-1914] the dominating ideas—and the reactions against them—were those based on middle-class idealism, middle-class prosperity, the whole system reaching its height in the sixties and seventies. . . . And in the main the literature of the period is literature about the middle class, for the middle class, by the middle class, even that written by the most violent critics of the edifice.

One violent critic, John Morley, with an enviable outspokenness that was also rooted in the great tradition of bourgeois independence and rationalism, polemically situated this Victorian literature in—

> a community where political forms . . . are mainly hollow shams disguising the coarse supremacy of wealth, where religion is mainly official and political . . . , and where literature does not as a rule permit itself to discuss serious subjects frankly and worthily—a community, in short, where the great aim of all classes and orders with power is by dint of rigorous silence, fast shutting of the eyes, and stern stopping of the ears, somehow to keep the social pyramid on its apex, with the fatal result of preserving for England its glorious fame as a paradise for the well-to-do, a purgatory for the able, and a hell for the poor (22).

But that same influential critic and editor, later Liberal cabinet member, also wrote a horrified attack on Swinburne's book of poems. . . .

   <u>3.1.</u> Determining the implied readership for Victorian
fiction thus has to start from two rock-bottom recogni-
tions. First, it is overridingly to be found in those
middle and lower classes having a yearly personal income of
£100 to £1,000.   They comprised between one twelfth and
one eighth of the UK population in the second half of the
century, and expanded in absolute numbers from 1 to 2
million income earners (and their families).   Second, the
dominant segment or core of this readership, the hegemonic
social addressee(s) of contemporary literature at the time,
were some groups from the upper-middle and middle classes,
that is, from the perhaps 2-3 percent of the population
that joined to economic affluence the dominant role in a
cultural and ideological consensus.   Thus, important and
fascinating as the conflicts or alternatives in this
fiction may be, they are nonetheless--with a very few
exceptions--situated within the bourgeois hegemonic consensus or cultural matrix.   For Victorian fiction, one could
thus adopt and adapt a statement made à propos the visual
arts:

> It is not far from truth to affirm, even in this exag-
> gerated form, that in all societies up to our times the
> history of the production of pictures is the history of
> ruling class visual ideologies.   Pictures are often the
> product in which the ruling classes mirror themselves
> (23).

Is it possible to approach the analogous "fictional ideologies" by providing a somewhat fuller breakdown of their
possible bearers?   The enterprise is hazardous, but it will
be hazarded.
   "Each section of the public has its own literary organs,"
remarked Matthew Arnold (Arnold 110), and one of the privileged ways of a more precise identification of the ideological profile for various social addressees of Victorian
fiction would, of course, be to study the "corporate personality" (Cox 202) of the reviews: from the older <u>Edin-
burgh</u>, <u>Quarterly</u>, <u>Blackwood's</u>, and <u>Westminster</u>,
through the high noon of "equipoise," to those of the fin-
de-siècle--for example, the <u>National Observer</u>, <u>Pear-
son's</u>, or <u>Strand</u> (where most of the important S-F texts
were first published).   Such a huge undertaking is, alas,
beyond the scope of this essay.   Nonetheless, Arnold's
observation can be taken as an encouragement to identify at
least the main social groups which underlay the "sections"
of the reading public.   This would provide a general framework for identifying the social addressees of Victorian

fiction; the attempt to particularize this for the S-F
corpus at hand will have to subsume also the internal
evidence of the texts themselves, and will therefore be
faced in a later section.

One way of going about such an identification would be to
induce from empirical evidence categories expanding slightly on a sketch such as:

> The middle-class market for print was divided into many
> interest-groups: the young, the religious, the fashion-
> able, the educated, the ambitious, the time-killing.
> As each of these audiences grew, publishers catered to
> it by finding writers and forms to meet its peculiar
> requirements (Altick VPI 62).

However, for the present purposes I would prefer to follow
a somewhat more systematic subdivision of this "middle-
class market for print," which would subscribe to neither
impressionistic empiricism nor economic determinism. It
is, of course, useful to note that, in terms of socioeconomic classes, the market for fiction embraced a spread that
went from the rich through the professional groups and
clerks to technicians, office and shop workers, and some
strata of manual workers. Yet important additional groupings, such as the young and various groups of women, can
only with difficulty be differentiated by such an analysis.
Further, economics are an indispensable limiting and
enabling factor, but they are not a sufficient explanation
of even the main cultural subdivisions in the fictional
public. It is best, then, to steer for a middle course
between the empirically particular and the societally
general. The most suggestive approach in this vein that I
know of is the one sketched for the popular culture in 1859
by Banks (Banks 207-13), who divides his "middling" or
"genteel classes" into seven groups; I shall supplement
this with some mention of the (largely overlapping) working
class and women consumers of this middle class market,
extrapolate it from 1859 to my whole period, take the liberty of modifying his terms and even some of his categories,
and finish by expanding on the professionals.

Though Banks mentions the working farmer, it is only to
say that circumstances allowed him very little book-reading; this was almost entirely impossible for the agricultural laborer, so that the following relates essentially to
the urban population (which had by the end of the century
expanded to three quarters of the whole). Banks's other
"classes" are the "leisured gentlemen," "professional
gentlemen," "professional men," nouveau riche capitalists,

clerks, and "teachers of the poor." With the help of table 1 (see also table 3) I would tentatively systematize this as follows:

1. The family reading of the richer bourgeoisie (Baxter's family income of about £500 to 5,000 yearly in 1867--or up to £12,000 by the end of the century), that is, of rentiers, industrialists, businessmen, bankers, upper merchants. This was an important part of the reading public; it was dominated by women, and the proportion of the male family-heads who participated fully in the family reading of fiction seems to have been small.

2-3. The learned professions, subdivided into: the upper professional gentlemen, attached to the upper middle class, whose income was within the same range as group 1, and the lower professional men, attached to the middle and sometimes even lower middle class, whose income ranged from as low as £100 to 1,200; more about them later.

4. The upper and possibly middle clerks in the larger cities, especially in banking, with a family income of perhaps £150 to 800 yearly; Banks notes that, being in good part sons of the upper working class, their tastes would be strongly snobbish, that is, conservative and "respectable." Clerks as a whole grew from 0.8 percent to 4 percent of the labor force 1851-1901, or about ninefold (Lockwood 23-32).

5. The junior clerks in banks, industry, railroads, law, etc., some middle tradesmen, upper employees (e.g., a railway stationmaster or tax collector), that is, the males of "lower middle class I," income range £80 to 200--more rarely to 300--in 1867 and not much changed by the end of the century.

6. The "unacknowledged" professionals, primarily Banks's teachers of the poor--that is, of the public but not "public" schools--who came mainly from the working class. They were a large but rather isolated group, for the most part paid under £300 per year and looked down upon by all the other professionals. Their numbers more than tripled from midcentury to the approximately 230,000 of 1901, of which more than three quarters were women (Reader 106-07, 147, 172, 181, 208-11, and passim; cf. Gray 89). To this should be added the 50,000 nurses; a number of parascientific professions, such as the chemists and the engineers below civil and mining ones but above foremen; and finally a great majority of the 90,000 actors, artists, authors, and musicians who in their fourfold growth from 1851 oscillated uncomfortably between this group (the census figures include, e.g., music teachers, engravers,

and shorthand writers!) and my group 3 or in a few cases
even 2 (Reader 69-71, 172-73, 181, 208-11).

7. Domestic servants, who also rose from 1.2 million
in 1851 to over 2 millions in 1901 (and possibly 25 percent
more--statistics differ according to whether one includes
the "outdoor" servants, etc.; see Mulhall 420-21 and 783,
Mitchell-Deane 60, Best 103-05) and nine tenths of whom
were female. In this highly striated group, no doubt the
slavey--even when she became literate--would have had relatively little time for book-reading, as opposed to the
lady's maid or the housekeeper. But even if the calculation is based on roughly one third of the "upper" indoor
servants (Best 78), this would be a readership of 700,000
by the end of the century. Admittedly very little is known
about this, and all guesses must be wilder than usual:
double or half of that figure is equally possible. How
aberrant was Richardson's Pamela, who had already in the
18th century desired "time for reading" (24)? And Mrs.
Wells, the housekeeper at Up Park mansion, whose son Bertie
had the run of the private library there?

It should be noted that women readers participating in
the above groups are generally supposed to have made up
more than half of all the readers; other women would tend
to be the penny-serial readers discussed earlier (see also
Cunnington, Reader, Altick VPI, Best, Cole SCS, and Laver).
The great bulk of three-decker buying would be concentrated in groups 1 to 4, and in the circulating libraries
patronized by the same groups together with group 5. Only
this gives full social meaning to the well-known fact that
the circulating library public "has always been . . . the
essential constituency to which candidates for novel-
popularity must appeal . . ." (TLS-CEL 343-44). Groups 3
to 6 would tend to be buyers of cheap reprints, while only
the very highest domestic servants would also buy some of
those. Groups 4 to 6 would also (together with the school-
children) form the bulk of free public libraries' borrowers.

It follows, then, that the hegemonic ideological position
of the three-volume, first-publication novel, can in terms
of social groups be read as the hegemonic position of a
"social addressee" cluster at whose core were middle and
upper-middle class women and the corresponding professional
and clerk groups.

Usually, a group called--in traditional European usage--
the intelligentsia is a disproportionately important part
of the reading public. In Britain, it was at this time
certainly less important than on the Continent, and in all
probability less important than group 1. Nonetheless, it

is both a significant grouping and one about which a better breakdown than usual is available in secondary literature. Its more detailed analysis might thus, beyond its intrinsic interest, suggest how rough and preliminary my sevenfold division is. First of all, it might suggest how very tentative are all its quantifications, depending as they do on shifting categories assembled for other purposes (see Reader 154). Even the global figures depend here on what was at different times understood by the very elastic term "professional class." The upper limit for 1901 can be indicated by about 200,000 for the civil service and 430,000 for professionals not employed by the government (25). But these "learned professionals" are more realistically estimated as shown in table 2.

Table 2
Learned Professions in UK 1901 (26)

Religious (all denominations)	50,000
Legal (barristers and solicitors)	25,000
Medical (physicians, surgeons, GPs, dentists)	35,000
Artistic (actors, artists, authors, musicians)	90,000
Other (accountants, architects, civil and mining engineers, midwives, surveyors)	50,000

This statistic does not comprise still other professionals such as actuaries, chemists, scientists and other engineers, merchant navy officers, nurses or pharmacists, many of whom were not considered to have a truly professional status in the Byzantine stratification of Victorian respectability. Nonetheless, even with all of them the sum would be considerably below 430,000. Attaching the nurses and the great bulk of "artistic" professionals to the teachers, as I did above in group 6, is the obverse of identifying the groups 2 and 3 as the "learned professions" in the stricter and culturally relevant sense of groups organized around a licensed professional body controlling professional education and membership. Numerically, I would assume that by the end of the century these groups had risen to upward of 150,000 families.

However, even this grouping of perhaps 350,000 people in the civil service and the learned professions was, as Banks observed, divided into an upper class of professional gentlemen and a lower class of professional men (cf. also Gray 89). This division was complicated but not basically overturned by the rise of new professions during the second half of the century, which were on the whole accommodated in my groups 3 and 6.

The professional gentlemen, my group 2, consisted of the upper reaches of the three traditional professions--clergy, lawyers, medical men--and of a very few top civil service professionals. (In many regards the navy and most of the army officers were akin to them, but in many others to the upper class. Further, their impermanence in the UK and frequent disinclination toward fiction makes it difficult to constitute them into a constant group of the fictional public. Still, the perhaps 20,000 officers "at home" [Reader 153] and a goodly number overseas must have been an important part of the readers of the just barely fictional "future war" tale.) While the professional men of group 3 all had the equivalent of a university degree, they only began to share with the professional gentlemen passage through a "public" (i.e., private) school later in the century and in a partial fashion. Otherwise, the watershed between groups 2 and 3 depended on many factors--

> . . . such as family lineage, education, professional success, and the social standing of their clientele. A London society physician, such as Dr. Lydgate in Middlemarch eventually became, was separated by an almost unbridgeable gulf from the small provincial practitioners, such as Mr. Gambit the midwife, who had been his resentful former colleagues. An even wider abyss separated a classics master, B.A., M.A. Oxoniensis, at aristocratic Eton, and a slum-born London schoolteacher like Bradley Headstone in Dickens's Our Mutual Friend (Altick VPI 30).

Nonetheless, as a general rule it can be said that barristers were in group 2, while solicitors (though if in business affairs, occasionally earning more than many a barrister) were not; that most Church of England clergymen --a prime case of status often, especially in the lower-to-middle ranges, overriding income--were in group 2, while ministers (and priests) of other denominations were not; that physicians were gentlemen, general practitioners lower professionals, while surgeons were on the divide but rising in the economic and status scale during the century. Since only a very few top people from the civil service and other professions--for example, from the laymen teachers--would also qualify, my group 2 can perhaps be estimated at 25-35,000 people and their families at the end of the century, or from one eighth to one sixteenth of the lower "professional men" (27).

The professional gentlemen constituted themselves as closed privileged groups. Their rise during the second half of the 19th century was sluggish (Reader 147, 207-11), much slower than that of the UK population, and economic benefits were correspondingly higher; but this meant that "opportunities in some of the highest employments, considered both socially and financially, were only increasing very slowly, if indeed they were increasing at all" (Reader 184). Group 2 was by the 1870s resolutely arriviste, conservative, and opposed to admitting women. Its yearly incomes seem to have been from £500 up to 12,000 with averages perhaps around 1,000-1,500 (Reader 200-01 et passim). "Below the social heights, certainly, professional men [i.e., all learned professions, DS] remained, but not hopelessly so, and they were at last unquestionably at a comfortable sneering distance above 'trade'" (Reader 146). This had not always been so; and a lingering tradition of political and religious radicalism in some barristers, medical men, and in a very few cases even clergymen (all of whom occasionally could still be living in wretched circumstances) will be testified to by some of our authors.

The lower group of professional men can be thought of as composed of all "learned" professionals above the free schools' teachers, the nurses, and most "artists" of my group 6, but below my group 2. This would comprise some--especially provincial--Church of England clergymen and surgeons, most ministers, priests, solicitors, and general practitioners, some teachers and artists (including many authors), and almost all the "Others" of table 2 (scientific, technological, and accounting professionals) as well as most civil servants--perhaps 300-320,000 families. They were mainly of middle-class parents, and very rarely from working-class ones. Their income might go as high as £1,200, or as low as near-beggary for anywhere up to 10 percent of them, with averages perhaps between £300 and 500 yearly (Reader 192-95, 200-01, et passim).

3.2. If one is now to reach toward a general conclusion about the social addressees of new Victorian fiction, the next question on the groups discussed is how many people--as different from income earners--were involved in all of them at their highest, that is, at the end of 19th century? This is even more difficult to estimate. Some light can be shed on it by an abbreviated update of Baxter's data (my table 1) to 1895 and for the UK as a whole, which follows (Mulhall 747; he does not give the number of paupers, but it might be estimated at roughly the same as in table 1, which would be about 10 percent of the 1895 "income-earning" population and thus necessitate dimin-

ishing all the percentages in the one-but-last column below
by one tenth for comparisons with table 1):

Table 3
1895 Distribution of National Income

	Income per year per person in £	Recipients in 000s	% of all income recipients	Equivalent Baxter % in 1867
UPPER CLASS	over 5,000	27	0.15	0.08
UPPER MIDDLE CLASS	1,000– 5,000	103	0.57	0.43
MIDDLE CLASS	300–1,000	360	2.00	1.53
LOWER MIDDLE CLASS I	100–300	1,600	8.89	8.64
LOWER MIDDLE CLASS II AND MANUAL LABOR CLASSES	under 100	15,910	88.4	89.1
Grand Total	--	18,000	100	100

With all due disclaimers about a large margin of uncertainty, I shall proceed to use this table for checking and
summing up the speculative results reached so far.

The public reading contemporary fiction can be envisaged
as a series of concentric circles. At the center is a
hegemonic cluster composed of my groups 1 to 4. Their
yearly income of, say, £200 to 5,000 (with a few thousand
families from £5,000 to 12,000) permitted them, and their
interests led them, to buy--and more importantly to patronize the circulating libraries that bought--new three-decker
fiction; groups 3 and 4 would also be large-scale buyers of
cheaper reprints. A core of articulate ideologists from
groups 1 and 2, as a rule with an income over £1,000, were
the key opinion-shapers of Victorian society (Gray 75, 78,
and 85). Allowing for three over-ten members per family at
any given time, and revising some of the earlier figures in
light of table 3, we would get the following rough

estimates for a possible <u>maximum</u> of readers in each of
them:
<u>Group 1--richer bourgeoisie</u>: about 230,000 families,
with two and sometimes three (wife, teenage child, father
or second teenager) readers . . . <u>450,000-700,000</u>

<u>Group 2--professional gentlemen</u>: 25,000-35,000 families,
with two adult and one to two teenage readers each . . .
<u>75,000-140,000</u>

<u>Group 3--professional men</u>: 300,000-320,000 families,
with two adult and one (sometimes two) teenage readers
. . . <u>900,000-1,000,000</u>

<u>Group 4--senior clerks</u>: 40,000-60,000 families, with two
and sometimes three readers (wife would not always read new
fiction) . . . <u>80,000-150,000</u>

TOTAL GROUPS 1-4: <u>1.5 to 2 million readers</u>, including
practically all the habitual three-decker buyers and circulating library subscribers.

    The second, outer concentric circle is a <u>subsidiary clus-</u>
<u>ter</u> composed of my groups 5 and 6, having a personal or
family income from £80 to 300 (in these groups one begins
to find more than one family member having income). This
income permitted them to buy reprints; occasionally (group
5 and some members of group 6) to patronize circulating
libraries; and to form--together with the highly skilled
workers--the majority of borrowers from free public
libraries. It must be assumed that this cluster was as
interested in new fiction as the hegemonic one, though not
necessarily in the same types of new fiction. Data are
especially scarce, and estimates especially rough, for
group 5:
<u>Group 5--lower middle class males</u>: if one subtracts from
the 1.6 million of "Lower Middle Class I" in table 3 one
third for women, and 100-200,000 each for men of group 6
and men not reading book-length fiction, the estimate might
be . . . <u>600,000-900,000</u>

<u>Group 6--unacknowledged professionals</u>: 350-400,000
people, often married to each other or without children or
with one teenager per family . . . <u>500,000-800,000</u>

TOTAL GROUPS 5-6: <u>1.1 to 1.7 million readers</u>, of which
few would be habitual three-decker buyers.

A further cluster of readers, most probably comparable in size to the 1-2 millions of the above two clusters, was constituted by the ·penny-serial readers. However, it seems that the overwhelming majority of these serials were not new but reprinted, so that this cluster can here be passed over. Should further research reveal that new, contemporary fiction was, in fact, abundantly represented in penny serials, our whole view of the fiction-reading public and indeed of British culture would have to be revised. From what we so far know, this seems unlikely.

A final group and cluster, the third and outermost concentric circle, is:

Group 7--domestic servants: about 90 percent women; discussed above as being perhaps betweenn 350,000 and 1,400,000 people. It is permissible to guess at . . . 500,000-1,000,000

TOTAL GROUP 7: 0.5 to 1 million readers, in the economically anomalous situation of not paying for books but mostly reading those of groups 1 to 4.

The above three clusters are, then, the hegemonic, the subordinate, and the parasitic social addressees for new, contemporary, volume-length fiction in the UK, and they can be tabulated as shown in table 4.

It would be fascinating to discuss whether and/or when social groups from the subordinate cluster groups (or perhaps even the "junior" groups from the hegemonic cluster) evolved into an oppositional or even alternative addressee. This could only be decided together with the internal evidence of the fictional texts. A number of other disclaimers have been touched upon, but perhaps it should be repeated that all the statistics are, first, quite approximate; second, applied to reading of new fiction only (which explains the different conclusions of 2.2); and third, oriented toward a potential maximum of readers for the whole of the fictional production--a maximum that has to be divided by a large factor for any subset (e.g., a genre or a writer's opus). In particular, the data would have to be modified if we knew more about the "family" reading, that is, the boys' reading (about which we know something, but little in quantifiable terms) and the girls' reading (about which we know next to nothing). Nonetheless, I trust that as rule-of-thumb indications of orders of magnitude and thus of basic relationships, qualitative as much as quantitative, they can be useful. A number of verifications both from the distrib-

Table 4

Victorian Social Addressees for New, Volume-length Fiction

	Family income in £ yearly	Persons in 000s (estimate)
1. RICHER BOURGEOISIE (mainly women and children)	500-12,000	450-700
2. PROFESSIONAL GENTLEMEN	500-12,000	75-140
3. PROFESSIONAL MEN (whole family)	100-1,200	900-1,000
4. UPPER CLERKS (whole family)	150-800	40-100

TOTAL HEGEMONIC CLUSTER: 1.5-2 million people, income mainly above £200 (only buyers of new three-decker novels, main clients of magazines and circulating libraries).

5. "LOWER MIDDLE CLASS I" (males)	80-300	600-900
6. "UNACKNOWLEDGED" PROFESSIONALS (whole family)	100-300	500-800

TOTAL SUBSIDIARY CLUSTER: 1.1-1.7 million people, income ca. £100-300 (buyers of cheap reprints when those existed, main clients of free public libraries).

7. DOMESTIC SERVANTS	not relevant	500-1,000

TOTAL PARASITIC CLUSTER: 0.5-1 million people, do not pay for books.

Sum Total of Reading Public for New Fiction: 3.1-4.7 million people.

uting end of the book-trade and from the internal evidence
of larger corpuses of fiction would now be necessary to
validate or invalidate these indications.

3.3. In conclusion, it should not be forgotten that
all of these three concentric circles, comprising between
them from 3.1 to 4.7 million readers of contemporary
fiction toward the end of the 19th century, were themselves
within the largest, final outermost circle of the 32.5
million literates. Thus, people who read volume-length
modern fiction at all came in the UK at the very best to 10
to 15 percent, or between one tenth and one sixth, of the
potentially available public. Even more importantly, the
hegemonic bourgeois cluster of social addressees--the inner
circle--came to 5-7 percent, or between one twentieth and
one sixteenth, of the potential public. Within this
cluster, the perhaps 1.5-2.5 percent of readers from the
rich bourgeoisie (and the cognate professionals) were that
social class whose interests and values delimited the
hegemonic ideological consensus (28).

Even if one were to increase the above percentages by any
amount up to their double, allowing for an unlikely margin
of error, such proportions--such a quantitative and qualitative distribution of social addressees--could not fail to
be of constitutive significance for further discussions.
To my mind, such clarification is indispensable if we are
to understand how Victorian fiction (including SF) was
shaped by the ideological, lived values and interests of
the dominant classes, and/or--to a minor extent--by alternative or oppositional values and interests. In brief, we
need to include an identification of social addressees, as
an entity within the texts themselves, if we are to understand the values in and value of Victorian fiction: or,
for that matter, fiction of any other period.

Notes to Section B

1. Altick VPI, p. x. This work, as all other frequently
cited ones, will be found in the appended select list at
the end, which will further be cited by abbreviation and
page number in parentheses within the text itself. The
list calls attention to works I found of particular interest and value for this essay and for those readers who wish
to pursue matters raised in it, but does not pretend to be
a complete indication "of the many sources from which I
have learned much and pilfered not a little" (Altick VPI
pp. x-xi). Secondary texts cited less frequently will be
footnoted. However, I shall follow, si licet, the excellent example and justification of Best: "I have tried to
give references for all actual quotations, and for the

sources of the more complicated figures. For the rest, my
good faith and professional self-respect may, I hope, be
thought sufficient guarantees that I have sought to be
accurate in my summaries of situations and developments"
(Best p. xvi).

    2. Hans Robert Jauss, Literaturgeschichte als Provoka-
tion (Frankfurt, 1970), p. 175--translation mine, as in
all cases where a non-English text is quoted without indication of translator. Jauss takes the term "horizon of expectation" from E.H. Gombrich, Art and Illusion (Princeton,
1972), p. 60 et passim, to which I am much indebted. Of a
number of precursors, perhaps the chapter "Pour qui
écrit-on?" in Sartre (original 1948) and Wayne C. Booth's
The Rhetoric of Fiction (Chicago, 1961) are the most
important titles, but see also Marc Angenot, "A Select
Bibliography of the Sociology of Literature," in Mullen-
Suvin, p. 321ff. Beside works by Jauss, see on the implied
social addressee also Wolfgang Iser, Der implizite Leser
(Munich, 1972) and Der Akt des Lesens (Munich, 1976); a
number of Polish studies--e.g., M. Głowiński, "Wirtualny
odbiorca w strukturze utworu literackiego," in idem, ed.,
Studia z teorii i historii poezji, I (Wrocław, 1967), pp.
7-32; three German anthologies of essays: Manfred Naumann
et al., Gesellschaft--Literatur--Lesen (East Berlin,
1973), Peter U. Hohendahl, ed., Sozialgeschichte und
Wirkungsästhetik (Frankfurt, 1974), and Rainer Warning,
ed., Rezeptionsästhetik (Munich, 1975); and Roland
Barthes, S/Z (Paris, 1970), passim, especially pp.
157-58. A number of other approaches, from Frye and Poulet
to Culler, Fish, Holland, and Ong, can be found in the
notes to Robert DeMaria, Jr.'s informative "The Ideal
Reader," PMLA 93 (1978), 463-74. In what follows, I am
contaminating and modifying some procedures within this
general horizon.

    3. "The bourgeois may be recognized by his denial that
social classes exist, and in particular that the bourgeoisie exists," writes Sartre in one of his most memorable
sentences (Sartre p. 145).

    4. Frederick Antal, Florentine Painting and Its Social
Background (London, 1948), p. 4; see also further discussions in Nicos Hadjinicolau, Art History and Class Struggle (London, 1978), pp. 79-102 et passim. Antal is, of
course, only one of the best practitioners of this demystifying methodology. See Angenot's bibliography (note 2) for
a number of others, from Marx on Sue, Lenin on Tolstoy, and

Gramsci on hegemonic and subaltern culture to Lukács, Schücking, Burke, Sartre, Goldmann, Hoggart, Watt, and Williams. Beyond Raymond Williams's four books in that bibliography, crucial concepts of this whole tradition have been summarized in Williams ML, to which I am evidently indebted.

5. First quote from Iser, p. 9. Second quote from V.N. Voloshinov (i.e., M.M. Bakhtin), Freudianism, transl. I.R. Titunik (New York, 1976), p. 110; see also his Marxism and the Philosophy of Language (New York, 1973).

6. Cf. D. Suvin, "The Social Addressees of Victorian Fiction," Literature and History 8, no. 1 (1982), 13-16.

7. Rowcroft, Confessions of an Etonian (1852), I, 302f., quoted in Myron F. Brightfield, Victorian England in Its Novels (Los Angeles, 1968), II, 2; see also Best pp. xvi and 250-51.--Perhaps this is the place to join one's voice to that of other students of the period, from Marx on, who have admiringly noted how nobody could point out the shady side of Victorian society more competently and fairly than the British official and unofficial inquirers of the time, nor could anybody chastise the dominant values and social groups more enthusiastically than some of the masters of the age's social discourse: Carlyle, Dickens, Mill, Morris, Ruskin, are only the best known among the most explicit of them.

8. The basic table is from Baxter, passim, and from the adaptation by Cole-Postgate p. 354. The "Wageless" category has been added from Perkin p. 420, and all the percentages recalculated accordingly; their "income" is official relief plus charity. The working class has been subdivided using data from Cole SCS pp. 56-57, his categories being redeployed by my retaining the "Most Highly Skilled" and the "Domestic Servants" as separate groups; their maximum yearly income is taken, with minor adjustments, from Baxter's and Cole's average wage for men, while the minimum one is modified by optimistically allotting to the women and juveniles 50 percent of the men's wages and weighting the whole accordingly. The incomes for all the "manual labor" classes are predicated on year-round employment, and ca. 20 percent should be subtracted from them for the frequent bouts of unemployment (Baxter p. 47, Ashworth p. 23, Burn pp. 94-96); this would more precisely fix the share of total national income (col. 6 above) for these two thirds

of the population at <u>less than 30 percent</u>. The higher
"family" incomes (col. 5) for the aristocracy, working
classes, and paupers derive from more than one family
member receiving income.

9. B.S. Rowntree, <u>Poverty</u> (London, 1901), p. 87.

10. My calculation from Ashworth p. 201, Hobsbawm pp.
159-62, and Cole-Postgate pp. 351 and 445; see also Marx-
Engels pp. 28-29, Perkin pp. 413-15, and Ensor p. 275. I
am only too painfully aware not only of the economists'
general caveat about all statistics of incomes and similar
matters in the 19th century (e.g., Ashworth p. 4) but also
of having sometimes rushed in where they tread with fear
and at cross purposes. On the other hand, the judgment
that the English "common reader," from the time of Macaulay
to that of Meredith, could have (apparently with equal probability) been "a member of the working class, or [. . . of]
the ever expanding bourgeoisie" (Altick ECR p. 7) seems
based principally on a general "democratic" vagueness but
at least in part also on statistics which have since been
impugned, e.g., Leone's (Perkin p. 414--see also Best pp.
91-94), so that it becomes essential to get some basic
proportions straight. Perhaps my calculation of the poverty line will seem but conservative when it is recalled that
as late as 1917 the first mass medical examination of young
men in Britain found 10 percent totally unfit for service,
42 percent with "marked disabilities," 22 percent with
"partial disabilities," and "only a little more than a
third in satisfactory shape" (Hobsbawm pp. 164-65; I
confess I cannot make this add up to 100 percent--perhaps
the fit third should be a quarter?).

11. See Guy Chapman, <u>Culture and Survival</u> (London,
1940), chapters 3-4, Vicinus, passim, and Best, chapter 3
(especially pp. 199-217).

12. See Michael G. Mulhall, <u>Mulhall's Dictionary of
Statistics</u> (London, 1884), p. 369. My calculation for the
working classes is based on assuming that Baxter's uppermost four classes would spend an average of £3.5 per
person while the fifth class (lower middle II) would keep
to Mulhall's average 107d. per person.

13. Karl Polanyi, <u>The Great Transformation</u> (Boston,
1968), p. 172.

14. Louis James, "The View From Brick Lane," <u>The Year-</u>

book of English Studies 11 (1981), p. 88. See for
working-class reading at the time first of all the numerous
autobiographies, such as those of Joseph Arch, Thomas Burt,
Thomas Cooper, Benjamin Gregory, Joseph Gutteridge, James
Hawker, John Hodge, George Jacob Holyoake, James Hopkinson,
Fred Kitchen, Charles Knight, William Lovett, Tom Mann,
James Nasmyth, and many more mentioned in Altick ECR and in
John Burnett, ed., Useful Toil (London, 1974), a collec-
tion of excerpts from 27 other autobiographies of working
people. See also comments in Burnett; Philip Corrigan and
Val Gillespie, Class Struggle, Social Literacy and Idle
Time, Studies in Labor History/Librarians for Social
Change (Brighton, 1978); Philip McCann, ed., Popular Educa-
tion and Socialism in the Nineteenth Century (London,
1977); Edward G. Salmon, "What the Working Classes Read,"
Nineteenth Century 20 (1886), 108-17; Stan Shipley, Club
Life and Socialism in Mid-Victorian London, History Work-
shop Pamphlet no. 5 ([Oxford], 1971); G. Stedman Jones,
"Working Class Culture and Working Class Politics in Lon-
don, 1870-1900," J. of Social History 7 (1974), 460-508;
James, Mayhew, Newburg, Vicinus, Wright CUP, and Wright GU,
passim.

15. The two most knowledgeable people I know in the
field hold somewhat divergent opinions. George Locke,
"Wells in Three Volumes?" in Mullen-Suvin p. 60, believes
that penny dreadfuls had an "Almost total preoccupation
with the past and its horrors, both mundane and supernatural, so that the amount of SF to be found there, even
in the form of isolated incidents, is minimal." John
Eggeling, however, has found (oral communication) at least
one Aldine S-F serial.

16. Allen was here particularizing a permanent complaint
of Victorian libertarians about the loss of means of subsis-
tence as societal penalty for voicing of opinions offensive
to the dominant consensus. This is perhaps best expressed-
--and characteristically followed by a discussion of ideological self-censorship--in John Stuart Mill's On Liberty
(in his Utilitarianism, Liberty, and Representative Government [New York and London, 1950], p. 122ff.) and repeated
in his The Subjection of Women (London, 1869), chap. 4.

17. Malcolm Elwin, Old Gods Falling (London, 1939), p.
329; he adds that public taste at this time was "the
crudest since the age of Boadicea. . . ." Innis p. 50ff.,
notes how Allen, Doyle, and other popular writers had to
use the magazines, whose editors prompted them to write in

a way that would inflict on readers "no effort and no
sacrifice" (pp. 125-26).

18. See Alec Craig, The Banned Books of England and
Other Countries (London, 1962), pp. 22, 40-52, 58, et
passim; from such evidence one must conclude that Altick,
VPI p. 198, is overoptimistic in affirming that censorship
applied only to obscene publications. As to the Bradlaugh-
Besant case, both the solicitor-general and the defendants
stressed that the contraception pamphlet--which had circulated freely for 45 years--was being prosecuted because it
was, at a price of only 6d., aimed at the working class
"unmarried female." In spite of being acquitted, the
divorced Annie Besant subsequently lost custody of her
little daughter on grounds of atheism and support for
contraception--see, e.g., David Rubinstein, "Annie Besant,"
in idem, ed., People for the People (London, 1973), pp.
145ff.

19. See Guinevere L. Griest, Mudie's Circulating
Library and the Victorian Novel (Bloomington IN, 1970),
Altick VPI pp. 196-99, Altick ECR pp. 295-97 and passim,
Sutherland p. 24ff., and TLS-CEL pp. 343-44.

20. Here I regretfully part company with Altick, who
believes--e.g., in VPI p. 66--that by the 1890s "most
readers could afford a freshly published novel," so that
"the average Victorian reader was well supplied with books
he could afford." If "well supplied" means buying, say,
more than two books per month (never mind "a" novel, which
I take to mean many, if not the majority of freshly published novels), I do not believe more than 50 percent of
British families could well afford over £3 yearly on books
(the "average reader" is a mythical concept anyway). Even
the yearly 21s. cheapest subscription for Mudie's was out
of reach for most people, so that the circulating libraries
were middle-class establishments, having less than a
quarter million readers--0.6 percent of the population--in
the mid-90s (Saunders p. 200, Altick ECR p. 312). My calculation tallies with the conclusion that in 19th-century UK
there was no "majority public" for reading as a whole
(Williams LR p. 189).

21. A. Halsey, "Leisure," in idem, ed., Trends in
British Society Since 1900 (London, 1974), has 823,000
registered borrowers in public libraries of Great Britain
and Northern [sic] Ireland in 1896, with a note that this
is unreliable (p. 564). The same table gives an average of
32 books issued per borrower that year.

22. First quote, Edith C. Batho and Bonamy Dobrée, The Victorians and After (London, 1962), pp. 1-2; second quite, John Morley, Critical Miscellanies (London, 1923), pp. 74-75.

23. Hadjinicolau, p. 102.

24. See Ian Watt, The Rise of the Novel (Harmondsworth, 1963), pp. 48-49.

25. I have added to the digest of the UK 1891 census, in Mulhall pp. 782-83, 15 percent as the average increase rate 1881-1901 from Reader pp. 207-11; I am not counting Mulhall's "teachers" and "students" rubrics, nor the armed services' officers who—except for the likes of army artillery and engineers—had a different social status.

26. Calculated by me from data in Reader pp. 207-11, adding 25 percent for the difference between England and the whole of the UK as in Mulhall p. 421 and p. 783. As different from Best pp. 85-86, in the irreconcilable quandary between these figures and those of Charles Booth I plump for Reader's smaller ones. At any rate, Booth too comes nowhere near 400,000.

27. My calculation from figures in Reader pp. 152-53 and 207-11 with the 25 percent extrapolation to the UK as a whole, see the preceding note.

28. My conclusion is diametrically opposed to the rich, painstaking, and pioneering investigation of Altick's ECR. The ideological perspective of his book, e.g., in the conclusion that "more and more, as the century progressed, it was the ill-educated mass audience with pennies in its pocket that called the tune to which writers and editors danced" (p. 5), seems to me either too vague or too Panglossian, at any rate too little realistic (see also note 20). Even for the antibourgeois French "high lit" writer of the period (i.e., 1848-1914), Sartre rightly notes that "It is the bourgeoisie that reads him, it is she alone that feeds him and that decides of his glory" (Sartre p. 154).

C. SF in the UK, 1848–1885

1. Narrative Logic, Ideological Domination, and the Range of SF

> Novels for housemaids?
> Since when are works of
> <u>belles lettres</u> classi-
> fied according to the cir-
> cle of their consumers?
> Indeed--unfortunately
> they are not thus classi-
> fied, or only too rarely.
> And yet, how much more
> profound an illumination
> would one expect from
> this than from threadbare
> esthetic critiques. But
> it is difficult to set up
> such a grouping. Espe-
> cially since the rela-
> tions of production are
> so seldom looked into.
> Formerly, these were more
> easily understandable
> than in our days.
>
> W. Benjamin, "Housemaid
> Novels From the Past
> Century"

1.1. A literary text has at least two strange groups of properties, pertaining to its extension and (to appropriate terms from logic as metaphoric suggestions only) its intension. Extensively, the text can in any sufficiently small period still be thought of as objectifying the central element of a circuit at whose ends are the original sender and the original receiver. However, this objectification--the apparent constancy of the text--lends itself to the creation of other communication circuits, with new receivers and often also new senders: synchronically and

(more often) diachronically, a text can have different
intensions--i.e., result in a number of different messages
for different social addressees. As to the latter, it is
clear that Marvell's ode to Cromwell, for example, is read
differently by monarchists, Puritans, and Levellers, as
well as by differing social addressees one, two, or three
centuries later; this also holds, say, for Dickens's Hard
Times read by a factory owner, a liberal reformer, and a
socialist, or for Heinlein's Stranger in a Strange Land
read by Charles Manson and by you, gentle critical reader.
Perhaps less evident but no less significant in the series
of strange metamorphoses undergone by the image of the
implied writer, which is the only aspect of authorship
relevant in a communication circuit (the "everyday," never
mind the "true," personality of the writer is not known
even to the original readership). Thus, while both
receiver and sender change, giving rise to a family of
messages, the text seems to remain unchangeable. Literary
studies--even taken in the widest sense, as studies of the
rhetorics of all "printed matter" or even of all discourse,
printed or oral--have therefore in a way rightly centered
on the text, as the one stable element of literary communication. The methodology of this essay too wishes to make
the preceding analyses of social addressees and of writers
subservient to analyses of texts in this section.

Yet if this is in a way right, it is also in a way wrong.
More precisely, if it is necessary to focus on this link
in the communicational chain--as against the temptation to
dwell on readers or (more often) on writers--, this is not
sufficient. The text is not an independent totality, a
closed monad within or atom of social discourse. Rather,
it is the frozen notation of a producing of meanings,
values, and structures of feeling, which results from the
writer's work on given materials within a given sociohistorical context. Outside of a context that supplies the
conditions of making sense, no text can even be read (as
distinguished from spelling out the letters). Only the
insertion of a text into a context makes it intelligible;
that is why changing social contexts bring different
messages out of the same text. Any reading ineluctably
invents a more or less precise and pertinent context for
the text being read. Any critical reading has at its
center the interaction between text and context, the unique
literary work and its collective addressee's world-view or
structure of feeling (a present world-view, and in case of
scholarly rconstructions such as this one wants to be, a
past one too). Thus, even the basic "formal" identifications of significant features in any narration are only

possible because we can approach it with some initial or
"zero" assumptions about people's relationships to each
other and to their world. And furthermore, these first
identifications will remain of little use unless they are
finally integrated into

> identifying those narrative bonds that can be defined
> as the relation between the set of elements in the text
> and the larger set of elements from which the textual
> ones have been selected (e.g. the relation of a blue
> sun to all other stars). In other words, the world
> that is excluded from the text cannot fail to be tacit-
> ly reinscribed into it by the ideal reader cognizant of
> that world: he will notice that the sun is not simply
> blue but blue-and-not-yellow. (It is of course possi-
> ble and not infrequent for readers to have a distorted
> perception of our common world, through ignorance,
> misinformation, mystification, or class interest: for
> them, literature will not be properly "readable" until
> their interests change. Nonetheless, a text contrib-
> utes to the education of its readers more than is
> usually assumed.) (Angenot-Suvin 169; see also Lotman
> passim).

The context indispensable for a text's intelligibility
could be analyzed at several levels. One could begin with
the historical semantics of any term taken separately--a
procedure the pertinence of which is more than usually
clear in the genre of SF, inevitably committed to new terms
that sketch in its novum (1). Such a specialized analysis
will not be attempted here, not only because it would be
too elaborate but primarily because its implications can be
subsumed under the implications of the text's presuppositions.
The presuppositions of an utterance (énoncé) and of
a text are--together with formal linguistic factors--a
necessary condition of its coherence (2). As such, they are
not external to the statement, but necessarily implied in
and by it: "The presupposed (Le présupposé) partakes of
the literal meaning of an utterance just as the posed (le
posé) does" (Ducrot 24). In other words, the presuppositions of a statement are a most intimate mediation between
what is "inside" and "outside" it, between text and
context. To take a famous example, the statement "The king
of France is bald" implies a complex and articulated
universe of discourse. Incompletely enumerated, in it one
can find: a) the anthropological presupposition that there
is in this universe a collective entity called France

(which implies that we are not omitting a classification by
anthropological entities, we are not talking about noncol-
lective anthropological entities nor about any anthropological collective entity not called France); b) the political
presupposition that France has one male monarch (i.e., we
are not omitting political classification, France is not
organized nonhierarchically, it does not have several
rulers nor one female monarch); c) the physiological presupposition that the king of France has no hair on his head
(we are not talking about his nonphysiological qualities,
nor about any other physiological characteristic of his,
etc.). The famous S-F sentence "The door dilated" presup-
poses--among many other things--that in this narration's
universe of discourse there are intelligent beings (psychozoa) who use sight, locomotion, and constructed edifices,
that these edifices incorporate building techniques not
used in human history up to the writer's period, that the
narration's "otherwhere" locus is normal for the implied
narrator, and that the categories of visual observation,
locomotion, constructed edifices, building techniques, and
historical normality are relevant for understanding this
universe of discourse. Obviously, presuppositions such as
the existence of nations, kings, baldness, edifices, doors,
sight, etc., exist _inside_ these utterances: they may
underlie the utterances but they are present within them
(not extrapolated) and necessary for them (not conjectur-
al). However, a synthesis of presuppositions implied in
all the utterances of a text amounts not only to finding
the rules that hold for this universe of discourse.
Insofar as the presuppositions simultaneously and equally
exist _outside_ the utterances, they are also ideological
maxims; in their most general form, they are principles of
verisimilitude or believability, that is, the cultural
invariants or ideological commonplaces of the context
common to the text's writer and addressee, and necessary
for understanding the text. The addressee's cultural
commonplaces unfailingly supplement and indeed shape the
"information" offered in the text (e.g., the Victorian
taboos on the body as sexuality and as source of physical
labor-force mentioned in the first section).

The presuppositions, the ideological givens, are thus
both logically prior and analytically posterior to the
text: its emergence as well as its interpretation is impossible without them. They are crucial factors of the
context; but they are also among the materials with which
the writer has to work, the building bricks which he/she
can manipulate in the text. Ideology is preeminently a
compromise between the discursive and the nondiscursive, a

representation (equally in the sense of subsequent presentation, of imagining, and of collective communication) of the
imaginary relationship between a subject and the situation
in which it practically exists. It is a negotiation
between the subject's (the ideology's collective bearer's)
inventing a place for her/himself in a historical process
that largely excludes his/her fundamental desires and
her/his accurate "mapping" of a societal reality which is
itself very difficult to represent yet must in any case be
represented either topologically or verbally. Directly to
the purpose of studying fiction, ideology is also a lived
structure of feeling "which simultaneously organize[s] the
empirical consciousness of a particular social group and
the imaginative world created by the writer" (Williams PMC
23, quoting Lucien Goldmann).

The presuppositions, the ideological maxims, the particular or common "places" (topoi) of a text as a sequence of
coherent utterances, are thus always intertextual--taken
over (possibly modified) from and shared with other discursive texts. In modern periods, they are mostly (or at
least most verifiably) shared with other printed matter
that coexists with it in a given moment of ideological history. This intertextual context, or intertext, is therefore not only an important means for establishing the horizon of expectation of a text's ideal reader (as in section
B). It is also the privileged way of establishing the
rules of believability or conventions of verisimilitude for
a text or a group of texts (3). This is particularly clear
in Victorian fiction, strongly oriented as it was toward
"the structure, internal movement, and moral atmosphere of
contemporary society. . . . The [major] novelists . . .
were especially concerned with the anxieties, envy, insecur-
ity, snobbery, and kindred psychological malaises that
stemmed from the ambiguities of rank and wealth in a time
of social flux." Practically without exception, Victorian
fiction took its themes from problems of the day, usually
already formulated in the intertext of an "enormous body of
printed argument and exhortation . . . [that] provided the
matrix for the masterpieces of social discussion . . ."
(Altick VPI 17 and 70).

Through such intertexts, various groups of texts may
usefully be linked with differing verisimilitudes, each of
which is the cultural invariant of another social group.
Often, this linkage is not a one-to-one correspondence
between a text, or group of texts, and the ideology of a
social group. Rather, it may show the text as a battleground of competing ideologies or "common senses." However, in the society as a whole, one of them--the structure

of feelings embodying the basic invariants of the ruling class(es)--is hegemonic (Gramsci MP and PN). Hegemony does not entail only "the articulate and formal meanings, values, and beliefs, which a dominant class develops and propagates":

> It is a whole body of practices and expectations, over the whole of living: our senses and assignments of energy, our shaping perceptions of ourselves and our world. It is a lived system of meanings and values-- constitutive and constituting--which as they are experienced as practices appear as reciprocally confirming. It thus constitutes . . . a sense of absolute because experienced reality beyond which it is very difficult for most members of the society to move, in most areas of their lives. It is, that is to say, in the strongest sense a "culture," but a culture which has also to be seen as the lived dominance and subordination of particular classes (Williams ML 110).

Such a hegemony is not simply a static domination. "It has continually to be renewed, recreated, defended, and modified. It is also continually resisted, limited, altered, challenged . . ."--either by pressures that do not defy its overall social validity and power (an alternative ideology) or by pressures that do so (an oppositional ideology). But even such counter-pressures are shaped by the hegemonic ideology: "the dominant culture . . . at once produces and limits its own forms of counter-culture" (Williams ML 112 and 114; see also Williams PMC 37-40).

Intertextuality is thus not simply an intersection and mutual influencing of different texts. It is primarily a way of developing, from within texts, the crucial scrutiny of their meanings and values as structures of feeling in a differential dialogue with other structures of feeling within the all-pervasive, complex, and shifting field of social discourse and its ideological tensions. The privileged, the most pertinent and significant, mediations in such a dialogue are, for fiction, the fictional forms, conventions, and genres. These mediations seem to be nearest to the actual processes of fictional production and reception. They make it possible to avoid both overly generalized concentration on ideology as direct, conscious, and pragmatic manipulation (though this aspect of ideology must also be taken into account, especially in SF) and overly particularized examination of atomized "influences" proceeding from a few texts isolated from the conditions that shaped their influences (though some works which are

fountainheads and/or summations of widespread tendencies
will also be taken into particular account in this section). Further, it is also possible to use the intertextual approach to discuss central fictional devices--in SF,
for example, the novum, the estrangement, the protagon-
ist(s) versus the setting, or certain themes crystallizing
as subgenres.
    1.2. What, then, are the central characteristics of
that formally and historically defined set of texts which
is in this book identified as Victorian SF? I have argued
that SF in general--through its long history in different
contexts--can be defined as "a literary genre whose necessary and sufficient conditions are the presence and interaction of estrangement and cognition, and whose main formal
device is an imaginative framework alternative to the
author's empirical environment," and that it is distinguished "by the narrative dominance or hegemony of a
fictional 'novum' (novelty, innovation) validated by cognitive logic" (Suvin MOSF 7-8 and 63). At the same time, I
suggested that the notion of an ineluctably historical
novum implies that SF in any particular period will only be
understandable by "integrat[ing] sociohistorical into formal knowledge" (Suvin MOSF 84). Further, it has been
rightly remarked that "'the author's empirical environment'
cannot be understood directly, that it is necessarily medi-
ated by epistemic categories, so that it presupposes,
outside the text, the contradictory whole of the social
discourse"--in particular, taking into account both intertextuality and institutional status (Angenot SSI 651). I
want to develop such discussions for further examination of
the narrative potentialities within the S-F genre.
    If an S-F narration hinges on the presence of a novum
which is to be cognitively validated within the narration,
then this novelty has to be explained in terms of the
specific time, place, agents, and implicated cosmic-cum-
social totality of each narration. This means that, in
principle, SF has to be judged--like "realistic" fiction,
and quite unlike mythological tales, fairy tales, and
horror or heroic fantasy--by the consistency, richness, and
relevance of the relationships presented in any narration.
Of them, consistency is not only intimately interwoven
with but also a basic precondition for discussing both
relevance (the value-fraught, ideological judgments of what
is true or radical change in human relationships) and
thematic or descriptive richness--both of which can only be
examined in a conclusion. Thus, consistency can here provide a central criterion for analysis.
    In a fundamental theoretical essay, "The Absent Para-

digm," Marc Angenot has shown that all S-F tales suggest--
in the very act of their reading as traced out in the
text--the existence of a both delusive and indispensable
"elsewhere," a missing or phantasmatic paradigm (in the
semiotic sense) bodying forth a differing world. The S-F
tale is constantly "shifting the reader's attention from
the syntagmatic structure of the text to a delusion which
is an important element of the reader's pleasure" (Angenot
AP 12 and passim). This carries important implications.
If the alternative world suggested, the alternative formal
framework, is not suggested consistently--if, that is,
the discrete syntagmatic novelties are not sufficiently
numerous and sufficiently compatible to induce a coherent
"absent paradigm," or indeed if the novelty is, without
regard for its logically to be expected consequences,
coopted into and neutralized within the current ideological
paradigm--then the reader's specific science-fictional
pleasure will be mutilated or indeed destroyed. "An
immanent aesthetics of SF is implied here: if the mechanical transposition of 'this-worldly' paradigms is sufficient
to account for every narrative utterance, we have a witless, even infantile, type of SF" (Angenot AP 16).

This tallies astoundingly well with an only recently published lecture of H.G. Wells's, "Fiction About the Future,"
in which he distinguished (to use present-day terms)
between the S-F story "at the lowest level," a middle range
of SF, and its highest form. Wells begins with the necessity of achieving "the illusion of reality. . . . the effect
of a historical novel. . . . a collaboration [with the
reader] in make-believe." He then focuses on the propensi-
ty of the S-F writer whose imagination breaks down to
"pretend that all along he was only making fun": this is
why so much SF "degenerates into a rather silly admission
of insincerity before the tale is half-way through." The
lowest level of SF, he ironically notes, stops at the superficial or defensive "first laugh" which is implied in the
strangeness of "every new discovery":

> Suppose--which is probably quite within the range of
> biological possibility--that a means is discovered for
> producing children--and feminine children only--without
> actual fathers. . . . Don't . . . probe into the
> immensely interesting problems of individual or mass
> psychology that it would open up, but just suppose it
> done. Then you have the possibility of a comic, man-
> less world. In order to be really and easily funny
> about it, you must ignore the fact that it would change
> the resultant human being into a creature mentally and

emotionally different from ourselves. That would
complicate things too much. You must carry over every
current gibe at womanhood, jokes about throwing stones,
not keeping secrets, lip-stick and vanity bags, into
the story, and there you are.

The middle range of SF comes about if the writer carries
out his hypothesis "to the extent of trying to imagine how
such a possibility would really work"--how would women grow
up and live in a manless world: "That would be a much more
difficult book to write; it would probably lose itself in
dissertations and unrealities, but it would be a much finer
thing to bring off if you could bring it off." However,
"the highest and most difficult form"--and Wells wryly
confesses that he has never written one--would be an
account of the struggle between opposed opinions, values,
and social groups that constituted the change in human relations as a consequence of the novum (here, directed parthen-
ogenesis). That would have to be a full-blown novel, probably narrowed down to a small group of figures, rather than
his own "romances or pseudohistories" (Wells 247-49). One
does not have to agree with all of Wells's details (there
are other forms of evasive inconsistency besides "I was
only making fun," for example, the "dissertations and
unrealities" he also mentions; nor does one have to accept
the usual self-disparagement of his S-F "romances") to see
both how closely this agrees with the approach of present-
day narratology and, more importantly, how useful it is for
an analytic grouping of the texts themselves. Wells too--
and who better qualified?--is here, clearly, pleading for
logical stringency and consistency in developing the implications of the novum.
    To systematize such leads: There is an immanent aesthet-
ics to (at least the novel-size) S-F tales, which fuses
formal and value criteria. It can be represented as a fan-
shaped spread with two limits, the optimal and the pessimal
one (see figure 1).
    In the optimum, a sufficiently large number of precise-
ly aimed and compatible details draw out a sufficiently
full range of logical implications from the central S-F
novum and suggest thus a coherent universe with overall
relationships that are--at least in respect of the thematic
and semantic field associated with the novum--significantly
different from the relationships assumed as normal by the
text's addressees. The narrative details (narremes) will
therefore be neither too sparse, nor too disparate, nor too
circumscribed. In order to bring about the most effective
estrangement, their arrangement will, on the other hand,

Figure 1

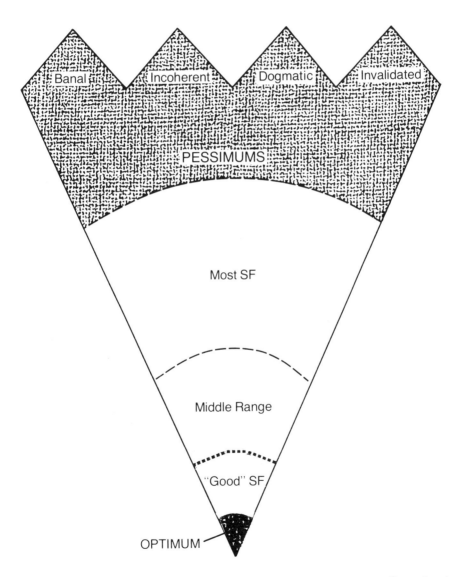

As all models, this could be improved upon; e.g., it should be a three-dimensional cone or pyramid, not a fan.

not be too explicit nor too repetitive, but will slyly
enlist the reader's imaginative activity to fill in the
gaps in the paradigm and create an "illusion of reality,"
analogous to that of the historical or "realistic" novel,
by a wise balance of the posed and the presupposed. In
such best cases, the balance or shuttling allows the S-F
estrangement to feed back into the reader's own presuppositions and cultural invariants, questioning them and giving
him/her a possibility of critical examination. In optimal
SF, the interaction of the vehicle (relations in the
fictional universe) and the tenor (relations in the empirical universe), makes therefore for the reader's freedom:
this freedom is rehearsed, traced out, and inscribed in
the very act of reading, before and parallel to forming a
conceptual system. As Wells suggested, such a freedom is
somehow connected both with personal relationships and with
power-conflicts of societal groups: a consistent narrative
logic is not only formal but also informed by ethics and
politics. Since freedom is the possibility of something
truly different coming about, the distinction between the
consistent and the inconsistent novum (as a special case of
the distinction between a true and fake novum) is, interestingly enough, not only a key to aesthetic quality in SF but
also to its ethico-political liberating qualities. Finally, as of the 19th century the only consistent novelty is
one that constitutes an open-ended or dynamic system.
     If there is only one ideal optimum, there are several
ways of falling short of it. These worst cases can be
divided into the banal, the incoherent, the dogmatic,
and the invalidated pessimum. In the first pessimum,
probably the most widespread type of S-F tale, the narrative details or elements that deal with the novum are too
sparse or too circumscribed. They are drowned in the non-
S-F details and/or plot gimmicks of a banal mundane
tale--adventure story, love story, etc. Wells's lecture
focuses on the SF being drowned in joke or whimsical inconsequentiality, a peculiar mode characteristic for English
class snobbery from the 17th century on, and as such not
without importance for Victorian SF. Beneath a certain
minimum of S-F narrative elements, the tale will cease to
be SF and become another genre which contains a localized
S-F element that does not determine the tale's dominant
narrative logic (see Part I.A.3 of this book): a grey zone
between SF and non-SF is evidenced by those books in the
main Bibliography whose annotations end with "marginal."
     In the second pessimum, the narrative details may be too
disparate, and then the tale is just not clearly focused,
in which case genological judgments become difficult, rely-

ing as they do more on the writer's guessed-at intention than on the incoherent execution.

The third, dogmatic pessimum is (in different ways) the obverse of the first two. In it the narremes are too explicit or too repetitive, so that the reader's return to his workaday world does not pass through an imaginary aesthetic paradigm. On the contrary, the reader is referred directly to the relationships in his empirical environment (which, conversely, severely limits the possible Other in the tale, the kind and radicality of the novum employed). In other words, these "empirical" relationships are redeployed so as to present merely a different conceptual grid or general idea. While a conceptual ideological field is always to be found in a work of fiction, it is (at the latest from the French Revolution on) in the significant cases not a static, preordained substitute for a specifically fictional insight or cognizing, but a questioning or problematic "attitudinal field" within the overall fictional cognition. In significant SF this means that the novum will, as explained above, allow for the reader's freedom--in literary terms, that the story will not be a project but a parable. Any S-F tale that is not a parable but a linear or panoramic inventory limited to a general conceptual grid--most clearly the static utopias of the 19th century-- partakes thus to a degree of non-fiction (of political, technological, or other kind of blueprint) and loses to that degree the flexibility and advantages of fiction. If in the first pessimum a banal plot is almost all there is to the tale, in this third pessimum the conceptual blueprint does not allow for interaction with the plot: the plot is here merely so that the reader should traverse the blueprint, and the narration has constant trouble with balancing events and lectures. (It follows from this that all uses of SF as prophecy, futurology, program, or any other form that claims ontological factuality for the S-F image-clusters, are obscurantist and reactionary at the deepest level--for example, all of Cabet and most of Bellamy, much of Gernsback's and Campbell's editorial policies, von Däniken and Manson, Scientology and Ufology.) (4)

Finally, the invalidated pessimum is akin to the banal one and competes with it for the lead in S-F statistics. However, it is more sophisticated: instead of the narrative details being quantitatively insufficient, they are qualitatively unsatisfactory in that they oscillate between a cognitive and a noncognitive or anticognitive validation --genologically speaking, between SF and fantasy, fairy tale, or kindred metaphysical genres. The details are plentiful indeed, in a way too plentiful: for the strategy here is to induce in the reader an ambiguity concerning the status of the fictive novum inside the story. Is it explainable as a set of logical events on the same level as the story framework, or is it a delusion, dream, or irruption of another level with different laws? An unambiguous decision for the second possibility would remove the story from SF and into delusional or horror fantasy, or into similar genres. The constant switching of indications and presuppositions, however, prevents any deambiguation and maintains a permanent hesitation between physical and metaphysical explanation. As the first pessimum is characteristic for British, so this last one seems to be for US and French literature (e.g., much of Poe and Maupassant's "Le Horla"--though dominant characteristics are not exclusive, and the hesitation can be found in UK fiction too). The estrangement is stressed but cut off from cognition or feedback into the reader's empirical world. Instead of a parable, the invalidated tale amounts at best to an unclear symbol suggesting the uncognizability of the reader's empirical reality (see Angenot SFF 65). Just as the old-fashioned and "realistic" banal pessimum does, this one also finally proclaims that the novum was not meant seriously; but it is a glossy, modernistic, nonmundane, occultist banality, correlative to the shift of ideological horizons from the surface-world of joyous market competition to the more threatening mysteries in the murky depths of the commodity logic.

Summing up, all the pessimums (the broad uppermost band of the S-F genre envisaged as a fan) amount to the hegemonic ideology denying, repressing, circumscribing, dispersing, invalidating, or otherwise neutralizing--and thus incorporating or coopting--the cognitive novum and the parable that allows estrangement to feed back into the reader's empirical environment (5). In all cases, the novum is prevented from full logical development and full narrative domination; to use Fourier's appropriate term, the "totally divergent" desire and cognition have been prevented. The wolf has been turned into a lapdog: tameness is all. Only the safe--indeed the deliciously titillating--memories of wolfdom are sometimes allowed to show through the dog.

No doubt, there is a middle range in between these good and bad extremes (which are ideal types rather than actually existing tales). One should in practice be thinking of how these models mingle and contaminate in each particular case. In the (inadequate) topological metaphor of the fan (see figure 1) most tales will be in a broad band say one

half of the way outward from the optimal fulcrum, a minority in the lower "middle range," and a few, singular exceptions near the optimum. This state of affairs seems to me
the handiest description of SF from the 1870s to the
present day.

What are the reasons of this dominant debility? Surely
not the malevolence, and not only the time-serving, of the
writers. Why did the imaginations of such a great majority
then, in Wells's phrase, "give out"? The reasons are to
be sought in the collective psychology that grew to be the
context of fictional discourse in the last 150 years. I
have discussed this at some length in a prepublication of
this section that contained a subsection focusing on comodi-
fication in the literature of bourgeois democracies (6). I
am here omitting that discussion partly for reason of
space, but also because the hypothesis developed there,
mainly on the material of the second third of 19th century
in France and US, can be fully applied to the more overtly
ideological and less commodified British printed discourse
only after my cutoff date of 1885. Nonetheless, I refer
the reader to that elaboration on Marx, Benjamin, and
Tocqueville, since I shall build on it in some discussions
of my corpus, for example, in the "Concluding Reflections."
For the conclusion of my hypothesis was that, as the mass
press comes to be the strongly tone-setting printed matter,
fiction under capitalism grows oriented "rather [toward]
its themes' saleability than [toward] their cognition"
(Benjamin II/1:383). This leads to literature as exchange-
value rather than use-value, and narratively to a domination of infinitely recurring superficial strangenesses;
thus, it constitutes the root-cause of the pseudo-novums
articulated in the fan-shaped model of figure 1.

2. The Phase of Inception, 1848–1870

2.1. It is then not a fortuitous coincidence that the
first truly significant writer in the Bibliography--that
is, the writer of the first truly significant SF published
in the UK after the mid-19th century--was Edgar Allan Poe,
Baudelaire's great _exemplum_ and Benjamin's prose example.
Poe was possibly the first important writer, and certainly
the first important writer of SF, totally--professionally,
psychologically, financially--exposed to a thorough-going
market and technology-oriented way of life and civilization, to the immensely pervasive capitalist societal web
that allowed the writer to survive only if trained in the
arts of a leisure-time entertainer for the middle social
groups, near to power but not sharing it (in the 19th
century, primarily middle-class women). Poe was--with the
partial exception of Mary Shelley--the first major figure
in the S-F tradition to make a living by writing for
periodicals and newspapers, directly or indirectly to
order. His complex social origins and status of a
marginal, ruined, bohemian intellectual with gentlemanly
pretensions made him both resentful of the existential and
cultural hegemony of "dollar-manufacture" (Poe 6:55) and
yet fascinated by its workings and scope. One of his great
strengths being an analytical and systematizing bent, he
became the first theoretician who had to reconcile the
conservative realm of eternal values with the dynamics of a
predominantly commercialized "tale-writing"--in other
words, who had to identify the particular psychology of
literary effect ineluctably constitutive for and of art-as-
commodity. Understandably, Poe became also--in his note to
"Hans Pfaall. . ."--one of the first theoreticians of SF,
which is discussed in terms of verisimilitude, analogy, and
plausibility for the wondrous story.
Poe's psychology of literary effect is of a piece with a
fairly consistent phenomenology and cosmology he eventually
evolved (the examples here will be taken only from his S-F
stories and nonfiction as--at least potentially--his con-

ceptually most consistent works). Life's supreme delight
lies in the creation of the absolutely new, shared by God
and the poets, and consubstantial with the epiphanic revela-
tions of knowledge and with individuality itself: "to
quench [the thirst to know] would be to extinguish the
soul's self" ("The Power of Words," see also "Marginalia"
XVI, Poe 6:93). However, true, consistent or angelic
knowledge, which perceives no barriers between intelligence
and the senses, presupposes cyclic universal catastrophes
for the world and regenerative death for the individual.
In a vein reminiscent of the radical romantics such as
Blake and Percy Shelley (minus the democratic politics), a
purified Earth should then become a smiling Earthly Paradise, "and be rendered at length a fit dwelling-place for
man:--for man the Death-purged--for man to whose now
exalted intellect there should be poison in knowledge no
more--for the redeemed, regenerated, blissful, and now
immortal, but still for the material, man" ("The Collo-
quy of Monos and Una"; similarly in "The Conversation of
Eiros and Charmion"). The mesmeric condition is an individual approximation to the "Death-purged" cognition, and
becomes obscenely horrible only when used to arrest death
itself and the attendant immortality and omniscience (as in
"the case of M. Valdemar"). The belief in noncatastrophic
development by means of mechanico-scientific knowledge and
liberal-democratic progress is for Poe the most dangerous
heresy, because dominant at large and because such utilitarianism corrupts true utility. It is savagely satirized
both explicitly and in Poe's favorite literary procedure
and form of hoax ("The Balloon-Hoax," "Mellonta Tauta,"
"The Unparallelled Adventure of One Hans Pfaall").
    Yet for all his airs of a consistent and systematic
natural philosopher, Poe was in a way highly ambiguous
about novelty and originality. He "played" it exactly as a
speculator plays the stock-market or his mariner the
Maelström, with a hectic excitement (the same one he
identified in Sue) on the verge of desperate gamble. Some
gambles--literally--paid off (e.g., "The Balloon-Hoax"),
some fell flat ("Von Kempelen and His Discovery"). He
despised "the wide-spread willingness of an ever-proliferat-
ing, journal-reading, stock investing, news addicted, male
and female public to be duped" (Beaver xvi). Progress as a
whole is a hoax, therefore the fitting and poetically just
form for presenting sensational instances of progress is
also a hoax--always connected with the fields of the
"Amriccan" idols of Wealth, Fashion, and Science. On the
other hand, himself poor and a victim of financial panics,
Poe was proud and intensely jealous on behalf of his

successful speculation (in both senses):

> The "Balloon-Hoax" made a far more intense sensation
> than anything of that character since the "Moon-Story"
> of Locke. . . . As soon as the first few copies [of
> the Sun newspaper] made their way into the streets,
> they were bought up, at almost any price, from the
> news-boys, who made a profitable speculation beyond
> doubt. I saw a half-dollar given, in one instance, for
> a single paper . . . (Poe's article cited in Beaver
> 369; see also Poe 6:328).

Thus, the final value and reality was, in his deep yearn-
ings, the permanently stable, "Out of Space--out of Time"
("Dreamland"), the sublime and the divine. Yet he observed
also that, in cognitive and literary practice, a novelty is
valuable insofar as it is strange and as it excites; excitement is, by "psychal necessity," a transient thing that
cannot be sustained for long (half an hour was Poe's pre-
scription for maximum poetic length); therefore, true
originality must be composed of novelty and vividness ("The
Poetic Principle" and "The Philosophy of Composition"). It
logically follows that "Nothing unless it be novel--not
even novelty itself--will be the source of very intense
excitement. . . . We are so habituated to new inventions
that we no longer get from newness the vivid interest which
should appertain to the new. . . ." ("Anastatic Printing,"
Poe 6:254): for each succeeding original and exciting
effect there must be a new novelty and a stronger vividness. The cursed idols of wealth and fashion, the despised
pseudocriteria of the "journal-reading, stock investing"
social addressee (half a century in advance of its UK
analog), keep molding and fashioning Poe's criticism and
fiction (7).
    In particular--as indicated by the publication of "The
Balloon-Hoax" in the Sun, the first penny newspaper in
New York, specializing in sensational scoops--Poe was deeply committed to breathless sensationalism. Sometimes, but
not always, hoax and/or satire gave his texts the breathing
space of ironic distancing. At other times, the theoretician of the infinite identity of universes considered as
God's heartbeats (Eureka), the satirist of mechanical
progress allied to power but divorced from imaginative
truth (e.g., "The Man Who Was Used Up"), became also a
purveyor of the novum as sensationalist horror, a presenter
of invalidated cognition. Skylark, the balloon of
"Mellonta Tauta," is halfway between Shelley's ecstatic
soaring principle of poetry and "Doc" Smith's leadenly

additive Skylark-series of pulp-magazine sensationalism.
For sensationalism is not simply an adventure-laden plot,
but the anxious, eunuchlike way such a plot avoids exploring the otherness of the novum that made those adventures
possible: the new locus, people, scientific element,
societal organization, etc. In it, curiosity--the interest
in causes and effects--is degraded into suspense--the
interest in effects sundered from causes. Many of Poe's
non-S-F tales are suspenseful horror-fantasies pretending
to a private supernatural reality that is in fact based on
prescientific lore. That aspect of his texts is at the
origin of what is most pernicious in the commercial "genre"
of SF--an adolescent combination of hysterical sensibility
and sensational violence, a dissociation of symbol from
imaginative consistency, a forcibly intensified style used
for creepy incantation. But at his best, in most of his
SF, Poe's tradition of the moral quest--which in his hands
turned urbanized, escapist, and heterodox--as well as his
analytical talent preserved him from such "Poeism." To the
mid-Victorian complacency, he brought an ambiguous but chal-
lenging legacy, ranging all the way to Wells.

2.2. However, for all his fountainhead significance
and influence, Poe was an eccentric intruder from outside
the UK social discourse--a curious blend of early Victorian-
ism and exasperated avantgarde. The other S-F texts of the
1850s-1860s were more typical for that period of doldrums.
As is characteristic for all SF before 1871, they are quite
heterogeneous; yet they can be grouped in clusters situated
within the fan-shaped model (fig. 1).

The first cluster contains texts dominated by sociopolitical prescriptions which are so strongly dependent upon
the nonfictional intertext (to "pre-scribe" means literally
that it has been written before) that they come close to
nonfictional popularization, and fall within the sphere of
what I have termed the dogmatic pessimum. It is useful to
divide them into utopias proper (whose intertext is the
social blueprint) and future histories (whose intertext
is the political tract as vision of positive development or
awful warning against decline): all such divisions being
effected on the basis of the narratively hegemonic aspect--
one that overrides any other aspect that may in some cases
be also present (see Part I.A.3). Utopias proper are,
then, Forrest, (the putative) Lamartine, and Pemberton,
while future histories are Imaginary History, Gale, and
O'Neil (8). I shall adjoin to the utopias also Harting,
appearing in the UK in 1871--probably as a result of the
surge of interest in such directly political SF--but first
published in the 1860s.

In the utopian group, Pemberton (1854) is something of an exception as it adopts the old-fashioned Enlightenment form of quasi-dialog supplemented with prospectuses and address- es, so that it is on the extreme margin of fiction. Though mentioning Utopia and Rasselas, it is nearer to Owen's entirely nonfictional plans and proclamations, not least in its unambiguous and spatial location (in New Zealand). Its only interest lies in the equally unambiguous intention to "emancipate the workmen from the tyranny and slavery of the capitalists" and found "the Millennium" on "productive labour and perfect education." To the contrary, Forrest, Lamartine, and Harting use the Romantic device of dream. In the eccentric Forrest (1848)—exercized as much by the eating of crude cucumbers as by the lack of State support for arts and education—this remains wedded to lacklustre lectures about an imaginary country, while in the others it is situated one or two centuries in the future. But there is really not too much to choose between these generally petty-bourgeois liberal visions: Forrest's variant is a mild, antiaristocratic ethical reformism; Lamartine's (1848) demagogic advocacy of middle classes stresses a united European continent against despotic Russia and capitalist England, whose Empire is dismembered; and Harting's (1871) scientific protagonist is given a balloon- tour of technological marvels by none less than Roger Bacon. In all of them, there is a perfectly soporific accord between signifier and signified.

The group of future histories is distinguished from utopians proper by stressing dynamics instead of statics, the process and causes of development instead of the final product. No doubt, there is a large grey zone between the two, further complicated by a difference between short and long range forecasts. As evidenced by Imaginary History (1857), the short range (here 30 years) lends itself to political and technological forecasting. The 2,000 years of Gale (1867) and O'Neil (1868), on the other hand, lend themselves to apocalyptic dire warning and to approximating the form of antiutopia, where the evidence of ruin justi- fies reflection on its causes. Both the latter texts adopt Macaulay's device of a future New Zealander on the ruins of London Bridge doing exactly that. Gale's slim booklet has a distinct edge, as its satire of the 1867 Reform Bill rather realistically foresees that even if Church and State are abolished, the armed forces and banks will reestablish the old regime (which is exactly what happened in Paris 1871); whereas O'Neil's long-winded sequence of epistolary disquisitions substitutes for Gale's class hatred from above laments on political reforms and commercial disasters

of the 1860s. O'Neil's only interesting element is that--
symmetrically inverse from Fourier--historical decline is
followed by mass volcanic eruptions and a shift into colder
climate. While these "long rangers" are distinctly Tory
reactionaries, Imaginary History focuses on semiliberal
developments: national independence, reforms, some technological improvements. Its main interest today lies, however, in its preface, which observes that "Histories of the
Future could hardly fail to influence the future, for the
mere proclamation of oracles often ensures their fulfill-
ment." Whether this is correct or not, it indicates the
raison d'être of this first cluster: to influence--to
further or to prevent--the developments presented in it.
Future history is as a rule a more urgent form than the
leisurely utopia, and both Gale and O'Neil are direct
responses to the 1867 Reform Bill agitation.

The second cluster has for its intertext the current
models of mundane tales--comic, love, and adventure
stories, often in uncouth combination--and falls within the
sphere of the banal pessimum. Its analysis is somewhat
more complicated both because of such entangled aspects and
because its writers are less single-minded than the political dogmatists; some texts will therefore tend toward the
"middle range" SF, and one (Rowcroft) will be discussed
under that heading. But most texts are a real hodge-podge,
so that they are best divided into a sequence by degree of
banality. Easily the worst offender is the once popular
Helps (1868), with its insufferable upper-class banter
masquerading as a lengthy series of glimpses into a
barbaric tribe. Its quintessential elitist ideology--not
too surprising for Queen Victoria's writing aide--is so
naked that it could almost be grouped under the dogmatic
pessimum, except for its lack of system. It is an almost
perfect example of what Wells meant by keeping at the level
of the shallowest laugh; for example, the title hero Realmah seems compounded of "Realm?--Ah!" and an anagram of
"Hamlear"! Whatever obscure place Realmah might keep in
the history of SF will be as a document of growing post-
Darwinian interest in prehistory and of influential use of
marginal SF by upper-class propaganda. A notch further
from the pessimum are two of the rare S-F three-deckers,
The Last Peer (1851) and Maguire (the latter published in
1871 but belonging to the atmosphere of the 1867 Reform).
They combine sentimental entanglements with a near-future
localization and are clearly addressed to the upper-class,
circulating-library circuit. The main novelty is in both
cases political: dispossession of aristocracy, with the
attendant rise in unemployment and crime--respectively,

suffrage for women, who lead the House of Commons. But the
novelty is submerged by the banality of a melodrama à la
Sue around the perfect aristocratic hero (Last Peer) or
of the "eternally feminine" traits in a Parliament and a
style of life where plus ça change plus c'est la même
chose (Maguire). A Catholic Irish M.P., Maguire does
present religious emancipation and a happy Empire which has
solved the Irish Question, as well as the poverty of lower
classes, but the supposed solutions are as inconsequential
and vague as the position of women (9). Wells's example of
how to botch a tale of female emancipation, cited in 1.2,
might almost have been coined for this text, and I cannot
forbear from quoting (even if I will absent myself from the
felicity of commenting upon) our heroine's response when
asked to take up a key political office and in effect save
the government:

> ". . . But I must, of course, consult Papa. But go,
> Mary dear, and leave me to myself; for I must put on my
> wisdom cap, and think--oh, so profoundly."
> "Grace, [for our heroine, being graceful, must of
> course have a speaking name . . . , DS], you are a
> positive love, a downright darling; and I am so glad,
> and John too will be so glad-- . . ." (Maguire).

Both of these three-deckers are in a way the fag-end of a
tenuous tradition of S-F consumption and production that
began in the 1820s, with Mary Shelley's The Last Man and
Webb's The Mummy! (the latter reprinted in 1872), and
combined horror or love melodrama with location in a
changed future. Always addressed to an elite, restricted
audience, this tradition became increasingly banalized as
the social addressee--the hegemonic, circulating-library
cluster of section B--grew more conservative. After 1848,
attempts to salvage the three-decker for nonbanal purposes
(Maitland, Blair) came to nothing, most probably because of
the inbuilt resistance of that communication circuit.
     Much less offensive, because frankly fanciful, are
Whiting, Heliomanes, and Chatelain. Whiting (1855) is the
richest among them, building upon motifs from Cyrano a curious, not quite coherent construct of dandified love-
romance, with some satire, some languid quasi-erotic utopianism, some spirit-fantasy and fairy tale, some science,
some adventures of a beautiful soul, and some snobbery.
Heliomanes's (1866) booklet, possibly published to cash in
on the third edition of Whiting's popular novel (Heliondé, in the same year), adds to details of flight to the
Sun taken from Poe's "Hans Pfaall" a general topsy-

turviness mixed with some political satire cognate to the
contemporary agitation. Chatelain's (1866) long story
details seven magical flights to venues variously taken
from myth, legend, and the 18th-century planetary voyage
tradition (English and French), with aliens suited to each
venue. These three works are all in the somewhat whimsical
area situated between the imitations of Cyrano and Swift,
Raspe's Munchausen and the 1001 Nights. Chatelain is
clearly marginal, Whiting attempts to justify his incoherence by invoking the dream-device, and Heliomanes is very
brief. Nonetheless, there are some strengths in these
works attendant upon their common element of flying.

Such strengths are perhaps best discussed within the "middle range SF," or third cluster, beginning with Rowcroft
(1848). This novel too has comical elements. But it bears
witness to the fact that comical incongruity always presents an otherness, which can easily become valid SF if
allied to consistency, that is, if cognitive rather than
whimsical, Swiftian rather than Munchausenian. In these
works at least (and probably in others too), a good test of
cognitiveness is the part played by science. Chatelain is
indifferent to it, Heliomanes and Whiting not quite consistent about but on easy terms with it: Rowcroft is in a way
under the sign of a scientific Other. True, much of its
science is alchemy and mesmerism, but these are motivated
as superpowers of a rational alien who discusses science
with a professor and falls in love with an astronomer's
daughter. It is also allied to a candid-eye, Voltairean-
type satire of erotic and other customs of a number of
countries he has seen in his flights. As in the above
three tales, but more clearly, the freedom of human flying
(significantly, the hero flies by power of will) is an
exhilarating analog to and signifier for the freedom from
social gravity and closed conventions. As in Whiting but
more consistently, this-worldly erotic happiness which over-
comes societal obstacles is the horizon of Rowcroft, and
the tale ends with the Neptunian (coming from a planet without women) wedding his Terran beloved—a final narrative
sign for the union of knowledge and happiness, science and
sentiment, suggested by the themes of the whole novel.
The Triumph of Woman is therefore superior to the sentimental banalities of, say, Maguire; while unclear on
reasons for and ways of overcoming societal obstacles,
Rowcroft's unpretentious tale is a good example of a
pleasant middle range of SF.

Two more examples can, strangely enough, be found in SF
written for younger readers. Hayward (1865) has some
Vernean elements: balloon and undersea voyage, a bizarre

sea-creature, and African exploration. If Hayward, a
professional writer, really took them from Verne's French
originals, that would be the first Vernean echo I know of
in the UK. Of course, Hayward could have taken the hidden
valley with beautiful ageless people from 18th-century
texts (Paltock, Dr. Johnson, etc.), and his submarine
voyage at least predates Captain Nemo's. What is in any
case important is that he was trying for the same institutional "landing point" as Verne--juvenile SF. As to the
parallel between the lower gravitation in the valley and
lesser biological wear and tear of its inhabitants, it
comes from the tradition of magical effects of the "weight-
less point" midway between the Earth and the Moon, from
Francis Godwin to Poe. Thus, Hayward is an indication what
possibilities were lost when Haggard appropriated the lost
race subgenre and ripped it bodily out of SF.

More important is "Herrmann Lang" (1859). It is however
an unresolved vacillation between adult and juvenile SF,
between radical novelties and old stereotypes. Its importance lies first and foremost in the racial ecumenicism,
which is in Lang's system of Providential "retributive
justice" and inversion fought out as the abolitionism of
white slavery, since the world is 5,000 years hence ruled
by a trio of black empires from the southern hemisphere.
After a victorious world war, natural cataclysms and a dead-
ly vortex on the site of London had radically remolded
British geography and reduced its remnants to barbarism (it
is possible that Jefferies took note of this). The basic
conflict is between "unchristianlike forms of religion,
slavery of white men, and absolutism" and "Christianity in
its simple purity," destruction of slavery, "a proper equality of rights, and a perfect equality of justice, and the
happiness of public non-interference for every one who
acted as a good citizen and subject" (Lang 100). Lang's
importance lies, secondly, in the form this conflict takes,
the air-battle between the wicked and the good, in which
echoes of set battles on sea or land mingle with the rout
of Lucifer and Armageddon. Aerial technology, though it
does not interact quite consistently with other elements,
contributes to the effect of an "absent paradigm," and to
the exhilaration of the reader. It functions as a literal-
ized symbol of his/her delight in rapid textual movement,
as a signified thematized or assumed into a signifier. A
further delightful touch is provided by epigraphs from
imaginary future poems (another possible and very rarely
found test of consistent novelty, of the paradigmatic
illusion of reality). On the inconsistent side, religious
ecumenicism does not accompany the racial one, so that Lang

has two blood-curdling villains, a dirty and grasping Jew and an uncontrollably irascible Catholic Irishman, as well as a comic servant-aeronaut midway between Dickens's cockneys and Poe's or Mrs. Beecher Stowe's darkies. Lang's "proper equality" of rights seems thus limited to the Nonconformist purity—it should be remembered that British abolitionism was very much a Nonconformist cause, and the publishing house of Penny seems to have been close to them too (see Clarke TF 4). On top of that, our heroine is a lovely hand-wringing maiden, while the second (Black) hero and heroine are carefully drawn as not too African, and the second heroine is allowed to wed our hero only after forsaking unwomanly wilfulness. Lang's happy ending, symbolized in the interracial marriages of the two pairs of protagonists, is thus a valuable emblem, but its price (the exclusions) is also quite high—as befits this middle range of SF.

The "future war" motif is an occasion to mention the inferior Fairburn (1867, probably distributed only in the 1880s), where the sympathies (not between Protestants and Blacks but England and Israel) are more mystical and exclusively used for victory in war. However, the culmination of UK SF between Shelley and Abbott is in my opinion Trueman's The History of a Voyage to the Moon (1864) (10), a work that should be situated somewhere between middle-range and optimal SF. The novel is fashioned as a system of binary oppositions: two parts, "The Voyage" and "The Ideal Life"; two novums, one per each part, the neutralization of gravity and the lunar state of affairs; two friendly protagonists, the first representing Catholicism, the second science and technology, the first a man of words and past tradition (he finds the "Monk's Legend" manuscript from 18th-century Spain that leads them to the enterprise of antigravity), the second a man of action and future-oriented dreams (he supplies the enterprise with a scientific basis and modern technology). The first novum is thus a blend of quasi-religious natural philosophy (levitation) and pragmatic mechanical technology: the repulsion is both a product of mixing (again two) new minerals and usable because iron is impervious to it, that is, both a blend and a limitable influence. The second novum, "perfect material existence," is a mixture of cosmo-biological Earthly Paradise (the soil is fertile, there are no diseases or predators, death is instantaneous and painless at about 70, people have a much higher capacity for pleasure than on Earth) and sociopolitical utopia (federation of self-governed workmen, no economic distinctions or sexual rules, short labor time). The first, natural-science or things-

oriented, novum is--given its premises--highly consistent
and leads to the calculation of an "island Earth" spaceship, complete with a greenhouse for oxygen, and to believable interplanetary travel (incorporating some elements
from Poe's "Hans Pfaall" but transcending them).

On the contrary, the people-oriented novum in and of the
second part is heterogeneous in two important and related
ways. First, together with already mentioned libertarian,
indeed socialist (probably Fourierist), elements it
contains a veritable mania for delimitation and negation
which introduces strong elements of dogmatic deadening:
each species subsists on one separate fruit and nothing
else, besides no disease and no predators there is
also no life in the water, there is only one sea and
one, wholly regular language, and even the music-
emitting flies are robbed of their charm by the fact that
they always sound only a harmonious octave! A symbol of
such world-excision might be seen in the abyss that
separates the further (the only inhabited) Moon hemisphere
from the barren hemisphere turned toward Earth. Curiously
for a federation of self-governing workmen, there is also a
'capital city and a chief Administrator. In fact, while
Trueman's sociopolitical machinery is not at all fully
delineated, it seems to share much of the spirit of that
Catholic communist, Thomas More: but what was economic
realism in Utopia becomes stifling statics after the
industrial revolution. Second, at the end of the novel we
learn that Lunarians are in fact select Earthmen reincarnated as a reward, though (incompatibly) without memory of
previous life, and there is speculation that the Lunarians
may reincarnate again on the further planets. Together
with the other cosmic and planetary features, this makes it
clear that Providence has shaped the Lunar ideal life.
Fourier and Percy Shelley thought that cosmic changes would
follow from political ones, that the novum would spread
upward from below. Here, Fourier is both reversed and
dominated by a divine, hierarchic framework, which accords
well with the Morean delimitations (King Utopus also cut
Utopia off from the continent). It also fits well with the
total absence of women and children from Trueman: was the
writer perhaps a Catholic priest?

The best test might, again, be provided by the two
instances of flying: the repulsion in part 1, and trans-
port by riding a giant bird in part 2. In both cases,
people accept and utilize the novelty; but in both cases
the novelty is mastered and harnessed. The "NEW PRINCIPLE
IN NATURE--. . . REPULSION" (Trueman's caps) is tamed by
the providential iron shields; the bird is simply a flying

horse. If there is a balancing between the radical and the
tamed Other, the latter clearly dominates. Equally, our
protagonists are sympathetic to their black laborers while
constructing the spaceship (an episode which Verne then
developed into the full saintsimonian euphoria of casting
the Columbiad gun): "to us a novel conception was always
acceptable." Yet such moral attraction does not extend to
the "savage," nonsubservient Red Indians. Thus, while many
elements of The History of a Voyage to the Moon remain
exhilarating and original, Trueman finally puts the stress
more on religious, hierarchic containment and framing than
on Shelleyan science and Fourierist politics, than on the
"upward" vertical. This text remains of great importance
in the development of SF (it is the missing link between
Poe and both Verne and Wells, not to mention Tsiolkovsky),
superior and in some ways astonishing for its time, but it
also remains an example of the upper middle range of "good"
SF: a rich and complex system of novums is gradually
contained, resulting in an only partial development of its
potentialities. The balancing act finally keeps the novelties under hierarchical (specifically, Catholic) control,
and harnesses them for a very good adventure story with
elements of both fitful cognitiveness and of dogmatic
limitations deduced from divine preestablished harmony.

In conclusion, this overview of the 1848-1870 prologue to
the constitution of UK SF has arrived at a distinction
which can be expressed as the communication of power
versus the communication of knowledge. The jockeying for
position and casting about for literary form, constant
social addressee, institutional "landing point" or intertextual plausibility that can be read off these texts has
to do with the various degrees of commitment to and oscillations between communicating domination or liberation. That
sociopolitical prescriptions--in utopias or future
histories--have as a rule more to do with power than with
cognition seems not to require special argument. But the
intertext of love and adventure tales as a rule is also--if
somewhat more subtly--oriented toward power: the bantering
tone of Helps exudes it, the presuppositions about natural
aristocracy of the "last peer" and natural womanhood of
Maguire's Women in Parliament contain it just below the
surface. The comic cluster begins to squint at cognition,
more openly when satirical and/or consistently wedded to
more or less erotic desire (Rowcroft, Hayward). At this
point, science and technology in alliance with the libertarian wishdream of flying emerge as the privileged way of
expressing knowledge of the Other opposed to power of the
status quo, and indeed they lead directly to a new and

(according to the writer's lights) just redistribution of
power--witness Lang, and much more swepingly and richly
though not quite consistently Trueman. To the contrary,
the basic strategy of the hegemonic power--of the ideology
of dominant classes--is an absorption and neutralization, a
containment and possibly cooption, of the discourse of
knowledge. "The characteristic method of securing this
objective is to eliminate antagonism and transform it into
a simple difference" (11)--that is, to substitute for the
radical novum an inconsequentially quaint or "wondrous"
one, a slumming sensation that does not give rise to a
parable on or counter-project to the established power.
This is, of course, most intimately involved with the constitution of SF as a coherent genre. The conflicting economic and ideological interests of a literary genre's
possible social addressees are a decisive factor in its
constitution and institutionalization.

The ups and downs of such a constitution will next be
examined in the period from 1871 to 1886.

3. The Phase of Constitution, 1871–1885

3.0. If ever there was in the history of a literary genre one day when it can be said to have begun, it is May Day 1871 for UK SF:

> [Bulwer-Lytton's <u>The Coming Race</u>] appeared on May 1st, 1871, the day when Blackwood's of Edinburgh also published Chesney's <u>Battle of Dorking</u> in their magazine, and by an even more extraordinary coincidence the day when Samuel Butler brought the manuscript of <u>Erewhon</u> to Chapman and Hall (Clarke PE 144).

This opens a period in British SF which culminates with the opus of Wells. It is still unclear whether that period should extend to 1901, to the First World War, or indeed to the mid-1930s; I have for practical reasons opted for the earliest date.

The reasons for this date of birth are complex, but there is no doubt that the immediate stimuli were the Franco-Prussian War and the Paris Commune of 1871, and in a more diffuse way the political regroupings in the UK attendant upon the 1867 suffrage reform. But as mentioned earlier, deeper reasons must be sought in a crisis of confidence in societal values and stability, which--significantly enough--began already during the economic boom of the early 1870s, <u>predating</u> the onset of the 1873-1896 economic depression. The term depression came to indicate "a pervasive--and for the generations since 1850 a new--state of mind of uneasiness and gloom about the prospects of British economy. . . . [The British boom] drifted inexorably downwards. . . . Prices, profits, and rates of interest fell or stayed puzzlingly low" (Hobsbawm 127). Clearly, this "depression," while codetermined by and possibly rooted in economic realities, was not confined to them, and it should be taken in the entire range of its meanings. The S-F outburst after 1871 was one means--one might almost say one organon--for articulating and attempting to explain that range.

However, even the basic quantitative indicators show that
such a macro-period has to be further subdivided. Taking
into account the main annotated Bibliography and the Appendix in Part I, it becomes clear that the extraordinary quantitative outburst of new S-F books in 1871 is almost
matched in 1886; the urgency and diversification of their
subject-matter confirms this indication. Of the 428 S-F
titles, 18 were published in the years 1848-1870 inclusive,
92 in 1871-1885, and 318 in 1886-1900; this gives a yearly
average of 0.78, 6.13, and 21.20 for the three shorter
periods into which I shall subdivide my corpus. The
publication frequency oscillated between 1 and 3 books in
1848-1871; between 2 and 10 in the 1871-1885 period (except
for the quite abnormal breakthrough year 1871 in which it
reached 17 items--of which 10 belong to the <u>Battle of
Dorking</u> controversy); and between 10 and 29 in 1886-1900.
A graph (figure 2) having for its abscisse the years and
ordinate the number of books published shows unambiguous
maxima in 1871 and 1886-1889.

The 1871-1885 period can be in its turn further subdivided into three subperiods. The first, 1871 to 1875 inclusive, comprises the breakthrough and its immediate consequences in stimulating texts of a similar nature. As

Figure 2

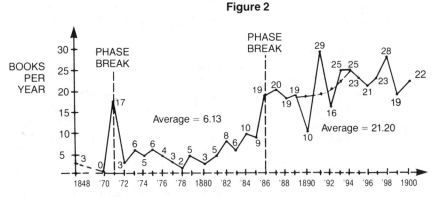

*The 1890-1893 and 1898-1899 oscillations are by themselves not statistically
significant; this is indicated by the broken lines.*

indicated by the slight dip in figure 2 (which would be
much stronger if one took into account only texts of over
100 pages), a reaction ensued roughly 1876-1879, due to the
falling financial and critical success in the previous
subperiod--itself due, no doubt, partly to the saturation
of the market by the "future war" spate as well as by
inferior examples of what I shall later discuss as "alternative history" works, but partly perhaps by other ideological considerations which remain to be identified. The
third and final subperiod 1880-1885 saw a renewed impetus
in S-F publication due to a renewed sense of political
urgency, which then reached new heights in and after 1886.
Bulwer-Lytton, Chesney, Butler, Verne, and Maitland could
be taken as the most significant authors of the first
subperiod, and Greg, Abbott, and Jefferies of the third,
while the middle four years were--except for the ubiquitous
Verne--a qualitative as well as a quantitative slump.
However, such chronological subdivisions will here be
subordinated to division by literary form or subgenre.

Chronology is, of course, not the same as deeper historical logic, which is often nonlinear, and it is in this
essay used as a rough guide, not as a shibboleth. In this
subsection I shall therefore use a corpus obtained by remov-
ing from the 1871-1885 entries in the Bibliography Maguire
and Harting, used in subsection 2, and six texts from the
1880s, which should be dealt with in a later study--four
dealing with Ireland (M. Pee, The Battle of the Moy,
Ulidia, Greer) and one each with prehistory (P.S. Robinson)
and the London municipality (Welch). The remaining 84
works (61 in the annotated Bibliography and 23 in Appendix
1) will be divided into the following clusters: outright
pessimums (3.1); the traditional generic "landing point" of
Extraordinary Voyage, as old as SF (3.2); the new landing
points, forms or subgenres of Future War (3.3) and--most
numerous--of Alternative History (3.5), which are new
avatars of and recombinations of elements from the earlier
utopian and antiutopian SF; the last being preceded by
Bulwer's Coming Race (3.4), a single work--or monotypic
cluster--of generically synthesizing as well as historically seminal significance. While the 1848-1870 formation of
a genre, with its tentative attempts and hesitations,
seemed to provide a good reason for dealing with each
single case, in this phase of more frequent and by the same
token more crystallized and stereotyped publications only
the examples significantly establishing or departing from
the norm of the cluster will be given fuller treatment.

3.1. A few texts which could on the basis of their
locus be allotted to other groups serve as an example how

the locus (island on Earth or in interplanetary space, near
future) is not necessarily a narratively dominant feature,
and cannot therefore serve as a meaningful basis for classification. Atlantis, Mars, or the 20th century are here
rather vehicle than tenor, and classifications based upon
such "hard facts" as the localization would make as much
sense as allotting the Biblical parable of the Mustard Seed
to "agricultural tales" or Brecht's The Good Person of
Szechwan to "Chinese tales." Rather, the 1871 Island of
Atlantis (which combines the New Atlantis model with Rosicrucians and magic) or Collins's (1874) reincarnation on
Mars (an anemic dreamland of the mid-Victorian bohème)
are both rather old-fashioned examples of the invalidated
pessimum, while Lumley's (1873) "Star City" and Cobbe's
(1877) newspaper report from 1977 are both eccentrically
incoherent variations of New Atlantis, albeit that the
first likes and the second fears scientifical and medical
progress. As opposed to these texts from the early 1870s,
the two anonymous three-deckers from the 1880s, The Dawn
of the 20th Century (1882) and John Haile (1885), try to
carry a political message on the wings of a mundane love
melodrama. The politics are in both cases right-wing and
antiliberal, but while Dawn is simply an orgy of Anglo-
Irish landlord wishdreams, John Haile mixes this with a
future war, Social Darwinist inheritance of two foundlings,
and a rise of three political parties based on the working,
merchant, and upper classes of the near future, concluding
in a Disraelian recipe for Tories and Radicals squeezing
the spineless middle. Nonetheless, in slightly different
degrees, both qualify for the banal pessimum.
    Together with these "classical" or pre-1871 pessimums,
the rise of the S-F genre created a secondary or parasitic
pessimum, the sensationalist cashing in on the genre's
images of destruction and downfall--mainly on Chesney's
future battles and retrospective narrator-witness, but also
on Bulwer's demagogy. Hemyng's 1871 Commune in London
threw together an "Anticipated History" (his subtitle) and
the red-hot theme of the day in a hasty concoction mixing
gory Paris-type street carnage with muddled political disquisitions, and principally aimed at making a fast six-
pence. A bit less virulent, hesitating between the old-
style political tract and the Future War was Back Again
(1874), a booklet on horrible world consequences of Liberal
disarmament. A step further toward transcendental general-
izing is Hay's Doom of the Great City (1880), where
immoral London is, like unto Sodom and Gomorrah, punished
by a killer fog. A preachy, prurient, pseudo-religious
brew of the dogmatic and the invalidated devices (the fog

is God's vengeance but also the result of coal-polluted air) narrated as an escapee's monotonous relation in old age from Macaulay's New Zealand, it ends with a gleeful description of corpse-filled London. The culmination of this trend is Watson Sr.'s Erchomenon (1879). It is much longer than Hay because it attempts to depict year 550 of the Commune, with a few political and technological changes strewn amid the moralizing casuistry, as well as a final Last Judgment, in turn validated by the "it was all a dream" ending. It is equally antimaterialist, antiscientific, and clerical, and it stresses the horrors of women dressed like men and smoking, of collective education of children, republicanism, euthanasia, and a "Religion of Humanity" (to which the writer, a staunch Protestant clergyman, has the Pope convert), all of which results in drinking, sex, gambling, and other assorted standbys of the pulpit.

It is quite interesting here to note two converse aspects. First, a preachment against evil fashions and novelties is conducted in the quintessentially fashionable and modern mode of sensationalism. Second (Benjamin and Poe seem to have missed that) sensationalism was readily used by clerics--ideologists on a "higher" level than professional hack writers like Hemyng--just because it could combine religious dogmatism with a presentation of evils that did not have to be consistently or at all logically argued: it simply had to be shrill, additive, and threatening but finally safe in narrative outcome just as in ideas. Laymen had difficulty competing with a hint of supernatural wrath in the business of aids to postprandial digestion. My last example, Robinson and Wall (1884), therefore comes off distinctly inferior. It also uses both scientific inventions (a kind of TV and a kind of elixir of life) and natural catastrophe (Panama sinks and Europe grows colder) within a melodramatic plot. But what is the death of an inventor as the ending of a sensationalistic novel, compared to a good Last Judgment?

3.2. In this period, the Extraordinary Voyage was quantitatively and qualitatively dominated by Jules Verne; as near as no matter, the Extraordinary Voyage was Jules Verne. But his overpowering model of the marvellous voyage through Terran and interplanetary space was itself a metamorphosis of earlier models, which did not entirely disappear. From the Renaissance on, as space became traversed (on Earth) or at least better known (in the Solar system), the original tribal, Antique, medieval or non-European feedback and equation between travelling and encountering radically different--strange, marvelous, extraordinary--

cosmic, biological, political, etc., states and conditions
began breaking down. In true as well as imaginary travel
tales (say, about the historical and the legendary
Alexander, or in Polo and Mandeville), there was earlier
little distinction between process and product: whatever
the reasons for travelling, from war and commerce to
religion and curiosity, almost all one saw while travelling
was new; locomotion and novelty were coextensive. After
Columbus and Vespucci, and more so after Magellan and Cook,
travelling on Earth could begin to be taken for granted.
There were still plenty of unexplored "white spots," where
one could imagine (and for all that was known, perhaps
really find) a radical Other; but the way to them was largely "normal," that is, largely a mundane space. The break
between the ordinary and the extraordinary, analogous to
the Aristotelian passage from imperfect sublunar to incorruptible heavenly space (still accepted by Francis Godwin
in the 17th century), now did not happen by leaving the
shore but by leaving the known shipping lane. An extraordinary tempest was the ontolytic agent usually motivating
this break, but while in the Odyssey as well as in the
Ulysses canto of the Inferno it is due to the wrath of a
god, in Bacon and Swift it is already a meteorological,
this-worldly accident (even if still capable of carrying
suggestions of Providential intervention--as is blatantly
the case with the lightning that destroys Robur's "Clipper
of the Clouds" in Verne). In fiction this meant that
travel could now be used as framework and justification,
which may be forgotten while the place found is described,
even if in all significant cases the two remained correla-
tive--as in practically all the loci of utopia and satire
in early SF, from More through Cyrano and Swift, and to
Bulwer and Butler. Thus, travel is used as a "getting
there" device in all the spatial locations of 19th-century
SF up to Verne, since the only other procedures available
in "realistic" verisimilitude, that is, dream or renunciation of fictionality (lectures, discussions, found manuscripts with displacement explanations missing), were
getting increasingly intolerable. Verne found a unique--
indeed a nonce, imitable but not creatively variable--
alternative: to focus on traveling itself as opposed to
arriving anywhere. This is one factor distinguishing the
new Vernean model from earlier historical forms of SF in
space.

Another factor, logically prior and at least as
important, has been suggested in the mention of Aristotle
on heavenly space. Even travel to far-off places on Earth
had in earlier times retained traces of the original tribal

numinosity attached to all space, and concentrated by mono-
theistic religions on central "holy places," associated
with the founder-prophet, as well as scaled-down local
replicas, associated with saints and miracles. The age old
communal dreams of Earthly Paradise, coopted by religion
both into Eden and Heaven, combined perfect freedom with
perfect order. The humanists laicized the freedom from
want and the perfect order, and built them into the early
utopias: Utopus and Utopia are a thisworldly, politicoecon-
omical transmogrification of Jesus and Jerusalem; Solamona
and Bensalem combined the sacred wisdoms of Plato's
Atlantis and Solomon's Temple. The humanists also laicized
religious numinosity onto mountain-tops, to which the
Romantics added the wide-open and untrammeled spaces of the
ocean, the waterfall, the volcano--all of them Verne's leading motifs. But divine numinosity lingered on longer in
the heavens, as yet less subject to human intervention.
Pursued by Galileo and Newton, God retreated to the further
stars. Yet while traveling to planets could begin to be
envisaged as a mundane activity, the Catholic Church burned
Bruno, who had dared to postulate an infinite universe with
an infinite number of worlds. Only totally subversive,
major SF dared to show people outside the solar system
before the 20th century: I can think only of Defontenay
(beside the semispiritualistic works of Flammarion and his
imitators) in France, and of nobody at all in the English-
speaking countries, where no revolution had broken with
religion. On the contrary, Flammarion was only a modern,
"scientific" refurbishing of an old and unbroken Protestant
tradition of supernatural visionary flights around the
universe (Milton) and divinely graded inhabitants of other
planets (Swedenborg--present, for example, in Maitland).
This tradition, reactualized in the 1870s by the renewed
interest in the "higher beings" of occultism and by the
post-1871 S-F boomlet, can be seen at work in Lach-Szyrma's
A Voice From Another World (1874), expanded into his
Aleriel (1883). The title hero is a winged Venusian "not
unlike the pictures we see of angels," and Venus is
(exactly as in Blair from 3.51) a tropical planet without
sin and death. Aleriel has mesmeric and other psychic
powers like the Vril-ya (though the writer prefers to
invoke Dumas père's Balsamo), and in the second text
leaves with the narrator a manuscript about visits to other
planets. Mars is a technologically superior theocracy of
lion-derived giants who migrate following the warmth;
illogically in view of the godlier Venus, Mars is also the
next stage awaiting Earth. There are giant aquatic
inhabitants in undersea cities on Jupiter, jumping life-

forms on Mimas, and the visitor has a couple of narrow
escapes. In brief, this is a perfect hodge-podge of mutually incompatible elements from religion and science (the
writer perpetrated two more S-F tales of declining
coherence as magazine serials after 1886). Yet it most
probably stimulated Wells to transmute it into The Wonderful Visit (via the Stewarts' text--see Locke VS), as well
as "In the Abyss." Also, it can serve as an example of the
unholy intertextual muddle that was the "qualitative" interplanetary tale before Wells. Another such example is Ryan
(1880), an eccentric, self-published booklet, whose
narrator levitates to the Moon by "extracting gravity,"
while the Moon inhabitants manufacture diamonds (as in
Bishop Godwin) and have airflight and monorails as well as
a sensory organ for long distance communication. This
muddle was to bear even more grotesque fruit between 1886
and 1900 (e.g., in Astor).

Lach-Szyrma and Ryan can, by contraries (and regardless
of their quite inferior texture), put into relief the other
factor distinguishing Verne's "quantitative" space-travel
from such typologically earlier forms: its resolute this-
worldliness or mundane refusal of transcendence (in spite
of the occasional melodramatic tricks such as the one
played on Robur). The development of traveling as end and
not means, within an exclusively mundane space, results in
a perpetuum mobile type of trajectory that is the topo-
graphical and orientational equivalent of the notion of
bourgeois progress:

> Progress was motion toward infinity, motion without
> completion or end, motion for motion's sake. One could
> not have too much progress; it could not come too rapid-
> ly; it could not spread too widely; and it could not
> destroy the "unprogressive" elements in society too
> swiftly and ruthlessly (Mumford 184).

Of course, there is no motion without stations through
which it goes; and Verne was capable of describing such
stations in his Alternative Histories, discussed in 3.51.
Yet progress, a formal ideological principle, is in a way
deeper and more exhilarating that any particular state
from, through, or toward which it is passing: while states
may develop dubious features or show logical incongruities
(as even The Mysterious Island does), motions are carried
forward by a momentum more difficult to scrutinize--like
the juggling of a prestidigitator, or indeed like commodity
circulation as distinct from any particular commodity and
use-value. This is the secret of Verne's success, present

in a pure state in his Extraordinary Voyages up to the mid-1870s; in SF, these are A Journey to the Centre of the Earth (1872), the "Moon dilogy" (1873), and Twenty Thousand Leagues Under the Sea (1873--further TTL), with Hector Servadac (1878) already a sign of decadence. I shall limit myself, in the case of this much and brilliantly discussed writer, to matters of immediate relevance for this essay, and for other aspects respectfully refer the reader to the overview in Suvin MOSF 147 ff. and to the bibliographies there and in this work.

Swift motion, the conquest of space, is rendered possible by machines: balloon (in Verne's first novel, not SF but influential in it, Five Weeks in a Balloon, France 1863 and UK 1870), submarine, interplanetary projectile, other means of surface locomotion (an anthology of which is found in the other very influential non-S-F novel Around the World in 80 Days, France 1872 and UK 1873), and finally, the quickest motion and the ultimate guarantor of them all, the "flight" of astronomical bodies such as the Earth and the comet of Servadac. Verne is interested in science insofar as it is applied to motion within clock-time and gives rise to a series of means for speedy locomotion in a closed circle, traversing already categorized horizons--thus escaping the time-anxiety discussed in 1.3. The resulting voyage has to be strictly continuous with the bourgeois North of our globe where it begins and ends, but it delivers that world of its everyday sedentariness; its whirl as it were liquefies the bourgeois solidity, which is yet preserved in the eye of the hurricane, the comfortably upholstered interior of the "space machine." As I have argued at length in MOSF, the voyage time is--as all other quantifiable elements in Verne--exactly measured and wholly filled by the traversing and filling in of known space. Even the voyage to the center of the Earth follows the pretraced route of Saknussem's. Indeed, this first S-F tale can be read as the key to Verne's epistemology: it shows how quantified time translated into quantified space constituted the book of Nature. The act of motion through it permits its decoding, the didactic verification of the information we already knew it contained but had not clearly visualized. The descent into Earth is at once a descent into the geological past and into the imaginative, intertextual space of textbooks of the pre-Darwinian, classificatory natural science--such a safe sitting on the ideological fence being the reason why, paradoxically, this text became the progenitor of almost all later evolutionary giant saurians and prehistoric men in SF. Verne's voyagers through geography, geology, or astronomy are always verify-

ing the triumphant plenitude and consistence of the
"positive," quantifiable, material, and above all closed--
circular--universe.

The only quality quantitative motion can have is to get
quicker--to accelerate; but it is unthinkable to accelerate
beyond the speed of Earthly--or cometary--rotation around
the Sun, into some radical exteriority (e.g., Flammarion's
faster than light speeds). The universe is in Verne identical with what pertains to the Earth and its immediate
cosmic neighborhood. Other planets, other times, aliens,
other mores--any threats of a radically "problematic Other"
--have been resolutely eliminated from his universe: the
only utopia imaginable is the paradox of a liberal utopia;
if there are any females, they are the Victorian girl-women
waiting to comfort the hero; the only lower class seen is a
loyal crew or dastards from the inferior races. As will be
indicated in 3.51, Verne's institutional "landing point" of
juvenile literature is well suited to the narrative form
which is the logical final horizon of movement on the
planisphere--the accelerating closed circle. Neither the
center of the Earth, nor the Moon, nor the Pole is ever
reached (except for one awful suffocating moment of his
supreme hero, Nemo), for nothing could be found there
except the death of circulation, asphyxiating stasis.
Verne's space is not analogical but digital: it cannot
harbor a hierarchy of values (in which, e.g., Utopia could
be better than England or Venus than Earth) but only the 1
of plenitude or the 0 of emptiness. Fulness is the
"positive" 1 of Being, which is therefore axiologically the
always identical, rendered exciting by progressive
traversing and elimination of the open and bland 0 of
Nothingness. All of his voyages go off toward a major
novelty, but after the joy of voyaging return to bourgeois
normality: even the limited novum of the wondrous means of
locomotion is at the end (necessarily) destroyed or
otherwise neutralized.

The always identical--a reference to Benjamin's application of the formal necessities of the "eternal return" in
commodity production to culture--leads to the heart of the
fascination exercised by Verne. The supreme, in fact the
only value of his Extraordinary Voyages: Known and
Unknown Worlds (as the collective title of his whole opus
goes)--the accelerating closed circle--is identical to the
supreme, and formally the only "value" of capitalism--the
Commodity-Money-Commodity circulation (Angenot JV). This
circulation "is an end in itself; for it is only within
this constantly renewed movement that value is turned to
account" (Marx chap. 4--translation mine). Practically all

of Verne's Extraordinary Voyages presuppose huge financial sums at the protagonist's disposal--a matter foregrounded in the subscription for the Moon projectile (as well as in Around the World and The Begum's Fortune). These sums are invested in the "space-binding machines" (Suvin MOSF 145)--vehicles or colonies--which as a rule come to nothing except the exhilarating periple itself: the circulation in the text is also the circulation of the text, its consumption by readers, and its sale as a commodity. The principle in the text is the principle of the text. What is "gained" is the warmth and energy in/of the rapidly circulating text; woman (sex) would only dissipate the investment of the readers' desire into them. By reading the text, we have, like Phileas Fogg, "gained" one day and shored it against menacing time, which can only be mastered by journeying through space. As time is money, money is spent to neutralize time. Verne's circulation seems to be Money-Space-Time-Money; and all of its terms are quantifiable exchange-values, formal but also existential equivalents of commodities. At the Pole, where the Earth does not move, there is no breathing space (spatially: oxygen, the circulatory principle of human energy; temporally: life; axiologically: Being). On the contrary, on Nemo's and Fogg's Great Circles girdling the globe, the maximum acceleration prevails. In the Moon voyage, where speed is constant, gravity is the great obstacle impeding circulation and overcome by the industrial arts translated from warlike to peaceful pursuits, as in the splendid saintsimonian epic of the casting of the Columbiad gun. Therefore, life and joy of being culminate in the oxygen inebriation at the point of zero gravity. This bouleversement is scientifically nonsense, but it is traditional in SF, from Godwin to Poe (see Bailey 242-43 and passim); it is in fact a remnant from the marvelous limit at which travelers enter Aristotle's incorruptible heavens.

Thus, both the Moon dilogy and TTL show there is more to the best half a dozen Verne novels than quantifiable certainties. They also incorporate the arithmetic enthusiasm of Saint-Simon's utopianism--or at least as much of it as can be accepted by a Christian liberal, that is, the bliss of individual affirmation within rapid technological circulation. This ambiguously touches even upon rebellious liberal radicalism in Captain Nemo, who is, together with Ardan, certainly the best developed S-F character until Twain, Morris, and Wells. This "Nobody," a disdainful Byronic political pirate, scientist, and visionary, is an avatar of the heroic Unknown Avenger from popular literature after Hugo and Sue. He circulates and lives with ease in the sea, the element of freedom, as a counter-power to the established tyrannies, the "iniquitous rights," of all the States above. He is the tutelary genius of a fully furnished world which, though on Earth, is as foreign to terrestrial life as a different planet would be. TTL--as well as Verne's other venture under the surface, A Journey to the Center of the Earth--is Verne's most extraordinary voyage, nearer to the radical exteriority of outer space than the astronomical voyages. The first sympathetic S-F rebel since Frankenstein's Creature, Nemo is equally wronged by civilization and revenging himself on it--but he surpasses the Creature by his openly political context (perilously close to the anarchists) and by the possession of a parallel and rival microcosm, the Nautilus. Verne's constant hallmark, and an indication of his textural richness, is such an equivalence between protagonist and S-F novum (the machine-vehicle or some other islandlike microcosm). They are connected by the strongest sympathies within a cluster of symbolic (one could almost say Symbolist) correspondence proper to the text's thematic and semantic field: Lidenbrock, the underground world, and geology; the conquest of gravity, the Moon projectile, and the ejected trio; Nautilus, the sea of freedom, and Nemo.

However, as discussed further in 3.51, Verne retreated precipitously from such perilous waters after the mid-1870s. In Servadac (1878), his whole system is hollowed out from within. The travel is not due to triumphant human will using science and machinery, but to a blind accident of indifferent cosmic Nature. Possibly the most memorable scene, the congealing of the supercooled sea, reverses the usual liberating liquefaction. The cosmic cold is, even more clearly than in The Begum's Fortune, barely kept at bay by the volcano's warmth; but tapping that energy does not lead, as it did in A Journey to the Center of the Earth, to accelerating movement but to sedentary hugging of its flanks. Most importantly, circulation grows increasingly impossible. Quite openly, the place of circulation is taken by the hoarding of gold, which for Verne constitutes the unacceptable face of capitalism; sadly, he falls into the petty-bourgeois racist mystification of blaming it upon a Jewish usurer, described in the usual terms of grotesque anti-Semitism. It is, of course, cognitively absurd to constitute the circulation of commodities into the supreme value and yet, simultaneously, refuse the consubstantial power of money and desire for conserving this tangible product of the Commodity-Money metamorphosis (see Marx, chap. 3). This is, however, exactly the insoluble aporia of Verne's basic societal philosophy. It had been hidden by the exhilaration of circulating with help of science, until politicoeconomic circumstances induced grave doubts in him whether capitalist progress was possible without domination by large capital, that is, without catastrophe. There is little enough exhilaration left in Servadac (an anagram of "cadavres"), almost no science, and the tired plot is finally threatened by the most tired excuse of them all, quite uncharacteristic for Verne, that it was all perhaps a dream. In terms of social addressee and addressor, the science-oriented fraction of the middle bourgeoisie and of the professionals was passing from saint-simonian euphoria to antiutopian gloom about the possibilities of capitalism. But while the euphoria lasted, Verne's breathlessly whirling plots and his fully furnished universes united his "landing point" of juvenile readership with the readership of serious periodicals interested in science, setting up the basic equation for S-F consumption in the generations to come.

Thus, from the mid-1870s on, Verne's belief in joyous human contact by way of mastery over nature, its mapping, and intimate penetration faltered. Concurrently, no SF by him was published in the UK from 1880 to 1885 inclusive. His influence in UK Extraordinary Voyages also declined in the later 70s. It probably began with Hayward in 1865, and continued in elements of Bulwer and (especially) in Blair as well as in geographic adventures in balloons, ships, and polar regions (see Part I.A.3). Of these, Penrice (1875) should be classed as SF: the first part of that hasty adventure-tale is a balloon flight to a sketchily described Moon and a Mars similar to Central Africa. In the early 1880s I can find only the interplanetary travel and polar hunt in Greg; the description of life on other planets, which rarely had Vernean ascendencies, begins at that time to be heavily indebted to Flammarion (in Green). It is only with Gillmore (1885) that the Vernean model reasserts itself, though it is not yet clear whether that story of an amphibious vessel traveling to North America etc. was taken hot off a prepublication of Robur le Conquérant or provided pointers to it. Though in this case not very likely, this would not be impossible. Verne read widely and excerpted carefully all sources of novelties, scientific and fictional, including English ones. He certainly used Trueman-Cathelineau for his Moon flight and Richardson for The Begum, and probably Hale's satellite idea (US 1872) for Servadac, not to mention the tradition from Hoffmann and Cooper to Hawthorne.

However, Verne gave at least as much as he got: from 1886 to 1900 around 30 UK publications testify to the influ-

ence of his Extraordinary Voyages—usually to clumsy plagiarism from him (Fawcett, Pemberton, Griffith, etc.); and
the clear influence on Wells, which led to counter-projects
rather than borrowings, has not yet been properly weighed.
On the UK readers his influence was unequaled. He was read
in French, he was pirated, he circulated from the preteen-
ager to the scientist and back. As argued above, the
perfect congruity of circulation as both signifier and
signified was what made his enormous success. He had come
at the right time and to the right place to describe the
conversion of quantified time into quantified space:

> The long and unbroken success of the <u>Voyages extraor-</u>
> <u>dinaires</u> . . . [and] their world-wide dissemination
> owed much to the commercial enterprise of the Hetzel
> company. For the first time in the history of fiction
> the much increased capacities of the publishing trade
> allowed an editor to plan production from the first
> appearance of a story in a magazine to serialization in
> the daily press, and then to special issues and the
> authorized translations into foreign languages and the
> long-term contracts with overseas publishers. (Clarke
> PE 95)

In the UK, Verne was after 1875 contracted exclusively to
Low, Marston, who published him in three types of editions:
the normal first edition at 6s. to 10s.6. per volume; the
plainer cloth edition at 3s.6d. to 5s.; and the cheapest
edition at 2-3s. (12). Thus, he was accessible to all
people who normally read fiction, and determined the dominant expectations from much SF. He therefore not only
inflected the Extraordinary Voyage form by creating its lay
or "scientific" (i.e., quantitative) variant, and by dominating it exclusively for 30 years. Much more fundamentally, together with his Alternative Histories Verne supplied
the whole S-F genre with the basic elements of careful
verisimilitude, exciting adventure, liberal didactics, and
safe circularity. In brief, positivism had arrived to SF—
which is why Wells so furiously (and rightly) fought
against the sobriquet of "the English Verne."
      It can be concluded, then, that the science-fictional
subgenre of Extraordinary Voyage was in Britain between
1871 and 1885 (as in France from ca. 1865) evolving from
the classical models of Swiftian satire and of travel to a
numinous Space—half transcendental in the religious sense
and half utopian in the sociopolitical sense—to a different model. The intertexts of the classical model of the
Extraordinary Voyage were the Earthly Paradise, satire,

utopia, tall tale, fantasy, and <u>roman planétaire</u> of the Cyrano-Godwin type. The basically new Vernean model focusses on traveling itself as a (literally) breathless circulation. Its intertexts were laicized travelogues and adventure stories as well as textbooks of the "positive" sciences. This situation would change only with the advent of the Social-Darwinist intertext that triumphs in the "scientific romances" of H.G. Wells, from <u>The Time Machine</u> on.

   3.3   The story of <u>the Future War</u> subgenre has been disinterred by the pioneering historical research of Professor I.F. Clarke, which fortunately allows this work to be relatively brief about it. Indeed, I have profited from this occasion to relegate almost all the "pure" Future War tales--defined as those which treat only of military matters and political changes (usually of boundaries) resulting from battles, without treating of technological changes more sweeping than a single invention or of radical economic and social changes--into the unannotated Appendix 1 to the main Bibliography. Thus, I wish to proceed from Dr. Clarke's surveys (Clarke VPW and Clarke TF) only into some considerations on the place of Future War in the development of SF as a significant part of UK social discourse. This will be here confined to Chesney's <u>The Battle of Dorking</u> (1871): it was not only the fountainhead and the model of this subgenre and form right through the rest of 19th century, but there were also no interesting modifications to this model before 1886.

   A first consideration concerns the ingredients for the astonishing rhetorical effectiveness of that text. Its first intertext is the economico-political tract on the need for military preparedness, which it translates into the much more powerful mode of a minutely realistic description of shocking events in a (wisely undated) near future. This is related as emotion recollected in tranquillity by a first-person narrator who combines urgent immediacy with judgments and reflections 50 years later, written down both as testimonial and awful warning for his grandchildren emigrating from a crushed England. The carefully detailed verisimilitude of battlefield confusion and carnage derives most probably both from newspaper reports of recent wars and from French Realists such as Erckmann and Chatrian (Clarke VPW 33), Stendhal, Balzac or Hugo. It is rendered shocking by substituting the topography of well known, peaceful, and affluent English Home Counties for Sevastopol, Waterloo, or the Vendée.

   The contribution of an S-F location to this is twofold. First, it ostends the events in a double future-present

that permits startling immediacy. Second, it finally
resolves the vivid present nightmare and the lamenting
hindsight into a possible expiating foresight: "it's all
happened 'in the future,' so it hasn't really happened:
it's just been a nasty dream--a description, incidentally,
that fits most modern genre SF" (Moorcock 9). The narrative tone tallies with the double temporal perspective,
being mostly that of a Clubland gentleman but rising at the
beginning and the end (and in some more awkwardly interpo-
lated comments) to bitter generalizations. Crucially for
the effect of Chesney, these are not simply military: the
army is a _means_ to economico-political ends, that is, to
secure England's position as the workshop and trading-cum-
financial hub of the world:

> . . . the wealth heaped up on every side was not
> created in the country, but in India and China, and
> other parts of the world; and . . . we ought to insure
> against the loss of our artificial position as the
> great centre of trade, by making ourselves secure and
> strong and respected. We thought we were living in a
> commercial millennium, which must last for a thousand
> years at least.

Thus, the military foresight can be used for preventive
action, for ruling out this alternative history, avoiding
the premature economico-political Judgment, and prolonging
the existing artificial Millennium. Going Clausewitz one
better, war is for Chesney the prolongation of political
economics by other means. The engineering precision is in
Chesney yoked to impassioned reasoning, the hardheaded
calculation of national profits is in the service of a both
nationalist and class myth or ideology.
    This quasi-mythical--in final analysis irrational--
fundament of Chesney explains the cavalier way he gets rid
of the British fleet by a combination of muddle and an
unnamed new invention. Much more importantly, it explains
his major presupposition, namely that once a however "artificial" world situation has come into being, it can be
upheld for an indefinite time by military force. The
discourse of power--here, a cynical vulgar Machiavellism
clothed in righteous lay millennialism--takes at this point
over from the discourse of knowledge. Their interaction is
Chesney's great strength: for power truly _was_ the final
reason of 19th-century rule. The horror-picture of the war
and of its price was exactly true (as the writer, a member
of the British government of India, was well placed to
know) of all other colonial and indeed class rule:

> Need I tell you the rest?--of the ransom we had to pay,
> and the taxes raised to cover it, which keep us paupers
> to this day?--the brutal frankness that announced we
> must give place to a new naval Power, and be made harm-
> less for revenge?--the victorious troops living at free
> quarters . . . our own magistrates made the instruments
> of extortion. . . .

But the totally unthinking subordination of knowledge to
nationalist power is also his major limitation. Usually
without Chesney's strengths, this will remain the hallmark
of all UK Future War tales until Wells's subsumption of
them--primarily and evidently of The Battle of Dorking--
in The War of the Worlds (see Moorcock 5-6).

This leads to the second consideration: who were the
social addressees of The Battle of Dorking? To begin
with the addressor: Chesney was a professional officer in
the Indian Army Engineers, who had after a quarter century
in India just been made president of the Royal Indian Civil
Engineering College in England. The Royal Engineers corps
as a whole was traditionally the home of people with the
only serious technological training in the UK and thus a
source of civilian State managers and scientists too:
surveyors, geologists, astronomers, communications (e.g.,
telegraphy) pioneers, railway managers, criminologists
(Burn 190 and 224, Reader 97-98). The initial pace of
Chesney's tale is rendered possible by the new communications systems of railways, telegraph, and submarine cable,
which break down because out-of-touch civilians and
admirals do not know how to manage them. His narrative
persona is a government civil servant, the exact social
equivalent of a colonel of Royal Engineers in the civilian
(read--militarily unprepared) agential system of his tale.
But further, Chesney was also a "nabob," son of an Anglo-
Indian officer, not trained via the normal R.E. route but
in a special military college of the Anglo-Indian establishment. He participated most directly in the creation of UK
wealth by extraction from India (and the first quote shows
he was perfectly aware of that). Within the ambiguous,
hinge character of the R.E. Corps between the professional
army officers and the professional gentlemen, that is, the
upper and the upper-middle class (see the section on social
addressees, 3.1), the Anglo-Indians must be seen as leaning
more fiercely toward the upper class, as Tory rather than
Liberal; The Battle of Dorking testifies to Chesney's
acute awareness of the thin red line of military might
holding the Empire together (13). His unique social position was to be at the meeting point of the Anglo-Indian and

the Royal Engineers Corps ideological traditions; his individual talent was that he found the right form and the right
time for their fusion.

The addressee is clearly indicated in the text. First,
by place of publication: <u>Blackwood's</u> magazine and publishing house was primarily addressed to the influential
bourgeoisie. Second, by the presuppositions of discourse
discussed above: national economic prosperity. Finally,
explicitly: the addressee whose mind has to be changed is
politically that dominant part of "our rulers [that] did
not heartily believe in the need for preparation," and
economically the businessmen whose concern was for "bills
[that] matured although the independence of the country was
being fought out under our own eyes. . . ." It is, in
short, the Liberal bourgeoisie, who should be weaned away
from antiaristocratic prejudices and brought under a new
political consensus. In this consensus, a new awareness of
technology would be the token for the ideological hegemony
of a technocratically updated protectionism and colonial-
ism. State intervention is--paradoxically but correctly--
seen as the precondition of a "free market" in which
Britain can remain dominant in the face of German (and
later US) competition. In the long-range and common
interests of prosperity and societal peace, the short-range
interests of the business class should be curtailed in
favor of higher budgets and a stronger war-machine. The
permanent cry of all Future War zealots was to be <u>si vis</u>
<u>pacem, para bellum</u>. The imperialist division of the world
was happily ushering in our own age of world wars.

Within the social discourse of SF, Chesney represents the
clearest, most consistent, and most intelligent right-wing
position of that fraction of the dominant group not directly dependent on the market (the aristocrats, top officers,
top politicians, and top civil servants discussed in the
essay on writers, in Part I) as against the pretensions of
the businessmen. "Power was passing away from the class
which had been used to rule," his narrator comments rueful-
ly. The top professionals of the new scientific professions should renew the imperiled ruling consensus by adjust-
ing it to the realities of technological power, strengthening the role of the State and the managerial fraction, and
bringing to heel undue liberalism which encourages "mob-
law" and foreign aggression. (Indeed, in some subterranean
ways, I believe that much of the force of this text comes
from an unacknowledged equation between fear of foreign
invasion and of revolutionary uprising, lurking always just
beneath the surface of all major conflicts in Victorian literature, and finally rendered explicit in <u>The Time Ma-</u>

chine.) On these conditions, and on these conditions only, English economics and politics--the very topography of English life--could go on without major disruption.

To suggest all of this in a slim booklet is an astonishing achievement, a stroke of ideological and rhetorical genius. To focus on the only ungainsayable and unavoidable new technology, the military one, as wedge against a bourgeoisie clinging tenaciously to the organizational forms and ways of thinking from the early, "free trade" phase of industrialization; simultaneously, to apply this wedge against the entrenched political and ideological expression of that class, "the party of William Ewart Gladstone, who looked forward to peace, retrenchment, and reform" (Hobsbawm 132)--this transcends SF. This text (with its huge success) is, in fact, one of the very first signs of the major shift in world economics and British politics that was to do away with peace, retrenchment, and the Liberal party. But conversely, it only transcends SF by first becoming SF: a new and, as it proved, powerful way of articulating social discourse.

Nobody in the Future War game was to repeat this pragmatic or aesthetic success until the new twist of Wells's. Chesney himself produced an aberrant specimen, The New Ordeal (1879), which is as exemplary in its escapism as the first text was in its realism: since new explosives have made war impossible, national conflicts are settled by a physical ordeal between selected champions. . . . Of the 25 other book-length UK titles, from the immediate replies to Dorking to The Battle of To-Morrow in 1885, only two were over 100 pages. They differed as to the enemy (the French pouring across the Channel and the Russians across the Hindukush came temporarily to substitute for the Germans around 1882, especially in connection with the outcry at the Channel Tunnel scheme), as to the particular military devices and strategies or political nostrums the writer was peddling, and as to the outcome (victory or defeat of our homeland as reward or punishment for its present course). But very rarely has even the most horrendous war any deeper sociopolitical consequences than changes of territorial sovereignty. "McCauley"'s Chapters From Future History (1871), with civil war in Germany and the sweep of republicanism across Europe, brings it into the vicinity of the Alternative History, as its title indicates. The only interesting aspect, the shift of social addressee from the upper bourgeoisie to a larger audience in which the petty bourgeoisie comes to predominate, and the attendant sensationalism, are best left to a discussion of the post-1885 period.

3.4. Bulwer-Lytton's The Coming Race (to be referred
to as CR, 1871) is, together with Verne and Butler, the
most discussed text of Victorian SF, so that I can again
focus on a few considerations cognate to this essay. If
the 19th century was "the golden age of the ideologists"
(Buckley TT 31), Bulwer stands out even among them for his
remarkable anticipatory intuition of the shifts in his
readers' ideological nuances and preoccupations, and his
equally remarkable talent for shifting literary genres as
well as for combining disparate intertexts and appeals in a
single text (14). But what is significant is that CR mixes
genre contexts and other basic presuppositions in logically
though not ideologically incompatible ways. It is much
like his Vril-ya paintings: "wanting, as it were, a
centre; so that the effect [is] vague, scattered, confused,
bewildering-- . . . like heterogeneous fragments of a dream
of art."
Before embarking upon an analysis of some key narrative
elements which show this up, I want to play the devil's
advocate and note where CR participates in a true--that is,
radical and unambiguous--otherness. I believe this is
confined to two areas: some physical surfaces of the Vril-
ya world--their looks, plants, singing birds; and some
reactions of the narrator-protagonist, for example, his awe
of the Vril-ya or daydreams of ruling them. These are
techniques of realistic credibility imported, probably for
the first time, into the utopia-derived societal anatomy--a
genuine novelty, to which both Bellamy and Wells are
indebted (and through them all utopian fiction and all SF
since). The novel of individualistic psychology and the
tradition of parabolic abstraction meet for the first time
in CR, the work of the first semirealistic "mainstream"
novelist to write SF. Even Verne's teen-oriented realism
focused on things more than on credible human relationships; for his social addressee realistic verisimilitude
could and had to be oriented toward the movement of space-
vehicles rather than toward their inmates--toward the
Columbiad or the Nautilus rather than Barbican or Nemo.
The twin striking novums of CR are the societal system
and the position of women. Both are weighty concepts,
treated in highly contradictory ways, both repose on CR's
keystone--vril. Vril is a material force that unites
physical (electromagnetic) and biological (mesmeric)
effects, a "mystical agency which art can extract from the
occult properties of nature." The depiction of this "all-
permeating fluid," which serves equally for destruction and
for preservation, was the culmination of Bulwer's life-long
interest in occult unity between matter and spirit. It is

a cosmic and societal principle which can manifest itself as sympathy between spiritual elements and as will that acts on material elements. But as in Hoffmann or Balzac, the natural supernaturalism of this superenergy can be divine or diabolic. Insofar as it permitted self-willed individuals to go in for a revolutionary storming of the heavens, from below upward, it was for him demonic (as with Margrave in A Strange Story; see also Zanoni, Caxtoniana, and Godolphin); insofar as it encouraged people to share sympathy with the ideal and the immortal, from up downward, it was angelic. In CR, vril is intertwined with the evolution of the race from proto-Aryans--if not proto-batrachians--to the eventual supplanters of Homo sapiens. Materialist evolutionism is (incompatibly) both guyed as false and emphasized as horrifyingly true. But vril is much more than a physical force (which informs such technological innovations as domestic robots, flying machines or sleep teaching); it is, even, more than an earnest of biological evolution with volitional control over nature. Vril's all-pervasive unity is also the analog, the "single first cause and principle" of the unified societal organization. The very terms for "civilisation" and "Civilised Nations," A-Vril and Vril-ya, build on and derive from "vril": in Bulwer's idealist metaphysics, language--which is accorded a separate chapter, just like religion--is significant and "realist" in the medieval sense (see A.C. Christensen 173-80, and Wolff, passim, in the Biographies entry).

The fundamental contradictions of Vril-ya society are glossed over by Bulwer's style of mellifluous vagueness or negligent imprecision and air of verisimilitude, and do not appear as dogmatic. Yet societal anatomy and political exemplarity are central to CR, and they are an incoherent admixture of dogmatic incompatibilities. A central illustration among many possible ones is the aporia between collectivism and individualism. Vril has eliminated physical labor and a separate working class so that civil society is a group of communities formed by an affluent aristocracy, without strife between classes or States. But the elements of Fourierist utopianism (Owen and Campanella also lurk somewhere near) are confined to children--adult individuals are differentiated by wealth, which also carries social and political obligations. The puzzling retention of degrees of wealth--totally unnecessary with unlimited energy literally at everybody's finger-tips-- makes this a strange "ideal of an aristocratic republic," which has less to do with Plato than with a tortured transposition of the situation of British bourgeois "aristocracy" and of capitalist individualism.

For, in the Lockean tradition, the individual is a
natural proprietor of his person and capacities, owing
nothing to society. Simultaneously, this individualism is

> . . . also necessarily collectivism (in the sense of
> asserting the supremacy of civil society over every
> individual). For it asserts an individuality that can
> only fully be realized in accumulating property, and
> therefore only realized by some, and only at the
> expense of the individuality of the others. To permit
> such a society to function, political authority must be
> supreme over individuals. . . . All [the propertied
> individuals] need to do is insist that civil society,
> that is, the majority of themselves, is supreme over
> any government, for a particular government might other-
> wise get out of hand. . . . the more thorough-going
> the individualism, the more complete the collectivism.
> (MacPherson 255-56)

As an extreme reactionary renegade from radicalism, a
radical Tory, Bulwer was much better placed than any
optimistic liberal to see that ideal bourgeois individualism (which, as in CR, needs to keep the State apparatus to
a minimum) issues in collectivism. For him, a thoroughgoing philosophical idealist who firmly held that consciousness creates being, this principle subsisted even after its
reason and cause--commodity production--had been abolished
by a wave of the magic wand of vril. But though "strife
and competition between individuals . . . render the many
subordinate to the few, destroy real liberty to the individual, whatever may be the nominal liberty of the state,"
competition remained a quite irreducible principle. Even a
perfect, aristocratic collectivism could abolish that
strife, together with class and national hatred, only by
issuing in soul-crushing mediocrity. The price of such an
"almost . . . angelic order" is too high for mere mortals,
if not for a superrace, concludes Bulwer. The basic contradictions of bourgeois individualism necessarily have to
envisage every, however desirable, utopian organization
first as unworkable (and CR incongruously mixes wealth-
gradations with equality of rank, constant volition with
"tranquil happiness," benevolent autocracy with ideal
freedom, class structuring with classless unity), and
second as supremely threatening for the very basis of this
individualism. In this structure of feeling, every utopia
which cannot accommodate individualistic property (a
competitive immortal soul) as the natural atom and axiom of

existence issues in antiutopia. Bulwer was the first
writer in UK SF to realize this, arriving at the furthest
edge of his social class's possible consciousness. Even
his idealist dogmatisms and incoherences articulated the
social discourse of the Victorian upper classes, and proved
by example that its fundamental problems could be envisaged
in the form of an alternative history--an alternative
locus where the hidden problems of the social system would
be incarnated in parabolic surface-relationships and thus
subjected to costless public scrutiny, explained or explained away.

Vril is biologically controlled by all the Vril-ya, but
the females are much better attuned to it. The sympathy
between vril and women reposes--though this is necessarily left unsaid--on their supposedly stronger sexual energy,
and Bulwer is again quite ambivalent about that. Being
closer to the unifying principle of the universe, the CR
females are not only socially equal to the males but physically and "mystically" (cognitively) superior. However,
just as the contradiction between the collective and the
individual, the contradiction between sexual equality
(i.e., freedom) and hierarchical nuclear family is quite
unresolvable within "possessive individualism" (MacPherson)
or "propertarianism" (Le Guin). In fact, Bulwer's inconsistent position of women is the private obverse and complement of the public, societal organization. His mechanism
is that basic device of bourgeois popular literature, the
invalidated novum, or narratively speaking "shock and
immediate tranquillization" (Eco 74 and passim). It is
radically new and shocking to present a social or a family
organization of full equals; but it is tranquillizing to
find, first, that this can happen only with the Vril-ya
(i.e., nowhere), and second, that social equality has not
abolished riches or autocracy, while emancipated females
are in practice prevented from using their superiority and,
once having married, become "the most amiable, concilia-
tory, and submissive wives I have ever seen . . ."! It is
as if the female sexual energy can have full play only when
"sublimated," before the deflowering. The murky phallo-
cratic logic of Bulwer's is fully analogous to his obscurantist political logic. All that remains of the radical
novum is the contained titillation of Platonic republicanism or of some gender-role reversals, for example, in
philosophy and--narratively well exploited--in courtship
(though this too is as old as the story of Joseph). But
again, Bulwer is important because he brings to the surface
--or at least near to it--such murky and most potent
psychic presuppositions. He is, in fact, uneasily fasci-

nated by the potent energies of political and sexual communism at the same time as he is deeply horrified by such a
principle of Evil. Bulwer's deep commitment to the discourse of power is matched by his constant attraction to
the discourse of freedom--to the Romantic radicalism of
correspondences between warmth, depths, energy, femininity,
and equality.

Perhaps the best way to encapsulate CR's hegemonic cooptation is--as in subsection 2--the presentation of flying.
Individual flying by means of vril and artificial wings is
possible for all the Vril-ya. However:

> A Gy [female, DS] wears wings habitually while yet a
> virgin--. . . in the boldness and height of her soar-
> ings, not less than in the grace of her movements, she
> excels the opposite sex. But from the day of marriage
> she wears wings no more, she suspends them with her own
> willing hand over the nuptial couch. . . .

I believe this revealing fragment fully confirms the equation of sex, freedom, and energy in CR, and my diagnosis of
uneasy fascination issuing in erotically and politically
obscurantist invalidation.

The sublimely beautiful, sphinx-like superscientific
superrace is another characteristical compromise. While
Swift's superior Houyhnhnhms were a clear lesson to the
effect that humans were not rational animals, Bulwer's sub-
Swiftian stance (which results in some feeble incidental
satire of Darwinism or democracy) exploits the helpless
hesitation between ideal and awful warning for a new
narrative recipe. This potent ideological brew contains
enough scientific and political cognition to suggest a
significant novum, but also enough neutralization and
tranquillization to invalidate the subversive novum as
impossible and/or inhuman. A superrace which can be suc-
cessively--as it becomes ideologically necessary--presented
either as thisworldly and subject to sympathy and parabolic
estrangement, or as transcendental and not subject to them,
is one of the best ways to do this, a stroke of malignant
genius. It will by way of Wells become one of the basic
mystifications of modern SF, shifting societal problems
into biology when not into magic.

The Coming Race's presentation of central dilemmas of
bourgeois individualism in a sensational yet tranquillizing
garb enabled it to aim for a cluster of social addressees
as wide as the whole book-market, soliciting them for its
particular ideology--a most important new tendency. At the
time, that market was still far from the 20th-century level-

ing. CR therefore sold 4,000 copies in 1871–1873, much
less than the immediately more shocking and urgent--and
cheaper--Battle of Dorking (yet as much in two years as
Erewhon in 26) (15). But its effect was at least as
lasting, and much wider: it was reprinted constantly to
1875, and again in and after 1886, with the new S-F wave.
More importantly, it contained the seeds of an almost
infinitely repeatable series of stranger stories and more
shocking sensations with correspondingly stronger dilu-
tions, for it articulated in mystified manner the addressees' central value-dilemmas. It is thus the exemplary
prototype of the invalidated but important novelty, of
hegemonic cooptation in narrative practice. This narrative
practice shifts toward the dynamics of the realistic novel,
introducing into the classical utopian anatomy the device
of narrator turning endangered plot-protagonist for whom
the anatomy of the new locus is a matter of supreme
importance, often of life and death (transmuted from hints
in Swift). This naturally latched on to the intertexts of
adventure-tale (with its cognates of detection mystery,
love romance, etc.) as a basic ingredient of the new S-F
recipe--CR already contains a few Extraordinary Voyage
elements stemming from Verne (the underground location, the
monster saurians). It also introduced the possibility of
functional character-sketches, of which perhaps the most
successful in CR is the superchild Taë. The new recipe
was to be fully codified by Wells, following a number of
leads--of which CR was (with Swift) formally the most important one. But already the publication of CR (together with
The Battle of Dorking and Erewhon) was sufficient to
usher in the first small boom of Alternative History SF in
the UK.

  3.5. Except for the thematically quite narrow and as a
rule brief Future War texts, no other cluster of UK SF in
this period comes even near approaching the 36 works
grouped here under "Alternative History." Alternative
History can be identified as that form of SF in which an
alternative locus (in space, time, etc.) that shares the
material and causal verisimilitude of the writer's world is
used to articulate different possible solutions of societal
problems, those problems being of sufficient importance to
require an alteration in the overall history of the narrated world. It subsumes but transcends and eventually
supplants the classical utopian (and antiutopian) form of
static anatomy--of pure wishdream or pure nightmare. In
its stead, it develops into a running through of extreme as
well as intermediate possibilities and outcomes. To this
end, its narrative procedures are--with Bulwer, Chesney,

and Butler, and then with Greg and others in the 1880s and
90s--gradually and haltingly adapted to needful "realistic"
dynamics. The result is analogous to (and midway between)
a formal game like chess and a military general staff "playing through" of realistic alternatives for future
campaigns. The Future War form is thus, among other
things, a signal for the model role of war for all societal
conflicts in class society, and particularly in the increasingly unified and totalizing world arising precisely in the
second half of the 19th century.

    It is a nice point of theory just what such literary clus-
ters as the Alternative History should be called. Provi-
sionally, I would hold that it is not a full-fledged literary genre, but a literary form or convention in the process
of aspiring to the status of, or hesitating on the verge of
becoming, a subgenre. This form comprises two main variants, the comico-satirical and the serious Alternative
History. There is no "pure" comical or satirical work in
my corpus, since such a tale would go beyond the limits of
even a generously interpreted SF; some marginal cases which
are predominantly whimsy or satire, can be found in Part
I.A.3 (e.g., Mackay, Burnand, Thompson). Rather, comedy
and/or satire is here always integrated with a more or less
serious depiction of an alternative historical locus, however perfunctory (e.g., Mammoth) and/or parabolic (Welch,
Abbott). On the other end of the Alternative History spectrum, the "pure" serious works, though possible, are always
in danger of crossing over into their nonfictional intertexts: blueprint, political tract--positive program or
awful warning--, prophecy (e.g., J.N., Dyas, or Theosopho
in Part I.A.3). The ascendancy of Alternative History at
this time can be seen in the fact that Harting and Maguire
from 2.2, the Irish Civil War and Welch 1882 entries from
3.0, and the sensationalist works in 3.1 genologically
belong here, that the same could be argued for Bulwer's
syncretic prefiguration of S-F aspects and subgenres in
The Coming Race, and that theoretically even the Future
Wars have to be thought of as a specialized alternative
history, both exemplary and narrowed down to military
matters for contingent reasons of daily politics (as is
palpable, e.g., in McCauley, in 3.3).

    In the terms of narrative logic, the comico-satirical
texts of Alternative History--in proportion to their non-
seriousness--do not induce a coherent but a fragmentary
"absent paradigm." Instead of cohering into the illusion
of an alternate reality, the comical or satirical elements
of the narration are each directly applicable to elements
or aspects of the addressee's view of the world--to the

ideological evaluations and certainties concerning particular matters of religion, politics, economics, etc.   Thus,
the comico-satirical Alternative History has to be evalu-
ated according to the relevance of the empirical domain it
is gunning for and to the radicalness of the estrangement
to which it subjects these matters; it is always transitive
and often on the verge of outright allegory. The incompatibility of the syntagmatic novelties in these texts is thus
not simple incoherence but a play with direct and frequently recurring transitions between each facet of a novelty
that can give rise to estrangement and the reader's
"normal" ideological view.   As a rule, the satire--however
vehement--will also be playful, that is, more concerned
with the multiplicity than with the focusing of its references (only the masters, such as Swift or Wells at his
best, manage to fuse both).   Nonsatirical comicality is
always more concerned with textual surface than with transitive effects, and it can therefore easily drift into the
vicinity of either whimsy or banality (the obverse of what
was discussed in 2.2).
  In proportion to the texts' distance from serious extrapolation, their fictional locus is (as already argued in 3.1)
of secondary significance (16).   To mention here works to
which it will not be necessary to return at any length:
the semiallegorical melodrama-cum-satire of Mammoth (1871)
is conducted from a vaguely liberal Nonconformist position;
it is aimed with equal vehemence against the slum mobs of
"Communism" in Paris, Darwinian and other scientific discoveries, or atheism or materialism in general, and against
the butchery of Parisians by the counterrevolutionary
government, British customs and politics, Popists, or
armies, churches, and courts in general. Soleman's (1876)
slim booklet is antifeminist persiflage of a Tory woman
premier who chooses ministers according to their looks and
passes nonsensical laws. Payn's long story "The Fatal
Curiosity" (1879) is a future in which coal is worth its
weight in diamonds, inventions abound, and people's status
is based on how many ideas they have. Brookfield's (1884)
political satire against radical liberals who give the vote
to a tribe either African or simian (but in both cases
subhuman, just like the workers) and thus subjugate England
is interesting only as a precursor of Animal Farm. Their
strengths (evident in Mammoth rather than in the other
three) or weaknesses do not depend on the location--
Mammoth's Symzonian transpolar world or Brookfield's and
Soleman's near future (in the latter it is also a dream).
Only Payn's 100 years in the future may be said to con-
tribute urgency to the projected coal-exhaustion, and in-

deed Payn's story is a mixture of comedy and extrapolation.

Finally, as the form became established and familiar to readers, it began increasingly to branch out and be used for ancillary purposes. Alternative History is basically a totalizing form on the level of the narrative signifier, and it necessarily suggests a global alteration on the level of the signified. However, it also began to be used for presenting limited historical alterations, single rather than multiple, brief rather than permanent, or individual rather than collective--for example, point-like political events, or techniques and inventions which inter-vene in an individual's life but do not change the societal totality. When it is not of small relevance, this develop-ment is always logically dubious and narratively strained, but it was destined to grow after 1886 and mushroom into giant proportions in mass 20th-century SF. Somewhat more legitimately, Alternative History began also to be used for focusing on separate problematic sectors of social life (e.g., the countryside in Jenkins). As ideological discourse, however, this form continued to move between the poles of knowledge and power, liberation and containment. Narratively, this means it increasingly blended the shocks necessitated by fiction's progressively decisive commodity status with the tranquillizations necessitated by the social disciplines of the age--so that, basically, even the sternest critics, such as Butler, were only battering at parts of the existing bourgeois consensus. However, this period culminates, in the mid-80s' texts of Abbott and Jefferies, with the first serious hints of a radical, pos-sibly catastrophic otherness.

3.51.   I shall deal first with the years 1871-1879, the time of the 1871 breakthrough and its immediate publish-ing consequences--first stimulating and from 1876 saturated--and divide the Alternative History texts into comico-satirical and serious. The comico-satirical ones, beside the mentioned Mammoth, Soleman, and Payn, consist of Butler's Erewhon (1872) and its direct echo in Dudgeon.

"Erewhon was not an organic whole," confessed Butler 30 years later (preface to revised edition); for all its quali-ties it might have been written by the Erewhonian professor of Inconsistency and Evasion. Not only are the half a dozen main thematic fields flimsily connected, they are often incompatible. Moreover, the argument inside each field proceeds through a bewildering if often drily amusing series of feints, reversals, and paralogisms which are also mutually incompatible. They range from simple topsy-turviness, through a dragging into open of the hidden British assumptions, to a debunking exposure which is as often as not finally balanced by some form of cynical justification:

> For property is robbery [Butler repeats after the anarchists, DS], but then, we are all robbers or would-be robbers together, and have found it essential to organize our lust and our revenge. Property, marriage, the law; as the bed to the river, so rule and convention to the instinct; and woe to him who tampers with the banks while the flood is flowing. (Chap. 12)

However, the Erewhonian rationale for the above two main subjects in Unreason studies is that they develop "faculties which are required for the daily conduct of affairs." Butler's satire may be additive and fragmentary, but it largely reposes upon two of the realistically most relevant social common denominators, or perhaps one twin common denominator: religion and money. This satire flows out of a deep revulsion from Puritan hypocrisy and the industrial civilization—which Butler with considerable acuity identified as the two main aspects of a single, if many-headed, monster. His best puns span this demominator: the classification of people by their horsepower, in which classes express "the number of limbs which they could command" so that "none but millionaires possessed the full complement of limbs," unveils the secret that "those who are worth most are the worthiest." The Erewhonian horror at offenses against health is, first, no sillier than the bourgeois horror at offenses against property (indeed health is intrinsically more important than social rules); and second, don't we all shun "those who are either poor or poorly?" His plot begins with an imitation of Swift translated into colonial prospecting for fortune ("hopes of making money"), and continues with a splendid Bunyanesque but anti-Puritan allegorical pilgrimage "up the river" to the sources, past the cruel, idiotic, and hollow—headed Evangelistic Ten Commandments whose chanting threatens to throttle him, and into the "promised land" of beauty and fertility. The plot ends, in some of the bitterest and most direct satire in the text, with the proposal to evangelize the Erewhonians by means of a limited liability society and a colonial gunboat. In between, the text is sprinkled with references to both money and religion in the most surprising places. In the middle of the charming fable of the Unborn, the latter are threatened with a life that is equated with a rentier's investments: "For you must live on your capital; there is no investing your powers so that you may get a small annuity of life for

ever: you must eat up your principal bit by bit, and be
tortured by seeing it grow continually smaller and smaller.
. . ." The obvious autobiographical echoes are not so
important as the light this dependence throws on the hate-
love for the industrial and banking system, for religious
institutions aptly named Musical Banks. Or: "Money is at
the bottom of all this to a great extent" explains the
relations between parents and children. Or, students of
painting have to pass exams in the prices of all leading
pictures: "The artist, [the Erewhonians] contend, is a
dealer in pictures, and it as important for him to learn
how to adapt his wares to the market . . . as it is for him
to be able to paint the picture." In brief, "Money . . .
is the sacrament of having done for mankind that which
mankind wanted."

The basic difficulty with this clever and very relevant
financial sacramentalism, pointing to the constant Victorian confusion of God with Mammon (17), is that the narrative attitude toward it is never clear. Sarcasm goes hand
in hand with "utter reverence . . . for the things which
are, which mould us and fashion us, be they what they
may; for the things that have power to punish us, and
which will punish us if we do not heed them; for our
masters therefore." The passages which I underlined above
(in a place as near as Butler gets to utter seriousness)
show up the cruel limitations of his bourgeois realism.
The discourse of liberating knowledge is in Erewhon held
in check by the discourse of power, the artist is balanced
by the dealer. The most famous--not necessarily the best--
segment of this work ingeniously extends Social-Darwinism
to the machines and ingenuously argues that they might grow
into masters of a mankind they render content. But what
might have become an important parable on Benthamite societal machinery, correlative to capitalist industrial revolution, dominating people is defeated by the overwhelming
literalness of the narrative vehicle. Yet the literal
hyperbole by itself is both absurd (luddism is incompatible
with Erewhonian prosperity) and retracted (the disturbing
menace is tamed by the unlikely combination of agrarian
monarchy and capitalist banking). Butler's "Book of the
Machines" fragments the space of knowledge and erects
causes into effects. Just as he separated money from
production, so he separates tools from uses they are put to
in a given economic system: both money and machines are
considered as transcendental entities, unmoved movers. An
anti-Puritan Puritanism, a compromise "neither-norism" as
Barthes would say, a hesitation between Swiftian bite and
final tranquillization is at the root of Butler's stance.

This corresponds well to his ambiguous social position of a cautious rebel from the upper middle class, revolted by its religious and business hypocrisies but relying financially on it (on his clergyman father and on speculative investment), and therefore hedging his bets, fearing his instincts and revering what he hates. The initially beautiful Erewhonians turn into grotesque grimaces, and the name of the conventional beloved with whom he finally flees--Arowhena--testifies that she is not only the genius loci of Erewhon but also, in Butler's anagramatic name-system, "a/an whore." Religious and business hypocrisy may be satirized (that was a staple pursuit of conservative preaching); however, the two dominant Victorian taboos-- work and the working class, sex and women--are dismissed by antiindustrial nostalgia (the explicit refusal of machines) or Victorian propriety (the tacit suppression of fertile beauty--that is, of the future).

Despite all that, Butler's discovery of the paradoxical place, the country where the ulterior motives within the writer's society could be brought to the surface, was potentially bold and for his time hugely stimulating. I would hold that his influence in SF was sustained, if much slower in coming and less apparent than Chesney's and Bulwer's explosiveness. It began with Dudgeon (1873)--where an eccentric friend of Butler's added to much feebler satire enthusiasms for optics and underwater life--, revived in the second half of the 1880s (Carne-Ross, Genone, Grove), and lasted well into the 20th century.

The serious Alternative History texts in this decade consist of the three "classical" utopias (Davis, Etymonia, Collens), as usual not too far from the dogmatic pessimum, of the Coming Cromwell, Jenkins, Maitland, Blair, and In the Future texts, and of Verne's Mysterious Island, The Begum's Fortune, and (perhaps) Child of the Cavern. They could be distinguished by location, but their overall effect is better explained by distinguishing between the classical utopian anatomy of a static situation and the modern process of historical development. A narration set in the future, a "future history," is in the long run the easiest form for presenting development (see 2.2), but a wily writer can use to that purpose even a contemporary island, as Verne managed in his foreshortened parable of the rise of bourgeois civilization in The Mysterious Island. It is still easier to take More's and Swift's (and Bulwer's) tack of recounting the coming into being of the present state, as in Collens's (1876) antediluvian semi-Eden, where labor was the measure of all values before it got supplanted by "our present

institutions," based on Cainite private property of land
and provoking the Flood. This strange Christian socialist
medley of economic tract, ethical theorizing, and imaginary
history is on the very verge of nonfiction. Etymonia's
(1875) direct leaning on Utopia bravely adds to More free
love, strict population control, even more thorough rationalist "geometrizing," and an adventure-cum-love story to
sweeten the by now anachronistic pill. Both Collens
(imported from the US) and Etymonia would surely not have
been published in the UK except for the popularity of
Alternative History, but the latter can also serve as a
late testimony to Owenite or Chartist echoes, a history-of-
ideas link between them (e.g., Pemberton or Bray--see Suvin
MOSF 138) and the socialists of the 1880s. Similar but
more original is Davis (1875). As in the above two texts,
it is an enlightened and communist society, and its decided
rationalism oscillates between Deism and Christian brotherliness. But the "cold," dogmatic systematization, nearer
to Campanella than More, is in part interfused by a consistent system of correspondences betraying a disguised
romanticism. The commune of Pyrna is under a huge glacier,
and the Pyrnians have adapted not only their architecture
and behavior but also their body temperature to it--an
interesting utopian twist to Swift's antiutopian conclusion
that new creatures are necessary if one is to have a rational utopia, cool security far from life's fitful fever.
Even the arts under the bluish ice-dome have adopted a
subdued but rich color scheme of precious metals and
stones, possibly in a Ruskinian vein (Dupont 444-45).

A further group in between the static utopia in space and
the full developmental "future history" are some expressly
short-range and therefore point-like presentations, without
much room for causes and effects. The Coming Cromwell
(1871) is a narratively quite blurred and unsuccessful but
interesting use of the Paris Commune scare (or hope) for
conjuring up a communist Cromwell who wins an analogous
Civil War against the monarchists and gives Home Rule to
Ireland. Hastily cashing in on the Future War vogue too,
it manages to translate it into class politics and throw
out an unusually large number of ideas for a slim near-
pamphlet. Jenkins (1873) is--for the nonce!--SF focusing
on the disastrous agricultural situation of the time, with
Liberal sympathy for striking peasants and in effective
local parlance, if with shallow prescriptions. Their adop-
tion results in universal satisfaction, presented as
ensuing ten years later.

As Bulwer had realized, recounting developments renders
possible a more direct political polemic. The "development-

al" Alternative History tales--the long-range future
histories and Verne--can be said to proceed along the lines
traced by The Coming Race; this does not necessarily
imply direct influence (Verne, Maitland, and Blair clearly
went directly to Saint-Simon) but merely that its model
developed central societal contradictions and thus became
for a time inescapable. The acute and all-pervasive bourgeois dilemma of collective versus individual is from CR on
articulated by some basic proceedings. First, validation
--a principle of believability--for both the isolation of a
given societal problem-expanse and the solution of the problems has to be found. The alternative situation is sometimes validated simply by ethico-religious necessity;
however, it becomes increasingly more believable to incorporate ideology into a postulated new technology, validated
by a natural science which had either fused with or
supplanted but in any case taken the role of religion, a
science that was in effect magical (e.g., vril). Further,
the problem-expanse is, in the best and norm-creating
cases, broad and twofold: overall politico-economic organization (crucially: the role of labor and the working
class) and erotics (the role of sex and women). Any sophisticated treatment contained close, often allegorical,
correspondences between these "public" and "private"
problems. Their radically subversive solutions were
communism and erotic freedom, both of which CR characteristically brought out and neutralized; they certainly haunt
all Victorian SF as its logical (if sometimes unacknowledged) furthest horizons. I shall therefore discuss the
remaining six texts first as concerns their validation
(science and religion), politics, and protagonist, followed
by the position of "problematic Others" (women, non-White
races, and laboring classes) and a conclusion.
    The validation for isolating and solving the problems
chosen is in Maitland (1873) individualist intuition which
is compatible with scientific technology (aeronautics and a
vague magnetic energy) but overwhelmingly directed toward
transcendental religiosity. The genius-hero's use of his
aircraft not only for his symbolic adventures but also,
above and beyond them, for communing with a superrace of
"angels," who live at the borders of atmosphere and ether,
exemplifies this mediating relationship of science. In
complementary alternative to CR Toryism, this religiosity
rejects collectivist societal organization, "ecclesiastic
or communistic" (i.e., gentry Catholicism or working-class
socialism), and takes Protestantism to its logical conclusion of elite individuals communicating directly with
higher, occult powers. His hero is therefore a latter-day

Christ in the guise of an international aeronaut, a millionaire from the English inside circle, uniting the best in
Teutonic heredity to royal blood of Arnold's Hellenic and
Hebraic descent, a saintsimonian planner and executor of
geographic (the Sahara Sea) and political remodeling of the
last holdout against enlightenment, dark Africa. He thus
puts the capstone on the world system of a corporate neocapitalism with partnership of capital and labor. In Blair
(1874) the union of science and religion is rather under
the sign of a positivist deism mixed up with various
utopian socialisms and progressing from one technological
wonder to another. History and nature (a Chinese invasion
and an earthquake) first had to wipe out the pride of
London, Oxbridge, and the Conservative aristocracy; but the
prudent hesitation between Jacobinism and antirevolutionary
declarations evades into quantitative expansion, from
scientific control of our planet to interplanetary contacts
and colonizing. The autobiographic narrator (going
McCauley and Lumley at the same publisher's one better) is
the president of the World Republic, the hero of a flight
to the Moon, contact with superior, unfallen beings from
the nearer planets, and a final flight to Jupiter. It is a
long, bombastic, and badly written medley of the most
disparate borrowings (underground and Moon journey from
Verne, Moon inhabitants from R.A. Locke, angellike
Venusians from Lach-Szyrma or Swedenborg, etc., ad nause-
am). But it is interesting both as evidence of a jelling
genre and as an expression of plebeian resentments and technocratic wishdreams of the middle professionals (Blair was
a young, probably poor medical officer in rural Scotland),
which influenced the young Wells--as did Blair's mixture of
science, political but antirevolutionary utopianism, and
extraordinary voyages. In The Future (1875) adopts the
cleanest variant: it assumes that after a revolutionary
period a scientific superstate has emerged, recapitulating
the empire of Alexander and the Caesars both in its
geographic extension and in its total etatism: State
possession of land and capital, but most importantly a
State religion obligatory for the citizens--only this time
a positivist rationalism. The validation is mostly left to
a fusion of the text's suggested "paradigm" of a coherent
new world and the reader's genological and intertextual
presuppositions--just as in much of the best SF to come,
from Abbott and Jefferies on. Its plot is the underground
struggle of Christians (as well as Moslems and libertarian
anarchists) for confessional tolerance, which looks well on
its way to success as the text, by happy accident or by
excellent narrative design, breaks off.

Finally, Verne's paradoxical utopian liberalism--to touch once more, briefly, on his well-known presuppositions (see 3.2 above and the references therein)--had as its primary inner logic the extraordinary voyage, but it could also deal with exemplary islandlike spaces, validated by the pre-Darwinian measuring and classificatory science in the guise of exploratory mapping. In his most optimistic parable, The Mysterious Island (1875), scientific knowledge and help from Providence allow a group of castaways, a collective Robinson Crusoe, to establish a community joyously united in the exploitation of nature and attainment of civilization. But if cooperative, this community is strictly graded. At its head is the ideal saintsimonian engineer, organizer, and thinker Cyrus Smith. He is flanked by two loyal seconds, an aide and an heir, both gifted classifiers, and by two comic servants; eventually, a repentant dastard and an agent of Providence are also discovered to complete this microcosm's Great Chain of Being. Only very marginally intersecting with SF but to my feeling still belonging here is Verne's Child of the Cavern (1877), set in a fantastically huge, underground mining grotto, where emblematic representatives of industrial progress and luddite obscurantism battle it out to the final triumph of the forces of Light. The parabolic microcosm grows both more threatened and more mawkishly simplified: science conquers working-class superstition and snatches renewed prosperity out of the jaws of catastrophe, but only in the nick of time. This theme is better developed in the still somewhat hasty Begum's Fortune (1879), whose memorable parts deal with the superindustrialized police mini-state of Stahlstadt rather than with the vaguely roseate countermodel or urban utopia of France-Ville. In this parable, capital can be equally invested in a collective concentration-camp hell or a hygienic city of free enterprise and family houses (based on the medical utopianism of another writer in my corpus, B.W. Richardson--see in the Bibliographies and Clarke PE 174-76) devoted to religion, science, and education. The final victory of the good needs by now a deus ex machina, and even more importantly, peaceful liberal enterprise has become antithetic to the most advanced technology. In a universe of irreconcilably opposed interests, utopianism breaks down with the divorce of science from religious morals. The validations of Verne's narrative worlds remain scientific, but science is turning from open-air harmony to strangulating prisons. In startlingly close parallel with the ascension to power of finance capital at the expense of industrial capital, or politically with the imperialist

division of the world, science is in The Begum's Fortune
allied at least as much with destruction and speculation as
with creation and commerce, with thermodynamic death as
with differentiated life, with the power of tyrannic collectivism as with individuals cooperating without the war of
each against each. In five short years Verne has advanced
from Saint-Simon and Scott to Dickens and Wagner (both
recognizable in this last text).

As always, the position of women is both a good ideological touchstone and a narrative equivalent to the
position of the text between the discourses of repressive
power and liberating knowledge. In Maitland's melodramatic
allegory, the hero's transcendence of physical instincts
and calculating reason is shown as two failed marriages
with women who incarnate these principles and who (somewhat
heterodoxly) are thus his equivalent of Christ's cross,
just as aeronautics are of Assumption. A compromise
between "the long conflicting ideas of the Home and the
Commune," that is, of the nuclear family and wider
interests, is embodied in a travesty of Fourierist "Clubs"
as well as in more flexible marriage and divorce rules.
However, women are physically, and therefore politically
(?!--in an age of magnetic aircars?), inferior to men. In
brief, Maitland is proposing to revoke the established
status quo of Victorian institutions in religion and sex in
order to make them more perfectly individualistic, but only
insofar as this makes for the more consistent development
of an elite. His most interesting ideas can therefore be
found in the long critiques of Victorian starchiness, but
the disestablishment of official religion does not basically alter the social role of women. It is also accompanied
by a naive argument for "Anglo-Teutonic" superiority and a
racist depreciation of Asians (the dastardly second wife is
of Eurasian "breed") and tropical races, the latter "[unwor-
thy] of preservation." A mixed treatment is accorded to
Jews who rule Palestine as powerful but grasping and vengeful capitalists (an idea probably taken from Bodin's Roman
de l'avenir, just as the aeronautic love melodrama mixed
up with empires might have been taken over from Lang and
Voss's Ini). Finally, the working class is still
dogmatic and prone to constituting hereditary castes. . . .
The sympathetic plea for full individual development turns
thus out to have been meant for White, male, and more or
less affluent individuals only. While the mawkish and
preachy text is today difficult to read, it is of considerable historical importance as the first detailed, if rather
melodramatic, UK examination of alternative world-politics,
and as a remarkably prescient answer to CR, bringing
capitalism, a ruling elite, and a family based upon private

property up to the age of super-Leviathans and corporate jet-setting.

The situation in Blair is in a way worse, as women, sex, and family are simply absent from his narrative world, and after the initial Chinese conquest of Britain so are the non-White races. His future Terran characters have one classical Greek and one English middle-class name-- signifying, I suppose, that class's assumption to classical status; the planetary aliens are simply nearer to God. In the Future's names are truly international and the inclusion of Godwinian anarchists is amazingly liberal in the best sense. On the other hand, its limits are indicated by the restricted focus; by the curious compromise on workers and women (the ethnically different lowest workers--of yellow race, but modeled on the Irish in Victorian England --are left unprotected, while native-born higher workers are protected by strict State rates; women can choose between being career "outdwellers" and home-making "indwellers" but cannot change or mix the two); and by the curious final suggestion of a second birth of Jesus. In Verne's worlds, as always, there are no women except pure Walter Scott maidens waiting for the protagonist. The industrial proletariat if found is menacingly correlative to dark satanic mills, and the supernumerary servants from other races when not absent either dastardly or comical. Chinese coolies are welcome to build the garden-city of France-Ville but not to live in it. In the perfect liberal utopia of Mysterious Island, there are no women at all (and thus no future--the island is destroyed by Providence in a volcanic earthquake and the heroes providentially saved), no aborigines, and of the two manual workers the White is a loyal crew-member and the Black devotion personified (which does not prevent him from having an instinctive affinity to a tamed orang-outang--Brookfield repeats the identical commonplace in his political satire). This boy-scout avoidance of erotics and industry might be explained by the juvenile audience aimed at. But such a "landing point" in turn testifies how even a writer of the greatest talent could break through only within "a more timid institutional framework, one more easily watched over by social censorship" and requiring the narrative form of an accelerating closed circle (explicit in the Extraordinary Voyages, see 3.2), the verisimilitude of bourgeois realism, puerile sexual morals, and interpolation into existing scientific knowledge--in sum "a taboo on all radical exteriority" (Angenot SFF 64-65).

This radical exteriority is in fact what the presentation of sexual, political, and biological Others (which for the male White writers of the bourgeois ideological consensus

meant respectively women, lower classes as workers, and
aliens) shows or avoids to show. Bulwer managed cleverly
to fuse the showing and the avoidance. Maitland and In
the Future are careful (just as Butler was) to claim that
they were composed before CR and to disclaim its influence.
But methinks they protest too much. As indicated earlier,
at the least all three (as well as Dudgeon, Blair, and the
"classical" utopias) would not have been published without the success of CR; and typologically, the serious Alternative Histories are all counterprojects to it. They have
their major differences in style, subject matter, etc.
Qualitatively, the utopian anatomies are all near the
dogmatic pessimum, and Blair is therabouts too; Maitland--
narratively undistinguished but ideationally important--I
would put in the middle range, while In the Future is
surely "a long-lost near-masterpiece of SF" (Mullen SFS6
185). But I hope their discussion has shown that they
touch on parts of the same set of problems, within the same
polarities of discourse (power vs. knowledge), or the same
horizons and dilemmas of the bourgeois individualist consensus. Verne affirms that consensus, though with increasing
precariousness, while the two main alternatives to the
consensus are represented by Maitland's partial moderniza-
tion (the obverse of Butler's satire) and In the Future's
presentation of a worse alternative updated from the past.
Blair's clumsy but sweeping book foreshadows a third
response, destined to be picked up by Green and then to
become dominant after 1886 either by itself or subordin-
ating the other two--that of dodging the qualitative issue
by concentration on quantitative technological expansion
geared to an increasingly plebeian reading public. But up
to the 1880s, the significant texts still had as their main
addressee the upper-middle classes, that is, the affluent
bourgeoisie and the upper professionals. This holds for
Maitland, In the Future, and Butler, as well as for
Bulwer and Chesney.

3.52. In the years 1880-1885 the Alternative
Histories are twice as frequent as in the 1870s, a very
significant statistical deviation from the 50 percent rise
of all SF (if the Battle of Dorking controversy in 1871
is disregarded). Furthermore, there are no more utopian
anatomies, and the comico-satirical variant is clearly
ebbing: except for Brookfield, discussed earlier, one can
find it only blended with the serious variant, in Welch,
Abbott, and partly in Lang-Tung, An Eye-Witness, Jefferies,
and The New Democracy. The Alternative History settled
down to become the dominant S-F form, overshadowing the
other two forms of Future War and Extraordinary Voyage.

This is also the time when it attracted UK writers known from other genres. Though this was already the case with Rowcroft, Helps, Bulwer, and Payn in the preceding decades, they now came more thick on the ground: Trollope, Abbott, Allen, Jefferies, as well as early works of the later more eminent Besant and Strachey.

The short-range or pointlike, limited historical altera-tions comprise the An Eye-Witness, Wise, Coverdale, An Ex-M.P., The New Democracy, and Strachey texts. They are all from 1884-1885, all anonymous or pseudonymous, and signalize the sudden strengthening of social tensions and urgency of political conflicts in the UK. Except for Coverdale's (a text from and dealing with the USA), they are all under 200 pages and deal with Britain's immediate political future (in New Democracy thinly disguised as "Caucusia"); except for Wise's, they are all awful warnings against radical takeover. "An Eye-Witness"'s The Social-ist Revolution of 1888 is the best of the lot, combining as it does a believable bloodless coup with the aftermath in which, for all its good will, the socialist government becomes detested due to both State supervision and loss of affluence following on the exodus of the rich and interna-tional financial pressure. The untying of the knot—an equally peaceful and forgiving return to the old regime—is a middle-of-the-road wishdream, but the first part is a not unshrewd nor unhumorous critique (Morris is made minister for industries since he knew how to keep expenses of produc-tion down). Wise is of interest in its generous indigna-tion against capitalist waste and pillage, but except for a dream of bloodless revolution through following an aristo-crat's example of Christian renunciation of property, it is scarcely fiction and largely a Christian communist tract. Of the other awful warnings, An Ex-M.P. foresees Britain in 1925 a republic under Joseph Chamberlain with such horrors as radical economic measures, women equality, and atheism; so, "Take care for whom you vote in the coming Election"—a final sentence that explains many of these works. Chamberlain is the villain of New Democracy too, though it happens in an allegorical country, with a muddled plot juggling technological wonders, love melodrama, political satire, and adventurous conspiracies. The young St. Loe Strachey depicts the horrors of a prolabor political organi-zation, tampering with free trade, in terms of the Whig mythology: the Corn Laws are reintroduced; the ensuing famine and socialist and anarchist riots have to be quelled by an upper-class plot and civilian volunteers (the latter a good forecast of how the 1926 general strike was to be put down). In this conjuncture, the Coverdale text—

depicting a left-wing takeover of a USA subverted by
radical immigrants, Irish dynamiters, and corrupt morals,
and quelled by Britain and Europe occupying the country to
protect business and order (and thus approaching a full-
scale alteration)--found an interested UK audience.

The by now established main tradition of full, developmental Alternative History, flowing out of Bulwer and
supplanting the utopian anatomy, was continued and sometimes developed further in the 1880s in a number of texts,
the most significant of which are Greg, Abbott, and
Jefferies. They may be divided into two groups, the coarse
and the sophisticated.

The coarse Alternative Histories comprise in 1880-1886
Greg, Hay, Lang-Tung, Besant, and Trollope. Greg (1880) is
a rather repulsive but historically important attempt to
combine the generic traditions of Extraordinary Voyage,
politico-religious propaganda through "realistic" developmental description, and historical-cum-sentimental adventure of the Fenimore Cooper or Dumas the Elder stripe plus
an admixture of exotic exploration. The part that has best
resisted time is, clearly, the long and careful account of
interplanetary travel. It is based on Poe and Trueman, the
latter being also present in the antigravity force and the
basic composition of the book--space-travel plus biological
and societal description of and travel through the planet--
as well as in some Martian details. But Greg translates
elements from these two writers into the careful verisimilitude of Verne, stripped of the juvenile euphoria: space-
travel is becoming a grim business rather than the
harbinger of utopian wonders to be found. Wells was to
remember this congenial ambiguity towards science both in
his space and in his time-travel tales. However Greg's
center of gravity is, as usual in these Bulwerian tales,
not in the travel frame but in the picture of the place
arrived at. This is a counter-project to CR, important not
simply in the overt ideology conveyed but in the analogous-
ly coarsened and diluted narrative form, whose reliance on
the intertext of sentimental and adventure melodrama points
to E.R. Burroughs (18) and the broad band of modern SF
approaching the banal pessimum even more strongly than the
intertexts of realistic space-travel and antiutopia point
toward Wells.

The diluting is at work in the not too coherent plot,
aimed scatter-shot fashion at valorizing all of Greg's pet
reactionary prejudices. Politically, not only had in the
Martian past democratic suffrage dispossessed "the intelligent, thrifty, careful owners of property" and led to
horrors of despotic political and unnatural erotic

communism, defeated only after bitter civil war, but the reestablished "order and property" was under the sign of an equally despotic State scientism. The common denominator of the two systems is an equal disregard for and suppression of religion and nuclear family, and thus of all affection. Therefore, the utopian absence of poverty, illness, and legal discrimination leads, in the tired old cliché, to the suppression of individuality. The logical fallacies in these constructs are abundant and wide enough to drive a truck through: Why should Communists be against science? Why should anti-Communists be scientific dogmatists? How can legal equality coexist with absolute monarchy and polygamy? etc., etc.? But it might be enough to note the entirely unresolved attitude toward science. It is unquestioningly adopted in the voyage part as well as in many Martian elements, from the ubiquitous electricity incongruously coupled with the labor of trained animals to the much touted notion of material, indeed "immediate and obvious self-interest [as] the only motive that certainly and seriously affects human action." Yet it is as mindlessly rejected whenever the writer remembers religion and forgotten as soon as he remembers women.

The coarsening can best be gauged through the most curious role allotted in Greg to women. Their legal equality being since the suppression of communism unaccompanied by economic equality and anyway unnatural to their central pursuit of marriage and maternity, "they are only too glad" to barter it for "the dependence, coupled with assured comfort and ease, which they enjoy as the consorts, playthings, or slaves of the other sex." The model followed is that of an Islamic seraglio: it is suggested that the narrator is an English officer familiar with West Asia. A tenuous hint of satire on the bourgeois marriage-market as well as the sentimental uplift of love for his child-bride Eveena (the prototype of Wells's Weena) are quite submerged in a pathological genteel gloating, where sadism is barely contained under a nobly forbearing masochism. These are Greg's most original and sickest passages, suggesting in its protracted descriptions of an exasperated pasha in an upper-class harem, spiced with references to an authoritative male amid adolescent inmates of an Italian convent, the pornographic, indeed paedophiliac wishdreams of the Victorian bourgeois, "decently" veiled (just as the wives are). The diatribes against science and logic suppressing affection, religion, and family draw their violence, no doubt, from this sexual suppression of Greg's. This first makes of the text a somewhat clumsy alternation of antiutopian sermonizing,

exotic travel-tale, erotic titillation, and finally political conspiracy. Further, this makes nonsense of the political anatomy and the conspiracy that provides the backbone
of whatever plot remains, by basing it simultaneously in
occult sciences and a Martian quasi-Christianity, as well
as in a revolt against a supposedly unnatural system and
yet on the part of an elite disliked by the people. In
Greg's Manichean universe, the conspiracy in the name of a
higher law that cannot count either on the reigning power
or on the people is necessarily a secret society (Eco 97-
98; see also Angenot RP). The germinal idea of a religious
conspiracy against a scientistic universal monarchy taken
at its crisis-point probably comes from the eminently
consistent In the Future, but that text's logic is
liquidated in a slapdash imitation of Sue or Dumas the
Elder. A secret society is the political equivalent of
Bulwer's vril: a magical way out of plot difficulties and
logical impossibilities. Consonant with Greg's extreme
elitism, it is a counter-ruler rather than an instrument of
liberation. But even with the help of it and a sentimental
sacrifice by the child-bride, Greg can end the text only by
leaving its world: the narrator flies back to Earth, where
he presumably crashes leaving his manuscript.
    Four works immediately following upon Greg remain within
the cheerless spectrum of reactionary banality in the SF of
the early 1880s. On the credit side of Hay's Three
Hundred Years Hence (1881) is a framing sustem, where a
historian introduces revised phonograph lectures by an
academic colleague, which was to be adapted by Bellamy's
Looking Backward. The hypothesis of a super-Malthusian
overpopulation running into 12 digits being balanced by
staggeringly developed technology, much as in Blair (trans-
portation, conquest of undersea and underground, a new
vril-like force), is also not without potential merit. The
scientific hyperboles are deployed as companion-pieces to a
super-Social-Darwinism. In connection with his other text
mentioned in 3.1, this indicates that Hay was more interested in the sensationalist narrative system of shock plus
tranquillization--evident also in his powerless "Empress"--
than in the nuance of sensationalist ideology used. The
text's long descriptions culminate in a chapter gleefully
justifying, after various superwars and the extermination
of all animals, the deliberate annihilation of non-White
races too "in order that the fittest and the best may
eventually survive." This frenzied genocidal racism is
validated both by biology and religion, and makes of Hay's
"Social Government" a true-blue example of proto-fascism,
destined to become influential in spite (or because?) of

its awkward style. Lang-Tung (1881--the pseudonym perhaps a take-off on Lyt-ton?) uses the similar form of a Chinese textbook of English history 1840-1981, with professorial howlers, for a brief hodge-podge of political predictions, which include Ireland's secession, civil war, and reunion, and issue in Britain becoming Communist (i.e., dominated by free love and atheism). At this, the climate changes to colder and Chinese send in missionaries to recivilize these barbarians.

Women were scurvily or at least ambiguously treated (when not forgotten) by almost all SF from 1848 through Bulwer, Maguire, Butler, and Maitland, to Watson Sr., Greg, and Hay, the only exceptions being a few Communist utopias-- notably _Etymonia_. Even there, the protagonists and/or narrators remained male. The first novel-length put-down in UK SF, however, in direct response to the women's emanci- pation movement, was Besant's _Revolt of Man_ (1882). Bulwer's ambiguous role-reversal is here absolutized and simultaneously isolated from Watson's linkage with commun- ism, evolution, humanism, etc., which, however, still operates between the lines (the two names stand here simply as present examples for widespread intertextual attitudes). Besant is an embarrassing text, another perfect example for Wells's hypothesis of a failure of imagination evident in going for the shallowest laugh. Besant's 21st-century England is constructed on one single device: that of heightening the simple reversal of male domination (women head the State, the armed forces, social life, etc.) with sub-Aristophanic hyperboles (males are totally repressed, young men are married off to ugly old women, politically England is an oligarchy, commercially, industrially, and culturally it is ruined, etc.). The unstated presupposi- tion that women's rule will not be like men's, but catas- trophically worse, reposes on the commonplace of women being by nature constructed for sentimental love and family life, and nothing else--neither _topos_ being at all argued in the text. When a few pathetic cases of persecution lead to a plot and eventually to a rebellion, the opposition is only half-hearted, and the younger women rejoice: "We shall take our place--we shall be the housewives; we shall be loving and faithful. . . . [M]an must rule outside the house." This earliest UK gender-role reversal novel already exhibits their stock assumptions: first, that their situation of

> . . . dominant women and subservient men . . . is a reversal of the natural order. Usually this is pointed out by having a truly masculine man . . . woo and win

> the most important female. . . . Second, that sexual
> relations, natural or reversed, require dominance and
> subservience. Hence the conclusion implied is that
> sexual equality is simply impossible. (Sargent WU 310)

Characteristically for Blackwood's readership, the higher
bourgeoisie, the novel was a decided critical and financial
success (it sold 12,000 copies in two years and was reprinted in a popular edition in the mid-90s--see Samaan 388,
397ff., and 404). In Hichens's The Green Carnation, a
dozen years later, the Oscar Wilde persona attempts to get
rid of his intellectual faculties by reading Besant's
complete works: he does not succeed, but the choice was
excellent.

In such company, Trollope (1882) looks a bit better than
it would otherwise, but it remains a perfunctory affair.
It is neither clearly satirical, as its antipodean location
on Butler's model might suggest, nor seriously consistent,
as its 100 years in the future might. The discussion of
its exclusive subject-matter--compulsory euthanasia at the
age of 67.5, which Trollope himself was just coming to--is
in fact on the border between a full-fledged Alternative
History and its use for personal or individual history
(about which see 3.43). The device of having the fanatic
antagonist--the political originator of the "fixed period"
law--narrate the tale is promising, but the promise is not
kept. The societal context is not related to the novelty:
"Brittannula" is simply a small Britain with some incidental burlesque (mechanized cricket) as well as echoes of
Trollope's enmity to democracy (and possibly to Irish Home
Rule), where nobody is eager to be the first to die. The
issue of euthanasia too was in bourgeois ideology of the
period inextricably connected with atheism, communism, free
love, subversion, etc., so that the satiric resolution of
Erewhon by means of a colonial gunboat is here taken up
seriously, with the perfunctory addition of a Bulwerian
supergun. Though The Fixed Period is not based on
adolescent but on adult--indeed, old-age--fears (and therefore had no success), sadly, it still belongs in the
shallow company of The Revolt of Man.

The remaining four works of "totalized" Alternative
History, on the contrary, testify to the use of the form
for more sophisticated and less reactionary purposes.
Green's (1882) 2,000 years of future history have a curious
narrative form, both interesting as to its implications and
clearly not under full control. A group of friends who
constitute a Cockney "Universal Discussion Society" find
themselves in 2882 (or possibly the narrator finds their

identical equivalents there--the matter is left without any
explanation, except for the final indication it was all a
dream). Interestingly, they are of various social classes,
from rich merchant to artisan and sailor (spaceship naviga-
tor in 2882); each is named after a color and devoted to
one societal function or cognitive category (statistics,
science, politics, travel, etc.), but all come together in
interclass amity, as parts of the spectrum. For the future
brings a fantastic increase in population and in the
achievements of science; as can be seen from the title, A
Thousand Years Hence, this is a counter-project to Hay's
Three Hundred Years Hence, using and improving upon
Blair's Annals of the Twenty-Ninth Century. A mass
welfare-State based on a democratic blend of workers'
cooperatives, huge corporations, and State enterprises, has
employed close calculation, some brutality, and a dreamlike
ease to emancipate women, unite the world, repress crime,
breed a new aristocracy of merit through sexual selection,
find a new energy, eventually reconstruct Earth, and go to
the planets. The spatial progression is consonant with the
temporal optimism: in Green's cosmos, each planet nearer
to the Sun exerts a discreet brotherly watch over its
outward neighbor--for example, Venusians watch over us,
while Mars is just repeating the 19th-century UK history of
Reform and progress. Our voyagers find that the Man in the
Moon has died out, but upon entering the Sun they find the
"Upper Solars" with an extra "causation sense," which
permits them (shades of Laplace!) to calculate conduct and
the future. Finally, in 3882 comets are mined for oxygen
and nitrogen, faster-than-light flight allows observation
of past history (most of this comes from Flammarion's
Stories of Infinity, and is probably the first echo from
him in UK SF), and at the end a Fourierist sympathy per-
vades the bodies of our solar system and begins to spread
throughout the stellar community. This anthology of disjointed science-fictional wonders is narratively amateurish
and politically a prefiguration of technocratic neocapitalism, but it is a historically important text "which very
effectively uses philosophical curiosity as dramatic
device, which fearlessly conceives of prospects in an
unlimited and dynamic future, and which already closely
approaches the most audacious anticipations of Wells,
Haldane, and Stapledon" (Dupont 468, and see his detailed
account 458ff.). Less radically but more coherently than
Blair, Green expresses the ideology of science-oriented
middle professionals, aiming at a significant updating but
not at a fundamental subversion of capitalism. Wells was
to hesitate between presenting some of its elements as

frightening (the mass cities in <u>When the Sleeper Wakes</u>)
or admirable (the classification of people in <u>A Modern</u>
<u>Utopia</u>), and one can find more than one foretaste of US SF
in it--all based on such writers' kindred social addressees
and ideologies.

  <u>Politics and Life in Mars</u> (1883), attributed to Welch
(but see the entry in the Biographies), reverts to Kant's
idea that the further a planet is from the Sun, the more
advanced it is. Its aquatic Martian society is not only
medically, technologically, and politically superior
(cooperative property and participatory democracy, women's
rights, disarmament with international police), it is also
used for sustained satire on Earth institutions, primarily
of English politics toward Ireland, religious divisions,
and political cum economic privilege. The planetary locus
for once helps to validate a fully fledged, libertarian
utopianism of the "warm" current within socialism, and insofar superior even to Trueman or <u>Etymonia</u>. Though the
text deftly interweaves satire and panorama, it is, unfortunately, narratively mediocre (possibly due to the haste
in which a Grub Street writer had to compose it), and it
will not stand comparison with the half-a-dozen best texts
so far discussed in this essay. However, it shows that a
large popular publisher believed there was a sufficient
amount of interest for quite radical views in the UK of
1883.

  This is confirmed by Abbott and Jefferies, works which
are the culmination of this period and which signal the
break-up of Bulwer's (and Verne's) model at least in "good"
SF. Both are built around a novum at once original and
authentic, that is, irreducible either to an earlier discursive model or to the witless "mechanical transposition of
'this-worldly' paradigms" (Angenot AP 16; see 1.2). Abbott
(1884) brings off the coup of most adroitly fusing lucid
geometrical didactics and a satirical parable on class-
society perception, politics, and behavior. The setting in
two-dimensional space peopled by geometrical figures is
simultaneously funny and the best kind of abstraction,
allowing Abbott to bring out the invariant backbone of some
central power-relationships in class society in a manner
not unworthy of the fertile analytic abstractions of Darwin
and Bacon (of whom he knew) or indeed of Marx (of whom he
did not know). The Flatland males "rise . . . in the scale
of development and nobility" from the "Soldiers and Lowest
Classes of Workmen," who are isosceles triangles, through
the Middle Class of equilateral triangles and the Professional Men and Gentlemen, who are respectively squares (as
the lawyer-narrator) and pentagons, to the Nobility, which

ranges from hexagons to increasingly many-sided polygons, and finally the "Circular or Priestly order." A male child has one more side than his father, but this "Law of Nature" does not always apply to tradesmen (the middle class), "still less often to the Soldiers, and to the Workmen; who indeed can hardly be said to deserve the name of human Figures, since they have not all their sides equal," nor to the offenders against morality, who revert toward Irregularity. This witty system, described by a narrator who is made to vary between the writer's mouthpiece and an unreliable dupe, is similar to but more consistent than the Erewhonian one, approaching (in spite of occasional lapses into headmasterly humor) the tone and effectiveness of Gulliver's Travels. The comparison extends to Abbott's political acuteness. Not only is the narrator, finally enlightened by a millennial revelation that there exist more than two dimensions, imprisoned for spreading that subversive gospel, so that his account is that new variant of "a manuscript found in a bottle"--"a manuscript smuggled out of prison," prefiguring the overtly revolutionary tales of Jack London and later SF. There are, furthermore, the remarkable demystifying passages strewn through the text, such as:

> The occasional emergence of an Equilateral from the ranks of his serf-born ancestors is welcomed, not only by the poor serfs themselves, as a gleam of light and hope shed upon the monotonous squalor of their existence, but also by the Aristocracy at large; for all the higher classes are well aware that these rare phenomena, while they do little or nothing to vulgarize their own privileges, serve as a most useful barrier against revolution from below.

> It is generally found possible--by a little artificial compression or expansion on the part of the State physicians--to make some of the more intelligent leaders of a rebellion perfectly Regular, and to admit them at once into the privileged classes; a much larger number, who are still below the standard, allured by the prospect of being ultimately ennobled, are induced to enter State Hospitals, where they are kept in honourable confinement for life; one or two alone of the more obstinate, foolish, and hopelessly irregular are led to execution. (Chap. 3)

Most significantly, however, a sample of the 120 major rebellions and 235 minor outbreaks recorded in the annals

of Flatland is given in "the Colour Revolt." This is
(after some approaches in In the Future, Collens, and
The Battle of the Moy) the first sympathetic and concrete
account of a plebeian rebellion in UK SF, in its way as
impressive as William Morris's more famous accounts in "A
Dream of John Ball" and News From Nowhere. Abbott's
Revolt blends elements of Roman history, the Middle Ages
(Wat Tyler's revolt), UK Reform struggles, and the French
Revolution, and he enthuses in Wordsworthian accents about
its early success which changed the whole of existence:
"To live was then in itself a delight, because living
implied seeing."

Women are the lowest class of Flatland, a simple straight
line, dangerous and inferior--"the Thinner Sex," whose
"miseries and humiliations" are "a necessity of their existence and the basis of the constitution of Flatland." Just
as in the case of political revolution, this is the first
work of SF that I can think of in which female subjection
is seen both as enforced by the ruling class and religion
to form the basis of the social order and as issuing in
desperate domestic circumstances with frequent murders and
suicides. (Abbott, moreover, acknowledges the psychologically oppressive effects of such a reality: reactionary
women organized by priests are also an important factor in
the defeat of the Colour Rebellion, which had initially
appealed to them.) Abbott's astoundingly radical vision
extends to a profound recognition of a male "bilingual, and
I must almost say bi-mental" double standard, which soothes
women with emotional pseudo-deference, reserving cynical
realism for male discourse; in this respect, the text is
unmatched in English-language SF until the modern
feminists. Our narrator's final vision includes thus the
realization that the despised "qualities of women"--
affectionateness, mercifulness--have to be integrated into
all humans. As can be inferred from this, the psychology
of Abbott's apparently two-dimensional figures is more
realistic and richer that the "realism" of Besant and Co.;
his narrator's panicky resistances to superior insight and
its slow fading are further touches of genius. Swiftian
satire, profound political and psychological realism, scientific analogy (reinforced by the delightful visions of Lineland and Pointland)--all of these fuse into a philosophical, cognitive and Promethean, parable:

> For why should the thirst for knowledge be aroused,
> only to be disappointed and punished? . . . like a
> second Prometheus, I will endure this and worse, if by
> any means I may arouse . . . a spirit of rebellion
> against the Conceit which would limit our Dimensions

to Two or Three or any number short of Infinity.
(Chap. 19)

Such accents had been unknown in British SF since Frankenstein (the tale of their exemplary retraction). They
lead directly to Morris and Wells, and indeed to the realization of Zamyatin's similar mathematician-narrator that
there is no final revolution as there is no final number.
Cleverly adapting Carroll's and Verne's strategy of subsum-
ing but transcending the juvenile reader, Abbott's is in
truth "A Romance of Many Dimensions"; in its thoroughgoing
democratism, it is addressed to the best minds in the new
reading public, issuing from the newly introduced obligatory primary schooling. In this text, a radical Protestant
is for the nonce protesting the unholy union of determinist
theology, clericalism, terror-based brainwashing, and class
privilege. The consistent and radical novum of such a
Flatland is correlative to its witty parable: it is not an
allegory of England but its (and therefore not only its)
hidden truth, arrived at by an interaction of science,
political philosophy, and satire. While Abbott's vision is
not without its limits (economic production and relationships are beyond his ken), it is certainly an S-F masterpiece. It is one of the very rare Victorian texts which
have had not only semi-indirect continuations (in Hinton;
in Schofield's Another World, misusing Abbott and Hinton
to prove Christian spiritualism; and through the "fourth
dimension" speculations of Hinton, and possibly Newcomb, in
Bierce and Wells) but also a direct, though feeble continuation in the 20th century (Burger's Sphereland). A
popularity that has persisted to the present day is the
poetically just reward of this delightful halfway house
between the Alice works and We.
  Jefferies's After London (1885) is in some ways both
more radical and less satisfying than Abbott. Its break
with the Victorian political system appears more complete,
for it envisages with equanimity and indeed with relief the
total obliteration of the bourgeois civilization. That is
symbolized by the terrible oozy mass and miasma of the
marshes covering what was London--the site of financial
wealth, aristocratic pride, luxury, and death (the gold
coins, china with heraldic animal, diamonds, and moldering
skeleton-impressions our hero finds when he accidentally
blunders into that evil place). These are--along with the
opening chapters--the finest passages of After London,
for they fuse into a nauseated and nightmarish vision the
impoverished countryman's and the yeoman-cum-artisan-
descended intellectual's loathing of capitalism, mechanical
"progress," urbanization, the "villadom" of Philistine

smugness--in short, of upper-class pride and prejudice
based on monetary power.

From Lang, Chesney, and Blair to Wells's War of the
Worlds and beyond, Cobbett's "Great Wen" of London is the
prime target of a destruction either arising out of or
playing on the fears of popular resentment: Jefferies is
possibly the clearest expression of that resentment. This
disappearance of bourgeois England is also more disturbing
than right-wing prophecies of doom, from O'Neil to Watson
Sr. and Hay, who follow the Apocalypse pattern by justifying the final catastrophe either as a cleansing followed by
the millennium or at any rate as a divine Judgment redeemed
(for the righteous) in Heaven. Jefferies is a thoroughgoing, if one-sided, materialist. Though the cause of "Wild
England's" coming is disputed in an age of barbarity and
confusion, his historian-narrator expressly shrugs off
"those whose business is theology," and clearly suggests it
is a natural one.

Thus, the shock in Jefferies is not induced for purposes
of titillation, nor is it offset by immediate tranquillization. The society arising "after London"--after "the
richer and upper classes made use of their money to
escape," no one knows where--arose out of the lower classes
and provincials and lost all knowledge of "the secrets of
the ancients," which persisted only as legends and rumors
(a staple of all catastrophic SF since). After many
generations, society consists of primitive villages and
small towns scattered amid a vast forest, feuding with each
other, with the Bushmen, gypsies, and bandits in the
forests, and with the powerful Welsh, Scots, and Irish
troops that range throughout the country. Most importantly, a vast geological change has hollowed out central
England into a large lake, a new geological dispensation on
whose shores the tale takes place. The social system is a
stifling petty feudalism, a concoction from classical,
medieval, and Oriental traits, analogous to industrial
capitalism inasmuch as for the overwhelming majority of
people it de facto means slavery (another important
contribution to S-F topoi, due more to analogous roots
than to writers reading Jefferies) (19). Only the nobles
(and their licensed merchants) retain knowledge of reading,
though they are more interested in fighting and court
intrigues. It is a "rotten and corrupted [society], coarse
to the last degree . . . held together by brute force,
intrigue, cord and axe, and woman's flattery." No wonder
such a picture had--and continued to have--small success
with the reading public of the bourgeois consensus. It is
neither a progressive future, nor a pleasant Haggard-type

evasion into the world of a superman hero.

And yet Jefferies is deeply ambiguous about his setting. In one way it is a Dark Age hyperbole, or reduction to the absurd, of the war of each against each that he himself felt victim of in the bourgeois society. But in another way it is also a setting where his usual sensitive, thoughtful, impractical, discontented, and proud young misfit can work out his destiny to a happy ending impossible in capitalist civilization. The aptly named Sir Felix passes through the liberating education of adventures around the lake; sailing is this technologically regressed world's equivalent of liberation from hugging the soil by flying in other 19th-century SF: "he left that hard and tyrannical land for the loveliness of water." His sailing adventures and some special prowesses finally lead him to the kingship of shepherd tribes, and we leave him as he goes to fetch his beloved into the fort being built for him. This open ending does not seem to me a blemish, since it is clear our hero has succeeded in finding himself. It is more difficult to imagine his life afterward, or indeed his life as anything but a questing adolescent: the second part of After London is pure quest-romance. Nor is the problem simply that the first part is a historian's account of "The Relapse Into Barbarism," an "imaginary chronicle" well known in the tradition of Alternative History (but never before so beautifully done), and that the narrative voice in the second part at times uncomfortably hesitates between that of omniscient narrator and that of the historian. Jefferies's puzzling ambiguity lies mainly in the incompatibility of stance and tone between, on the one hand, his splendidly unremitting and pitilessly precise observation of (vegetable or human) nature and its blind processes of wasteful fertility, a mature Darwinian objectivity, and, on the other hand, the fairy-tale wishdream with the focus on the boy-man hero, his courtly love, and his kingship--an individualist, escapist salvation outside the world of the chronicle. The break with the political system is not accompanied by the break with its underlying world view or structure of feeling.

This logically, but not ideologically, untenable ambiguity between fatalism and voluntarism stems, no doubt, from a personal refracting of his societal position. It is remarkable that Jefferies is the only son of working people among UK S-F writers so far (and with Lee probably the only one until 1900). His father was a financially unsuccessful, small dairy farmer, hard hit by the severe agricultural depression; his mother came from a London artisan family of draughtsmen, engravers, and printers (the class

that had at the time of the French Revolution produced
Blake). Just because Jefferies was intelligent, sensitive,
and personally idiosyncratic, he was also typical for--and
a limit-expression for the structure of feeling of--the
class with "two souls," the small working farmers. On the
one hand, they were manual workers, producers who felt,
feared, and hated the power of the city, the moneyed
classes, the capitalist industry, and whose exasperation
over their blighted lives was such that practically no
price, not even the downfall of this civilization, was too
high for getting rid of what Jefferies called that "machinery for extortion." He himself became a radical plebeian
democrat, admirer of Whitman and Swinburne, consistently
and vigorously anticlerical, antiaristocratic, anticapital-
ist, at times (e.g., in "Saint Guido," The Open Air)
practically an agrarian communist: there is far more
parabolic satire in After London than usually, allowed
for. This is no mean feat when it is remembered that provincial farmers were the political reserve of the Tories
(their last revolutionary period having been Cromwell's
one); it was helped along by his mother's class heritage of
plebeian near-intellectuals. On the other hand, the small
farmers were also small landowners, and Jefferies's ideal
too was the independent small homestead (hyperbolized in
Felix's royal fort). Most important, his class ideology
was one of an exasperated individualism: the more the
blind forces of society (rather than nature) pressed on and
oppressed that individualist independence, the more pronoun-
cedly it clung to its individualism, to the sense that
one's destiny should and could be resolved by standing
"free" and alone against the world--as Felix does. It is
clear that Felix's adventures on the farm and on the site
of London are a transposition of Jefferies's existential
struggles; I suspect the intervening sections are such too.
Thus, the second part of After London seems to be a kind
of private allegory, not integrated with what is presented
as a glaringly nonprivate, caste world. Only Felix's final
magic kingship is pure compensatory wishdream. The split
consciousness of the small farmer class seems to me, finally, also why the reasons for the catastrophe oscillate
between cosmic and politico-economical (e.g., the ruin of
the farmers!).
   Nonetheless, this is finally an important and seminal
text. It is very significant to have translated the Ruskinian metaphor of "the storm-cloud of the 19th century" into
a consistent framework of a decisively different world and
history, even if Jefferies oscillates between satirizing
and welcoming that world. The tacit consensus between the

writer and the existing ideological hegemony has been
radically broken, even if instead of a counterhegemony we
fall back into petty-bourgeois fairy tale. And after all,
even that fairy tale has, ever and anon, romantically exhilarating, Hugoesque aspects: and principally, that basic
innovating delight in redrawing maps, in new, often
pristine and unexplored shores of the great midland lake
that our lucky protagonist explores in his buoyant canoe.
After London too remains a near-masterpiece of Victorian
--which here means anti-Victorian, upsettingly Other--SF.
It contributed significantly, if mostly by negation, to
shaping the vision of a future which would be truly alternative to the framework of bourgeois civilization. True, the
joyous relief of fertile nature--the free forests and lakes
--obliterating all traces of the old did not extend to
ushering in a human collective freedom. Beside the ideological dead-end of Jefferies's individualism, this was due
to the imperative necessity not to offend the middle-class
public on which the ailing writer depended for his liveli-
hood and which was prepared to accept any strangeness and
even critique that did not present a workable, positive
Otherness--a subversive challenge. Even so, after reading
this text, a socialist like William Morris could feel
strengthened in his convictions: "I know now ['civilization'] is doomed to destuction . . . ; what a joy it is to
think of! and how often it consoles me to think of
barbarism once more flooding the world, and real feelings
and passions, however rudimentary, taking the place of our
wretched hypocrisies . . ." (20). Thus, if Jefferies
influenced few S-F writers, perhaps only Hudson and Morris,
through Morris he reached to Wells and beyond.

   3.53. As mentioned at the beginning of 3.5, Alternative History turned in the 1871-1885 period also to presenting limited societal alterations. Beyond the short-range
political alternatives, there appeared what might be called
the private Alternative History. This is the presentation of one particular novum (entity or process) which does
not interact with the common, public framework or background of the tale, but is confined to its interstices or
foreground. The novum is not totalized, it does not affect
the whole narrative universe; it is instead an unexpected,
as a rule shocking impact upon a strictly limited circle,
often merely the sentimental environment of the protagonist
--an actualization of exasperated cleavage between the
public and the private. Thus, it is of Romantic descent,
and it was developed first outside the UK. Its earliest
and clearest masterpiece is Hoffmann's The Sandman,
apparently published in a UK book only in 1884, though

known earlier (in part through a US publication in the 1850s). Its Olimpia—a creature embodying human loveliness but later revealed to be a disgusting mechanical construct —is presented solely through the perceptions of the dazzled and mortified narrator-protagonist, within a system where fiends, physics, and finance are inextricably bound up, while individual sentiments are diametrically opposed to such public matters and to societal conventions. Although Poe liked suitably reinterpreted physics, he (as well as some other US writers such as Hawthorne) primarily picked up and developed the horrific aspects of both the artificial creature and the novum focusing on one individual.

Even such masters felt the stringency of the question how come the novum's effect does not extend to the whole society implied in the framework or background, and wisely limited themselves to the short story. Thus they minimized the importance of the pragmatically inescapable answer that the new invention was a nonce aberration, which is at the end of the tale expelled from its universe by being lost, destroyed, etc. When Bellamy developed the form into a novel, Dr. Heidenhoff's Process (1884), in which the first female near-protagonist in our corpus submits herself to erasure of unpleasant memories by galvanic current, the problem became acute. This was compounded by Bellamy's constant interest in the general problems of personal and public security. Madeline takes the treatment because she had been seduced; and furthermore, this is a possible means for treating criminals medically instead of penally (Butler rendered serious), that is, for global societal reform. The question is suspended rather than resolved by the (male) protagonist's waking up. But even this fairly tired dodge is given a new lease of life when he learns the humiliated Madeline has committed suicide. As usual with Bellamy, brute reality is opposed to ideal possibility. In his endeavor to formulate an at once deeply personal and deeply general anguish, he had here chosen a rather imperfect form, where the anguish could be stated but its alternative could not be developed; he was to do much better later. But he is quite distinct from entertainers in the "middle range" SF, such as About and Allen.

If the private Alternative History is limited to individualist psychology, its strengths, which lie in the resources for detailed, "depth" probings, should at least be used. Hoffmann, Poe, and Bellamy—in descending order— used it thus. About (1878) uses it only superficially. He has a "dessicated" colonel of Napoleon I revive under Napoleon III, brimful of an imperial enthusiasm which is

more than a little ridiculous and more than a little
parodying the Bonapartist ideology of the Second Empire
(when it was first published). For the rest, the
tongue-in-cheek premise is used for a two-volume meandering
through his reactions to the new environment in a dilution
of the Rationalist "philosophical tale," helped along by
the somewhat refurbished standbys of attempting to obtain
his money, which has grown by compound interest, and
falling in love with the homonymous granddaughter of his
past beloved (both picked up in later SF, the latter from
Collins through Macnie to Bellamy). Of Allen's two short
stories (1884), "Pausodyne" is also about suspended
animation; the protagonist who emerges after a century is
suspected of being insane. "The Child of the Phalanstery"
is a two-handkerchief tale detailing the euthanasia of a
deformed child imposed by the State Socialism of a
Positivistic and scientific future--a strangely
sensationalist concoction from the pen of an ardent
Darwinist, Spencerian, and self-proclaimed iconoclast. Its
merit is confined to having cleverly transferred the
private history from the present to the future, where it is
easier to treat it as a part representing or standing for
the whole which it allows to be glimpsed--an updated form
to be perfected by Wells.

Clearly, all of these are only the first steps of a new
form on the brink of emerging. Its tentativeness can be
seen in the fact that of the five titles three are imports
and three short stories, while the longest text, About,
flirts with both the comic and satirical alibis. But it
was one of the waves of the future, so that the publishing
of Hoffmann and Bellamy in 1884 is a signal of the readers'
interest outrunning the availability of British texts, and
the two texts by Allen in the same year of a polygraph's
quick reaction to the market. Their ranking should take
into account, beside consistency and relevance, how representative is the private microcosm of the public macrocosm
suggested. Based on all these criteria, Hoffmann's "The
Sandman" has long been recognized as a masterpiece,
Bellamy's Dr. Heidenhoff's Process is in the lower
reaches of good SF, About's Colonel Fougas' Mistake a
typical middle-range work, while Allen's two "Strange
Stories" are in the broad band of my figure 5, between the
middle range and the pessimums.

Notes to Section C

1. This exordium and therefore the whole analysis of
section C utilize--at times to the point of close para-
phrase--two main sources. First, the theoretical and

historical conclusions arrived at in Suvin MOSF, to which
the reader is respectfully referred. Second, for further
developments, a number of Marc Angenot's texts on narrative
semiotics and on SF. I cannot adequately show my fundamental debt to him in my references; of the several reasons,
one is that a number of them come from his manuscripts or
from oral discussions.

2. See for the following discussion Angenot PT, Irena
Bellert, On the Logico-Semantic Structure of Utterances
(Wroclaw, 1972) with further bibliography, and Ducrot.
Also Angenot AP; Communications, no. 16 (1970); Teun A.
van Dijk, ed., Pragmatics of Language and Literature
(Amsterdam, 1976); W. Dressler, Einführung in die Text-
linguistik (Tübingen, 1972); "Groupe Mu," Rhétorique
générale (Paris, 1970); M.R. Mayenowa, Poetyka
teoretyczna (Wroclaw, 1974); M.R. Mayenowa, ed., O
spójności tekstu (Wroclaw, 1971); Cesare Segre, Le
strutture e il tempo (Turin, 1974); V.N. Volosinov (M.M.
Bakhtin), Marxism and the Philosophy of Language (New
York, 1973); and Williams ML.

3. See Marc Angenot, Glossaire pratique de la critique
contemporaine (Montréal, 1979), s.v. "Isotopie," "Pré-
supposée," "Idéologème," and "Maxime idéologique," and
his "'Intertexte,' 'intertextualité,'" unpuplished MS;
Communications, no. 11 (1968); Jonathan Culler, "Presupposition and Intertextuality," Modern Language Notes 91
(1976), 1380-97; Jameson PU; Laurent Jenny, ed.,
Poétique, no. 27 (1976), special issue on "Intertextuali-
tés"; Julia Kristeva, Séméiotikè (Paris, 1966); and
J.S. Petöfi and D. Franck, eds. Präsuppositionen in
Philosophie und Linguistik (Frankfurt, 1973).

4. See Charles Elkins, "Science Fiction Versus Futurology," Science-Fiction Studies, no. 17 (1979), and Rafail
Nudelman, "On SF and Futurology," Science-Fiction Studies, no. 18 (1979).

5. Besides the literary aspect, discussed theoretically
in Williams ML and historically for paraliterature--
beginning with Sue--in Marx-Engels HF, Eco, Angenot RP, and
Angenot SFF, see on coopting Herbert Marcuse, One-Dimen-
sional Man (Boston, 1966) and Counter-revolution and
Revolt (Boston, 1972).

6. Darko Suvin, "Narrative Logic, Ideological Domination, and the Range of SF," Science-Fiction Studies, no.

26 (1982), 9-14. Besides Marx, Benjamin, and Tocqueville,
see also Jameson MF, some caveats in Williams ML 103-07,
and my essays "Some Introductory Reflections on Sociological Approaches to Literature and Paraliterature," Culture
& Context, no. 1 (1980), 33-55, and "Transubstantiation of
Production and Creation," Minnesota R., n.s. no. 18
(1982), 102-15. Much too little has been written about the
commercial strictures profoundly inflecting modern SF, but
cf. Dieter Hasselblatt, "Reflections From West Germany on
the Science-Fiction Market," in Mullen-Suvin pp. 282-89.
Cf. also the various titles cited in the notes to the SFS
essay, in particular those by Christian Enzensberger, Ernst
Bloch, Georg Simmel, and Arnold Hauser.

7. Beside the articles cited, cf., e.g., also Poe's
"Tale-Writing: Nathaniel Hawthorne," in Robert L. Hough,
ed., Literary Criticism of E.A. Poe (Lincoln, NE, 1965),
p. 45; I am indebted for a reference to this essay to
Barbara Lanati, "Una Ligeia, cento Ligeie," Calibano, no.
2 (1978), a special issue on mass literary forms which also
partly builds on Benjamin. See on Poe also Beaver,
Franklin, and other works listed in Suvin MOSF 300-01, and
on the new press that made of money "the common denominator
of cultural life," as well as on its intimate permeation of
both the bohème and the "high lit" in 19th-century
Paris, Kracauer 71-76 and passim.

8. Here, as in all further instances of section C, the
names stand for texts in the annotated bibliography of Part
I; for easier orientation the first mention will be accompanied by year of publication. No distinction is made
between true names and unresolved pseudonyms, but true
names are used whenever a pseudonym has been resolved.
Anonymous works are referred to by the first two words of
their title. Discussions of each text are, from here on,
based on the annotations in the bibliography.

9. On Maguire and Harting cf. "Fictions of the Future,"
Dublin R. 70 (1872), 76-103, significant only as possibly
the first critical echo on the type of writing identified
in its title.

10. It should be clear that "Chrysostom Trueman," the
clergyman-narrator of the introduction who supposedly found
the story MS, is a fictional figure; the "speaking name" is
not to be found in any of the 1848-1900 biographical
sources, including Crockford's Clerical Directory. The
situation is complicated by the fact that the text was

published in France 1865 as Cathelineau, <u>Voyage à la Lune</u>. Chronology suggests, and Messac (see in sources for the annotated Bibliography) and Angenot SFF p. 59 concur, that the latter is a translation of "Trueman"; however, I have not compared the two texts. Some--not all--of "Trueman's" ideas sound like those attributed to James Hinton (1822-1875, father of C.H. Hinton--see Biographies) who was much exercized by parallels between religion and science and by the metaphysics of pain, and had traveled to the Gulf of Mexico; but I have not read Hinton Sr.'s texts, and this is no more than a preliminary stab.

11. Ernesto Laclau, "Towards a Theory of Populism," in his <u>Politics and Ideology in Marxist Theory</u> (London, 1977), p. 161--Laclau specifically mentions as the classical example of this transformation the hegemony of the British 19th-century bourgeoisie.

12. Michael Sadleir, <u>XIX Century Fiction</u> (London, 1951), II, 77.

13. Chesney fought in the great Indian uprising of 1857, and later wrote a novel on it; he also wrote the largely autobiographical <u>A True Reformer</u> on Anglo-Indian life and an M.P. who tries to reform the UK army, as well as a number of works on Indian government--see Biographies.

14. For a first approach to CR see the five works of secondary literature in the Biographies entry; a long bibliography in Allan Conrad Christensen; Raymond Williams, "Utopia and science fiction," in Patrick Parrinder, ed., <u>Science Fiction: A Critical Guide</u> (London, 1979), pp. 56-57; and the German works by Schepelmann and Seeber listed in Suvin MOSF p. 302.

15. See Angele Botros Samaan, "The Novel of Utopianism and Prophecy," Ph.D. dissertation, University of London 1962, chapter 2; I could not find the publication in article, "Bulwer Lytton and the Rise of the Utopian Novel," Cairo Univ. <u>Bulletin of the Faculty of Arts, European Section</u> (1964).

16. The trickiness of exclusive categorization by surface elements such as the narration's locus, without regard to their narrative importance, is one reason why the pioneering and bibliographically very meritorious lists of Clarke TF, Locke VS, and Sargent UL--which mention many of the texts in this and the following subsections--have often

one-sided annotations. Other pioneering and fact-laden
secondary works dealing with many texts of 19th-century
Alternative History are Dupont, Samaan (see preceding
note), and, most comprehensively, Bailey; however, their
judgments are by now largely superseded, and this holds in
my opinion also for I.F. Clarke, "The Nineteenth-Century
Utopia," Quarterly Review 296 (Jan. 1958), 81-91. More
recent partial surveys include Philmus, Sargent WU, J.
Christensen, and Hillegas. To my mind much the most stimulating, if brief judgments are to be found in R.D. Mullen's
reviews of 19th-century reprints in Science-Fiction
Studies, nos. 4 (1974), 5 and 6 (1975), and 10 (1976);
even where I disagree, I have learned much from them.
Significant works dealing with a smaller number of texts
are sometimes mentioned when these are discussed, but see
also Suvin MOSF pp. 301-3 for the works of Barron, ed.,
Beauchamp, Beer, Bloch, Cohen, Elliott, Gove, Messac,
Morton, Mumford, Nicolson, Parrington, Patai, Sargent,
Schepelmann, Schwonke, and Sussman, as well as the bibliography to this essay.

17. Cf. Max Weber, The Protestant Ethic and the Spirit
of Capitalism (London, 1930), R.H. Tawney, Religion and
the Rise of Capitalism (Harmondsworth, 1938), and Jerome
Hamilton Buckley, The Victorian Temper (New York, 1964),
chapter 6: "God and Mammon." For secondary literature on
Butler see Suvin MOSF p. 302 and the Biographies entry.

18. This is suggested, with none of my negative connotations, by Sam Moskowitz, "Across the Zodiac: A Major
Turning Point in Science Fiction," introduction to the
reprint of Greg's novel by Hyperion Press (Westport, CT,
1974), pp. i-v, who also notices its intermediary position
between Trueman and later interplanetary tales. See on
Greg also Bailey, Dupont, Henkin, and Mullen SFS5.

19. This is borne out by the fact that the After
London slavery is a financial one! The parallel to
capitalist relationships is openly present in his Dewy
Morn and some other works (e.g., "Thoughts on the Labour
Question," cited in the splendid Edward Thomas, Richard
Jefferies [London, 1978], p. 271). See also W.J. Keith,
Richard Jefferies (Toronto, 1965), and Fowles, Salt, and
Williams in the Jefferies entry in Biographies—though
there is still a place for a thorough reevaluation. The
prescient idea that capitalist society was devolving into a
new feudalism was at the time just becoming popular among
"alternative" intellectuals, and in SF eventually issued in

a flood of works beginning with Wells and London. But already in 1873, Bellamy was writing on "The Feudalism of Modern Times," drawing analogies between "the old political and modern commercial feudalism" (quoted in A.E. Morgan, Edward Bellamy [New York, 1944], p. 108), while Brooks Adams set up a Law of Civilization and Decay (London, 1895) and, fuming against monopolies, announced that Americans were "passing from contract to servitude" (in Centralization and the Law [Boston, 1906], p. 134). Though perhaps less vehemently debated, this would have been even more believable in Britain, where some feudal trappings have persisted to this day. In particular, it would have been near to Jefferies, who hated the rich bourgeoisie and the aristocracy with equal, deep fury—see the secondary literature in the Biographies.

20. Letter of May 1885, in Philip Henderson, ed., The Letters of William Morris to His Family and Friends (London, 1950), p. 236.

D. In Conclusion: A Tension between Knowledge and Power

> . . . first, I made him
> know his Name should be
> <u>Friday</u>. . . . I like-
> wise taught him to say
> <u>Master</u>, and then let
> him know, that was to be
> my Name.
>
> Daniel   Defoe,   <u>Robinson</u>
> <u>Crusoe</u>

<u>0.</u> In conclusion to this interpretive essay--as well as
to this whole work, beginning with the Bibliography and the
data on the writers--only a few of the most important
aspects can be recapitulated, developed, and brought into
relief.   A full evaluation of the great amount of data
available within these covers could only be achieved after
a lengthy study of the 1886-1901 period; I hope to undertake this in the future, and I hope some other critics may
be stimulated to do so too.   But perhaps here is the proper
place to repeat that in this book I wanted to identify an
almost unknown, and yet historically significant, genre of
discourse delimited in space, time, intertextual affinities, and structures of feeling or ideological horizons.
Historically significant means, as Benjamin's epigraph to
my Preface explains, that 19th-century SF is interesting
for us today as the birthplace and baby figure of the giant
mass of SF--indeed, in some significant ways, of all mass
or "popular" literature--to come.   Here one can observe, in
an urgent discursive polarization between domination and
liberation and yet in the estranging situation of our ancestral century, both how and why the central ideological
vectors of hegemony, alternative, and cooptation shaped a
social discourse between the poles of power and knowledge.
   This conclusion bears principally on the 1871-1885
period, that is, on the phase in which Victorian SF is con-

stituted as an uninterrupted field of social discourse.
This <u>phase of constitution</u> was rendered possible by the
1848-1871 <u>phase of inception</u>. Further research will have
to elucidate what would be the most useful division into
following phases. I would today envisage a third one (characterized by the heightened virulence of political anticipations and alternatives already prefigured by Abbott and
Jefferies, in particular the "future Civil War in Ireland"
tales, the catastrophe utopias à la Hudson, and the
philosophico-scientific analogies à la Hinton--all of
which leads further to Bellamy, Morris, Twain, and
Flammarion) from 1886 to roughly 1893, and a fourth phase
(comprising the best of Griffith Jones and Wells) from
about 1893 to 1901. A possible major historical break,
analogous to the 1848 one, could then be situated either in
1901 or during World War 1.

Within the 1848-1885, but mainly the post-1871, period, I
shall then focus on a few salient points: the ideological
preconditions of S-F narratives; the division of SF into
subgenres and its relationship (in particular, the relationship of Alternative History) to the communication system of
British class discourse; the crucial thematic problem-
fields of History as Destiny and their logical furthest
horizons; and finally, a conclusion about the discourse of
power or domination and the discourse of knowledge or
liberation, which situates all SF as a dialog of class
values.

1. The Preconditions of Victorian SF

The preconditions of the narrative structures in my corpus are, then, to be sought in the ideologies of various social groups in contemporary Britain, as they were trying to come to grips with and work upon the largely new historical force-field taking shape in their lived experience. Conversely, the significance of any individual text (or writer) lies primarily in the clarity and consistency as well as in the referential richness of its narrative unfolding, that is, in how it articulates the implications and meanings of this force-field: which is simultaneously an ideological context and a "literary raw material" that is never "initially formless . . . [or] contingent, but is rather already meaningful from the outset" (Jameson MF 402), composed as it is of people's ongoing relationships to each other and to the societal objects, institutions, and values. The force-field burst upon British public consciousness at the beginning of the 1870s. SF, always an early-warning system, constituted itself, coalesced as a recognizable and henceforth uninterrupted genre, precisely in 1871 (a few years after the less insular but also less thoroughgoing and comprehensive French SF, which appears to have constituted itself around 1865--cf. Angenot SFF). It is in the 1870s that the sense of a secure society began to be openly and frequently doubted within the wide upper and middle-class ruling consensus itself. Though radicals possibly exaggerated when they claimed that "every man of any cultivation and a grain of imagination . . . , not absolutely absorbed in politics or business, . . . [was] visibly mocking at the whole apparatus (Parliament, Bible and Free Trade) in his heart" (1), both the efficiency and the morality of the apparatus were being widely put into question. Where in midcentury an ideologist like Bagehot could expect little demurral from within the hegemonic consensus when claiming that the British society was not only one of removable inequality but also one where each striving individual could rise by one step, in the 1880s a

highly respectable—if still exceptional—educator and theologian like Abbott could successfully pour sarcastic scorn
upon this quaint concord of physics and politics (see the
discussion of Flatland in 3.52). Centrally, what was
being discredited was the notion of immutable values,
validated in the final instance by the illusion of automatic progress on the basis of laissez faire economics, of the
impersonal and "natural" market mechanisms relegating the
State to a "night watchman" that protected property by
means of the police, army, and law system. Alternative
value-sets could now be articulated, exploring different
existential structures, often a more or less purposeful
intervention by some societal agents or agency. Such
alternatives could be narratively presented either in
active form, as better or worse developments, or in passive
form, as awful warnings of collapse of values should no
restructuring come about (the fourth possibility, an
unchanged state of affairs persisting as a positive value,
is by definition incompatible with SF).

Thus, a rich ideological discussion of values is—
paradoxically—the obverse of their experiential evan-
escence:

> What is paradoxical about such an experience [of the
> absence of values] is obviously that it is contempor-
> aneous with one of the most active periods in human
> history, with all the mechanical animation of late
> Victorian city life, with all the smoke and conveyance
> inherent in new living conditions and in the rapid
> development of business and industry, with the experi-
> mental triumphs of positivistic science . . . , with
> all the bustling parliamentary and bureaucratic activi-
> ty of the new middle-class regimes, the spread of the
> press, the diffusion of literacy and the rise of mass
> culture, the ready accessibility of the newly mass-
> produced commodities of an increasingly consumer-
> oriented civilization. (Jameson PU 251)

Carlyle had, very early on, acerbically observed that the
preoccupation with the future is a sign of lack in happiness or wisdom: "It is no very good symptom either of
nations or individuals, that they deal much in vaticina-
tion" (Carlyle 27:78). The sudden rise of S-F texts—and
primarily of Alternative Histories—after 1871, as well as
after 1886 and to a lesser degree after 1893 (see figure
2), grows directly out of the lived urgency of this casting
about for satisfactory value-sets. As one of the more
interesting S-F writers, W.H. Hudson, remarked in the 1906

preface to his utopian romance A Crystal Age (1887):
"Romances of the future, however fantastic they may be,
. . . are born of a very common feeling--a sense of dissat-
isfaction with the existing order of things combined with a
vague faith or hope of a better one to come" (2).

Within fiction, the rise of SF was correlative to--often
indeed a prefiguration of--the huge post-1880 expansion of
fiction in general, and in particular of a more controversial type of fiction which was partly displacing the
dominant mid-Victorian currency's twin faces of digestive
entertainment and moral preachment--the "novel of ideas."
Though all 19th-century publication statistics are very
imprecise, it is possible to discern an overall trend by
which fiction increased from the approximately 380 volumes
yearly in the 1870s to nearly 1,000 in 1888-1889 and 1,800
in 1896-1897. Simultaneously, its percentage within the
published titles increased from 9 percent in 1880 to 31
percent in 1896-1897, mainly by taking the place and
primacy of the (correspondingly decreasing) religious nonfiction (Ensor 159-60, Mulhall 465 and 791). In close
parallel, S-F titles rose from an average of 5 yearly in
the 1870s to 19 in 1888-1889 and 22 in 1896-1897, oscillating during that period--first upward and then downward
again--between 12 and 20 per mille of all fictional works.
Yet--dialectically--this upswing of fictional discussion
testified not only to a challenged but also to a not yet
seriously undermined stability. Only given--parallel to
significant doubt--a still strong sense of a "knowable
community" (Williams EN passim), scope and leisure were
available for looking at all steadily and fully at society
as a collective protagonist, to which all fictional characters related as its interacting parts and/or representatives. It is the unique combination of ideological
instability and loss of values encroaching upon a still
centrally unchallenged political stability and viable economics that provided the fertile ground for the growth of
both the "novel of ideas" and SF.

In comparison to all other European countries, even to
France, all of this--together with an earlier rise of the
English bourgeoisie and industry--meant that the UK public
sphere relied in ideology (as in economics) more on open
market rivalry than on State leverage, more on the social
disciplines resulting from a parallelogram of competing but
complementary forces within the bourgeois hegemony than on
the legal disciplines enforced through the State apparatus
(which, of course, existed too--see B.3.2.). This reliance
was rendered possible and guaranteed by the practical
absence from the public sphere, until the 1890s, of serious

forces outside the hegemonic ideological consensus, as
witnessed by the presence of armed rebellions in 19th-
century France and their absence in the UK (outside of
Ireland): "Free discussion was possible only because a
relatively small number of people took part in it" (3);
"the philosophers, scientists, government officials,
lawyers, clergymen, higher journalists . . . were the real
opinion makers" (Altick VPI 70). As to the S-F writers, it
was shown in the section on their social classification
that of 186 UK ones from 1871 to 1901 only 11 were women,
while of the 74 writers of known social origin only between
one and three were from the "manual laborer" classes in the
widest sense. Thus, the roughly 90 percent of the UK population comprised of workers, paupers, and women (see table
1 and Mitchell-Deane 6-7) were represented by between 7 and
13 percent of writers, if one counts by social origin. It
was as if Locke's restrictive judgment still held in the
British public sphere two centuries later:

> Where the hand is used to the plough and the spade, the
> head is seldom elevated to sublime notions, or exer-
> cised in mysterious reasoning. 'Tis well if men of
> that rank (to say nothing of the other sex) can compre-
> hend plain propositions, and a short reasoning about
> things familiar to their minds, and nearly allied to
> their daily experience. (24)

Furthermore, the overwhelming majority of those who succeeded to publish books--even at their own expense--had by that
very fact moved out of the manual laborer, farmer, or even
small employee or tradesman class of their origin. Thus,
among the UK writers one can count the serious disturbers
of the hegemonic ideological consensus before the mid-90s
(and they are more often than not transfuges from the
upper classes) on one's fingers: Abbott, Jefferies, Lee,
W. Morris, and the two ambiguous feminists Corbett and
Dixie. To this should be added such reprinted Americans as
Bellamy, Twain, G.N. Miller, and Donnelly, as well as a
couple of proindependence Irishmen. In all, this would
again come to about 7 percent of the texts before The Time
Machine, none of them prior to 1884, and few of them
consistently oppositional.

It should not be forgotten, however, that the situation
of writers was significantly different before and after
1886, up to which time S-F writers had a social position
very similar to those of "high lit." Table 5 will supplement the overall 1871-1901 data given in the essay on S-F
writers from Part I (cf. table 4 there).

Table 5

Comparison of S-F Writers, 1886-1901 to 1871-1885

	1886-1901 number	1886-1901 %	1871-1885 number	1871-1885 %	Comments
A. FEMALE WRITERS	11 (of 186)	6	1 (of 34)	3	
B. SOCIAL ORIGIN--UNADJUSTED					(Names, 1871-1885)
1) Upper class	6	11	4	20	Bulwer, Chesney, Cobbe, Strachey
2) Rich bourgeoisie	6	11	2	10	Dudgeon, Greg
3) Professional gentlemen	20	37	6	30	Brookfield, Butler, Maitland, Payn, P.S. Robinson, Trollope
4) Professional men	7	13	5	25	Abbott, Allen, Collins, Davis, Jenkins
5) Middle bourgeoisie	8	15	2	10	Greer (?), Lumley
6) Unacknowledged professionals	3	5 } 9%	-	- } 0%	
7) Petty bourgeoisie	2	4	-	-	
8) Manual labor classes	2	4	1	5	Jefferies
TOTAL	54	100	20	100	

C. SOCIAL ORIGIN--ADJUSTED

	1886–1901 number	%	1871–1885 number	%	Comments
1) Upper class	6	4	4	12	Half again larger percentage of upper class origin before 1886
2) Rich bourgeoisie	6	4 } 21%	2	6 } 35%	
3) Professional gentlemen	20	13	6	17	
4) Professional men	17	11 } 23%	8	23 } 38%	Ditto for middle class origin.
5) Middle bourgeoisie	18	12	5	15	
6) Unacknowledged professionals	52	34	5	15	
7) Petty bourgeoisie	21	14 } 56%	2	6 } 27%	Percentage of lower-middle &
8) Manual labor classes	12	8	2	6	
TOTAL	152	100	34	100	

D. "SURVIVING" WRITERS, BY SOCIAL ORIGIN

W. Morris (class 2), Griffith Jones (class 3), Shiel (class 4), Doyle (class 5), Wells (class 7); except for working classes (8), considerably more representative than the pre-1886 writers.

Bulwer, Chesney (class 1), Greg (class 2), Butler, Trollope (class 3), Abbott (class 4), Jefferies (class 8, but ambiguously so given the position of small farmers.

E. SOCIAL POSITION

	1886–1901 number	%	1871–1885 number	%	Comments
Wealthy dominant group	19	12.5	5	15	
Upper professionals	45	30	8	23	
Middle professionals	34	22	16	47	See section on S-F writers.
Lower professionals	21	14	–	–	
Tradesmen, employees	1	0.5	–	–	
Unknown lower class	32	21	5	15	
TOTAL	152	100	34	100	

It is clear, therefore, that both by social origin and by social position S-F writers after 1886 are—with the perennial exclusion of the working classes—considerably more representative of the English and Scottish social class system than those of 1871–1885.

2. S-F Subgenres and British Class Discourse

The discussion of S-F texts published in the UK has led to
the identification of some forms which can tentatively be
called subgenres, and which will here be used together with
the writers' social positions and ideologies to situate SF
with sufficient precision into the social discourse.
Before 1871 these are: the static or classical Utopias
proper (intertext--the social blueprint); the Extraordinary Voyage, old style (intertexts--fantasy, satire,
utopia, planet romance, tall tale); the more dynamic
Future Histories (intertext--the political tract as
positive vision or awful warning), divisible into long-
range and short-range ones, and constituting a transitional
form between the static classical Utopia and the post-1871
Alternative History. While it is not at all clear that the
location into the near or into the far future is absolutely
wedded to a given type of message, within the particular
ideological preconditions of mid-19th-century UK it was
found that the short range was used for political and
technological forecasting (specific intertext--the predictive essay) and the long range for apocalyptic and antiutopian warning. As always after Swift (see Suvin MOSF
112-13, 174, and passim), static Utopias were threatened by
the pessimum of dogmatic paralysis.

From 1871 to 1885 the picture changes. The subgenres
are: the Extraordinary Voyage, evolving from the
classical model of Swiftian satire and of getting to a
numinous--half transcendental and half utopian--space
(whose intertext was the Earthly Paradise and genres
mentioned in the previous paragraph) toward Verne's focus
on traveling itself as a breathless circulation (inter-
text--laicized travelogues and adventure stories, textbooks
of "positive" sciences); the Future War, codified for
this whole period by Chesney's Battle of Dorking (inter-
text--newspaper war reporting, general-staff planning); and
most importantly, the Alternative History, an alternative
but believable locus used to articulate different possible

394

solutions of problems possessing a sufficient magnitude to alter the overall history of the narrated world (inter-text--all the varieties of historiography). Stripped of Verne's inimitable whirl, the Extraordinary Voyage tended to revert to a "getting there" device for the alternative locus, just as any tale about future wars transcending the professional limitations of officers amd military corres-pondents tended to spread into the war's politico-techno-logical causes and socio-economic (but almost never psycho-logical) effects; thus, both were constantly attracted back into the Alternative History, which in that period became the basic form of SF. It was found that the partly comico-satirical Alternative History (e.g., Butler), historically the older form harking back to Cyrano and Swift, was in constant danger of becoming incoherent by neglecting a consistent depiction of an alternate reality in favor of its single narremes referring directly to the addressee's discrete opinions. Thus, they were under the threat of collapsing back into their intertexts of allegory, satire, whimsy, or similar, from which they were in the successful cases (Abbott, Welch's Politics and Life in Mars) saved by a combination of satire and parabolic consistency. To the contrary, the serious Alternative History, developing from Utopia proper through Future Histories to "realistic" dynamics, is threatened by a regress into social blueprint or political tract. Furthermore, as the Alternative History subgenre developed, it began to behave with a kind of semiautonomy, "as a cultural structure which can then know an unforeseeable history in its own right, as an object cut adrift from its originating situation and 'freed' for the alienation of a host of quite different signifying functions and uses" (Jameson FA 95). Thus, besides the initial global or totalized uses, it began to be used first for limited (single and/or brief) and later for individual historical alterations or alternatives (e.g., Bellamy's Dr. Heidenhoff's Process)--again a harbinger of S-F developments to come. Such developments faced it with the other intertextual threat--the reversion into the banal mundane tale. Nonetheless, the rise of Alternative History in lieu of utopia, old-style extraordin-ary voyage, and satirical dystopia, as a more dynamic and more encompassing subgenre, is the major change in the inner workings of SF in the 19th century.

The resulting distribution can be chronologically charted as follows:

1) In 1848-1871, Utopias proper were Forrest and Lamartine (both 1848), Pemberton (1854), and Harting (1871); there were two precursors of the Future War story,

History of the Sudden . . . Invasion (1851--see Appendix
1) and possibly Fairburn (1867), and one interesting early
Extraordinary Voyage, Hayward (1865). The other works have
to be divided between Future Histories (The Last Peer--
1851; Imaginary History--1857; Lang--1859; Gale--1867;
O'Neil-1868; and Maguire--1871) and a catch-all category I
shall call Other, consisting mainly of belated "planet
romances" (see Suvin MOSF 103ff.) such as Whiting (1855),
Heliomanes and Chatelain (both 1866), but also of a belated
conte philosophique (Rowcroft--1848) and an immature
prehistoric tale (Helps--1868). Finally, the major text of
that period, Trueman, spans Utopia, Extraordinary Voyage,
and planet romance.
     2) For the 1871-1885 period of constitution in SF in
the UK, an overview of book-length texts is given by table
6; caps indicate the most important texts, and works mixing
subgenres are written across their divide. In all, with
Bulwer, there are 86 texts, of which 24 are brief Future
Wars,, listed in the Appendix (all of them, except for W.F.
Butler and Welch, under 100 pages). The "Other " category
comprises as a rule inferior works with elements of classical utopias, political warning, eschatology, and/or melodrama, not rarely equally brief. Thus, half the works of
over 100 pages are Alternative Histories; qualitatively,
the situation is even better, as of the 12 works capital-
ized (not counting Bulwer), 7 are Alternative Histories.
This confirms the earlier impression of their rise to
dominance.
     The specific positions of single subgenres within
Victorian social discourse appear to be somewhat different,
with the Extraordinary Voyage and the Future War having
much smaller ideological spreads than the Alternative
History. As Wells was to demonstrate in his triumphant
assumption of Extraordinary Voyage and Future War into
modern SF, from The Time Machine and The War of the
Worlds on, a narrative stringency is at work here: for,
that assumption or canonization was only possible by also
being a subordination and incorporation into Alternative
History. The Extraordinary Voyage contained the fag-end of
its traditional usage as a vehicle of residual, semireligious but by now safely coopted, structures of feeling, as
in Lach-Szyrma; Verne's new formula of laicized, liberal
and positivistic, accelerated circulation addressed to a
combination of bourgeois teenagers and adults interested in
"positive" domination of the material world; and the incipi-
ent commercial dilution and banalization of his formula in
Gillmore (later in Grousset, Griffith Jones, Causse-
Vincent, M. Pemberton, Fawcett, Pallander, Stockton, etc.).

Table 6
Distribution of S-F Texts, 1871–1885

Year	Extraordinary Voyage	Future War	Alternative History	Other
1871	B U L W E R – L Y T T O N	CHESNEY, BATTLE OF DORKING	Mammoth	Hemyng The Island of Atlantis
		McCauley		
		8 more texts (in App. 1)	M., The Coming of Cromwell	
1872	VERNE, A JOURNEY TO THE CENTRE OF THE EARTH	An Octogenarian (App. 1)	S. BUTLER	
1837	VERNE, "MOON DILOGY" VERNE, 20,000 LEAGUES		Dudgeon Jenkins MAITLAND	Lumley
1874	Lach–Szyrma, A Voice	Adams (App. 1)	Blair	Back Again Collins
1875	Penrice	The Battle of Pluck (App. 1)	IN THE FUTURE VERNE, THE MYS-TERIOUS ISLAND	Davis ETYMONIA

Year	Extraordinary Voyage	Future War	Alternative History	Other
1876		Cassandra The Invasion of 1883 (both in App. 1)		Collens Soleman
1877		Fifty Years Hence (App. 1)	Verne, The Child of the Cavern	Cobbe
1878	Verne, Servadac			
1879		Chesney, The New Ordeal Dekhnewallah (App. 1)	About Verne, The Begum's Fortune	Watson Sr.
1880	Ryan		GREG	Hay, The Doom of Great City
1881		Budge (App. 1)	Hay, 300 Years Hence Lang-Tung (M. Pee)	

				The Dawn of the 20th Century
1882		W.F. Butler The Demure One Welch, How John Bull... (all in App. 1)	Besant Green Trollope (Welch, The Monster Municipality)	
1883	Lach-Szyrma, Aleriel	The Battle of Port Said Forth (both in App. 1)	(The Battle of the Moy) (Ulidia) Welch?, Politics and Life...	
1884		How Glasgow... Posteritas (both in App. 1)	ABBOTT Bellamy Brookfield An Eye-Witness Robinson & Wall Wise	
1885	Gillmore	The Battle of To-Morrow	Coverdale An Ex-M.P. (Greer) JEFFERIES Strachey	John Haile The New Democracy
TOTAL 9		26 (1)	30	(9) 10

The Future War contained the ideologically "pure" awful political warnings addressed as a rule by upper-class officers and their allies, the military correspondents, to the wealthy bourgeoisie in order to stimulate its patriotic feelings and ensure higher military budgets (Chesney); but again, a mass sensationalist variant was emerging in the 1880s, addressed by hack scribblers to the middle and even working classes and veering into crass jingoism (Welch's How John Bull . . ., The Battle of To-Morrow; later: Le Queux etc.).

The greater flexibility of Alternative History is correlative to its wider ideological use and spectrum. Taking into account only the central body of more or less global alternatives proposed in a coherent way (i.e., disregarding the sensationalist melodramas and incoherencies as well as the classical utopias, both in my "Other" column of table 6), a corpus of 30 texts remains. From among them, it is possible to identify 18 UK writers by social origin and position--the names adjoined to table 5B from which Chesney, Cobbe, P.S. Robinson, Collins, Davis, and Lumley are subtracted, while Besant, Blair, Hay, and Welch are added (see for the following also the essay on social classification of S-F writers in Part I). These identifications provide some important pointers for ideological grouping within social discourse. First of all, the post-1885 dominance of professional writers is already more or less in place, if Butler, Besant, Payn, Allen, Greg, Jefferies, and Welch are taken together with the halfway-house cases of Bulwer, Jenkins, Trollope, Dudgeon, and Maitland. Thus, in the 1871-1885 period there is already a balance between men of letters and other professions within the addressors of this central corpus of Alternative History. The writers, whether gentlemen amateurs or already men of letters, were by the intensely moralistic readership still thought of (and largely--though decreasingly--thought of themselves) as a residual clerisy or wisdom preachers; as moral persuaders rather than commercial profit-makers.

Such an "author image" stems, in significant opposition to the post-1885 period, largely from the fact that all the addressors of Alternative History belong to the upper three classes of table 5E--the already wealthy dominant group (Brookfield, Bulwer, Butler, Stachey), the upper professionals (Abbott, Besant, Jenkins, Payn, Trollope), and the middle professionals (Allen, Blair, Dudgeon, Greer, Greg, Jefferies, Maitland, and the somewhat less clear cases of Hay and Welch). Thus, on the one hand there seems to be no representation at all from lower professionals, tradesmen, and employees, nor also from unidentified and therefore probably lower-class social positions. The lowest that can be found here are, apparently, prolific middle-rank writers such as Allen, Jefferies, and Welch, or lower medical men such as Blair, Dudgeon, and Greer—all of them probably still within the upper 10 or 15 percent of contemporary social positions. This is, of course, not always accompanied by financial affluence, which was in particular questionable in Allen, Blair, Jefferies, and Welch—coincidentally (together with Abbott and possibly the financially unstable Butler) writers of the most ideologically deviating or least consensual texts in this entire period. On the other hand, the two uppermost categories of social position (wealthy dominant group and upper professionals), with a yearly family income upward of £500, most often over £1,000, account for an astounding half or 50 percent of the above 18 writers, as compared to 0.44 percent in the total UK population. At least two of them, Bulwer and Strachey, were among the most affluent and powerful people in British public life—a bit as if Nelson Rockefeller and Henry Kissinger were to write SF in our day.

Second, combining social origin and social position, the following groupings result:

a) Bulwer and Strachey were both by origin and position in the ruling upper class, and aggressive political ideologists.

b) Brookfield and Butler came from families of prominent Anglican clergymen and rose to the lower fringes of the dominant group, though both at important points in their life had serious financial difficulties.

c) Abbott and Jenkins came from respectable middle professional families and rose to the top professional positions of Oxbridge lecturer and member of Parliament; both were reform-minded liberals and indeed libertarians.

d) Payn and Trollope were of upper professional origin and successfully stood their position.

e) Besant, from unclear and probably lower class origin, had made it to a leading man of letters and pillar of the Establishment; he was also the most virulently reactionary ideologist outside of the wealthy dominant group.

f) Greg, and less clearly Maitland and Dudgeon, had descended in social rank from an origin in either an affluent bourgeois or a prominent clerical family to the lower, socially less respectable fringes of professional men; correlatively, their writings tend to eccentricity and a partial alternative, altering some elements but not the basic principles of the hegemonic ideological consensus.

g) Allen and Greer (the latter not discussed further in

this essay--see C.3.0), originating from middle professional groups, had chequered careers oscillating around the
level of their origin, which made them to a certain degree
receptive to alternative viewpoints.

h) Finally, only Blair and Jefferies can be called of
possibly plebeian origin (classes 6 to 8 in table 5B and
5C). In Blair's case this is a probability extrapolated
backward from his biographical data and position of Scottish provincial medical officer, and makes for a mixture of
plebeian resentments and technocratic wishdreaming. In
Jefferies's case his origin in a family of small, impoverished farmers, simultaneously owners and laborers, makes
both for his characteristic ideological illusion of exasperated individualism and for his growing sense of hatred
against the urbanized bourgeois civilization (see for both
C.3.51).

None of the above should be taken--as explained in subsection C.3--to imply simple economic determinism. Juxtapos-
ing the above eight groups to the structures of feeling and
ideological systems within the texts at hand, it becomes
apparent that the most important questionings came from
either the top (Bulwer, Butler, and Abbott) or the bottom
groups (Jefferies), while the somewhat less significant
works came from threatened middle-class origins (Greg and
Maitland; Allen should be added to this on the strength of
his later S-F novel The British Barbarians). Enlarging
this conclusion to all S-F subgenres would add Chesney and
Verne to the top groups and strengthen my case. Nonethe-
less--with the possible exception of Abbott (as well as of
the unknown writers of Etymonia and In the Future),
testifying to the power of sympathetic cognitive consistency to overcome class limitations in exceptional cases--it
is not too difficult to correlate the ideologies and the
social positions-cum-origins of the writers, even on the
basis of this rough grid which could be significantly
refined by further biographical research. As important as
any other conclusion is the overall picture of some
segments from the top 10-15 percent of the social scale
talking within this S-F corpus first to themselves and to
other specialized groups of a similar social rank, and then
to their inferiors. This clearly correlates to the consensual limits of even the most ingenious satire or alternative. Even Abbott remains within a radical ethical
critique disjoined from economic power, even Jefferies
remains within an escapist individualism disjoined from
collective hope. Both can therefore, in the final analysis, just barely be acceptable at the furthest limits of a
petty-bourgeois radicalism shaking and restructuring but

not abolishing the capitalist hegemonic consensus--though both have, for the same reason, been shamefully neglected by the hegemonic literary criticism and history.

In order to reach sure conclusions about the social role of this S-F corpus, a full investigation would, besides further biographic data, require much more information than I have on the distribution data and what inferences about addressors could be gained from them. One of the most startling facts my Bibliography has uncovered is that my S-F corpus was mainly published in single-volume books. In other words, at least up to 1893, it seems that SF circu-lated overwhelmingly outside the principal--i.e. the three-decker, circulating-library--fiction circuit, as well as outside its principal alternatives so far identi-fied, the penny-serial and the self-improvement circuits (see section B) (5). The very fact that SF as a rule func-tioned within what must be seen as an alternative communica-tional system of reading, and presumably of feedback, is highly significant--even though we do not know and can only guess what this circuit was like and how it functioned. For some first reflections, one should start from the reasonable assumption that there are significant correla-tions between forms, institutions (such as publishers and distribution networks), social addressees, and ideological presupposition-systems in the texts. This suggests that the bulk of Victorian SF from 1871 and at least up to the mid-90s was not principally aimed at either the central bourgeois family-reading of fiction or the working classes' nonfiction circuit or the lowest middle classes' escapist circuit, but at a communication with some other sections of the public with a profile yet to be determined. Indica-tions from the textual system point to one of those groups comprising mostly upper-middle and middle class males with special interests in politics, religion, and public affairs in general. This is a circuit very close, perhaps even identical, to that of the bourgeois nonfiction reading-- which would explain the intertextual closeness to SF of such nonfiction genres as the social blueprint, the politi-cal tract, the predictive essay, even the semireligious apocalypse.

The clearest limit-case is the Future War one, addressed in the 1870s by officers and military writers in the first place to other officers, politicians, influential business-men, and equipollent opinion-makers, and only in the 1880s and 90s evolving into a yellow-press subgenre addressed to a mass reader. This could serve as a model for understand-ing other interventions by groups or segments of the dominant classes, using other forms of SF initially as an

instrument for both flexible and effective intraclass discussion of gathering threats. Once in place, this circuit
would--as usual--acquire some autonomy, considerably
strengthened by the irruption of profit-oriented mass publishing in periodicals as well as in the book-trade during
the great depression after 1873 and in particular since the
1880s (cf. Williams LR, especially 222ff.); it would therefore become available for alternative structures of feeling
too. Another group of addressees was, no doubt, the juvenile readership; Verne's great strength, discussed at length
earlier, lay in his unique formula for combining important
segments of what might be called the "publicly minded
adults" with the teenagers, and thus reinventing a new,
male rather than female-oriented, family reading-matter.
(Later, Bellamy's outstanding success will be due to recom-
bining certain segments of female readers with certain male
"publicly oriented" ones.) In sum, it seems that most SF
in the UK circulated in a newly formed, peripheral and
therefore relatively open, circuit, which could carry a
whole spread of discourses, up to alternative ones. Of the
69 titles in my main Bibliography from 1871 to 1885, 15
were published by the "popular" publishers Low, Marston
(including 6 Vernes, Watson Sr., Green, and Coverdale), 5
by their lower competitor Tinsley, and 5 by the resolutely
bourgeois Blackwoods (both Chesneys, Besant, Trollope, and
Brookfield). Yet the case of News From Nowhere teaches,
obversely, that an outright oppositional discourse was,
even in 1891, possible only after serialization in the
author's self-financed periodical with a particular, politically captive audience, and when the writer's name and fame
were that of William Morris. The new communication system
of SF was up to 1885 in an overwhelming majority used for
one-way communication from above.

3. History as Destiny and Power: Containing the Other

Approaching some (provisional) conclusions about the great collective and intertextual discourse of which SF was a dynamic part that significantly contributed to articulating the whole, the notion of discourse ought first to be clarified. For discourse is in class society always a confrontational dialog between disparate social groups, ultimately organized around the central axis running between the ruling and laboring classes. The geometric metaphors of segments, fractions, or strata of society are misleading if and insofar as they imply that these are closed monads, isolated one from another in such a way that the analysis of their value-sets folds back into independent world-views, each of which inertly reflects its particular social group. If, then, forms in art—in fictional literature—are "possibilities of a . . . shared perception, recognition, and consciousness [to be] offered, tested, and in many but not in all cases accepted," if they are in each case "the activation of specific relations, between men and men and between men and things" (Williams ML 189 and 190), then the fictional forms can be correlated only to differential group ideologies grasped as relational systems.

In the case of the SF at hand, I hope this essay may have shown that my central notion of narrative consistency (set up in C.1) is that strategic enactment of the societal within the formal which permits analysis to illuminate the relationships—presupposed in and by the texts themselves—between the dominant and submerged, ruling and subversive ideologies. The social discourse revealed by the texts is a battleground, and the metaphors proper for it are those of military manoeuverings and confrontational pressures rather than those of static divisions and stable borders. To take a crucial example for fictional narrative, that of its ending (6): it is well known that Victorian novels in general end "with a series of settlements, of new engagements and formal relationships" (Williams LR 313), with the reaffirmation of a dominant and central social order (at

whatever cost to individual agents in exceptional cases).
Adopting the same horizon of consistency, one would expect
the S-F texts to end in an analogous, indeed formally
identical, reaffirmation of a different but equally
central social order--the difference being the reason for
writing, the raison d'être of SF. And yet in most cases
this did not happen. The overriding ideological needs and
taboos led instead to strategies of containment, consisting of ingenious devices constructed in order to avoid the
ultimate consequences of a genre's insights. The successful strategies of containment result in what I have earlier
called cooptation or neutralization--in inconsistent narratives with diluted or fragmented insights. While within
the limits of the effective and hegemonic ideology there
may be, and often are, found both subsidiary probings and
sometimes also real conflicts (as in Bulwer, Maitland,
Greg, or the best Verne), overwhelmingly the ending of any
S-F text in this corpus is what George Moore, in a different context, chastized as a false ending, which breaks
the logical sequence of events, and/or the dominant "key"
of the novel, and/or the concord of plot with character.
One of his strictures in particular, referring to the
mixture of "realistic" characters and romance situations in
writers such as Besant and Haggard, could be applied to
much SF almost literally: the "inchoate . . . folly" of
combining "pa and ma, and dear Annie who lives at Clapham,
with the Mountains of the Moon, and the secret of eternal
life" (7).
    In the particular case of the SF from 1871 to 1885 a
distinction should be drawn between focusing on subsidiary
probings addressed to one's own class or to a cluster of
classes of similar rank in the social hierarchy, and focusing on talking at least as much to a lower class or cluster
of classes (with the strengthened political agitation from
the 1880s on). Politically speaking, only the latter is
predominantly containment, while the former is rather
preemption or forestalling. But narratively speaking, the
consequences are very similar--they are always inconsistencies. This justifies the general appellation of containment, and testifies that subsidiary probings too are, in
fact, largely refractions of unspoken, contextually implied
or even repressed, but very real pressures from the lower
classes. To take the example of family reform, both
Maitland's and Greg's gropings toward polygamy or at least
a relaxation of the monogamous hearth are finally defined
by the tension existing between the strongly repressive
bourgeois consensus and such radical lower-class desublima-
tions as formulated by Fourier's utopian socialism and its

expansive sexuality. Even the probings of preemption are
in this narratological sense--decisive for an analysis of
fiction--in an antagonistic dialog with serious threats,
possibly in the "political unconscious" rather than in an
explicit intertext. This is amply confirmed by even a
superficial glance at the "social discipline" of the whole
spectrum of British literary criticism, say from its fight
against the radical romantics and up to the end of the
century. Beyond all changes of fashion, Byron and Shelley
just as Hardy and the naturalists were condemned in the
name of morality, good taste, common sense, and a depiction
of social relationships that should be faithful and healthy
and yet not sordid, "not too disturbingly precise and political" (Cox 200) (8).

The clash of dominant, enforced class value-sets with the
emergence and articulation of radically other values and
structures of feeling is fought out in the "master code"
common to all the ideologies of the 19th century--the
convention of development in linear historical time. The
Whig optimism could be, and increasingly was, offset by
Tory laudations of the safer, less stressful and less
commercialized, past, and also by increasing bourgeois
pessimism--in SF perhaps best followed in the evolution of
Verne, analyzed at length earlier. But in all cases,
history was thought of as a strict causal sequence going
upward or downward. This seems to me the main drive behind
the establishment of Alternative History--together with the
Future War, always in the near future--as the main subgenre
of SF. Such a participation in the master code of History
as Destiny and Power, of man as the historical animal,
permits the comparison of SF to the historical novel (9), a
genre that emerged as coherent social discourse half a
century earlier than SF, precisely in the same accelerating
societies of Britain and France (the obvious differences in
national destinies being the main reason for the relatively
stronger American role in SF than in the historical novel).
Further, just as the historical novel was an analogy to
some conflicts in the writer's present, so Alternative
History too is not an extrapolation from but a dramatiza-
tion of the present as a moment pregnant with the choice of
futures. The basic historiographic and conceptual image
constitutive of modern SF is one of a node in branching,
from which different paths or branches may issue. This is
why SF has so many not only ideological but also formal
affinities with its Victorian twin brother, Darwinism (cf.
MOSF chap. 10), echoing in it right from its 1871
founders, Bulwer, Chesney, and Butler, to Wells, Haldane,
Stapledon, and further--often using biology also as narra-

tive vehicle. This might help to explain why SF's own "historical novel," the prehistoric tale, is universally acknowledged to be a subgenre of SF--the one turned towards the evolutionary past--, confounding all definitions that insist on a literal future locus or on scientific gadgetry. Finally, the central conception of alternatives which exemplify results of historical branching also explains why-- though the narrative is in the majority of cases set in the future--the locus of estrangement is a secondary narrative convention, inflected by other factors such as the prestige of the older models of Plato, More, Swift, etc., and most importantly by the encroachment of the protean time/space of parable (the literary form most appropriate to dramatizing choices instead of inevitable extrapolations) upon linear time. In direct proportion to its significance, the loci of SF are analogies thinly masked by extrapolative verisimilitude, and not narrative dominants usable as a serious basis of classification (see more in C.3.1 and Suvin MOSF passim).

If History is Destiny,, it follows that the constellations of societal forces which go to make it up have to be articulated with equal attentiveness as the designs of the gods in Hellenic culture or the earthly strategies of divine salvation in the Middle Ages. No doubt, such constellations could be extrapolatively commingled with forces from biological or indeed cosmic history, this extrapolation being anyway also and fundamentally an analogy to societal processes (a proceeding so logically brought to a head by Wells). As induced and analyzed in C.3, the key thematic fields of the forces in question presented themselves to the texts' addressees and addressors in guise of "natural" (i.e., ideological) problem-expanses, which focused on the positions or roles of the Other as defined by opposition to the cultural norm of male-bourgeois-White. Thus, these roles were crucially an ideological view of the existential, lived exclusions from power (and therefore from equal value) of women (and the body), the working classes (and the labor-force as creator of economic goods), and the ethnic aliens (from different civilizations, through other "races," to biological Aliens). The lack of attention to these fields, the first two in particular, is in itself an important critical fact--especially for texts above short-story size, to which the rest of this subsection will confine itself.

To begin with a quick recapitulation bringing to a point earlier discussions, in the 1848-1871 period the substantial limitations of all the texts (except for some singled out further on) can be read off the fact that their ignor-

ing, repressing or--in the best case of the two utopias--
patronizing the laboring classes and labor is strictly
homologous to their ignoring, or clichetizing within gender
chauvinism (sentimental melodrama) respectively national
chauvinism, the women and the aliens. As it has been noted
with regard to a different but equally representative
Victorian work, the texts of that age "subtly imbricat[e]
the questions of the production of sexuality and the production of political power. . . . [and] there are other [anal-
ogous] codes . . ." (10). The "first shallow laugh" level
of Maguire's women in Parliament can be defined precisely
in terms of the absurd inconsistency between political
leadership and sentimental subjugation, of a piece with his
inconsequentiality about poverty and the Empire. The Extraordinary Voyages of Whiting and Hayward are precisely
circumscribed by the patchiness of the former's semierotic
and the latter's semiscientific utopianism. Symmetrically
obverse, Rowcroft's compensation for the absence of women
on the alien's planet, thematized even in the title The
Triumph of Woman, is accompanied by some satirical estrangement of manners within the comic bonhomie of his
slight but pleasant Biedermeyer tale. On top of the
value-scale, Lang's Air Battle hesitates between sturdy
liberal abolitionism and religious prejudices as well as
patriarchal cliches. Finally, Trueman's History of a
Voyage to the Moon was earlier discussed at length as a
similar, though more significant, hesitation between,
first, a consistent natural-science and inconsistent political novelty, and second, between communist self-government
by workmen and Catholic hierarchical containment, most
obvious in the total absence of women.
     Continuing this overview with the 1871-1885 period, it
first of all becomes striking just how cognitively limited
--for all its momentary political importance--the Future
War form was. Whether Liberal or (usually) Tory, it was
exhausted by manoeuvers of foreign policy and armed
battles. Women are practically nonexistent, even Chesney's
realism about the army being a means to economic world-
domination cannot encompass nonmilitary production, while
the foreigners are always bloodcurdling despoilers, by
definition wrong, evil, and to be killed. The rhetorics of
power speaks here, literally, in naked forms. Any contamin-
ation of Alternative History with Future War--for example,
in Lang, Verne's Begum, or Lang-Tung--is strictly proportional to rhetorical stridency, chauvinism, and marginaliza-
tion of women. Even Wells will testify to this necessary
correlation, which overrides and everts the otherwise
liberating associations of navigating the air or the sea.

The Extraordinary Voyage is complementary and parallel to
the Future War insofar as its dominant Vernean variant,
which neutralizes its earlier association with utopianism
and Earthly Paradise, also bows to the two great Victorian
taboos on labor-force and laboring classes, women and sex.
This is clearest in Greg, but even Butler's satire—and
both are situated within the narrative frame of extraordinary voyage—is clearly bound by these limits; even
Trueman's union of utopia, voyage, and alternative history
is able to cope with workmen but not with women. The deepest convictions of the Victorian hegemonic bourgeois consensus about women and workers were identical: if they ever
became their own masters, chaos would be let loose. The
heroines of a more critical realism, for example, met with
a revealingly horrified refusal by the writer of She
(which only its pruriency distinguishes from the well-known
chastisements of workers as basely materialistic) for being
"Lewd, and bold, and bare, living for lust and lusting for
this life and its good things, and naught beyond . . ."
(11).
Now Trueman is on the whole a glaring positive exception
in this whole S-F corpus, where—except for half a dozen
reformist and rationalist utopias old style—workmen are
very rarely mentioned (and women workers, as opposed to
princesses, lovely ladies, and even matriarchs, seem totally nonexistent except for vague hints in two or three texts
such as Etymonia; but then this is the case even in
Wells). When they are mentioned, it is never as economic
protagonists or important roles but as a faceless mob fit
for upper-class or divine repression (Hemyng's Commune in
London, Mammoth's Gorilla Origin of Man, Watson Sr.'s
Erchomenon, Strachey's Great Bread Riots) or as equally
faceless pawns in some scheme of reformist regulation
(e.g., in Green's Thousand Years Hence, or melodramatical-
ly personalized as loyal crew and criminal dastards in most
Verne). Besides Trueman, I know of only six exceptions:
Jenkins's largely present-day but sympathetic and protagon-
istic agricultural workers of Little Hodge; the self-
governing though still faceless workers of Etymonia and
Welch's Politics and Life in Mars; and the bottom-of-the-
heap victims of dystopian regulation in In the Future,
Abbott's Flatland, and Jefferies's After London,
forerunners of Orwell's Proles. As in Victorian
"realistic" fiction generally, "[t]he limiting factor is
commonly one of social class." Many contemporary critics
pointed out "that lower-class characters by virtue of their
position in life can never evoke [full] sympathy. . . . It
is as if the social . . . snobbery has become . . . a

principle of artistic selection" (12). If democracy means sympathy for the desires (never mind the rule) of the majority, that is, of workers and women, there are half a dozen democrats, and another half a dozen reformists willing to include the majority in some form of partnership with the minority, within our approximately 75 novel-size texts 1848-1885: one twelfth each for the democrats and the reformists. This is what I meant by a predominantly bourgeois hegemonic and intraclass discourse.

It is, thus, understandable that the rhetorics of a number of texts of sensationalist and bloodthirsty antipopular propaganda in the wake first of the 1867 reform (Gale, O'Neil) but mainly of the Paris Commune and the women's emancipation movements, and later of Irish Home Rule agitations, is largely identical to the rhetorics of the Future War. From journalistic sensationalism and near-future horrors they progressed to the apocalyptic sensationalism of far-future ones, exemplarily demonstrated by Watson Sr.'s Erchomenon, which in one fell swoop settles the hash of communism, atheism, female equality, collective education, sexual freedom, euthanasia, Russia, Germany, Popery, humanism, Darwinism, etc. Revealingly, it manages to do that without referring to labor, workers, or economics at all; being shut out of public discourse, this must presumably be left to the interaction of the Bible and private ethics. It becomes clear that writers concentrating on parts of these interlocked problem-expanses--as in Besant's antifeminist Revolt of Man or Trollope's antieuthanasia Fixed Period--always assume that the whole complex will be triggered in the addressees by contact magic. It is only unfortunate that they associate ideologically negative elements on the parochial basis of opposition to the historically contingent dominant ideology--as if atheism could not go with the bourgeoisie or Darwinism with anticommunism--so that this type of ideological coherence has to result in narrative inconsistency. From Butler to Greg and beyond, this is the major problem of texts in my corpus.

As I argued earlier, from case to case, no examined text wholly escapes either referential poverty or narrative inconsistency, if measured by the standards of the best Wells. However, the main works of Chesney and Verne (as well as some minor works, e.g., Rowcroft and Jenkins) achieve consistency at the price of referential impoverishment; Bulwer is skilled--and was for a whole generation successful--in evoking the appearance of consistency by employing the dynamics of the realistic novel and devices of what might be called "sensationalist tranquillization,"

in particular the omnipotent superrace and its occultist
superenergy, to paste over the antinomies of The Coming
Race; while in Trueman, Abbott, and Jefferies the alternative ideological horizons break the magical circle of narrative illogic in favor of the discourse of knowledge, which
to a significant degree counteracts their omissions and
inconsistencies. Concerning Bulwer, I want to recall only
how strictly congruent is his hesitation between superior
utopian girls and submissive women with his hesitation
between elitist collectivism and possessive individualism,
magical technology and suburban decorativeness--a congruence on which then Maitland and Greg ring changes.
Maitland's By and By can be characterized as exasperated-
ly elitist individualistic reformism in religion and marriage accompanied by unabashed male superiority, White
racism, and an offer of a decidely smaller share in
technology-based prosperity to workers. From that angle,
Maitland is an interesting prefiguration of coopting the
individualist elements in Fourier and the technocracy of
Saint-Simon for a global and corporate neocapitalism.
Greg's Across the Zodiac is equally, if not more interesting. Just as he strips Vernean travel of the liberal
remnants of utopian euphoria, so he also hints as broadly
as possible--given Victorian censorship--at a sado-
masochistic absolute patriarchy, complete with polygamy and
paedophilia, in full congruence with a use of science
subordinated to occultism and of supposedly liberating
revolt by an elite secret society.
   It was also discussed earlier how all the more interesting texts feature flying (or at least navigating the sea)
as a possible physical analog to liberation from societal
gravity and oppressively closed social relationships.
While it would be fascinating and very useful to extend the
discussion of this device to all SF in my Bibliography and
beyond (e.g., to the role of antigravity and space-travel
in all modern SF), I shall here indicate only its significance in the system of correspondences at hand. At the
outset, from Rowcroft to Trueman, flying is associated not
only with unknown powers of nature accessible to human
control but also with utopian political organization and--
as in the old orgastic metaphor--sexual liberation. But
parallel to the first use of balloons in war, the "realistic" reduction of flying to simply an improved technology,
sundered from radical liberation in the direction of either
superficial strangeness or technocracy (a reduction already
present in Lang and Trueman), is fully articulated by
Bulwer. But perhaps the primacy in making flying--and all
SF--safe for the bourgeoisie belongs to Verne, from his

first novel of ballooning explorations in prospective
colonies to the culminating euphoria of the Moon dilogy and
20,000 Leagues in the 1870s--still partly associated with
significant liberation--and the later disenchantment of icy
cometary orbits in Servadac and orbiting missiles in
Begum (which will finally lead to the complete retracta-
tion of Robur). The technocratic, politically elitist
strand is followed up by Maitland and the space travel in
Blair's Annals of the 29th Century, more interestingly in
Green (welfare-state reformism), and most interestingly in
Welch's Politics and Life in Mars (utopian socialism).
The strand of associating flying with superficial strangeness, hailing from the Munchausen-type tall tales, whimsy,
and occultist take-offs from Bacon such as The Island of
Atlantis, is developed in the religious farrago of Lach-
Szyrma's Aleriel and of Ryan, and in the sub-Vernean
adventures of Penrice and Gillmore; by the time of Greg and
of Hay's 300 Years Hence--the beginning of the 1880s--it
is so fully neutralized that it can even be hitched to antiscientific sermonizing and extreme political reaction. In
keeping with societal, or even cosmic, catastrophe,
Jefferies returns to the more modest and individual liberation of navigating an inland sea--almost in a Vernean
boyish vein. Henceforth flying is a neutral device, usable
within all political horizons but not necessarily associated with integral--political and sexual as well as
physical--liberation. Women as well as collective freedom
are already absent, marginalized, or neutralized in Trueman
and Bulwer, while Verne sets up the standard S-F transfer
of libido from sex to machine and/or to politics as armed
manoeuvers of males for power, so clearly explicated in the
veiled brutality of Greg's seraglios. Again, the only
exceptions are works going against the stream,, in which
(as both Mill and the early socialists, from the utopians
through Engels to Bebel, agreed) the status of women is the
gauge of civilization--and in SF, also, the correlative to
free movement upward, away from the level of everyday life:
positive examples, such as Welch's amusingly aquatic Mars,
or generously indignant satires, such as Abbott's equally
amusing dimension shifts. In view of all this, flying
indicates among other things also the attitudes within this
SF toward science and reason in general: together with the
correlative position of women, it is the benchmark of the
discourse of knowledge and the indicator of its front-line
with the discourse of power.

4. The Furthest Horizons of S-F Discourse

A further privileged way of discussing the import of my corpus could be to focus on the agential system in it: the persona of narrator opposed to the dramatis personae shown, the various actantial roles (protagaonist, antagonist, value) and its personifications, more in representative types than in individualistic characters. Another way would be to analyze the imaginative spaces in the "absent paradigm." However, in the space at my disposal, I shall now attempt to come to a conclusion about the position of SF in the UK social discourse of History as Destiny, understood as an antagonistic dialog or polyphony. In C.2, I concluded that the pre-1871 SF can best be systematized as a field of ideological tensions polarized between the discourse and communication of knowledge and the discourse and communication of power. These tensions are of a piece with the institutionalization of the genre, the identifications of its social addressors and addressees, the intertextual plausibility used, and the literary forms evolving within it. It is now clear that this applies also to the post-1871 UK SF, indeed in my opinion to all SF since. Knowledge is communicated by means of referential richness and narrative consistency, power by barriers to knowledge in the shape either of formal narrative inconsistency (dilution, fragmentation, incoherence, etc.) or of intertextual dependence on dogmatic systematization (mostly in residual Enlightenment structures of feeling), on banality (in dominant Victorian structures of feeling), and finally--ominously swelling on the horizons even of conservative England with the victorious march of total commodification--on superficially sensational strangenesses. The discourse of knowledge is therefore the productive or creative principle, and it is visible only in an active or positive form--by the knowledge conveyed in the text as a whole. The discourse of power is the more insidious limiting or uncreating principle, and it can be seen both in the active or positive and in the passive or negative

form--by the power-relationships openly conveyed in the
text, as well as by the knowledge prevented from cohering
in it. Knowledge is, as it were, the land reclaimed by
irrigation, power the desert waves whipped up against it:
an image to my mind not ahistorical but, on the contrary,
drawn from the "long duration" of all class history. In
SF, power--always the power of the Powers That Be, of the
actual class domination--is most clearly knowable by the
taboo on all radical exteriority. It was found that for
the dominant British bourgeois consensus of the period and
its male White writers this meant the sexual, political,
and biological Others--respectively women, laboring
classes, and aliens as subjects on their own, that is, as
protagonists pursuing at least some specifically different
values of their own. To the contrary, the fictional presentations of alternative human relationships to each other
and to the cosmos are--in proportion to their radical
otherness--true novums, potentially subversive of existing
class domination and its lived ideology.

In this light, final conclusions about the place of
19th-century SF in the social dialog that was its element
and about its narrative consistency cannot avoid the
question of the furthest logical horizons of its central
problem-expanses. If one eliminates the existing societal
status quo as both contingent (history not being very
logical) and by definition representable in SF only as
reacted against, the two logical alternatives remaining
are: first, to exasperate the discourse of power into
total repressions of the basic problems of sex, labor, and
ethnic alienness; second, to abolish the discourse of power
by total acceptance of these three variants of radical
exteriority or difference. The latter solution is the age-
old dream of communism; the former, a new thing under the
sun, we can today identify as proto-fascism. Communism
means centrally the organization of labor by structures of
self-managing workers (politico-economic communism or classless society), the organization of sexual companionship and
family groupings by the self-managing men, women, and
children (erotic communism or "free love"), and the organization of intercommunity relations by the self-managing
communes and larger cultural structures (polycentric inter-
nationalism, working out contradictions by political
arguments and pressures instead of wars of possession). As
different from primitive or tribal communism, it must in
modern times be based on high technology, affluence, and a
planetary--if not interplanetary--scope. It is the
ultimate discourse of knowledge or liberation. Fascism, on
the contrary, means the total fusion of the apparatus of

physical repression (the State) with that of economic property as well as of political, sexual, and generational control into one huge Leviathan of patriarchal, "chosen nation," racist, and militarized domination over people and nature. It is the ultimate discourse of power or domination.

Tangentially, it should be stressed that such delimitations presuppose that the modern reader suspend many of the meanings given to the term "communism" after the 1917 Russian Revolution, either by its adherents or enemies: the always contingent history has in the case of this "State communism" fused liberation and repression, knowledge and mystification, in ironic ways. Since my analysis, fortunately, deals with theoretical logical horizons as present in the 19th century, I believe I can legitimately demand such a suspension of semantic overlays. But it also ought to be stressed, in all fairness, that although I believe the term "totalitarianism" to be of very limited cognitive use, the horizons of both communism and fascism include an (in theory diametrically opposed) enmity to private buying and selling of labor-force and sex-partners and to the world market--that is, to liberal capitalism. Even further, though communism as well as fascism pick up and valorize opposed aspects of liberal capitalism, it must also be acknowledged--against most of the present-day defenders of both communism and fascism--that their roots (in particular, the 19th-century ones) in a kind of right-wing populism often intertwine in very close ways; as knowledge and power, paradoxically, always do in class society.

Fear of communism was, of course, widespread and perennial in the 19th-century bourgeoisie and upper class. Not only conservatives fulminated against it. A liberal bourgeois like Macaulay was against democracy because it necessarily led "either to communism and the end of 'civilization' or to dictatorship and the end of liberty" (Houghton 56, and cf. the whole of 54-59); Greg was to dramatize such sources in the muddle of his Martian history. I have argued (in MOSF 127ff.) how the rebellious Creature in Frankenstein is a transposition of the unrestrainable plebeian forces unleashed in revolutions such as the 1789 French one. At the end of the century, The Time Machine will openly deduce societal anxiety from the existence of a repressed proletariat, neatly evolved also into a biological alien. In between, the spectre of communism was not only haunting the old Gothic castle of ruling Europe but also the cognate literary genre of SF. Even within its transposing distanciation, insurgent, usually communist mobs are present from the early texts of Gale, Hemyng, Mammoth, and M's The Coming Cromwell to An Ex-M.P.'s Radical Nightmare and An Eye-Witness's Socialist Revolution of 1888, and working-class strike or sabotage in Jenkins and Verne's Child of the Cavern; both are preempted in almost all the works that show a reformed society, from the classical utopias of the 1840s, through the reformist and technocratic works of the post-Bulwerian period, to the Ruskinian Christian communism of Wise's Darkness and Dawn. A few works may show a utopian, not always consistent sympathy for federations of self-governing workmen, as in Trueman, Etymonia, Collens's Eden of Labor, or Welch's Mars. On the other hand, Greg envisages an elite coup d'état against the atheist rationalists (having already disposed of the communists in an earlier bloody civil war), while Hay's 300 Years Hence even has sympathetic German and British national socialisms as instinctive responses of the human race for survival in a Malthusian future. Both of them assemble so many characteristic fascist traits that they deserve to be called proto-fascists. But very many other texts can serve as confirmation of the thesis that fascism is one of the two logical mutations from liberalism, and the more frequent one at that. Having gone in several places into the more pressing attitudes toward women (e.g., in C.3.52) and workers, I want to exemplify this briefly in the less inhibited problem-expanse of chauvinism and racism. Piecing it together with the other two congruent problem-expanses comes near to providing a full picture.

Ethnic aliens either do not exist in the 1848-1885 SF, or they are brutal enemies to be slaughtered (all Future Wars), or an often frantic racism prevails (Maitland, Hay, Brookfield). Interesting aliens or outsiders--even so, often confined to one particular, favorite ethnic group, or inconsequential, or ambiguously treated--can be found in Rowcroft, Lang, Trueman, Bulwer, Butler, in Verne's exceptional Nemo, in Blair, Davis, Etymonia, Ryan, Green, Welch, Abbott, and Jefferies. However, I would say that they receive the status of fully envisaged protagonists only in Bulwer, Verne's Captain Nemo, and Abbott (they are, of course, the supreme value in three or four utopias, from Davis to Welch, but neither fully delineated nor protagonists). To clarify the picture, one might usefully pose the question, which of the S-F writers would sympathize with a colonial liberation rebellion? One trusts that, of the later writers, the Morris of John Ball would demonstrate for them and be willing to go to jail; probably, the mature Jefferies might be in his company. One rather

uneasily hopes the same for Abbott. Verne would only sympathize if they were White and anti-British (e.g., Hindoo
aristocrats or Québécois Catholics), but would be
horrified if they were against White "civilization."
Bulwer, as secretary for colonies, might appoint Chesney,
as officer who fought the Sepoy uprising, to suppress the
rebellion, administratively supported by Trollope (loyal
civil servant with a predilection for gunboats), Strachey,
and Besant. Greg, Gale, Brookfield, "Coverdale," Hay, and
Watson Sr. would rush to volunteer for a punitive expedition as officers or chaplains (Greg preferably if there
were plenty of native women around), and Maitland would
hover overhead in an air-fleet threatening annihilation
unless a Semitic prince can be produced to lead the insurrection back to capitalism. It is a bit difficult to
envisage extirpating the workers, and even more so the
women: not so for other ethnic groups. In this hegemonic
consensus, it is only in the most mature cases, as in
Abbott or Wells's First Men in the Moon, that the aliens
(or Aliens) are an estranging mirror for human problems.
Otherwise, they are either angels (Lach-Szyrma) or devils.
In both cases, they are not subject to the discourse of
knowledge but of power: either to adoration of dominion,
or to the final weapon of power, the ultima ratio regum--
military subjugation, with more than a hint of genocide.

5. Liberating Knowledge versus Hegemonic Power

Thus, in sum, SF can be grasped as a genre in an unstable equilibrium or dynamic compromise between two factors. The first is its cognitive--philosophical and political--potentiality as a genre that grows out of the subversive, lower-class form of "inverted world," within the horizons of knowledge and liberation. The second is a cluster of powerful upper and middle-class ideologies that has, in the great majority of texts, sterilized such potential horizons by contaminating them with mystifications which preclude significant presentations of truly <u>other</u> relationships, with the horizons of power and repression. Given the historical power-constellations, presentations of true fictional novums mean, at the latest from the 18th century, contesting the dominant social addressees and their hegemonic consensus. Yet for a writer to do so, "he must have become conscious of a contradiction between himself and his public, i.e., he . . . must feel the astonished gaze of alien consciences (ethnic minorities, oppressed classes, etc.) weighing upon the little community which he forms with his readers" (Sartre 116). This alien gaze--the true novum of an estrangement that permits cognition of power and of knowledge itself--clashes with the ruling class limitations, often within the same text. That clash, always articulated in autonomous "possible worlds" of alternative history as urgent human destiny, determines the importance and place of this--and of all--SF. For it puts into question the way of ascribing meaning to relations between people that became dominant in discourse with, say, Machiavelli, Bacon, Descartes, Hobbes, Locke, or Defoe (see the epigraph to this section!), and in practice with the rise of a bourgeois and capitalist reality. Finally, Victorian SF produces a specific and very revealing variant of the question posed by all the discourse of art at the time. It asks how is each reader, how are all of us, to conjoin freedom and order, joy and utility, happiness and sovereignty, knowledge and power: knowledge as happiness

419

integrated into a new, nonoppressive power, or (the obverse
of that) as happiness opposed to the dominant power.

Notes to Section D

1. Frederic Harrison, <u>Order and Progress</u> (London,
1875), p. 186.

2. <u>The Collected Works of W.H. Hudson</u> (London, 1922),
p. v.

3. This remark by Asa Briggs, <u>Victorian People</u>
(Harmondsworth, 1967), p. 13, was intended for 1851-1867.
However, in view of my conclusions about the social
addressees of fiction constituting a hegemonic cluster of
5-7 percent of the population, within which ca. 1.5-2.5 percent of addressees from the affluent bourgeoisie successfully imposed their interests and values as the limits of the
ideological consensus, even the undoubted numerical rise of
partakers in the public ideological discussions would not
change the applicability of the remark up to at least the
1890s.

4. John Locke, <u>The Reasonableness of Christianity</u>
(1695), <u>Works</u> (London, 1759), 2:585-86; see also
MacPherson, and the end of B.3.2.

5. See John Sutherland's essay in Part I, section A,
"Nineteenth-Century SF and the Book Trade"--to which, as
well as to further discussions with him, I am much indebt-
ed--and the pioneering article by George Locke, "Wells in
Three Volumes?" in Mullen-Suvin pp. 59-63.

6. Cf. my essay "'Formal' and 'Sociological' Analysis in
the Aesthetics of the Science-Fiction Novel," in Z.
Konstantinović, et al., eds., <u>Proceedings of the IXth
Congress of the ICLA, vol. 4: The Evolution of the Novel</u>
(Innsbruck, 1982), pp. 453-58, expatiating upon the ending
as a narrative dominant in SF from Wells on, with secondary
bibliography.

7. George Moore, <u>Confessions of a Young Man</u> (London,
1888), p. 274 and generally pp. 266-81.

8. Cf. many crass examples in Kenneth Graham, <u>English
Criticism of the Novel 1865-1900</u> (Oxford, 1965), which
make their class standpoint quite clear.

9. Not only is my term "master code" from Jameson PU 84,

but my argument here--as in the whole conclusion--is strongly indebted to two unpublished lectures of his and discussions we have had over a number of years.

10. Terry Eagleton, "Tennyson," in Francis Barker et
al., eds., 1848: The Sociology of Literature ([Colches-
ter], 1978), p. 98.

11. H. Rider Haggard, "About Fiction," Contemporary
Review 51 (1887), 176-77.

12. Graham, op. cit., pp. 30 and 31; see also the Part I
essay on the social addressees of Victorian fiction, subsections 2 and 3.

Secondary Bibliography

Standard bibliographies, histories, and surveys of society,
politics, culture, and literature have as a rule not been
retained.

Sections A and B
Adams=[Adams, Henry.] The Education of Henry Adams. New
    York, 1931.

Allen=Allen, Grant. Introduction to his The British
    Barbarians. London, 1895.

Altick ECR=Altick, Richard D. The English Common Reader.
    Chicago, 1967.

Altick VPI=Altick, Richard D. Victorian People and
    Ideas. New York, 1973.

Arnold=Arnold, Matthew. Culture and Anarchy. Cambridge,
    1960.

Ashworth=Ashworth, William. An Economic History of
    England 1870-1939. London and New York, 1960.

Banks=Banks, J.A. "The Challenge of Popular Culture:
    Introduction," in Philip Appleman, et al., eds., 1859:
    Entering an Age of Crisis. Bloomington IN, 1959, pp.
    199-214.

Baxter=Baxter, R. Dudley. National Income: United King-
    dom. London, 1868.

Best=Best, Geoffrey. Mid-Victorian Britain 1851-1875. London, 1971.

Burn=Burn, W.L. The Age of Equipoise. New York, 1965.

Clapham=Clapham, J.H. An Economic History of Modern Britain, vols. 2-3. London, 1932-1938.

Clark=Clark, G. Kitson. The Making of Victorian England. London, 1965.

Cole SCS=Cole, G.D.H. Studies in Class Structure. London, 1955.

Cole-Postgate=Cole, G.D.H., and Raymond Postgate. The Common People 1746-1946. London, 1964.

Cox=Cox, R.G. "The Reviews and Magazines," in Boris Ford, ed., From Dickens to Hardy. The Pelican Guide to English Literature. Harmondsworth, 1958, 6:188-204.

Cunnington=Cunnington, C. Willett. Feminine Attitudes in the Nineteenth Century. London, 1935.

Ensor=Ensor, R.C.K. England 1870-1914. Oxford, 1949.

Gattie=Gattie, Walter Montagu. "What English People Read." Fortnightly Review 46 (1889), 307-21.

Gray=Gray, Robert. "Bourgeois Hegemony in Victorian Britain," in Jon Bloomfield, ed., Class, Hegemony and Party. London, 1977.

Hardy=Thomas Hardy's Personal Writings. Edited by Harold Orel. London, 1967.

Hobsbawm=Hobsbawm, E.J. Industry and Empire. The Pelican Economic History of England, vol. 3. Harmondsworth, 1980.

Houghton=Houghton, Walter E. The Victorian Frame of Mind 1830-1870. New Haven, 1975.

Innis=Innis, Harold A. Political Economy in the Modern State. Toronto, 1946.

James FWM=James, Louis. Fiction for the Working Man: 1830-1850. Harmondsworth, 1974.

James PP=James, Louis. Print and the People, 1819-1851. London, 1976.

Laver=Laver, James. The Age of Optimism. London, [1966].

Lockwood=Lockwood, David. The Blackcoated Worker. London, 1966.

Lynd=Lynd, Helen Merrell. England in the Eighteen-Eighties. London, 1945.

MacPherson=MacPherson, C.B. The Political Theory of Possessive Individualism. Oxford, 1962.

Marx=Marx, Karl. Capital, vol. 1. New York, 1967.

Marx-Engels OB=Marx, Karl, and Frederick Engels. On Britain. Moscow, 1962.

Mayhew=Mayhew, Henry [et al.]. London Labour and the London Poor, 4 vols. London, [1861-1862].

Mitchell-Deane=Mitchell, B.R., with Phyllis Deane. Abstract of British Historical Statistics. Cambridge, 1962.

Mulhall=Mulhall, Michael G. A Dictionary of Statistics. London, 1899.

Mullen-Suvin=Mullen, R.D., and Darko Suvin, eds. Science-Fiction Studies: Second Series. Boston, 1978.

Neuburg=Neuburg, Victor E. Popular Literature. Harmonds-worth, 1977.

Perkin=Perkin, Harold. The Origins of Modern English Society 1780-1880. London and Toronto, 1969.

Plant=Plant, Marjorie. The English Book Trade. London, 1939.

Reader=Reader, W.J. Professional Men. London, 1966.

Sartre=Sartre, Jean-Paul. What Is Literature? New York, 1949.

Saunders=Saunders, J.W. The Profession of English Letters. London, 1964.

Sutherland=Sutherland, J.A. <u>Victorian Novelists and Publishers</u>. London, 1976.

TLS-CEL=<u>The Times Literary Supplement</u>, 1 May 1937: "A Century of English Letters" (special issue).

Vicinus=Vicinus, Martha. <u>The Industrial Muse</u>. London, 1979.

Webb VRP=Webb, R.K. "The Victorian Reading Public," in <u>From Dickens to Hardy</u> (see Cox above), 6:205-26.

Williams IP=Williams, Raymond. Introduction to idem, ed., <u>The Pelican Book of English Prose</u>, vol. 2. Harmondsworth, 1969, pp. 19-55.

Williams LR=Williams, Raymond. <u>The Long Revolution</u>. Harmondsworth, 1971.

Williams ML=Williams, Raymond. <u>Marxism and Literature</u>. Oxford, 1977.

Wright CUP=Wright, Thomas. "Concerning the Unknown Public." <u>Nineteenth Century</u> 13 (1883), 279-96.

Wright GU=A Journeyman Engineer (pseud. of Thomas Wright). <u>The Great Unwashed</u>. London, 1868.

Young=Young, G.M., ed. <u>Early Victorian England</u>, 2 vols. London, 1934.

Section C

Subsection 1
See also Altick VPI, Marx, Mullen-Suvin, Reader, Williams LR, and Williams ML from section A-B.

Angenot AP=Angenot, Marc. "The Absent Paradigm." <u>Science-Fiction Studies</u>, no. 17 (1979), 9-19.

Angenot JV=Angenot, Marc. "Jules Verne," in Patrick Parrinder, ed., <u>Science Fiction: A Critical Guide</u>. London, 1979.

Angenot PTI=Angenot, Marc. "Présupposé--topos--idéologème." <u>Etudes françaises</u>, no. 1-2 (1977), 12-34 (now also in his <u>La Parole pamphlétaire</u>. Paris, 1982, chapter V.2).

Angenot RP=Angenot, Marc. Le Roman populaire. Montréal, 1975.

Angenot SFF=Angenot, Marc. "Science Fiction in France Before Verne." Science-Fiction Studies, no. 14 (1978), 58-66.

Angenot SSI=Angenot, Marc. "La science-fiction: genre et statut institutionnel." R. de l'Institut de Sociologie, no. 3-4 (1980), 651-60.

Angenot-Suvin=Angenot, Marc, and Darko Suvin. "Not Only But Also: Reflections on Cognition and Ideology in Science Fiction and S-F Criticism." Science-Fiction Studies, no. 18 (1979), 168-79.

Benjamin=Benjamin, Walter. Gesammelte Schriften, 4 vols. Frankfurt, 1980.

Carlyle=The Works of Thomas Carlyle in Thirty Volumes. Centenary Edition. London, 1899.

Ducrot=Ducrot, Oswald. Dire et ne pas dire. Paris, 1972.

Eco=Eco, Umberto. Il superuomo di massa. Milano, 1978.

Gramsci MP=Gramsci, Antonio. The Modern Prince and Other Writings. London, 1957.

Gramsci PN=Gramsci, Antonio. Prison Notebooks. London, 1970.

Jameson MF=Jameson, Fredric. Marxism and Form. Princeton, 1971.

Jameson PU=Jameson, Fredric. The Political Unconscious. Ithaca NY, 1981.

Kracauer=Kracauer, Siegfried. Jacques Offenbach und das Paris seiner Zeit. Frankfurt, 1976.

Lotman=Lotman, Jurij. The Structure of the Artistic Text. Ann Arbor, 1977.

Marx-Engels HF=Marx, Karl, and Friedrich Engels. The Holy Family. London, 1957.

Suvin MOSF=Suvin, Darko. Metamorphoses of Science Fiction. New Haven and London, 1979.

Tocqueville=Tocqueville, Alexis de. Democracy in America, vol. 2. London and New York, 1900.

Wells=H.G. Wells's Literary Criticism. Eds. Patrick Parrinder and Robert M. Philmus. Brighton, 1980.

Williams PMC=Williams, Raymond. Problems in Materialism and Culture. London, 1980.

Subsection 2
See also subsection C.1.

Beaver=Beaver, Harold. The Science Fiction of Edgar Allan Poe. Harmondsworth, 1979.

Clarke TF=Clarke, I.F. Tale of the Future . . . . London, 1978.

Dupont=Dupont, V. L'Utopie et le Roman Utopique dans la Littérature Anglaise. Toulouse and Paris, 1941.

Franklin=Franklin, H. Bruce. Future Perfect. New York, 1968.

Locke VS=Locke, George. Voyages in Space. London, 1975.

Poe=The Works of Edgar Allan Poe in Eight Volumes. Philadelphia, 1906.

Subsection 3 and section D
See also Burn, Cox, Ensor, Hobsbawm, Houghton, MacPherson, Mitchell-Deane, and Sartre from sections A-B and subsections C.1-2.

Bailey=Bailey, J.O. Pilgrims Through Space and Time. Westport, CT, 1972.

Buckley TT=Buckley, Jerome Hamilton. The Triumph of Time. Cambridge, MA, 1966.

A.C. Christensen=Christensen, Allan Conrad. Edward Bulwer-Lytton. Athens GA, [1976].

J. Christensen=Christensen, John Michael. "Utopia and the Late Victorians." Ph.D. dissertation, Northwestern

University, 1974.

Clarke PE=Clarke, I.F. The Pattern of Expectation 1644-2001 [sic]. London, 1979.

Clarke VPW=Clarke, I.F. Voices Prophesying War 1763-1984 [sic]. London, 1966.

Henkin=Henkin, Leo J. Darwinism in the English Novel 1860-1910. New York, 1940.

Hillegas=Hillegas, Mark R. "Victorian 'Extraterrestrials'," in Jerome H. Buckley, ed., The Worlds of Victorian Fiction. Harvard English Studies 6. Cambridge, MA, 1975.

Himmelfarb=Himmelfarb, Gertrude. "Varieties of Social Darwinism," in her Victorian Minds. London, 1968, pp. 314-42.

Jameson FA=Jameson, Fredric. Fables of Aggression. Berkeley, 1979.

Le Guin=Le Guin, Ursula K. The Dispossessed. New York, 1974.

Moorcock=Moorcock, Michael. Introduction to idem, ed., Before Armageddon. London, 1975, 1:3-18.

Mullen SFS5=M[ullen], R.D. "The Hyperion Reprints." Science-Fiction Studies, no. 5 (1975), 95-96.

Mullen SFS6=Mullen, R.D. "The Arno Reprints." Science-Fiction Studies, no. 6 (1975), 179-95.

Mumford=Mumford, Lewis. Technics and Civilization. New York, 1963.

Philmus=Philmus, Robert M. Into the Unknown. Berkeley, 1970.

Roemer=Roemer, Kenneth M. The Obsolete Necessity. [Kent, OH], 1976.

Sargent UL=Sargent, Lyman Tower. British and American Utopian Literature 1576-1975. Boston, 1979.

Sargent   WU=Sargent,   Lyman   Tower.   "Women   in   Utopia."
    Comparative   Literature   Studies   10   (December   1973),
    302-16.

Williams   EN=Williams,   Raymond.   The   English   Novel   From
    Dickens to Lawrence.   London, 1973.

Index

This index has two types of entries: first, all the names of writers and all titles from the primary bibliographies on pp. 11–122 (they are printed in upper case); second, selected writers and titles of other fiction as well as the names most relevant from the intertext of the 19th century, of the historical tradition, and of other SF. Names and titles of secondary literature have not been indexed; they are grouped in several copious bibliographies to the various sections of this book.